W9-CRW-814

INSIDE CORPORATE AMERICA

Also by Allan Cox

The Making of the Achiever
Confessions of a Corporate Headhunter
Work, Love and Friendship: Reflections on Executive Lifestyle

INSIDE CORPORATE AMERICA

ALLAN COX

St. Martin's Press
New York

INSIDE CORPORATE AMERICA. Copyright © 1982 by Allan J. Cox. Preface to the Paperback Edition copyright © 1986 by Allan J. Cox. All rights reserved. Printed in the United States of America. No part of this book may be used or reproduced in any manner whatsoever without written permission except in the case of brief quotations embodied in critical articles or reviews. For information, address St. Martin's Press, 175 Fifth Avenue, New York, N.Y. 10010.

Library of Congress Cataloging in Publication Data

Cox, Allan J.
  Inside corporate America.

  1. Executives—United States.   2. Corporations—
United States.   3. Industrial management—United
States.   I. Title.
HD38.25.U6C69   1986   658.4′09   86-13787
ISBN 0-312-41869-8 (pbk.)

First published in the United States by Delacorte Press under the title *The Cox Report on the American Corporation*.

*For the woman of still waters and
the man who knew how to laugh*

Managing a business corporation, as distinct from
a government agency, does require a substantial
degree of entrepreneurial skill. But it is also the
case that they [the managers] are as much
functionaries as entrepreneurs, and rather
anonymous functionaries at that. Not only don't
we know who the chairman of General Motors is;
we know so little about the kind of person who
holds such a position that we haven't the faintest
idea as to whether or not we want
our children to grow up to be like him.

—IRVING KRISTOL
in *The Public Interest*

Contents

Section II
How Corporations Function

Section V
How Executives Succeed

Tables

Preface

This is a report on thirteen major American corporations. I think of these corporations as the *lucky thirteen.* They're lucky because recently they have undergone a study that gives them a fresh new way to know themselves. Knowing themselves better allows them to improve their performance.

We on the outside looking in are lucky, too. Because these corporations have been willing to look at themselves in exhaustive detail, and to let the outcome of such study be known, we, too, can learn what makes them tick.

Most people are curious about business life and the corporation. Some of us work in a corporation or serve several of them as advisors or suppliers. Others don't work in corporations, but their spouses do. Others are students who plan careers in business. Others work in fields apart from business, such as medicine or education, but feel its impact. There are still others in those fields apart from business who contemplate a career switch into business and wonder what working for a corporation is like. Then there are those who do not work at all, such as children, the elderly, and the unemployed, who are touched by the corporation as consumers and by the state of the economy itself.

Most of us, then, want to know more about the corporation. The rapid growth in the size of the business sections of our daily papers over the past few years shows that business itself is *news.* This book is intended to help satisfy our appetite for information and knowledge about corporate life.

The thirteen corporations in this study are representative of American business life and the slice of corporate America that produces the overwhelming bulk of our gross national product. The annual sales of these corporations range from approximately $300 million to $3 billion. This means our study does not include the behemoths such as Exxon, nor those small, primarily family-owned businesses that number in the thousands and dot the landscape.

Three of our thirteen corporations are in fact privately held, but they are larger than most. The remaining ten are publicly held, with their shares trading on the major stock exchanges. The corporations are divided among the three segments of business: (1) service, (2) consumer, and (3) industrial. Each segment contains one privately held company. The 115 operating units of the companies we studied are located in twenty states throughout the country; Washington, D.C.; and Canada.

24	Ohio
15	Illinois
14	California
9	Pennsylvania
8	Washington, D.C.
7	Wisconsin
6	Massachusetts
5	New York
4	Virginia
3	Indiana
3	Michigan
3	Oregon
3	Texas
2	Canada
2	Georgia
1	Delaware
1	Florida
1	Hawaii
1	Maine
1	Maryland
1	New Jersey
1	Oklahoma
115	Total

Brief descriptions of the corporations included in this study appear in Appendix B. I'll simply name them here.

Service

ARA Services, Inc. (Philadelphia, Pennsylvania)

Consolidated Freightways, Inc. (San Francisco, California)

Hyatt Hotels Corporation (Rosemont, Illinois)*

Woodward & Lothrop, Inc. (Washington, D.C.)

*Privately held

Consumer

Anchor Hocking Corporation (Lancaster, Ohio)

Encyclopaedia Britannica, Inc. (Chicago, Illinois)*

Sherwin-Williams Company (Cleveland, Ohio)

Taft Broadcasting Company (Cincinnati, Ohio)

Industrial

Allen-Bradley Company (Milwaukee, Wisconsin)*

Ametek, Inc. (New York, New York)

International Minerals & Chemical Corporation (Northbrook, Illinois)

James River Corporation of Virginia (Richmond, Virginia)

Scott Fetzer Company (Lakewood, Ohio)

A word on how this book came about is in order. The idea to undertake a corporate study of this breadth and depth did not originate in my own mind. It was brought up by my friend Dominick Abel in the spring of 1979 and struck an immediate, responsive note with me. To design a study that would be an X ray on corporate innards was irresistible!

As an executive search consultant, I have spent the past seventeen years involved with a broad variety of executives—the types that are the subject matter of this study. These years gave me opportunities to observe the corporation and draw conclusions about it. But such exposures often raised as many questions as they answered. Those unanswered questions are what made me take on this project.

The first step in getting started was to draft a questionnaire to prompt quality responses from corporate executives. I had completed graduate training in sociology, so this alone was not formidable. But to go further was something else. I had just enough exposure to social science research to be dangerous. In short, I needed an advisor. Professor Allan Schnaiberg, sociology department chairman at Northwestern University, agreed to be that advisor.

Our collaboration produced a refined questionnaire (see Appendix C for its final form), a means of processing questionnaire returns, a research design to generate a representative, valid response, and a report format useful to the participating corporations. Refining the questionnaire, pretesting it, revising it, printing it, completing the research design and arranging for data processing occurred from mid-1979 to mid-1980. Recruiting the corporations, distributing the questionnaires, collecting them, processing the data, and sending the computer reports to the corporations occurred from mid-1980 to

*Privately held

mid-1981. For further details on these processes, see Dr. Schnaiberg's remarks in Appendix A.

The questionnaire was pretested among executives attending seminars at the Kellogg Graduate School of Management at Northwestern during the summer of 1979. Their suggestions were adopted in our final revision.

Our research design called for distributing the questionnaires to five top-level and five middle-level executives within each unit of the corporations. This would give us the differences and similarities of thought between these two levels of management throughout a corporation's subsidiaries, divisions, and headquarters.

With the exception of three of the corporations, my staff and I distributed the packets of ten questionnaires (more or less, depending on the number of executives at each level) to each division, subsidiary, and headquarters. Each executive was instructed to send his completed questionnaire himself back to a post office box in Wilmette, Illinois. He thus was assured that his superior would not see his responses. Each set of ten questionnaires, divided between top and middle executives, was marked by the *same* number within a corporate and unit code, so they had further assurance that, at most, a questionnaire could be tracked to only one in five.

At the deadline when a corporation's questionnaires were to be returned, we knew how many had come in because of our broad coding. But we didn't know which executives had not completed their questionnaires. That was when we learned the executives believed their responses were anonymous. We took cold comfort from them claiming they had returned their questionnaires when we knew they had not. The comfort came from their feeling they could not be traced.

A nice thing happened. A follow-up mailing produced responses "mysteriously" from executives who earlier claimed they had returned their questionnaires. It is understandable that a busy executive would be reluctant to give the time to such an exhaustive questionnaire. The reluctance is even more understandable when that executive questions if his responses will be held in confidence.

The three companies that distributed the questionnaires among their own units were Woodward & Lothrop, Allen-Bradley, and Encyclopaedia Britannica. They did so after we coded them and gave the same assurances of anonymity. The executives returned their own questionnaires.

The task of recruiting representative corporations for the study fell to me. This was accomplished by contacting chief executives. My pitch to each was that we could provide him with a report on his company's collective response to the questionnaire. That would be valuable. More importantly, we would provide him with the composite report of all the other corporations participating. This sample, which had not existed until now, would allow him to compare his firm's makeup and performance with all others combined. This book was sufficient to gather an outstanding group of companies to undertake the study. While each corporation's participation would be known, I pledged to each chief executive that his firm's responses would be kept confidential. Where I might make reference to it in some way, I would be sure to disguise its identity.

Not every corporation I sought was willing to participate. For example, 3M, a company I admire, was one I hoped to include. They enthusiastically considered it, then declined because they were engaged in other surveys, different in scope from ours, but requiring their executives' time nonetheless. That was a reason for staying out I could understand. But a few others gave inane reasons for not participating, leading me to wonder if some chief executives have a *need not to know*. Knowing what is on the minds of their executives was information they seemed all too eager to do without. They fit the description given to some corporate leaders recently by Commerce Secretary Malcolm Baldridge: "fat, dumb, and happy."

Having satisfied ourselves that we were getting valid responses from the executives, we turned to the rate of response, worked hard on follow-up, and kept our fingers crossed. We were pleased there, too, as it turned out, because we got exceptionally high returns.

Across all thirteen corporations, 1,173 executives were asked to complete the questionnaire. Of that number, 1,086 executives complied, providing a response rate of 93 percent, an extraordinary one. Five hundred fifteen top executives responded out of a possible 552, for a rate of 93 percent. Of middle-level executives, 571 responded out of 621, for a rate of 92 percent. One corporation gave 100 percent participation. The corporation with the lowest level of participation did so at a 78 percent response rate.

Voluntary studies trouble me because of their low response rate, inviting fringe types to unburden themselves of extreme views. When I read a study where the results are published on the basis of, say, a 3 to 5 percent rate of response, I wonder what the other 95 to 97 percent of the study universe thought about the matters at hand. While this study was not coercive, and assured anonymity, it had enough thrust to achieve full, representative participation.

So there you have the backdrop on how *Inside Corporate America* came into being. The book is divided into five topics I believe will be most important to you. They are: (1) what corporations value, (2) how corporations function, (3) how corporations succeed and fail, (4) what executives are like, and (5) how executives succeed. My views on these topics stem from my own experience plus the research I've just described. While that research has been rigorous and its findings significant, I have tried not to be "heavy" in presenting them.

Inside Corporate America is comprised of data analysis and commentary sprinkled with advice and anecdotes. Although it is not a "how-to" book in a strict sense, it readily can serve as a manual for any person who seeks to improve his or her performance in the corporate setting. *Its main purpose is to get at the veiled truths of the corporate world.* Access to these truths should enhance the careers of every man and woman who is now a corporate executive at any level from the most junior to the chief executive. The executive hell-bent on reaching the top will find revealed how others not only do it, but do it with finesse. An executive looking to make his organization more responsive will be shown alternatives for effective action. An executive considering a job change will see how others make such moves to ensure their growth. A woman seeking to advance her career will be made privy to the hidden biases she must overcome to take advantage of the opportunities that are hers alone. The middle-aged executive will be made aware of the issues in striking a balance between his or her changing life commitments and those demanded by the corporation. The student contemplating a career in business will learn how to come off the blocks fast. The business-school professor looking for hard data on his subject will have fresh findings for his inquiry. And the professional—such as a lawyer, accountant, consultant, or advertising executive—who serves the corporation as advisor will gain new insights on ways to help his client.

In short, I think *Inside Corporate America* will be an eye-opener to all people who are curious about this remarkable phenomenon called the corporation, which, for better or worse, so shapes the lives of us all.

As with most books, this one could not have come to fruition without the contributions of many people. I express my appreciation to them here.

Officers of their corporations who gave me suggestions for making the study most useful to participating corporations are James Andress of Abbott Laboratories, Robert Bennett of FMC, Roger Briggs and Robert Palenchar of Esmark, Richard Collister of Chase Manhattan, David Diana of Jewel Companies, David Dickson of Carnation, William Hood of Norton Simon, Harry Niemiec of Beatrice Foods, and William Watchman of Revlon.

Douglas Gray, Louis Kislik, and Melvin Marks painstakingly read the manuscript and made constructive criticisms along the way. William Taylor, partner with Deloitte Haskins & Sells, along with his colleagues, likewise offered help and counsel at various points.

Northwestern University was not involved officially in this study. However, several individuals and facilities connected with the institution were a part of it in significant ways. Raymond Mack, provost, made a key recommendation to me early on that I adopted. Allan Schnaiberg's contribution already has been noted, but that in no way captures my sense of debt to him for his expert, good-natured guidance.

Two of Allan's students, both Ph.D. candidates in sociology, proved their competence and commitment throughout the study. Rosanna Hertz tallied the questionnaires as they were returned and supervised their preparation for key punching. Wayne Baker designed the coding system, wrote the computer program, and supervised the final processing of the data at the University's Vogelback Computing Center. Executives at the Kellogg Graduate School of Management, as previously mentioned, made valuable suggestions on improving the questionnaire.

Louis LaPorta worked tirelessly in meeting our stringent demands in key punching. Likewise, Dennis Frantsve met the highest professional standards in our repeated revisions of the questionnaire before its final printing.

Barbara O'Hara, my secretary, maintained the patience of Job during the course of my picayune revisions while she typed the early drafts of the manuscript. To Georgia Nikolopoulos goes the credit for the expert typing of the final draft.

Bonnie Cox efficiently coordinated the questionnaire's distribution and follow-up. She also generated numerous workable ideas, and took the right action at the right times to ensure the smooth continuation of the project. Jeanette Almada, who served as my assistant on the project, has my gratitude and admiration. Without her research and editorial contributions, this book would not have been possible. I also am indebted to my editor, Cynthia Vartan, who believed in this undertaking from the beginning.

Finally, my special thanks go to the thirteen progressive corporations who agreed to join the study, and to their executives who took the time to share their thoughts with us on an exhaustive array of questions.

Allan Cox
January 1982

Preface to the Paperback Edition

This book was published in November 1982, with the title *The Cox Report on the American Corporation*. Its new title is more apt, for while it is a detailed study of thirteen major, identified corporations, in the last analysis it is a book of lessons.

The lessons aren't derived from "best-managed companies" or any other particular "exemplary" category. Rather, my zeal for the study group was to assemble *representative* corporations—firms that symbolize "corporate America" in most respects, and are the kinds of places that most people work.

As has become apparent, excessive glamorization of any group of companies at a given point shows its flaws as time passes, and these companies are unable to sustain outstanding performance. Moreover, the isolated anecdotes that are selected by an author to serve as examples for her or his lionizing an organization are often not representative of its overall climate. They tend to be romanticized.

I know some of this from my experience with this book. In it, I take a strong stand affirming corporate responsibility and hold up Control Data, Levi Strauss, and Bank of America as models for the rest of us to emulate. However, since I wrote about them, they all have fallen on hard times, and as profit-makers have been anything but exemplary.

None of this makes me admire these corporations any less, doubt their ability to rebound, or believe less in what they were attempting to do. But it remains a fact of life that they were—at this time at least—unable to balance overt social concern and profitability.

What other changes have taken place since this book was published? For one, the executive from Continental Illinois National Bank and Trust, who is quoted at the end of Section III, didn't know how prophetic he was about that organization's coming status. Said he, "If we're one of the best, God help the rest."

Everett Olson, chief executive of Carnation, and Donald Kelly, chief executive of Esmark, were named in *The Cox Report* as masters of time management, priority-setting and delegation. Carnation has been acquired by Nestle's, and Olson died in November, 1985. Esmark was acquired by Beatrice; Kelly quit; James—live by the sword, die by the sword—Dutt (see Chapter 15) was fired as Beatrice chief executive by the board of directors to ward off a palace revolt, and on April 11, 1985, that company's stockholders ratified being recipients of the largest leveraged buyout in history, and for the company to be run by—you guessed it—Donald Philip Kelly!

Of the thirteen corporations in the study, ten were publicly held, three were private. Allen-Bradley, one of the latter three, has gone public by being acquired by Rockwell International. ARA Services and Woodward & Lothrop, two of the public companies, have gone private.

Another participating company—Scott Fetzer—entered several negotiations to be bought out in one way or another, and in January 1986, was acquired by Berkshire Hathaway, Inc. The company also changed its name to Scott & Fetzer, which it had been originally. Undoubtedly, some consultant won a large fee earlier for persuading them to drop the ampersand!

Apart from coming under new ownership, the company that has changed its makeup the most is James River Corporation. Since 1981, when company annual sales were 773 million, James River has grown markedly through acquisitions. In 1982, they more than doubled sales by acquiring the consumer paper products group of American Can. In 1986, they acquired the bulk of assets of Crown Zellerbach Corporation, and after spinning off certain of those, sales in their fiscal year ending May 1987 will exceed $4 billion.

Charles Swanson of Encyclopaedia Britannica retired as chief executive and has been replaced by Peter Norton. The same is true of Richard Lenon of IMC, succeeded by George Kennedy. The same goes for William Fishman of ARA Services, replaced by Joseph Neubauer, and Claude Whitney of Allen-Bradley, replaced by J. Tracy O'Rourke. Finally, Consolidated Freightways moved its headquarters from San Francisco to Palo Alto, California.

Other changes, evolutionary in nature, are in full bloom and predicted in the book's six conclusions, drawn from the study's findings.

Some reviewers were critical of my conclusions. But these "nuggets of insight," as one called them in a tone belying his words, seem to have been borne out. And as a special example, my first assertion—made during the 1981–82 recession—that the American corporation is basically healthy, prompted another to say this was Pollyanna in light of the strength of West German companies and the Japanese miracle.

Nonetheless, this view has acquitted itself well in the interim. All around us is ample evidence of the re-emergence of American management and industry, and that these currently are helping to stir all of Europe's (including Germany's) slumbering economy. Moreover, when we experience our next recession, which we inevitably will, Europe will feel its pain just as we will. Meanwhile, signs are popping up increasingly to suggest all is not well at Japan, Inc.

This leads to my final point. When this study was first conceived, a few people at my publisher thought it was a great idea because it could be repeated every five years. You get the point: just like (oh so hopefully) *Rocky I*, *II*, *III*, and *IV*.

I had to tell them, no, it wouldn't work that way. I said that in my opinion, despite the current rhetoric to the contrary, significant change in corporations is evolutionary, and much of what people refer to as "unprecedented change" is most often just novelty.

I had to tell them that the *earliest* date to repeat the study in order to generate enough substantial changes to capture anybody's interest was ten years away. I asked them then (and ask you now) to recall how much their company had changed "radically" in the past ten years, and they had to admit: "Not all that much."

Is your answer the same? Perhaps not, but just think how impatient you have been when wanting to introduce changes in *your* department or company's way of doing things. Actually, many of us wish change would occur faster.

So then, my point to you, the reader, is that it is my belief that the findings of this study, first reported in 1982, have a long shelf life and can be useful to you. You can have reasonable confidence that in your own thinking about corporate life, improving your management style, and in the interest of your career development, the information and observations here are timely.

This is especially so because far more than being about how things ought to be, *Inside Corporate America* is a looking glass on how things are.

Allan Cox
Chicago, Illinois
June 1, 1986

Section I
What Corporations Value

Appearances are to us in four ways: for either things appear as they are; or they are not, and do not even appear to be; or they are, and do not appear to be; or they are not, and yet appear to be. Further, in all these cases to form a right judgment is the office of an educated man.

—EPICTETUS

1

The Novice from Whitewater State

"My *god*! What am I doin' *here*?" That's what you exclaim to yourself as you stare blankly at the run-down heels of the haughty maître d' who is crisply ushering you upstairs to the dining room of this restaurant with the weird name of "21." It never occurs to you that it got its name simply from its address on West Fifty-second Street.

What does occur to you, however, is how fast the mind races when you find yourself in a life-threatening situation. In the few seconds that have elapsed between your entering the front door—quickly announcing whom you were here to meet—and now approaching the top of the staircase, dozens of thoughts have crowded your brain, forcing you to an inescapable conclusion: *You are out of your league.*

First of all you remember arriving in the city last night, your first trip ever to New York, more specifically Manhattan, and the borough had been every bit as dazzling and frightening as you always had heard. Though home is Beaver Dam, Wisconsin, you arrived at Penn Station on the Metroliner from Philadelphia, where you had come from another interview. Upon alighting from the train, bag in hand, you had it taken from your grasp immediately by an aggressive youth who told you to follow him up the escalator and he would find you a cab to take you to your hotel. When you got to street level and he put your bag down beside a taxi, he told you the charge for his unasked-for services was five bucks. You were shocked, but he seemed menacing enough that even though you were bigger than he, you reached into your pocket and meekly paid him.

When your taxi dropped you off at your hotel, you noticed the ride took only about eight minutes, which was a relief, since you were afraid he might take you by way of Montauk. What would have been most embarrassing about *that* is you wouldn't have known the difference.

As you approached the hotel entrance, the waiting doorman offered, "Welcome to the Regency." You nodded, gave him your bag, wondered if you were supposed to tip him, and followed him into the lobby. You gave him a buck and sighed. You'd been in town ten minutes, and your major actions had been to follow two hustlers around, both eager to relieve you of your scarce cash.

3

Once well into the lobby, standing at the registration desk, you looked around and had to be impressed. No question about it, the company that had invited you to town was no piker.

What really blew your mind was, as you were escorted down the corridor to your room by yet another man, the bellhop, who for payment (of course) carried your threadbare suitcase, who should pass you on his way to the elevator but Paul Anka. Can you believe it? You already knew Joni Mitchell kept a suite here. You had read that in *Rolling Stone.* Later on, after you caught your breath, you went down to the bar for a beer to settle your nerves. There, huddling in the corner with a group, smoking a cigar, was Melvin Laird, former congressman from your home state and Nixon's secretary of defense. Now, for sure, you knew you were someplace special.

Before turning in, you walked down the west side of Park Avenue to the Pan Am Building. There you crossed over to the east side and, halfway back, stopped in front of the tall, black skyscraper that bore the name and served as the headquarters of the company that might want you to go to work for them. You couldn't deny the sense of pride that welled up in you as you saw that this building more than held its own, standing tall in this corridor of raw corporate power and big-city architecture more impressive and overwhelming than you ever could have imagined.

You stood there rehearsing what had brought you to New York, and remained surprised at those unlikely developments. You had just completed your M.B.A., but it was from a small school; not a prestige degree at all, and you thought these big New York companies insisted that their eager novices come from Harvard, Wharton, Chicago, Stanford, and the like. But when the company recruiter came to your campus, and you signed up, he saw something in you he liked.

Next thing you knew, you were visiting the company's regional offices in Minneapolis. Your pleasant day there ended with the regional sales manager telling you he'd like to have you on his staff. If you were interested in this job that would get you on your way to a promising business career at an attractive starting salary, you had to clear only one more hurdle. You had to go to New York headquarters, meet the big boss, the VP-Sales, and pass his muster. . . . Boy, let's have at him. . . . I'm ready. . . .

That was last night. Now, as you reach the top stair at "21," knowing he's sitting at a table waiting for you, knowing what's at stake, knowing you can blow this job you so badly want with one dumb move, you would welcome any intervention short of an epileptic seizure to prevent this imminent encounter. It suddenly burns into your brain, making you feel more inadequate than ever, that you're one helluva long way from Whitewater State* and Beaver Dam!

As you are on your way across the room, you get giddy thinking that, by

*University of Wisconsin at Whitewater

God, if anybody has to tip *this* lackey leading you around by the nose, it won't be you! You see the big boss you're to meet sitting at a table neatly tucked away in the far corner. He gets up from his seat to greet you as he sees from the maître d's signal that his quarry has been bagged.

You regain your composure enough to smile broadly as you approach his table and offer the man a firm handshake. You exchange greetings, notice that your voice comes out tenor rather than its normal baritone, and make a mental note to do something about that. He beckons you to sit down, which you do and politely place your napkin in your lap and begin twisting it so hard that it could be used to tug the *QE II* firmly into dock.

The big boss is friendly, engaging, warm; disarming all the way. He's totally at ease. He's handsome, in good shape, well dressed, has an unjaded face, and, overall, cuts an impressive figure. All this is apparent in the short time since you shook hands, seated yourselves, and began to respond to his question of how your trip into New York went.

Right then the waiter comes to the table and asks if you would like something from the bar. Aha, even though you can feel the perspiration running down your sides beneath your shirt, you're ready for that one! You don't subscribe to *Playboy* for nothin'. You remember reading an article recently at the back of the magazine entitled "How to Survive an Interview Lunch," and some executive recruiter gave advice on this very trap. You look at your host and parry: "I can go either way. I'll join you with something if you like, or not; it doesn't matter." Your host turns to the waiter and says, "Fine, bring us the wine list, will you, George?" You settle back in your chair and begin to feel this thing may just go all right after all.

Later on, after you get to know each other slightly through some small talk, and you manage to find one thing on the menu you recognize—striped bass—and order creditably enough, he begins to probe into your background and schooling. He deftly and engagingly learns you are the youngest of four children, have two sisters and a brother, and are the son of a Congregational minister. He nods at that; seems interested. He mentions he grew up in a serious Catholic family, even graduated from Notre Dame, but is no longer practicing, and in fact, is married to a woman who is Presbyterian and raising their children according to her religious traditions. You like this guy. He has asked you a lot of questions, but when you turn the tables and ask him a few, he answers forthrightly. When you ask how many children he has, he tells you two; a daughter seventeen and a boy fourteen. When you ask him where he lives, he tells you Darien, Connecticut, and you promptly make another mental note to find out about that place. When you ask him how old he is, he tells you forty-four. It's obvious to you that this man may go all the way.

Back and forth you go, throughout lunch, asking and answering questions. He wants to satisfy himself on your character, habits, energies, sense of team play, and potential for leadership. You want to satisfy yourself that this man is as good as he seems, that he is representative of a company of which you can be proud and enjoy working in, where your talents will be appreciated, where you know you'll have a contribution to make, and that in this entry-level job you won't be lost and forgotten out in Minneapolis as you trudge an upper-Midwest sales territory.

Lunch comes to a natural conclusion and he asks you to come back to the office with him. He says he wants to show you around a bit and introduce you to a few people. It turns out that one of the people he wants you to meet is a nice enough fellow who happens to be the president. President! True enough, it's just a courtesy visit and you spend only five minutes with him in his awesome office. But it dawns on you what a classy gesture it is and that it was for your benefit, not his. The big boss, who is now "Jim" to you, who sat in the office with you for your brief visit with the president, takes you back to his office and, after a few pleasantries, tells you he'd like to have you on board.

Again you lean back in your chair, thrust both your feet out in front of you with your heels resting on the floor about a foot apart. This is your unwitting symbol of triumph to yourself. You know the game is over. No more time for coyness. You look at Jim. Grinning from ear to ear, you tell him at just barely below a shout. "You're on!"

Walking back to the Regency to get your bag, you remember the advice Professor Caldwell (good old Caldwell; he didn't even have a doctorate) gave you business students back at Whitewater. "Never choose a job," he said, "for the money. Never choose a job for the company name. Never choose a job for geography. But choose a job for the *people*." Funny, that practical advice came out of a course called "Business and Ethics."

It also was at that moment that you knew, or hoped you knew, that you just had joined a company that places great store and value on most of the same things you do.

Your exhilaration shows in your stride as you come out of the hotel and leap into a waiting taxi. "LaGuardia; Fifty-ninth Street bridge, please." Your voice has the sound of command. No cabbie's gonna take *you* to Queens by way of Brooklyn.

Look out, world. Here you come!

It makes sense to examine what it is about this young hypothetical hero that made him attractive to this fictional company. For a beginning, let's look at some startling information about so-called prestige degrees. That is the area in which this young man (and thousands of women and men like him), felt most vulnerable in the mating dance. He believed his lack of such a degree would work against him.

Not so. The prestige degree is not all it is cracked up to be. We found from our study that executives judge their companies to be more likely to place higher value on—and are more likely to hire for entry-level management positions—a graduate from a large state university with a B average in business than either a Phi Beta Kappa literature major from Princeton or a C political science major from Dartmouth.

We asked these 1,086 top executives and middle managers from thirteen major corporations to evaluate hypothetical job candidates of various backgrounds and credentials. We made them do so by indicating the level of desirability of these candidates on a scale of 1 to 7. A candidate who would be disqualified rates a 1; an excellent prospect earns a 7. The responses of these two levels of management are summarized in Table 1.

Of top executives—those executives on the top tier of their pyramid organization chart, whether at the parent company or at the same level in divisions or subsidiaries—less than half rank the Princeton graduate average or above. The Dartmouth student fares even less well. Middle managers— those executives occupying the three or four tiers on the organization chart between the top executives and front line supervisors—follow their seniors closely on both the Princeton and Dartmouth graduates. In contrast, when evaluating the large state school graduate with a B average in business, the top executives are far more positive. Eighty-six percent ranked this graduate average or above. The middle managers follow suit with 88 percent ranking him average or above.

I can hear the howls from some quarters for my lack of logic on this matter. They properly might chide me for comparing oranges and apples, and ask that I compare a prestige-school undergraduate degree with a non-prestige-school undergraduate with the same major. "Or, better yet," they would say, "compare a prestige-school M.B.A. graduate with a nonprestige-school M.B.A. graduate."

"Okay," I reply, "let me do the latter." But first I would like to ask this: You would think for sure that an M.B.A. graduate from Stanford would have it all over this large-state-school undergraduate business major, wouldn't you? I certainly did, until I saw our findings. Among top executives, the Stanford M.B.A. scores are only slightly higher in the 6 and 7 cream-of-the-crop categories, but not *as high* as the state school undergraduate in the 4 and 5 categories. Also worth noting is that 15 percent of top executives consider the Stanford M.B.A. a below-average or worse candidate. One percent would disqualify him altogether.

In comparing the nonprestige-school M.B.A. with the prestige one, equally fascinating findings present themselves. When we asked top executives to evaluate as a job candidate a "twenty-four-year-old male student who just finished his M.B.A. at a B-school you know little about," 66 percent ranked him average or above.

When we asked top executives to evaluate this same male if he were graduating with the M.B.A. from Harvard, 83 percent ranked him average or above. In the higher 5, 6, and 7 categories, Harvard M.B.A.'s exceed the

Table 1
Evaluations of Candidates' Schooling

| | TOP EXECUTIVES | | | | | | |
	1	2	3	4	5	6	7
Princeton Lit. PBK	3.5%	19.0%	32.2%	28.2%	11.4%	4.3%	1.4%
Dartmouth Poli/Sci	5.1	22.7	35.6	27.6	6.7	1.8	0.6
State School Bus.	0.6	3.1	10.2	34.1	32.9	14.3	4.9
Nonprestige M.B.A.	0.4	6.8	26.4	41.6	18.0	4.7	2.1
Harvard M.B.A.	0.6	4.5	11.9	30.5	30.3	14.3	8.0
Stanford M.B.A.	1.0	3.0	10.4	31.0	28.2	17.6	7.8

| | MIDDLE MANAGERS | | | | | | |
	1	2	3	4	5	6	7
Princeton Lit. PBK	3.9%	17.7%	31.4%	29.6%	12.9%	3.5%	0.9%
Dartmouth Poli/Sci	5.3	19.9	37.8	28.2	6.6	1.6	0.7
State School Bus.	0.9	2.1	8.5	30.0	34.8	15.6	8.0
Nonprestige M.B.A.	1.4	7.6	25.0	36.5	20.7	5.3	3.5
Harvard M.B.A.	1.8	5.8	11.8	27.6	26.9	18.9	7.2
Stanford M.B.A.	1.6	3.6	13.7	25.2	29.3	19.0	7.6

1 = disqualified   2 = very poor   3 = below average   4 = average   5 = above average
6 = very good   7 = excellent

rankings of nonprestige-school M.B.A. s. But in the 4 or average category, Harvard graduates fare much worse in the rankings than their nonprestige counterparts. Similar to the pattern with the Stanford M.B.A. s, Harvard M.B.A. graduates totaled 17 percent who ranked in the below-average and worse categories. Combined with the 31 percent who find Harvard M.B.A. s average, that hardly constitutes an across-the-board cheering section in American business.

The score category that intrigues me the most is the 5, or above-average, one. There, the state-school *undergraduate* outperforms everyone in desirability, including Harvard and Stanford M.B.A. s. It seems that quality state-school undergraduate business majors are viewed by many corporations as eminently trainable.

As you can see, the middle-manager scores on most of the above questions are similar enough to the top executives so as to make unnecessary a discussion of their responses.

What Made Him Attractive?

The question still goes begging as to what makes our hero attractive. What can be said simply at this point is that his lack of a prestige degree didn't hurt him.

His background and family's socioeconomic circumstances didn't hurt him, either. When we asked executives how much their corporations supported the recruitment of executives with high social status backgrounds, we got responses that aren't as startling as those on schooling, but quite revealing nonetheless.

Fully 71 percent say their companies have no position on this matter. Only 11 percent of top executives say their companies give the recruitment of such executives strong or some support. Five percent indicate their companies offer some or strong opposition to this practice. The remainder indicate they do not know how their companies think on this issue. Middle managers' views match those of top executives.

This young man could not claim third-generation wealth, experience with world travel, or a father who knew the ropes and had many business contacts to open doors for him. The clumsiness that comes from a lack of social exposure is a problem he would have to overcome with keen powers of observation and being a quick study.

Getting down to mundane matters of craft and moxie, the young man showed himself to be an able and well-studied performer, despite his case of nerves. Obviously, he brought them under control. His astute handling of the drink before lunch is proof. When asked to evaluate a potential candidate for employment "who orders an alcoholic drink when you take him to lunch," top executives such as Jim respond in a diverse way.

Since Jim didn't tip his hand on his feelings about drinking at lunch, our man might have ordered something and risked offending a man who was a Mormon rather than a wayward Catholic. Or he simply might be a man who has taboos about drinking at lunch for reasons of fitness or beliefs about his efficiency at work in the afternoon. What's clear from our findings is that some executives feel strongly on this matter, and an unwary candidate can jeopardize his chances needlessly over a minor incident.

Candidate who:	1	2	3	4	5	6	7
Orders drink at lunch	1.4%	5.8%	17.8%	54.0%	13.2%	5.4%	2.4%
Asks reflective questions	0.2%	0.4%	3.4%	15.0%	37.2%	30.7%	13.1%

Where the young comer from Beaver Dam truly excelled and made himself attractive was in his give and take, his genuine and penetrating questioning about the company of which Jim is a senior officer. What were its general policies? What were its major products? Which ones were showing signs of weakness in the marketplace? What promising new ones were in development or recently introduced? What expectations would the company have of the young man the first year? What kind of training would he undergo? At what point might he be asked to come to New York to serve in some corporate staff assignment? What are the ultimate measurements for reaching top management in the company? On and on, in a genial fashion, the young man put such questions and more to his soon-to-be employer.

You can see that here, too, he was on solid ground. Top executives indicate that this is the most impressive behavior of all in a prospective candidate. A candidate who "asks reflective questions about your company during your job interview" gets high marks. Ninety-six percent of all top executives consider such a candidate to be an average to excellent prospect.

The evidence is indisputable. This novice from Whitewater is no slouch!

2

Lions, Dolphins, Hippos, and Gophers

Anyone setting out to achieve a rewarding career in business needs a broad comprehension of the spirit of his organization. One cannot know any corporation or be effective within it unless he first understands its value system. The astute Whitewater candidate isn't just trying to be impressive with his reflective questions about a corporation's policy and procedures. He is assessing its values, hoping for genuine compatibility between them and his own. In fact, way back at that first campus interview, he already had begun such an assessment.

Corporations pride themselves on their values in much the same fashion that individuals do. All we say and do reflects both our individual and internalized collective values. The large degree of self-interest that leads to development of such systems justifies and explains the pride with which we regard our value systems.

Now and then someone ludicrously states that corporations have no values. But complex structures have a complex web of values, and there is no institution more complex than the corporation. Granted, those values often may be difficult to discern, but they are there—and demand careful attention. Like all other groups, corporations cannot exist without objectives; their objectives cannot be met unless action is taken; action cannot be taken without making choices; and choices can never be made without values.

If you are an employee or aspiring candidate seeking corporate employment, you would be unwise if you didn't attempt to ascertain and understand the uniquely developed values within the organization you are a part of or are considering. Constant flux of daily business in any corporation— with a brisk, changing climate—usually results in values that also are in constant flux and difficult to pinpoint. But pinpoint them you must.

If you remain ignorant of the assets and behavior codes most important to your corporation, you are denying yourself unknown opportunities. **11**

Before you can ever assess your own ability and chart your growth in a corporation, you have to grasp the underpinnings and components of its atmosphere and the image it seeks to maintain. If you lack such knowledge, you merely whistle in the dark, feel your way around, and bluff your way through blind negotiations that lead to unknown results. Most important, not knowing what is valuable to your corporation is a severe handicap when competing for career growth at all levels. It is comparable to a dog trying to please his master without knowing his favorite trick.

The Corporation as Animal

You may have heard or seen the corporation compared to an anthill. No matter how disturbing this comparison is to some purists, the analogy is useful. Much like the anthill, corporations depend on employees to inform them and relay their needs to the outside world. And like ants, employees within the corporate entity communicate by conforming to an elaborate matrix that facilitates their responding to the ongoing needs and sudden changes presented inside and outside the organization.

The commitment major corporations make to being adaptable is most responsible for their success in the ever-competitive wilderness of commerce and industry. Just over 80 percent of the executives we queried agree that if corporations were animals they would have to be of a kind mostly possessed of predatory instincts and ability. No corporation grows to conglomerate or "Fortune 500" size and success without such predatory bearings. But corporations aren't animals, and these same executives (77 percent) hold convictions that being merely predatory is no longer enough. They believe that corporations cannot hide from social responsibility to their employees or communities.

Old tendencies to ignore problems at community and employee levels—having resulted perhaps in less profit and more grief than anticipated—have been discarded in favor of dealing with such issues head-on. At last the magic dragons have come out from hiding. Pounding their chests, they now let us know that their business and purposes aren't all bad. They have contributions to make to society aside from generating profit and hiring (thus feeding) the local citizens.

Top and middle executives are successful in assessing and complying with the values of their organizations. They are most deeply involved with the policies, needs, and procedures of their companies. They have risen to a level where they are representatives of their corporations' values. Moreover, they are decision makers who also contribute with varying degrees to the makeup and change of these value systems. No group can shed light on corporate values with as much firsthand experience. No group can tell us the corporate story as well or with as much clarity.

So when we asked them to describe their corporations as animals and support their classifications with corresponding characteristics, what we wanted were responses based on intimate knowledge of their organizations, but generated in such a way that they might be more revealing. What we got is their unguarded reactions about how and why their organizations operate and place value on the things that they do. They are fascinating.

Specifically, we asked, "If you could describe your company as an animal, what would that animal be?" Then in follow-up we asked, "What characteristics of that animal make it a good analogy for your company?"

Animal Analogies and Corporation Types

Animal classifications chosen by executives symbolize their relationships with their corporations and their organizations' relationships with outside communities and competition. Degrees of identity with their companies, degrees of pride, satisfaction, fulfilment, dissatisfaction, frustration, and contempt are seen in their choices of animal analogies and characteristics.

Overall, executives place their corporations into one of four general categories:

Aggressive and strong: always ready to pounce, these corporations are impressive, widely respected, feared by the competition, provide leadership and a degree of protection to employees.

Aggressive and smart: can rise to any challenge because they are clever and have maintained concerns for the future as part of their strategy, have developed quick and skillful maneuvering abilities.

Hardworking: are impressive and successful mostly because of high energy and industrious atmosphere rather than because of clever manipulation and maneuvering in business affairs.

Restrictive: overwhelming inertia and complexity of the organization is seen as hampering the achievement of objectives and growth within the company, at times viewed to be without direction.

Aggressive and Strong

Aggressiveness and bigness are the most commonly named major characteristics of their corporations by executives. These attributes still are viewed as the major requirements for success in business. Sixty-two percent of executives describe their corporations as predatory or large animals. Typical examples of such animals and their distinguishing characteristics are listed below.

Wolf or wolverine—"fiercely competitive," "can provide leadership," "takes care of the pack."

Tiger, lion, panther, and other large cats—"aggressive," "feared by others," "predator and individualist," "cautious," "superaggressive," "fast growth through persistence," "aggressive, quick, quietly advancing," "strong, aggressive, opportunistic," "tremendous endurance and stamina—heavily results-oriented—adroit at capturing larger and stronger prey."

Bear—"cumbersome, hard to outguess, potentially dangerous," "operates in unfavorable environment," "endangered," "big, but not vicious," "hibernates periodically, liked by most people, but can become a fighter if threatened," "protective of own, angry when riled."

Bull—"charges ahead—does whatever it decides to do," "strong and determined about things—changes mind often," "sometimes snarls horns on underbrush."

Hawk—"very positive and strong in field," "image of born leader—respected by competition."

Shark—"smart, adaptable," "consumes others of its own kind."

Badger—"aggressive," "not as well known as other animals, but tenacious," "can defend against larger animals."

Elephant—"slow moving in early stages, powerful once rolling."

Bulldog—"small, aggressive, tenacious."

You can see from these descriptions that executives regard their corporations as highly aggressive; usually winners in major competition, successful enough to be able to protect employees and their domain, capable of providing leadership, and occasionally dangerous even if slow moving.

Aggressive and Smart

Some executives view their organizations as still aggressive and competitive, but also cunning and intelligent; entities capable of artful application of their powers. Fourteen percent of executives describe their companies as animals capable of intelligent maneuvers, possessing physical or natural attributes that serve aggression. They see their organizations as achieving objectives through tactical planning, clever manipulation and maneuvering in business environments, and timely application of their power. Their animal choices and characteristics include:

Fox—"wily," "alert to environment," "avoids pitfalls and adapts and responds to environment," "anticipates future," "aggressive when confident," "cautious when uncertain."

Deer—"graceful," "adapts to environment," "always on the move."

Others underscore their companies' priorities of innovation, sometimes even in unfavorable environments:

Turtle—"moves slow and steady—sticks head out for good reason," "adaptable on land and sea," "has hard protective shell," "moves slow, but gets where it wants to go," "good hard shell—willing to stick neck out to get somewhere," "can beat a rabbit when has to," "stays in its proper element so as not to end up helpless on its back," "starts out behind, often wins."

Dolphin—"intelligent, perceptive, strong, and particularly adept in environment, but confined to environment."

Eagle—"farsighted, aggressive, soaring above others."

Chameleon and other reptiles—"highly adaptable," "quickly adjusts."

Owl—"reputation for wisdom."

These descriptions indicate that managers of some—though relatively few—organizations perceive their companies as fast, smart, dynamic, fairminded, agile organizations who use more than size and power to get what they want. They suggest that winning and competing in these companies is regarded more like a sport. In such companies the traits stressed are agility, flexibility, shrewdness, and cleverness; all leading to perceptive interpretations and resourceful actions in the face of daily problems and opportunities.

Hardworking

Other executives see their companies' success coming more from the coordination of massive energy than aggressiveness or cleverness in daily operations. Fourteen percent reveal that their organizations are achievers because of high energy or persistence. They choose the following animals and characteristics to make their point.

Hippopotamus—"top heavy, too much staff, more emphasis on condition than action," "reliable, few teeth, has happy disposition," "conservative and reliable—heavy body."

Horse—"able to do various jobs," "versatile," "works hard but dumb," "hard worker, not too creative."

Ox—"strong body, slow mind," "slow, inflexible movement, but very strong."

Whale—"long life, big, can't be ignored," "proceeds in predictable and efficient way."

Beaver or squirrel—"industrious and dull, but a good citizen," "hard worker, builds strong structures, avoids public limelight," "a builder, structures, strong, but not artistic."

Buffalo—"herd instinct, hard to change direction or policy," "stodgy, slow moving—impressive and effective because of bulk," "not innovative, but plods down same path year after year."

While managers of these organizations believe their companies are big and fairly successful, their descriptions suggest that challenge and sportsmanship are less operative in their companies than in more aggressive and cunning organizations. Though not entirely negative, these descriptions offer a hint of possible boredom and frustration among their executives.

Restrictive

The smallest group of animal classifications is indicated by 10 percent of executives who operate in cramped quarters. They reflect unsatisfying and incompatible relationships with their companies. It is unlikely that such executives can or will grow within these settings.

Gopher—"puts head in ground," "ignores problems or pretends not to see them."

Hippopotamus—"slow, not too bright."

Kangaroo—"we are well protected in mother company's pouch, hopping around in mother's pouch, rather than on our own."

Armadillo—"hard shell, soft belly."

Elephant—"cumbersome, slow," "no one can see the whole animal," "awkward and slow moving."

Operating Values

As much as these analogies and characterizations reveal about major traits of executives' corporations, they also mirror the nature of the executives' relationships with their corporations. In many cases where largeness of the company is perceived by some as a positive trait, others present the same characteristic as negative. It is easy to see how an aggressive sales manager can use the large size and aggressive nature of his corporation to impress prospective customers. But others experiencing isolation and frustration with its cumbersome and time-consuming bureaucratic procedures may be more inclined to see the huge complexity of a company as a factor leading only to alienation and frustration. For example, within one company, some managers labeling their organization as an elephant described it as an impressive and powerful entity. But others using the same label described the same company as a slow, cumbersome, and overly complex enterprise.

For good or ill, depending on the views of an individual executive, such companies *operate* as an elephant would. Their operating *values* are blended around strength, slower movement, and longer gestation periods; but also around staying power and a massive show of force. If you are considering a career in such a company, it is important to determine if those operating values are consonant with your personal values and operating style. If you are already with such a company, but by virtue of your preferences would rather be with a gazelle-type company that is more swift and graceful—but also more fragile—you had better get on with the realignment for the sake of your contribution and consequent self-esteem.

I gather this kind of sorting out has pretty well taken place by the time executives reach the higher levels of middle management. Most executives give strong evidence of identifying with their corporations' operating values. While 25 percent positively reflect that their companies are quick, for example, only 15 percent indicate that their organizations are slow. While 55 percent believe that traits of innovation characterize their organizations, only 17 percent indicate inflexibility and bullheadedness characterize theirs. In stark contrast to the 18 percent of these executives who contend that their organizations are stupid or dull, 73 percent see brainy maneuvering as primary characteristics responsible for the success of their enterprises. Opposed to the 14 percent who view their organizations as weak, passive, or unresisting are 50 percent who think that their companies are highly aggressive.

The strong evidence of executives' identification with their corporations speaks well of the overall health of corporate America. Despite ritual griping by executives, by and large they seem well placed within their corporations, serving the ebb and flow of an enormously complex, worldwide commercial enterprise. Square pegs. Square holes.

The negative views among these executives show either personal incompatibility with their corporations' value systems or insight into what improvements are needed to build a smoother operating network within those organizations. The positive views, very much in the majority, show personal compatibility and the executives' belief that their corporations are functioning well in their environment.

I began this chapter by saying that to have a rewarding business career, you need a broad comprehension of your organization's spirit. I have shown how corporations fall mainly into one of four broad categories and that you must judge which of these types is most suitable for you. For example, even restrictive companies offer opportunities for you if you have shown yourself to be persuasive and skillful in turnaround situations.

The remaining chapters in this section deal with more detailed material; questions on which corporations express their values in specific ways. Some of these expressions are surprising and dispute traditional rhetoric. Others confirm what most of us believe to be true. Knowing both is useful in improving your executive performance.

3

Corporate Image and Grooming

Aggression always has been integral to corporate competition and survival. But executives believe that how companies employ aggression has changed over recent years. Their responses to our inquiries show how today's corporations seek to improve their public image; how they bring about better attitudes among employees and outsiders; how they recruit and train employees to help project a positive image to the public; how they implement policy to support such an image inside as well.

Corporations hope to give off images that express their own value to the society they serve. Policies concerning such positive images are issued from only a few leaders within the organization. Just *how* these policies get carried out is dependent on individual understanding of policy purpose by each company manager. The frequent result, as with all institutions and groups, is that gaps occur between policy intent and translation.

We asked executives to relate their corporations' concern for:

Being perceived as a socially responsible company.

Having media attention regarding corporate stances on industry issues.

Being perceived as a high technology company.

Being perceived as innovative.

Social Responsibility and Public Image

The emphasis placed on public image by managers when characterizing their corporations is well documented. Almost 90 percent say that their organizations want to be seen as socially responsible. Yet corporations either hide their light under a bushel or are not aware of the benefits of good public **19** relations. Only 52 percent of executives think their corporations are concerned with having media attention on their stances on industry issues. While this may not be social responsibility as such, it's related.

Though corporate chiefs themselves agree overwhelmingly that their enterprises suffer a negative public image, nearly 50 percent fail to participate directly in a solution. A 1980 *Wall Street Journal*/Gallup survey conducted among thirteen hundred large American corporations' chief executives relates their concern for reeducating the public about how corporations function. Steps suggested by them to narrow the gulf between business and public include a need for improved media coverage of business affairs. They also believe that more enlightened approaches by educators—explaining how and why corporations function as they do—will establish better corporate images.

The conclusion to be drawn is clear. Corporations have become more aware and concerned in matters of social responsibility and public involvement, but just about half fail to make that concern known. Failure to announce or publicize stances on most industry issues muddies the effect of any corporation's growing social concerns. Controversial issues that lead to antagonism and hostility when misunderstood by outsiders need clarification rather than evasion from companies. Publicized stances on issues are effective tools to educate the public about technical and political problems faced by corporations.

Technology and Innovation

Technology is back in a leading role on the corporate stage. It had a brush with infamy a few years ago. During the sixties, people became mistrustful of technocrats and their machinery and routinely made allegations about their evils. Flower-child literature spread its gospel about how technocrats could bring about the end of civilization as we know it. Fortunately, we learned in the seventies that to be afraid of change is to be afraid of life.

There is a definite and growing place in our world for ever-advancing engineering and technology. Sixty-one percent of all executives report that their companies like to be perceived as high-technology enterprises. This figure is likely to grow in future years. Some industries such as services and retailing have relatively little primary concern for the development of technology as we typically think of it. But they are increasingly dependent on it for the operations of their own companies. The tremendous advances in word processing and information systems in computer-based technology have had an enormous impact on companies in these industries.

On the other hand, some companies depend on technology entirely for their bread and butter. Most companies are not as devoted to it as the 3M

Company is. 3M is so supportive of technological developments that they give an award annually to executives for lofty scientific achievements. There isn't a Carlton-Award holder at 3M who doesn't cherish that honor almost as much as a Nobel-Prize winner does his. Invigorating support for technology has led 3M to its reputation as one of the most highly innovative companies in the world. The worst thing that can be said about an executive at 3M—that makes him a pariah—is that he killed an idea.

Most American companies are committed to the notion of innovation. The word itself is almost an elixir, possessed of magical properties. They *like* to have it used as characteristic of them. Eighty-six percent of executives say that their corporations are concerned with being perceived as innovative. Whether corporations actually are innovative or not, and to what extent, is another matter.

Truly, innovation is a significant attribute of any company that grows and changes to meet its changing environmental needs. No major corporation could have achieved its size and stature if it were not innovative in some fashion. Many observers complain technical innovation is lacking in many American businesses today, especially when compared to those of Japan, Inc. This charge loses ground, though, when one considers other nontechnical priorities that have been addressed in a highly innovative spirit in recent years.

Recent innovative energies among American corporations have been addressed to image and employee problems, marketing developments, and management and administrative affairs. In effect, organizations have been busy getting their houses in order. Many of the newly developed participative management experiments and various campaigns are designed to involve employees more directly in understanding and dealing with the trade-offs of their businesses. They are imaginative approaches that have been overlooked too long by many observers.

Corporate Grooming

Corporations have come to realize that good-spirited, healthy employees are more productive. Not so long ago, this wasn't the case. Corporations deemphasized employee work surroundings. They held that salaries were enough to provide incentive and motivation. Gould Inc., a large electronics technology company in Rolling Meadows, Illinois, is a good example of companies that have rejected this position.

Jack Jackson, vice-president of facility planning for Gould, believes that lower turnover, better production rates, and healthier and happier Gould employees are direct results of the pleasant surroundings in which they work. "Our chairman basically believes that a work area should manifest aesthetic and health considerations as well as efficiency, for productivity." So Gould developed a facility that includes a health club, residential management education center, quality artwork throughout the facility, and pleasant relaxation areas for employee use. The aesthetic nature of the entire complex has resulted in a community that considers itself fortunate to have the corporation in its midst, and has contributed to improved employee relations.

According to Jackson, the change is a direct result of Gould chairman William Ylvisaker's incorporation of aspects of his own philosophy into corporate philosophy. "He's a man who believes in physical fitness. He runs. He's an active man. His belief that health and positive aesthetics in a work environment are important to productivity are reflected throughout the complex."

How corporations dress themselves up accurately reflects concerns regarding their newly evolved relationships with employees and their publics. Nowhere is this interest in image improvement more apparent than in the new trends of what could be called corporate grooming. Through such trends you can see that corporations are ready to take affirmative steps to improve their own images, whether they verbally admit to such steps or not.

We asked executives to what extent their corporations pay attention to the following items:

Having quality artwork displayed in executive offices.

Architecture of the corporation buildings.

Landscaping around corporate facilities.

Decor and furnishings of the facilities.

Supporting the arts financially.

Contributing funds to community service agencies.

Their responses indicate that corporations have acquired new vanities and narcissistic leanings. Like peacocks, they increasingly are prone to strut their stuff—with the result, it must be admitted, that the workplace and the communities in which they are located are made more attractive.

As much as corporate leaders are concerned with a larger outside viewership and opinion, they are equally interested in how they are perceived in their immediate communities and from the inside itself. It seems to be more functional than trendy that corporations pay more attention to atmospheres projected by their corporate buildings, facilities, and surroundings. Sixty percent of executives claim their organizations pay attention to landscaping around their facilities. These statistics convey a desire for tidy, functional, and, in some cases, grand first images to outsiders. Well-maintained facilities surrounding these organizations also assure their welcome within their local communities.

If America is the land of the Philistines to Europeans judging our regard for culture, then they must see American corporations as pathetically barbaric. Corporation executives seem not to give a hoot for "culchah." But that doesn't mean that these enterprises don't care at all about the atmosphere within. They do. Though over 60 percent of executives say that their organizations don't have Calders, Renoirs, Modiglianis, or even Whistlers or Dalis hanging in their executive suites, roughly 70 percent think their companies do pay attention to the decor and furnishings of their facilities. The inferences to be drawn are obvious. These organizations care more about what is functional than what is simply aesthetic. And when aesthetics are functional, most organizations will leap to apply them.

Traditional views of corporate decor are changing, and they are changing within some of our most traditional companies. For example, Chemical Bank recently embarked on a move from its old offices in the Wall Street district to a more conveniently located office in midtown Manhattan. The first thing bank executives did was consult with their employees to assure that all functional requirements were met. One hundred executives within the bank were interviewed by space planners. Employees were able to evaluate and revise prototypes of the new offices before the final move was made.

The changes at Chemical provide flexibility with an eye to the future through interchangeable panels, artwork, and desks. New designs combined traditional looks in furniture with modern color schemes and lighting. Most dramatic of all is a glass-enclosed garden and atrium that allows outsiders to view the progressive and happily functioning world within. "Employees at Chemical Bank are lucky" is the message to future employees and passersby. Objectives in the move were numerous. Providing flexible work space for executives was a primary motive, of course. But officials also hoped to enhance the bank's image as a world-class institution and accent the bank's reputation for quality and solidness.

If you were to stroll along Biscayne Boulevard in Miami, you would come upon a captivating piece of architecture in which the entire sides of a six-story building are a ceramic mural. This building is the American headquarters for the Bacardi Corporation. If you looked behind this building, you would see another, even more visually exciting building made up mainly of bright stained glass that serves as the data-processing center for the company. Today, Bacardi Rum is the number-one consumed spirit throughout the world. Bacardi was built over the better part of the last forty years by the delightful and slightly mischievous José "Pepín" Bosch. I toured these facilities on one occasion with Mr. Bosch and marveled over the architecture. He turned to me with a twinkle in his eye and said, "Our buildings are billboards." And make no mistake about it, Miami is very proud of its Bacardi Buildings.

Other projects throughout the nation attempt better work and business environments. Eisenhower 280 Corporate Park in New Jersey, with its lobby floor-to-ceiling atrium and six-foot-high, sixty-foot-wide waterfall, is typical of the environments businesses create to instill an improved work atmosphere. The race is on to make work space more pleasant and productive, as well as enhance corporate image.

Absence of quality art in corporate offices does not necessarily mean that companies have no interest in the arts. A lower, but still substantial, 34 percent of executives report that their companies place some emphasis on supporting the arts financially.

Patricia Colbert, assistant secretary of the Mobil Foundation, suspects that corporate support of and involvement in the arts is likely to increase. "Oil companies ten years ago were concerned only with bottom-line drilling and exploration. But they follow the lead of their top executives. While the arts didn't play a big part in the lives of top executives who tended to be a little older a few years ago, they are a bigger part of the lives of executives tending to be somewhere in their forties today."

Mobil Oil's support of quality art, as in the funding of *Masterpiece Theater* or the sponsorship of museum exhibits, confirms Pepín Bosch's view that this constitutes tasteful advertising. Funding of the Mobil Foundation and its consequent support of numerous local art programs that has expanded from twenty-five to eighty cities since 1974 express commitment to direct community involvement. Awareness is growing regarding the part that art can play in society. Colbert sees corporate funding as vital to art programs and their influence and benefit at the community level. "Supporting the arts is like having a double-edged sword. It benefits the company's image but also it assists the community and therefore current and future employees."

Some corporations prefer to fund and support direct efforts to combat social problems they think plague and hinder progress in their own communities. Over 70 percent of executives say that their organizations contribute to community social service agencies.

4

Corporate Policies
for Executives

Finely meshed management networks are the arterial components through which corporate enterprises achieve their goals. How well these networks are developed, maintained, and controlled depends on how successful the corporation is at propagandizing.

In America propaganda is a distasteful word. It smacks of brainwashing. But indoctrination is simply a form of enculturation—merging new values with old ones; individual values with group ones—and is employed more often than most care to acknowledge. Military groups, governments, football teams, and even churches employ such indoctrination to establish common goals, enthusiasm, and cooperation among their populations. Without propaganda Moses himself would have been at a loss in steering his beloved but quarrelsome people, with their tribal values, to the Promised Land. Without such common objectives established through well-articulated propaganda, no group survives. Wars are lost, corporations fail, football teams lose (more than they already do), and churches split.

Comparisons of corporations to various groups are common. They are compared to military groups, football teams, and even the church. In the July 27, 1981, issue of *Fortune*, Kenneth Mason, former president of Quaker Oats, expresses his view of today's corporation as "what the Church must have been in the middle ages." He was referring to the corporation as the central institution in our society.

Upon induction into corporations, the pervasive tone of the relationship between executives and their companies begins. Policies serve to apprise executives of performance standards. The acceptable patterns of communications between them and the organization and between them and other executives are made clear. How successfully they navigate the waters in a career sense, and how much guidance they will get from their companies, become apparent early on in their employment. In setting policies for executives, corporations express their desired relationships between top executives **25** and the board of directors on one level, and among top executives, middle managers, and supervisors on another.

To determine the degree to which executives think their corporations achieve desired corporate/executive relationships, we asked them to indicate how typical it is for their companies to engage in the following:

Education

Articulate its intended corporate destiny and business strategy
   for all its employees.

Encourage its executives to add to formal education.

Provide company-sponsored management education/training/development.

Paternalism

Fire marginally performing executives.

Transfer executives only after careful consideration.

Provide coverage in health-care policies for psychological counseling.

Provide counseling for executives with drinking problems.

Guidance

Provide career counseling for executives.

Education

The role of educator is one of the most important roles that corporations play with employees. Successful indoctrination depends in part on articulation of objectives and strategies to all employees. Articulation of strategies and objectives has primary value in achieving the kind of loyalty and cooperation companies desire from employees who can be far off in some distant subsidiary or division. Most corporations employ various means to communicate these strategies and objectives to their employees. Sixty percent of top executives and 55 percent of middle-level executives believe their companies devote much energy to such education. How they accomplish spreading the word throughout their ranks varies among corporations.

In a July 21, 1980, *Business Week* article describing a study by McKinsey & Company of ten well-managed companies, considerable focus is placed on the one value stressed by each company's chief executive. According to McKinsey, the CEOs stress these values to employees "with an almost religious zeal." For example, one chief executive hammers away at his executives about improved quality. In times past, Thomas Watson of IBM wrote memo after memo "on the subject of calling on customers—even discussing how to dress for the call."

For most companies, policy statements are a routinely employed method of indoctrinating or informing employees about company objectives and expectations. Issued to management and employees, these statements begin the education process. Managers carry the word to subordinates, and ideally, these objectives are translated into action.

However, objectives communicated in employee newsletters and through numerous memos are seldom fully absorbed. McKinsey argues that when CEOs fail to concentrate on one particular concern, their communications lose effectiveness. A chief executive who stresses improved quality in production from his executives risks diluting his main message when he also stresses innovation, higher production rates, and better communications with customers at the same time. While all of these are important, executive energies spread thin to cover all of these areas may result in no concentration in any one of them. One executive complained about his CEO: "Sure he's for quality, but he's for everything else, too."

Repeatedly circulated policy statements, newsletters, and bulletins are worthless if they are not absorbed. And this is precisely what so often occurs. One major fault of these communications is that they often are not read by employees. Even when they are, they may seem so unintelligible or irrelevant to the reader that they go unheeded.

In recent years some companies have developed precise and sophisticated ways of communicating objectives to employees. In reaction to crucial problems among employees, some corporations have responded with impressive speed, and with impressive means of gaining employee comprehension.

For example, when selling off 25 percent of its operations, Gould Inc. concluded that effective education and communications with employees were imperative. Carefully planned campaigns were put into action. Films were made, scripts written and distributed. Division heads and plant managers personally carried the rationale to all employees for why the company was making the sale. Future security for employees was assured and the company's objectives spanning the next ten years were articulated. Marion Durk, public relations director at Gould, believes that such an approach to employee communication is "the wave of the future for most corporations. When our employees understand our objectives, they will articulate them when talking to outsiders."

In contrast to the example at Gould, one well-known large oil company instituted a package of generous perquisites to be distributed only to middle managers in one subsidiary. An executive I know there expressed his dismay at his company's not announcing the decision, but simply having supervisors inform those who were to receive the new perks. Rumors ran rampant about the new policies while dire predictions of woe grew to alarming proportions. Though these perks were largely matters of compensation requiring private discussion between supervisors and each subordinate, the explanation for the company's departure from long-standing policy, well justified in this case, would have allayed fears of other executives and subordinates throughout the organization.

Probably the biggest danger in private presentation of corporate objectives and strategy to employees through their immediate supervisors is that the effectiveness of such a procedure is dependent on accurate, uniform interpretation and explanation. The ability to so communicate to their subordinates is sure to vary among executives within the company. True enough, many policies actually may need to be understood by only a few individuals when these policies directly affect only their jobs. Those situations invite trouble, however, and must be given careful thought to avoid the sort of debacle that took place at the oil company. Contrary to erratic and arbitrary communications, most policies should be understood by all employees.

Progressive companies also have found other ways to stress indoctrination. IBM rewards every newly promoted manager with a trip to its sanctuarial management development center in Armonk, New York. There, these recently boosted executives are drilled on corporate philosophy. Enhanced skills, inculcated company spirit, and aroused loyalty to the corporation are achieved through these sessions. All this, bathed in the afterglow of the recent pay increase, can't help but reinforce the company philosophy in business activities back home.

Procter & Gamble sponsors an annual "employee dividends" day in which employees have ample opportunity to get acquainted with the company's objectives. The outcome of these meetings is that employees are given an understanding and sense of participation in corporate goals.

Corporations always must prepare their executives to help the enterprise meet its competition head-on. As one means of doing this, many corporations insist that executives add to their formal education periodically. Fifty-four percent of executives say such additional education is encouraged in their corporations. Continuing education not only enhances existing skills and keeps executives up on current developments in their fields, but it also equips them with new tools as an overabundance of M.B.A.'s crowd their corporate offices and take aim at their jobs.

Some business analysts speculate that many executives will take on second careers, in effect, within their corporations as a result of stiff competition. Many B-schools already have added continuing education courses for these executives. This latter career adaptation phenomenon is often a reflection of what is called the midlife crisis in executives in their mid-forties.

Company-sponsored training programs are more commonly encouraged than adding formal education requirements to the schedules of busy executives. Seventy percent top executives and 60 percent middle see them as highly valued in their companies. These training programs ordinarily are more beneficial to executives than is formal education. They expose them to other executives in the corporation who face the same problems and challenges. This company-sponsored education in some cases becomes almost a technically oriented therapy session. Executives can exchange ideas on ways of handling day-to-day business problems.

Such sessions usually serve as a sabbatical, however short. Benefit from such peer-group exchange for executives ultimately is good for the corporation as well as the executives involved. Further indoctrination in accordance with organization standards is achieved while the executives learn new developments in their fields. In addition, the executives may establish cooperative problem-solving relationships among themselves.

Paternalism

It's "all but dead," according to Peter Drucker in his classic *Concept of the Corporation*, published in 1946. But this study shows that paternalism is far from dead in today's corporations. As some corporations lean toward humanizing executive work conditions, their relationships with their executives become more paternalistic.

Most large and successful corporations harbor average or mediocre executives. The perception of 45 percent top executives and 39 percent middle that their corporations actually fire marginally performing executives lets us know, in fact, that such tolerance is the norm rather than the exception. Whether it is more humane to cut loose a consistently mediocre performer or to keep him on the job is an old debate. If he is fired, he may become alert to the seriousness of his shoddy performance. He may shape up and find more compatible placement elsewhere.

Considering that just under 60 percent of corporations retain such people, they are faced with the weighty problem of training leaders. Since quality leadership is in such short supply in companies, training procedures and programs are essential to overcome the shortfall. But even as training programs are established and conducted, organizations simply cannot expect to be free of marginal performance from some of their executives. Such is the human condition.

Failure to fire so-so executives may be viewed as paternalistic sheltering. But it is particularly gratifying if some marginally performing executives benefit from their training and outgrow their mediocre performance. It is something akin to the rejoicing in heaven at the return of the prodigal son. However, there is no denying that in many corporations marginal performance is tolerated in numerous quarters beyond the capability of educational remedy.

Some extraordinarily successful companies such as IBM, GE, Kodak, and Caterpillar are quite paternalistic. Caterpillar is known as "big yellow brother"—named by its employees after the color of its world-dominant earthmoving equipment. Many executives of these companies are of average or mediocre ability, yet do their jobs just well enough to serve the system. Mediocre performance is mainly what is required except from those who someday will run the place. Until a progressive Charles Brown became AT&T's chief executive, it was said to be nearly impossible to get fired from this monolithic company. The executives of average abilities never reach the top of these companies, but are simply grist for the corporate mill.

Other companies may seem ruthless. They cut loose mediocre performers. Demanding companies such as Cummins Engine are uncompromising with their executives. From the start they put them in rigorous competition with their peers. Constant attention to quality performance in such organizations produces hard-charging (albeit sometimes overly political) executives. According to Arjay Miller, former dean of Stanford's Graduate School of Business, quality executives are harder and harder to find, despite the high turnout of M.B.A.'s from B-schools. "There is still a shortage of really good managers. Executives who know how to cope with external change, and handle really big assignments, will always be in short supply," says Miller.

Generally, paternalism is thought to be a negative approach to management. However, in moderation it can be of comfort and benefit to both corporation and executive. The resulting feeling of security is well received by employees, while a stable, loyal work force is the payoff to the corporation. According to an article in the July 27, 1981, *Crain's Chicago Business*, Motorola has made such paternalism work. The brand of paternalism that is touted at that company is based on mutual respect between corporate leaders and their employees. There, workers do not punch clocks; they haven't for twenty-five years. The corporation acts as a protector of employees, offering monthly bonuses that can equal as much as 41 percent of their base salary. The impossibility of firing any employee who has worked for the company for more than ten years without the consent of CEO Robert Galvin makes any executive less likely to fire someone out of pique or impulsiveness.

Bob Galvin comes by his inclinations for running a company honestly. When his late father, Paul, founder of Motorola, instituted a profit-sharing plan many years ago, one of his competitors told him, "You will get so damn generous with your heart that someday you'll give up running the company with your head." In those days it was common for the Galvin family to assume medical bills for employees and their families and sometimes pay the college tuition for an employee's children.

In desperate need to see an executive's relocation through, some companies have been maneuvered to unbelievable compromises. An August 10, 1981, *Industry Week* article describes unconventional and extravagant perks awarded to reluctant relocation candidates. Two Midwest executives about to move to distant offices persuaded their companies to add shipment of their pets to their reimbursed costs. Ordinarily, this wouldn't sound like much. But one of these executives had twenty horses and a groomer. The other had fourteen sheep and a tractor. A Floridian persuaded his company that a move to Detroit would work hardship on his wife, who was accustomed to year-round warmth. The company hastened to provide her with a mink coat to make wintry Detroit a little more pleasant.

Some companies engage in job hunts for spouses of relocation candidates from two-career families. Engaging in spouse placement activities is only one type of response from corporations to the magnified problems encountered by the families of relocating executives. For example, children placed in new schools and new social environments often incur problems that are difficult for both a family and executive to overcome. Increased awareness of possible adjustment difficulties seems to have discouraged corporations whenever possible from ordering moves that might result in troublesome times for executives and their families.

When it comes to aiding executives or encouraging them to find social outlets for coping with high stress and pressure on the job, paternalism does a fast fade. Only 30 percent of both level executives report that their corporations provide coverage in health-care policies for psychological counseling or counseling for executives with drinking problems.

Guidance

Because executives are supposed to be leaders within their organizations, they are expected to demonstrate purpose and drive. This is essential for all upward-bound executives because, whether or not they realize it, they are on their own. Except for occasional mentor relationships, most young executives cannot look forward to a helping hand. Only one-fourth of executives assert that their organizations provide career planning or counseling for executives.

However, in some of the better-managed companies, the concept of "career path" is given much credence. Here's how it works: It is made clear to the younger, promising executives what is expected from them and what they must accomplish to be considered for plum jobs higher up on the corporate ladder. The resourceful ones act on these expectations articulated by their bosses. They use these demands as benchmarks to choose tasks to work at to round out their experience. Their superiors observe their performance and growth and devise additional exposures and responsibilities for them. Their achievement, or lack of it, serves as the basis for future promotions and project assignments. Through their running of the gauntlet, the company tests the mettle of these upcoming executives and at the same time provides them with a sense of direction and continuity (a path) in their careers.

5

Executive Workstyle

Companies require workstyle habits of executives that comply with and enhance their corporate image. As corporations groom themselves for presenting the best possible image to the public and employees, they also groom their executives to follow suit. With any company, its executives represent the *crème de la crème*. They are the supreme achievers within that entity; talented individuals who meet stringent work standards in order to gain and keep their positions. Skill in mirroring the corporate sense of good grooming, carrying out corporate policy, and projecting a professional image are all characteristic of executives to one extent or another. In that sense, these corporate leaders have more to do with success or failure in the corporation than some boardroom decisions.

Executives have to cope with varying degrees of stress and pressure. In matters of workstyle, it isn't difficult to imagine how their grueling routine has produced reputations for workaholism of near-mythical proportions. In reality, corporations demand extreme effort and competence from their executives. Behavioral requirements placed on executives to greater or lesser degrees are: (1) shouldering a heavy workload, (2) mastering mandatory job execution skills, (3) displaying an appropriate degree of congeniality, and (4) partaking of and displaying their corporations' images.

No matter how strenuously corporations attempt to humanize their climate and work conditions, results are still the order of the day. In fact, in certain cases, the attempt to humanize the workplace is likely to produce negative countereffects. Such modification can support less effective and committed executives. To determine the degree to which corporations *may* have modified their expectations and demands regarding work habits for their executives, we asked them if their companies encourage or discourage the following:

Heavy Workload

Understaffing executives.

Sixty-hour or more workweeks.

Heavy business traveling.

Taking only short vacations.

Job Execution

Speed in decision making.

Consistently displaying energy and a fast pace on the job.

Being a good writer.

Congeniality

Executives being "well liked" by their peers.

Executives being feared by their subordinates.

Proper Image

Following an active physical fitness exercise program.

Working in suit coats.

Their responses (outlined in Table 2) confirm my suspicion that corporate executives are gluttons for punishment—masochists, some might call them. Generation after generation, following the lead of earlier role models, they ask for more. But bless them, really. They are a special breed who still thrive on challenge.

Shouldering a Heavy Workload

Along with the old Protestant work ethic came adages about maximum productivity and how to achieve it. One of these is a byword in corporate management. That is, the more work one does, the more one can do. Busy people tend to produce more, and more of their work is quality work.

Many corporations pay attention to one of Parkinson's Laws. They see their employees inflating their work to fill available time slots. They especially agree with the reversal of that law put forward by Wallace Bell, director of Britain's Industrial Participation Association: "It is always possible for more work to be done by fewer people with less effort."

Corporations encourage understaffing. This means heavy workloads for executives. Whether or not such workloads actually bring higher-quality work, 40 percent of the larger corporations in America still believe so. The McKinsey study mentioned in the last chapter states that operating with a lean staff is a characteristic of ten of America's best-managed corporations. Since managers are potentially in training for still greater leadership positions, it often makes sense to overload them, forcing them to set priorities for work. This encourages executives to complete the important projects and disregard matters of secondary importance or pass them down to their subordinates.

Clear policy on understaffing cannot be presumed in a good many companies. Twenty-eight percent of top executives don't know whether or not their companies believe in maintaining lean staffs. Perhaps this group is not an overworked population. Or they may not be versed in corporate policy. Then, too, this finding may indicate that corporations are backing away from the notion that efficiency is increased by overloading executives.

Disparity regarding these views seems to be rising within corporations. Thirty percent of executives say their organizations actually *discourage* understaffing executives. Their report leads me to conclude that some corporations are retreating from the pressure/production concept of achieving greater efficiency. Many of them may never have believed it in the first place. The encouragement or discouragement of understaffing varies among corporations. Every organization has its own philosophy for training its executives.

A *Wall Street Journal*/Gallup survey published in the August 19, 1980, edition indicates that chief executives typically put in sixty- to seventy-hour workweeks. They don't do so because their corporations insist on it. The fact is, the question about excessive hours never even comes up. Simply put, given the array of CEO responsibilities, the job requires it. I work with two CEOs who put in forty-hour weeks. One is Everett Olson of Carnation; the other, Donald Kelly of Esmark. Their limiting working hours this way is rare among their peers. They are able to do it by virtue of setting firm priorities, being incredibly bright, and not meddling in the affairs of their subordinates, to whom they have delegated authority along with responsibility.

Chief executives responding to the *Wall Street Journal*/Gallup survey say they are willing to carry as much as seventy-hour-a-week workloads. Career dedication is so intense among them that they list their priorities as business, family, and personal. Among a few Spartans, only business and family are listed; they have no time for personal priorities. These are the executives whose minds keep coming back to the job, even when they're not on the job. While work is borne well on their shoulders, leisure is not.

Only 36 percent of executives say their companies expect executives to work sixty-hour (or more) workweeks. Thirty-seven percent believe their companies take no position on work hours. Most companies expect their executives to recognize if long hours are required to get the job done. Getting the job done is the rule; aside from that there are no rules.

As with heavy workloads, there are signs that long and tedious hours are

Table 2
Workstyle Preferences

	TOP EXECUTIVES		
	Strongly or somewhat Encouraged	**Strongly or somewhat Discouraged**	**No Position**
	(%)	(%)	(%)
Understaffing	38.7	30.4	28.0
60-hour or more workweeks	37.3	24.4	37.2
Heavy travel	21.1	28.7	43.7
Short vacation	26.5	14.8	56.1
Quick decision-making ability	73.9	4.9	19.9
Displaying energy; fast pace on job	72.8	2.2	23.7
Being a good writer	70.4	0.2	28.0
Being well liked by peers	58.0	3.1	37.9
Being feared by subordinates	8.2	58.5	31.9
Following active physical fitness program	50.5	1.0	46.6
Working in suit coats	39.4	9.8	49.9

"Don't Know/Inapplicable" responses not included.

beginning to be discouraged by some companies. A quarter of executives report that their organizations actually discourage long hours. It is becoming recognized in some companies that though it is vital to be able to work under pressure, there is no law that says continuous work under such conditions assures greater productivity.

Corporations are evaluating the necessity and efficiency of sending their executives on out-of-town trips as much as in the past. To some extent Ma Bell can substitute for extensive travel among businessmen. Perhaps phenomenally increasing air fares have discouraged corporations from sending

	MIDDLE MANAGERS		
	Strongly or somewhat Encouraged	**Strongly or somewhat Discouraged**	**No Position**
	(%)	(%)	(%)
Understaffing	39.7	24.6	31.0
60-hour or more workweeks	35.6	25.9	36.7
Heavy travel	16.3	30.8	42.7
Short vacation	35.2	14.1	48.1
Quick decision-making ability	67.0	7.0	23.9
Displaying energy; fast pace on job	75.3	1.5	21.9
Being a good writer	65.2	1.6	30.7
Being well liked by peers	60.3	2.5	35.1
Being feared by subordinates	12.7	53.5	30.7
Following active physical fitness program	39.2	3.2	54.0
Working in suit coats	47.0	8.3	42.8

"Don't Know/Inapplicable" responses not included.

executives to chase down some shadow of a prospect or solve some inkling of a problem. Only 21 percent top executives and 16 percent middle think their corporations encourage them to spend 130 nights per year or more away from their homes and families. Again, the idea is to get the job done the easiest way possible. Among executives who have had the moxie to climb the corporate ladder, chances are good that their jobs come first. For example, 43 percent of executives cleverly take the fifth, implying that even though their corporations may not like it, "if you gotta travel, well, you just gotta travel." Those who deplore needless travel, as I do, can take comfort in the fact that 30 percent of executives believe their corporations discourage spending as many as 130 nights away from their families.

Regarding both understaffing and long work hours, corporations at first glance may seem to maintain no policy. But getting the job done is always the policy. As much as heavy workloads appear to encourage efficiency, it is actually the determination to steer through them that cultivates leadership and astute decision-making abilities. For the most part, executives are free to decide how they best can get the job done.

Taking time off for a badly needed breather also is decided arbitrarily by executives. The 27 percent top executives and 35 percent middle who say their corporations strongly or somewhat encourage *short* vacations suggest that even these backbreaker organizations recognize the need for their executives to get away from time to time. The over half who believe their corporations maintain no position in determining the length of their vacations affirm that getting results is what determines practice.

Job Execution Skills

Despite the stress of long, arduous hours on the job, with sometimes only occasional vacation time available to them, executives are expected to maintain sharp mental faculties to make quick and timely decisions. Approximately 70 percent of executives report that their corporations strongly or somewhat encourage both speedy decision making and a high energy level and fast pace on the job. They are expected to think and act with verve.

Despite long hours and the pressure to act and decide quickly in response to the challenges that arise in daily business, the purpose of all this energy and thinking will go misunderstood if it is not communicated efficiently throughout the corporation. Any executive lacking skill in written communications is without a prerequisite for leadership. Seventy percent of top executives and 65 percent of the still-climbing middle report that good writing skills are strongly or somewhat encouraged by their corporations. Writing clear, persuasive letters and various communications both within and outside the company is necessary to job effectiveness.

Congeniality

Congeniality is vital to getting any job done, not to mention getting a promotion. While 58 percent of top executives state their corporations encourage their being "well liked by peers," and 59 percent think being feared by their subordinates is discouraged, their middle-management counterparts differ, though only slightly. Sixty percent of middle managers think being well liked by peers is encouraged. Fifty-four percent think being feared by subordinates is discouraged by their corporations. Authoritarianism is a bygone mode.

Proper Image

Personal appearance of executives is clearly perceived as adding to or subtracting from corporate image. While 51 percent top executives and 39 percent middle perceive their organizations as encouraging them to engage in physical fitness programs, a near-opposing 47 percent top executives and 54 percent middle maintain neutrality. Though some corporations have their own gyms or workout facilities for executives, corporate emphasis is placed on health and longevity as well as suitable appearance. Good appearance jells with a corporation's desire for good public image. A minuscule 1 percent top executives and 3 percent middle actually contend their companies discourage physical fitness. They must believe their top management sides with the writer of Ecclesiastes: "Vanity, vanity; all is vanity."

Dress codes tend to vary markedly between corporations. When they are stringent, emphasis is placed on image projection. Among top executives, just under 40 percent report they are encouraged to work in suit coats, while 47 percent of the aspiring middle managers believe their corporations encourage work in suit coats. About 45 percent of both levels are neutral, suggesting that such adornment is left either to personal discretion or is expected when dealing with clients or in public contact situations. Otherwise it is unimportant.

Corporations that make dress-code demands upon their employees usually have specific image reasons for doing so. You will not find sportcoats worn by top executives in the executive suites in our largest companies. That is taboo, particularly in the big cities. Dyestuff manufacturers may require their executives to wear colored shirts, promoting their own products. On the other hand, Mr. Watson at IBM used to say that his executives could wear any color shirt as long as it was white. This white shirt requirement no longer is etched in granite, but it remains predominant. The IBMer still is clad most commonly in long-sleeved white shirts, rep ties, dark, pin-striped suits and wing-tip shoes. Brooks Brothers lives!

Corporations in the textile business might look more kindly upon executives who wear long-sleeved shirts with more material—more textile product—used in their making. Others might require long-sleeved shirts so "ugly" and "hairy" arms don't protrude out of coat sleeves, or long socks that keep those blue-white lower legs well covered.

A couple of years ago Coors began a new image campaign by assigning red T-shirts and duckbilled caps emblazoned with COORS—THE GOLDEN REFRESHMENT to its workers. The company's hope was for a looser, lighter, more favorable image in contrast to that of the beleaguered brewery that has suffered considerable bad publicity since its 1977 clash with its union and has lost market share to its avaricious competitors.

6

Personal Style

If you fall in love with a machine, there is something wrong
with your love life. If you worship a machine, there is
something wrong with your religion.

—LEWIS MUMFORD

Executives are free to live their private lives pretty much as they please. This may be surprising because, as you have seen, they are hard pressed in demanding, well-defined corporate roles. After such grueling performance one might expect their social lives to be minimal. While most are not in love with machines, they are in love with their work. Some are quite cozy in machinelike bureaucracies. And true enough, many executives put business matters before all else in their lives.

However, unlike the depressing picture painted in Sloan Wilson's *The Man in the Gray Flannel Suit* (1955), businessmen (and increasingly, businesswomen) maintain active family and social lives. Their performances in these roles take on meaning to the corporation only when they impinge on the company image or daily business.

You can assess how executives manage their personal lives by their responses to our questions of how much importance their corporations attach to:

Executive involvement in community activity.

Spouse's involvement in community activity.

Marriage: with regard both to male and female executives.

Membership in a church.

Having large families (four or more children).

Having small families (two or fewer children).

Living in prestigious residential areas for:

—middle managers.

—top executives.

Avoiding divorce.

Avoiding extramarital affairs.

Avoiding discovery of extramarital affairs.

Maintaining hobbies off the job.

Executives socializing with other executives.

Overall, executives are autonomous where their personal lives are concerned. But, like the church, the corporation seems to maintain a kind of father image, hovering in the background, to be considered after all is said and done. For example, responses indicating corporate impartiality as to whether executives are married is contingent on how marital status plays into their corporate performance. Single executives are less resistant and more economically feasible to relocate than are married ones. Managers from two-career families especially undergo cumbersome family and social problems when relocated. The corporate stance on divorce, though tolerant, is still partial to happy marriages that breed happy children who grow up to be stable citizens contributing in one way or another to the corporation's healthy environment. The corporate disapproval of affairs is no more than concern for bad effects from possible divorces that can result from such activity. Scandal, of course, is abhorred by the corporation. It is the commonsense responsibility of the executive to avoid bringing scandal on the corporation by being discovered in a media-event dalliance. In other words, if you must mess around, keep it low profile.

Community Involvement

In essence there really are no individuals. Aside from the occasional monk, like Mendel, who is lucky enough to discover genes amidst his solitude, most of us establish and enhance our worth through various sorts of relationships with others. The community is the mirror that shows us that worth. No matter for whom the bell tolls, or who responds to it, everyone is affected by its chime. Perhaps more than any other institution, the corporation benefits from a healthy society, and therefore has great vested interest in social conditions. It is more for these reasons than from pure altruism that corporations increasingly encourage community involvement among their executives. Sixty-six percent top executives and 58 percent middle report they believe their corporations regard their involvement in community activities as important. Surprisingly, only about 18 percent of both levels think their organizations care at all about their spouses being involved in community activities. So relax, spouse. You're not on trial, at least not in this area.

On reflection, this statistic should not have surprised me. It is of less benefit for a corporation manager's wife to be involved in community affairs. After all, she is representing herself and not the corporation, except in the most indirect sense. But an executive himself involved in the community serves two purposes for the organization. First of all, he is in a hands-on position to determine what are the concerns and general atmosphere of the community. He is exposed to social trends that may affect his corporation.

Directly or indirectly, most social events and trends affect corporations. Over the short and long range, corporations are affected by problems existing in their communities. For example, current nationwide statistics show that grade and high schools habitually are churning out students who simply cannot read. Students who are victims of a "new math" epidemic reportedly cannot add and subtract. Such inadequate educational processes lead to eventual problems for all American corporations when they begin to recruit from that population of poor readers and mathematicians. Their poor education will have a drastic effect on corporate needs for effective communication skills. You'll remember that 70 percent of top executives report their corporations place considerable emphasis on written communication abilities. For these reasons, many corporations encourage their executives to get involved in various reading programs for community youth.

A second purpose is served when the executive carries the social message back to corporate leaders. In this activity, the executive further involves himself and his corporation in community matters. His back-and-forth presence diminishes overall perception by civic groups and social organizations that his corporation is indifferent to their concerns. Understandably, there is give and take on values between executives and community. This involvement satisfies the corporation's responsibility to be a good citizen, but also enables the company to do its business on peaceful, mutually beneficial terms with the community.

What corporations expect from an executive in the matter of his personal life reflects the organization's desire to function smoothly. Corporate concern with altruism for altruism's sake, art for art's sake, or morals for morals' sake is not a factor in their policies for desired executive life patterns. Morals at any level, much like values, are functional codes within a corporation's subculture that aid in sharing turf and achieving objectives. The demands made upon executives' private lives are mere expressions of the corporate benefits this productive conduct holds.

Changing Marital Codes

While trendiness is not necessarily a corporate preference, even these organizations cannot avoid the impact of certain social movements. Nowhere is this more evident than in the corporation's commitment to marriage and maintenance of the family unit as the focal unit of society. With no particular intent of imparting moral judgment on marital activities, corporations are as negatively affected as any other organization and institution by disintegrated marriages and families. Yet, not able to stem the tide, corporations bend when failure to do so could cause them to break. Graduates coming out of college who remain single longer force organizations either to insist on expected stability in individuals through the trademark of marriage, or to be flexible and overlook the marriage requirement.

Some time ago, being married indicated that an individual was likely to be more stable in his life patterns. Rather than carousing, indulging in party life, and pub-crawling, he went home at night to his family. Marriage also implied that individuals were capable of making a commitment. Ability to commit is of course a major asset to corporate leaders and managers. But since 17 percent of executives report marriage among male managers is somewhat unimportant to their corporations, and 34 percent think male managers being married is *not at all* important to their corporations, you can see that making such a commitment is not nearly as important as in times past.

Women, please take note. For you, being married becomes more problematical. As opposed to the 34 percent of executives who think it is not important that males be married, that figure goes up in your case.

According to 57 percent of all executives, corporations put even less emphasis on female executives being married. Actually, your being married is a touchy issue when considering how marriage affects your winning of promotions. Issues arise questioning a woman's freedom to do her job and meet her family responsibility, too. Concern regarding her availability of time—time enough to do her job effectively—takes on more importance. Many women today are attempting to blend family and professional lives. Pregnancy issues that clearly affect the corporation are beginning to be dealt with in management policies. As more and more women occupy higher rungs on the corporate ladder, gaps occur in management structures as women over thirty elect to start families. Women who want it all—family and fulfilling career—present a dilemma to corporations interested in promoting women and meeting demands for equal opportunity between the sexes.

The relevance of marriage to business conduct has changed. That people are electing to stay single longer because of career objectives cannot be a totally unappealing social development for corporations. Single males or females have more freedom to put in the longer hours that are required of top and middle management. In the July 26, 1981, *Chicago Tribune*, Elaine Markoutsas writes about a recent study funded by Exxon. It was conducted by the Career and Family Center, a division of a nonprofit organization named Catalyst. The study reveals that companies are newly absorbed with two-career families. Some companies mentioned in the study express a willingness to experiment with flexible hours and other less traditional employee benefits.

Freedom of Choice

No particular judgment is implied by corporations to executives regarding most other personal choices. For example, corporations don't care much about what church their executives belong to, or what size their families are. Most corporations are more concerned with maintenance of highly productive personnel and atmospheres within their organizations than with matters of moral commitment. Having large or small families is not deemed important by 81 percent top executives and 77 percent middle. Likewise, 72 percent top executives and 64 percent middle do not believe that membership in a church is important to their organizations. While it isn't likely that one will hear Hare Krishna chants within the executive suite, most concerns regarding religion are strictly between the executive and his family.

Neighborhood selection also is considered inconsequential by most managers. Views regarding social status tend to reflect as much about the respondent as about the organization he is describing. Only 25 percent of top executives are of the opinion that their living in a prestigious neighborhood is important to their corporations. Eighteen percent of them believe such residence selection is important for middle managers. But a slightly higher 33 percent of middle managers perceive a prestigious address as being of consequence for senior executives; 20 percent perceive one as important for themselves.

The greater number of middle managers who think their corporations place emphasis on an impressive address suggests they are convinced such an address can be helpful to advancement. Their feeling is that if they are ever going to make it to the top, it helps to live with top executives; to prove they'll do what they have to in order to make it. It makes them more impressive. Some companies do value impressive addresses. When matters such as a high-status residence, prestige degree, or even dress code are deemed of consequence by corporations, they are *really* important. If you're bent on success, you have no choice but to play by the rules. If you won't, start looking for a new corporate home.

Generally, there aren't wide differences in perceptions among top and middle executives. However, they do have different views about what their organizations expect from them in life patterns and work habits. These varying perceptions are more reflective of uncertainty on behalf of middle managers. Top executives are more privy to official policy than are their middle-management counterparts. They are more certain of themselves on these subjects while middle managers are subject to more second-guessing.

Part of the need for middle managers to second-guess their organizations' policies on such undefined issues is due to communications styles and quality within these organizations. Given the channels and various interpretations and translations through which any given order or policy is directed, perfect communications are never likely. Communications within corporations will be treated in more detail in Section II.

By and large, personal lives are important to corporations only insofar as they affect the corporations' business or image on a large scale. For the most part, executives have considerable freedom to exercise their personal lives in just about any fashion they choose. Their primary concern is that they avoid bringing any negative effect on their corporations' images or their conduct of daily business.

For example, at current epidemic proportions, divorce is considerably more tolerated among corporate leaders than it used to be. Divorce is deemed unimportant to the corporation by 55 percent of executives. Though it is clear that divorce is not necessarily smiled on by corporations, tolerance is usually unofficial policy. But extramarital affairs, being likely to take time and energy away from the corporation, cause corporate frowns. Additionally, this activity, which may well lead to divorce, is viewed ultimately to have a negative effect on family, thus community, and finally, corporate welfare.

So when corporations frown on extramarital affairs, it is a function of pragmatic social concern. In the old Spartan tradition, if extramarital affairs are offensive to corporate standards, getting caught is worse. Half of all executives say their companies disapprove of extramarital affairs. Fifty-five percent top executives and 48 percent middle believe their companies disapprove of getting caught. Of course, these numbers can be looked at from the other side. That is, every other executive can conduct amours, even be bold about it, without serious repercussions in the way he is evaluated by his company.

You have seen how corporations vary in their degrees of paternalism. However, when it comes to personal coping, paternalism is kaput. Though increasingly aware of problems confronting their executives, few corporations actively encourage outlets and temporary forms of mental escape. While not restricting executives in matters of rest and recreation, these organizations take no position on how executives seek to escape pressures of their daily routine. For example, maintaining hobbies off the job is perceived by only one in five executives to be important to his organization.

Nor are executives required to associate with each other regularly. Fifty percent of them report that such routine socializing with other executives is not viewed as important to their organizations. In fact, as a rule their companies offer plenty of freedom to separate work and personal life. Ordinarily, this freedom is viewed as a plus. Sometimes, however, executives' pressures lead to problems that cause corporate ambivalence on such compartmentalizing.

Law of the Jungle

Aware of the stress and pressures faced by their executives, some corporations seek to act as coach rather than father figure for them. They encourage the utmost in positive performance and contribution to the team's success. By means of this, executives are trained to accent the positive and disregard the negative aspects of their jobs and consequent mental pressures. Corporations thus pass on the macho notion that strong men can overcome anything. Indeed, most executives prove that philosophy to be true. The random few who eventually may crack under such pressures typically are considered tragedies. They are viewed as casualties of the corporate struggle; individuals who have failed to adapt to the "survival of the fittest" law of the jungle.

Executives are expected to cope with personal problems on their own. The callousness apparent in such evasion of personal problems encountered by executives under stress is arguable. This is where the ambivalence comes in. Corporate conditioning of their executives toward toughness is somewhat like a military maneuver. It enables these organizations to staff up with suitably competitive, durable, unsinkable executive teams.

If corporations divert their attentions to such plights as drinking and psychological problems, much of their time and energy will be given to attending to the needs of a select few. Further, extending such attention to these few sets a precedent—an example for others to call on the corporation for help. High standards may begin to disintegrate when mercy for the failing few interferes. From a survival standpoint, if it is fatal to nurse an ailing few, the ailing few are sacrificed. As Irving Kristol has said, "Dependency tends to corrupt, and absolute dependency corrupts absolutely." By choosing to evade such problems, most corporations encourage their executives to deal with them discreetly.

7

Favored Fields for Promotion

> Give him a trial . . . if he can win the race, he is our racehorse.
> If not, he goes to the cart.
> —ANDREW CARNEGIE

Training and promoting those who excelled in their field was a common practice in Carnegie's Scotland. But in the late 1800s such promotion policies were nearly unheard of in the United States. Dispersing power to hired help was viewed skeptically as a dangerous policy by most big business families. As a consequence, many of those family businesses suffered duress, tension, fatigue, poor planning and execution, and sometimes even failure. For example, Eli Whitney nearly destroyed himself and his firm trying to run it entirely by himself. In *American Made*, Harold C. Livesay recalls that Cyrus McCormick, near nervous breakdown, appealed to his nephew to come to his rescue. McCormick complained, "My affairs have been so numerous, embarrassing, and oppressive that I am almost driven to delirium. I find that it is absolutely impossible for me to accomplish . . . the most pressing necessities."

Carnegie, however, remembered well the drawbacks of working around the clock from his early days on the railroad. Delegating authority was the sanest and most effective method for achieving his company's objectives. In the early years of his business operations, forty men rose through the ranks to enjoy partnership status.

It's not hard to imagine how such promotion policies have served to change the face of the American work force. The workingman since Carnegie's time has been more hopeful, capable of reaping greater reward from his labors. Earlier promotees who received fractions of their companies' profits were actually more capitalists than managers. Nonetheless, bureaucratic managerial structures began to evolve in the American workplace, allowing more people on lower levels to prove themselves and move up within the corporate pyramid.

Promotion from within brings results as well as fulfilment. By the time World War II had come and gone, promotability was the right and aspiration of many common workers. Accompanying the evolution of bureaucratic structures within corporations across the country was the evolution of the world's largest middle class.

Because of what generally was viewed to be insufficient sources for the in-supply of leaders, companies were compelled to promote from within—a potential they touted to all incoming applicants—letting the applicants know they might well fit into the companies' plans for a developing, customized leadership. As in Carnegie's day, promotion policies serve to encourage company loyalty and boost productivity. Carnegie readily realized this benefit when he teased that "Mr. Morgan buys his partners—I raise my own." Today, corporate chiefs still follow his lead. According to 89 percent of executives, promotion from within is widely encouraged and whenever possible implemented in their companies. When asked, "How much does your corporation support promoting individuals to senior positions (vice-president or above) from within its ranks?" executives overwhelmingly assert that promotion from within is widely observed policy.

However, 55 percent top executives and 60 percent middle report their companies go to the outside to fill senior positions. This means top managements believe that promotion from within is not always practicable. Figures like these should make the aspiring executive see to it that he or she continues to broaden his or her experience. When the time comes to be considered for a key spot, that executive will be ready.

In searching for the special formulas involved in getting a promotion, however, one is led to conclude that no such formulas exist. There are no yellow brick roads leading to the corporate executive suites of America. Rather, those who win promotions do so through sound strategies developed early in their careers. No one aspect of their career strategizing is more important than any other. Serendipity seems not to be a major factor in getting promotions within large corporations. Being in the right company, at the right time, with the right acquired skills is not so much an accident. Lucky breaks are terribly overrated when it comes to planning, implementing, and achieving successful careers. "Luck is in love with efficiency," says Walter Rose, an old friend who is also a successful senior vice-president. The individuals who possess the right combination of workable skills within a given corporation, who are capable of filling the unique needs of that organization, are likely to grasp the brass ring.

Though factors considered in promotion decisions seem random and arbitrary at times, there are prerequisites that must be completed before anyone is even considered for promotion to key-level management. Some of these relate to two questions that might be asked right from the start in planning a career as a senior executive:

What are the select fields that are more often preferred for preparing a manager for promotion to senior executive positions?

What are the ages when major promotions occur?

The answers executives give to these questions confirm the importance of seeking the right combination of experience in due time.

Importance of Field

The fields most likely to bring consideration for promotion are:

General Management

Finance

Sales

Field Operations

Manufacturing

Marketing

Line Positions

Staff Positions

Research and Development

Legal

Personnel/Human Relations

Percentages of responses in each category make clear that one field or another may be influential depending on the specific needs of a particular corporation. But like aggression, it is *how* time and experience in these fields have been used that argues for or against a promotion. Their usefulness in a candidate's portfolio depends on how they are blended with other traits and assets.

Preference ratings for these fields are shown in Table 3.

I have cited the views of the top executives only. This is because they are the ones who actually make decisions regarding promotions to senior-level positions. Their opinions on what fields lead to such promotions are most pertinent.

General Management: 78 percent of top executives think their companies support promoting those from general management. Contrary to the upbeat reaction to sales people (as you'll see shortly), this strong preference isn't surprising at all. It is as it should be. Someone who has run a small division or subsidiary with profit-and-loss responsibility is the best-equipped person, on average, for assuming similar responsibility on a larger scale. General managers also have wider experience, have faced more vagaries, have had to

Table 3
Evaluations of Field Preferences for Promotion

| | TOP EXECUTIVES | |
Field	Strong or Some Support (%)	No Position (%)
General Management	77.5	14.6
Finance	75.4	14.3
Sales	73.6	14.4
Field Operations	71.5	17.2
Manufacturing	70.6	16.4
Marketing	67.9	19.5
Line Positions	64.5	21.4
Staff Positions	46.4	30.6
Research and Development	32.5	43.7
Legal	31.6	41.5
Personnel	29.7	40.2

"Strong or Some Opposition" and "Don't Know/Inapplicable" responses not included.

be more flexible while maintaining broader perspectives, and have achieved less parochial objectives.

Finance: 75 percent of the top executives believe their corporations support promotion of individuals from finance. Since the seventies, this field has enjoyed high status as a training ground likely to produce candidates for promotion. It retains that status. Finance is a discipline that helps harvest profits. It also is a retentive and defensive discipline that is employed by senior management to bring the best possible returns per invested dollar. Armed with a valuable, specific knowledge, financial analysts and other finance managers are cushioned with favor from most executives likely to consider them for promotions. Key buzzwords begin to appear in the rhetoric of top management when they bestow the privilege of promotion. "Profit planners"—those who have made profit or loss recommendations—tend to gain favor. So do the practitioners of "cost-benefit analysis" and believers in high "return on investment." These individuals are positioned well when it's time to call someone up from the lower rungs of the corporate ladder.

Sales: 74 percent of top executives express the opinion their corporations look with favor on those from sales when considering people for promotions. Frankly, this is a pleasant surprise to me. Since the marketing discipline was assumed to have replaced sales in the sixties as a likely path to promotions, many of us thought sales had been given short shrift, despite its contribution to corporate success. Salespeople have to be gutsy to be effective. Contrary to my beliefs, business seems not to have forgotten this.

The sales area itself is a kind of historic, heroic discipline in American business. Salesmen of old played tactical parts in building most businesses. In fact, along with manufacturers, salesmen were *the* early heroes of American business. In today's one-upping business atmosphere, with increasing numbers of technological and scientific corporations, sales managers who are adept with technical products and display interpersonal communications skills are perceived as premium people.

Successful sales managers already have mastered the skill of combining their own specialized and technical knowledge with the ability to persuade people. They demonstrate strong leadership skills as well as versatility. Having sold themselves, their corporations, and their products or services effectively, these individuals have what corporations require from top executives. What is more important to any business than the ability to sell an idea?

Field Operations: 72 percent of top executives believe their corporations support promoting individuals from field operating positions to key management positions. Much like those from the sales area, their work involves fine-tuned blending of specific industry or technical knowledge with an ability to work through and with people. District and regional operations managers daily face the challenge of preventing problems—and solving them when they haven't been prevented. Their work provides broad experience and excellent background for overseeing large groups within complex operating structures. Individuals from field operations combine many of the most important elements required to fulfill needs of key management positions. One of them is that "they know the territory." They are adept at working with people, are the recipients of good leadership training, and, most of all, are effectiveness oriented. Success in their discipline requires that they demonstrate farsightedness and competent decision making. This combination results in efficient and timely troubleshooting and avoids problems down the road.

Manufacturing: 71 percent of top executives think their corporations support promoting individuals from this specialization. Manufacturing is the other discipline that has had heroic sagas spun about it, dating from the days of yore in business. Old-time entrepreneur manufacturers used to "straighten out the problems at the plant" in the morning, then go out in the afternoon to sell their wares. It is a rich historical precedent that leads to the placement of high value on manufacturing executives today. Their contribution is every bit as significant as it was in the past. They can have a marked effect in cutting the costs of running a business.

Marketing: 68 percent of top executives believe that people from the marketing discipline receive support for promotions. Level of support for promoting marketing managers is likely to vary among companies. For example, in several highly competitive food or other packaged-goods industries, marketing is the vital organ within their system. But for other more technical or service-oriented organizations, marketing is likely to be valued less as a major function of the business. The tendency to stress advertising and packaging over technical developments led to much corporate favoritism toward marketing functions during the sixties. But such favor dwindled during the seventies as financial planning and control became more vital to the corporation's survival.

Line Positions: 65 percent of top executives think their organizations support promoting individuals from line positions. Much like the pure general manager (in some cases they are one and the same), the line manager is the one who sits behind the desk where the proverbial buck stops. He is the fellow who hears the arguments from all his support staff and analysts, and after considering all their views and recommendations, makes a final decision. Final-decision makers are more exposed to high-stakes responsibility on a daily basis, unlike analysts and others whose decisions or recommendations don't carry as much weight or consequence.

Staff Positions: 46 percent of top executives believe their corporations support promoting individuals from these non-profit-responsibility positions. Staff people rate much lower than line for promotability to senior positions. Often they are uncomfortable making bold decisions of the nature that line people are required to make. Usually they are more comfortable exercising strong analytical abilities and then making recommendations to their line bosses. Sometimes exceptional staff people are promoted to key management positions. Staff people considering such promotions should give much consideration to their possible incompatibility with the responsibilities of a senior general management position.

Research and Development: 33 percent of top executives believe their corporations support promoting individuals from this field. Researchers and other scientific people tend to be more parochial in interest and knowledge. They often see their own fields as most important, are more loyal to those fields than to their corporations, are more aware of happenings and state of the art in their disciplines than of the "big picture" affairs of their corporations. Such limited scope is mostly what inhibits individuals from research fields being promoted.

Legal: 32 percent of top executives think their corporations support promoting people from their legal department to senior management positions. Naturally, the tendency to promote or not promote from legal is affected by unique considerations within the corporation itself. Many companies place high value on legal training for their senior executives. Indeed, many CEOs are lawyers. But as far as our research is concerned, it is generally the case that legal professionals are still considered by most top executives to be overly specialized, detail-minded, and parochial for top management positions.

Personnel/Human Resources: 30 percent of top executives think their corporations support promoting personnel managers to senior executive positions. This could be viewed by some as surprising since personnel managers are required to maintain an awareness—in theory at least—of the overall present and future corporate staffing needs and functions of their organizations.

The lack of practical and applied overview in the personnel/human-resource person's daily routine is probably his most handicapping feature when it comes to being considered for promotion to top management. Despite establishing guidelines for hiring, deploying, and firing personnel, along with responsibilities in compensation programs and employee benefits, combined with responsibilities for management development programs, this person still is perceived by his superiors not to be getting the hands-on experience with corporate problems that individuals in other fields do.

Looking beyond the Labels

Limitations or blessings affecting promotions are as superficial or as deep as an individual allows them to be. The upfront desirability with which these fields are invested in making promotion decisions is indicated in the percentages of "no position" responses (meaning the percentage of executives who believe their company maintains no strong views one way or the other on the field in question) expressed by executives. Highly favored fields are embraced with little hesitation. Between only 14 and 17 percent of top executives maintained "no position" on disciplines receiving over 70 percent of support from these executives. But disciplines perceived as likely to receive support for promotion by between only 30 and 40 percent of our respondents received a high 40–44 percent "no position" response. This conveys an unenthusiastic—or neutral at best—sponsorship within most companies for the field *itself* for spawning future top executives. However, it is important to remember that no one is frozen out from consideration for promotion simply by virtue of his or her discipline. Rather, the effort of individuals to broaden their experience beyond these fields of specialization is what matters in influencing promotion decisions. Examples in the real corporate world are numerous.

Though scientists are viewed as parochial in scope and interest, they are not barred from the grand suites of senior executives. On August 6, 1981, *The New York Times* heralded startling news: SCIENTIST TO BE PRESIDENT OF

AIR PRODUCTS AND CHEMICALS EUROPE. Somehow that read like VILLAIN TO BE COUNTY SHERIFF or ACTOR BECOMES PRESIDENT. It just didn't seem likely, even to business journalists. Obviously, the *news* was that a scientist, in the person of J. Robert Lovett, had been named president of Air Products and Chemicals' European division. Mr. Lovett, who holds a doctorate in chemistry, is somewhat of a novelty and living proof that there are exceptions. So is John Welch, CEO of General Electric, also a Ph.D., and John Richman, CEO of Dart & Kraft, a lawyer. Their qualifications and experience comply with the needs of their corporations. Charles Brown, CEO of AT&T, is a graduate electrical engineer. Before he assumed his current post, he served the company as chief financial officer. These dramatic success stories are proof that in many corporations professionals who make it their business to become broad executives as well stand excellent chances for rapid advancement.

To repeat: as a rule, there is no rule. Executives come from all fields, all disciplines, all types of backgrounds. The only item that far and away marks most promotable executives is an expressed desire to be a senior executive in the early planning stages of their careers.

Age at Promotion

Senior management positions aren't for kids. Sixty-three percent of top executives say their corporations support promotion of executives thirty-five and over. Age preference for promotion considerations are shown in Table 4.

Top management believes that individuals who have garnered the proper exposure and are at least thirty-five years old are suitable for promotion to vice-president positions. Middle managers see the ages between forty-one and forty-five as the golden years before *the* golden years—a time when they will be tapped for management positions that will reward their efforts and loyalty shown over the years.

Top executives agree with them. They believe that forty-one to forty-five are the years in which their corporations *prefer* to promote middle managers to top-level positions. These people are looking backward somewhat, thinking their own prime years may be past, but also are once again showing that they are privy to corporate policy. High ratings for candidates thirty-five years of age and over, combined with low ones for those under thirty-five, make clear that is the age an executive has to reach before he can be considered for key spots in top management.

In the mid-sixties, Boise Cascade got a lot of favorable press for promoting M.B.A.'s in their late twenties and early thirties into the topmost positions in the company. Soon thereafter, the company underwent a precipitous

Table 4
Age Preferences for Promotion to Senior Positions

| | TOP EXECUTIVES | |
Age	Strong or Some Support (%)	No Position (%)
35 years and over	63.3	30.5
Between 51 and 55 years	36.5	42.6
Between 46 and 50 years	45.8	42.5
Between 41 and 45 years	54.0	37.6
Between 35 and 40 years	48.0	38.8
Under age 35	24.8	37.1

| | MIDDLE MANAGERS | |
Age	Strong or Some Support (%)	No Position (%)
35 years and over	65.0	21.2
Between 51 and 55 years	36.7	33.7
Between 46 and 50 years	47.4	34.2
Between 41 and 45 years	55.0	31.6
Between 35 and 40 years	51.4	29.3
Under age 35	24.0	33.0

"Strong or Some Opposition" and Don't Know/Inapplicable" responses not included.

slide, with CEO Robert Hansberger—author of the kiddie policy—getting a fast heave-ho. John Fery stepped in, restored order, and set the company on a steady growth course that continues today. Talented as they were, those young executives just hadn't been over enough track to develop the judgment needed for top-management decision making.

Just as there is no special discipline offering a boost for promotion seekers, there is no special age. But again, there are magic combinations. If you are able to perceive an obstacle to your promotion residing in a corporate or managerial mismatch, you're lucky. You're simply observant and progress-oriented. In striving for growth in your career, you have to be able to perceive such mismatches, recognize them for what they are, and go on from there. On such occasions, you would be wise to apply the lesson of the prayer composed several decades ago by Reinhold Niebuhr and used by Alcoholics Anonymous. The executive who changes things that are changeable, accepts the things that can't be changed, and has the wisdom to know the difference between the two is the one who is capable of placing himself in a winning environment.

Today's promotion policies have evolved with the changing business environment. They are complex, in a state of flux, and riddled with problems. A *Business Week* special report of February 20, 1978, notes that companies will experience increasing difficulties in finding seasoned managers in the next ten years. As technology becomes more sophisticated, new areas of growth develop, and mass production creates demands for more experienced leaders, specialized managers capable of a general grasp and attention to broad corporate needs become rarer and more valuable.

Considering the variety of corporate atmospheres and philosophies, it isn't hard to imagine that a poorly placed individual within one corporation could be received gladly and thrive in another. The major finding in this report for you is that there is no existing formula for success, nor a foreclosure on your talents in achieving management promotions.

Read the stream. Do your job. Go get 'em.

8

Standards for Recruitment

The primary task before corporations is to merge their own values with those of individuals inducted into their systems. The trick is to do this without arousing major life crises in the new recruits or in the corporations themselves. This isn't easy. Throughout the world, corporations are the largest and most complex embodiment of social and personal values and value conflicts.

Most valuable to any corporation is the depth and variety of experience and knowledge provided by its employees. Recruits are brought into a company with the intention that they will assist in achieving a corporation's objectives and complement its image; an image derived from the organization's set of values.

Top- and mid-level executives are the designers and implementers of corporate recruitment policies. To determine what corporations value in making recruitment selections, we asked executives how much their corporations would support hiring these candidates:

Education Background (holders of):

A degree from a prestige college or university.

An M.B.A.

Other type of master's degree.

An undergraduate engineering or technical degree.

An undergraduate liberal arts/humanities degree.

Personal Background

Female executives, only after evaluating their husbands.

Male executives, only after evaluating their wives.

Executives with high-social-status family backgrounds.

Executives with low-social-status family backgrounds.

Executives from any particular region in the United States.

Executives who are not overweight.

Executives who are women.

Education

Contrary to popular belief, student suicides do not seem to increase during exam periods. Of twenty-three suicides during a ten-year period at Berkeley, for example, only one occurred during an exam week, while sixteen occurred during the first five weeks of a semester.

—*Harper's* magazine/*Wraparound*

For anyone hoping to do anything that resembles a profession, doing time at the university level is a mandatory first step. All pain aside, a college degree remains the priority of young adult life. Freshman students reading the above inscription in May probably will be relieved. Despite talk about the rigors of college life, there's no decline in college applicants. Students still faithfully flock to take SATs and ACTs. They compete fiercely to win a cubbyhole in some run-down or less-than-quaint dormitory. At registration, the frenzied cramming and sleepless nights during exam week are rarely anticipated. That is to the good.

In an essay written in 1921 entitled "What College Did to Me," Robert Benchley relayed less than impressive views of his liberal arts education. Benchley reported learning in his freshman year that "Charlemagne died or was born or did something with the Holy Roman Empire in 800. . . . French nouns ending in 'aison' are feminine, almost everything you need to know about a subject is in the encyclopedia. . . . The law of diminishing returns means that after a certain margin is reached, returns begin to diminish. This may not be correctly stated, but there is a law by that name."

We can guess that Benchley, degreed or not, is not the ideal corporate candidate. Though his remarks are not necessarily typical of all liberal arts majors, there are science, engineering, and business disciples inclined to think they are. While corporations put premium emphasis on college education, they do so only so long as the curriculum is right.

M.B.A.'s

Remembering the successful candidate from Whitewater State, you may be secure that where you went to school is not the primary focal point of a job interview. If you're not from a prestige school, don't be disheartened. If you

Table 5
Recruitment Preference

For candidates:	TOP EXECUTIVES		
	Strong or some support (%)	Strong or some opposition (%)	No Position (%)
With degrees from prestige school	49.9	1.6	43.4
With M.B.A.'s	64.4	2.7	27.7
With other master's degrees	59.9	1.2	34.1
With undergraduate degrees, engineering/technical	60.6	1.2	30.8
With undergraduate degrees, liberal arts/humanities	33.1	10.6	47.8
With high social family status	10.5	5.1	71.0
With low social family status	2.4	9.3	74.4
From one region in United States	10.8	2.0	77.1
Female; only after evaluating husband	6.2	4.9	71.0
Male; only after evaluating wife	12.9	6.0	65.9
Not overweight	33.5	3.3	54.2
Who are women	48.5	29.4	14.9

"Don't Know/Inapplicable" responses not included.

are, rejoice. When reviewing the executives' responses in Table 5, you certainly know by the perceptions of 50 percent of executives that prestigious education backgrounds surely can't hurt. But 43 percent top executives and 39 percent middle say their organizations take no particular position regarding hiring candidates from prestige schools. As I have said, other factors affect their final decisions. Ratings outlined in Table 1 in the first

For candidates:	MIDDLE MANAGERS		
	Strong or some support (%)	Strong or some opposition (%)	No Position (%)
With degrees from prestige school	50.1	2.5	38.7
With M.B.A.'s	60.8	1.6	29.3
With other master's degrees	53.0	1.4	37.0
With undergraduate degrees, engineering/technical	57.0	1.8	28.6
With undergraduate degrees, liberal arts/humanities	34.2	8.4	45.9
With high social family status	14.2	4.1	66.4
With low social family status	3.9	9.6	71.1
From one region in United States	10.3	2.2	74.3
Female; only after evaluating husband	6.6	5.9	66.5
Male; only after evaluating wife	10.0	6.4	64.7
Not overweight	27.3	2.1	58.1
Who are women	40.1	17.9	33.5

"Don't Know/Inapplicable" responses not included.

chapter make clear that judgment of students or executives from prestige schools is reserved. Executives who hire would rather wait for further evidence to support the candidate. They look for integrity, capability, and motivation.

The numbers also show that a degree from a prestige school can be interpreted negatively by some managers. It isn't difficult to conceive of a manager from, say, South Dakota—who worked his way through a state university, then up the corporate ladder—being suspicious of a prestige-school graduate. Such an executive might be concerned about this candidate's willingness and ability to roll up his sleeves to get the job done. You already have seen from 70 percent or so of our middle managers that hard work—high energy and a fast pace with lots of sweat and toil—comes long before the rise to the top. Most executives endure many years of arduous tasks before being elevated to top executive positions.

Executives are openly impressed by the holder of the almighty M.B.A. Premium value placed on M.B.A. degrees is shown in the perceptions of 64 percent top executives and 60 percent middle who contend their organizations seek to hire such candidates. But once again look to the almost 30 percent of both levels who reserve judgment until all the evidence is in. Some M.B.A. s have acted like prima donnas in many organizations. Such behavior has discouraged corporations from recruiting them. In addition, high starting salaries required to attract M.B.A. s have been a deterrent to some companies. Graduates holding these degrees also are increasingly selective, leading to the criticism (often not fair) that they are more concerned with advancing their own careers than with fitting into a corporation's scheme of things. As a result, undergraduates holding a B.A. or B.S. continue to be given serious consideration for employment by almost all companies.

Some companies resent paying M.B.A. s high salaries (fifty thousand dollars starting salaries for those from prestige schools are not unheard of) and keeping them challenged and satisfied that they are moving along fast enough in the company. Some M.B.A. s also resist taking assignments in divisions or subsidiaries they believe may retard their growth, or worse yet, lead to stagnation.

It seems like eons now that M.B.A. s have been touted in some business circles as the miracle component for corporations achieving success. But the pampering required to keep some of them satisfied with their progress is turning many companies away from recruiting them exclusively. Obviously, wise M.B.A.'s will not consider their ownership of this degree an automatic license to special treatment. They will go to great lengths to assure their new employers and coworkers that they fully intend to earn their way.

Undergraduate engineering or technical degree holders are rated second to the M.B.A. in recruitment desirability. Sixty-one percent top executives and 57 percent middle give them the thinnest of margins over other master's degree holders. Other types of master's degrees receive third largest support from executives. Executives with master's degrees other than the M.B.A. are perceived by 60 percent top executives and 53 percent middle to have strong support for recruitment at their corporations.

No matter how college life is viewed by corporate executives, they remain biased in favor of business degrees. If college has more to do with routine than education, it serves as a suitable method of honing, processing, and standardizing a wide variety of individuals and temperaments. No matter in

An M.B.A. is a favorable alternative, provided that the liberal arts student knows where he wants to go. According to career counselor Marilyn Moats Kennedy, "Being a confused career planner with a master's degree is no better than being a confused planner with a bachelor's degree."

Liberal Arts Majors

Business majors are wooed. Liberal arts graduates are shunned. There are worse labels to bear than that of liberal arts major. Murderers, thieves, and hijackers are examples. The plight of liberal arts majors, rebuffed repeatedly after experiencing a late awakening to the drama and excitement of business, is real. It is shown most in the serious obstacles they face in achieving a satisfying corporate career. Sometimes these obstacles seem no less debilitating than bubonic plague.

Despite my barbs directed to corporations for their low view of liberal arts majors, I must admit that while subject to initial exasperation, they do have alternatives available to them for breaking into a business career. The best one, if they can swing it, is to get an M.B.A. Our hypothetical M.B.A. from Stanford received his undergraduate degree in liberal arts at a small church-related college. He ranked among the highest in the cream-of-the-crop categories of all prestige-school candidates.

An M.B.A. is a favorable alternative, provided that the liberal arts student knows where he wants to go. According to career counselor Marilyn Moates Kennedy, "Being a confused career planner with a master's degree is no better than being a confused planner with a bachelor's degree."

Executives often think liberal arts students are less farsighted than business majors. Planning and executing are qualities valued by corporations. Business majors have anticipated problems and demonstrated frugality in applying their educational energies toward their future. The liberal arts student, however, may be perceived by many executives as one who doesn't contemplate likely career obstacles until he comes to them. For such executives this orientation, contrary to the canons of business planning, only serves to prove the lack of direction characteristic of a generalized education. Still, and here is where a critical contradiction presents itself, such a general education provides broader, richer backgrounds and more encompassing, elastic perspectives that are required of top executives.

Some businesses are opening their doors with more enthusiasm to liberal arts majors. Some always have done so. However, opportunities for placement of the generally educated individual in the specialized business world are still relatively limited. Recent attempts have been made to close the gap between liberal educators and the corporate world. Businessmen are concluding that liberal arts students may be better qualified to make complex, speedy decisions. Hesitation prevails, however, over taking on lengthier and perceived-to-be riskier training programs for these candidates. In a June 28, 1981, *New York Times* article, Gene Maeroff writes that liberal arts graduates are attracting the serious attention of businessmen. He quotes Dwight Allison, president of The Boston Company, who says that "liberal arts students are an undiscovered secret for business." But to date, in my view, Allison's optimism is shared by precious few executives.

Personal Miscellanea

The types of recruitment considerations that follow are much like the prestige degree, but weigh less. Depending on what impression a candidate makes, they serve as either a cherry on top, or the last straw. For example, when 71 percent top executives and 67 percent middle express no opinion on evaluating a female candidate until evaluating her husband, certain assumptions can be drawn. Most important, we can assume that provided the husband doesn't pick his nose at the dinner table, drink himself into oblivion, or spill his wine on the interviewer's suit, he won't play a crucial part in this decision. The same holds true for evaluating male candidates based on the performance of their wives.

Actually, the only importance a spouse should possibly play in determining whether or not a corporation will hire a candidate has to do with that spouse's tolerance of the inconveniences that accompany executive positions. Spouse support for executives who may be exposed to long, grueling hours, heavy travel, and shortened vacations will be appreciated by corporations. But if the candidate has successfully displayed impressive integrity, ability, and technical skill, chances are that favorable or unfavorable spouse performance (unless it is totally outlandish) will barely affect a company's decision to hire.

Neither do executives set great store by family status or regional origin of executive candidates. High or low social family status background is perceived by over 70 percent top executives and over 66 percent middle to be of no consequence to their organizations. Regional screening is usually conducted by recruits. A marketing executive from Hawaii who works for a Texas-based company recently told me he would never consider working east of Chicago. This executive felt that his cultural elasticity just about reached its limit somewhere along the western shores of Lake Michigan. Whether his notions are or aren't justified, I hear comments like his every day.

You may be aware of the complaints and legal action of obese candidates who charge that because of their weight they have been overlooked when it comes time to promote or award jobs of interest. While our data suggests they have a point, this bias has not reached epidemic proportions. Fifty-four percent top executives and 58 percent middle report no position on hiring an executive who is not overweight. On the other hand, 36 percent top executives and 27 percent middle offer that their corporations give strong or some support to hiring executives who are not overweight. This does arouse notions that overweight candidates might receive less favorable consideration.

Finally, a fascinating and presumably generous 49 percent top executives and 40 percent middle suggest that their organizations offer strong or some support in recruiting executives who are women. I merely want to mention this here. The subject of recruiting and promoting women deserves special consideration and therefore will be treated separately later in the book.

The numbers reported so far in this chapter deserve careful scrutiny before arriving at any conclusions. While they may reflect accurately whether candidates are viewed at first glimpse as good, very good, or excellent by these executives, it is necessary to ponder what first appear to be evasive "no position" ratings. Actually, rather than demonstrating evasiveness, these responses indicate the concern that executives have for more than any one item in evaluating a prospective employee. They can be interpreted as a means of keeping themselves open until all the supporting information is in.

The successful student from Whitewater State obviously has defied some of these statistics—upper-range preference for students from prestige schools, for example. But while he may have received low ratings in some categories, he more than compensated for them in others.

Though corporations remain traditional and conservative in their values, they become highly flexible when assessing background combinations that underscore success.

Varied Backgrounds and Considerations

Corporations are as staunch and traditional as ever when it comes to evaluating an executive. They continue to look at past performance. Though it is reported that more people from all walks of life are seeking second careers, such career and life shifts are difficult to make, and are viewed skeptically by corporate leaders.

To determine how executives perceive such changes, we asked them to "assume you were considering the following people for positions in the departmental function or division for which you are responsible. Indicate how highly you would rate them."

Executive who was fired from his last job.

Executive who was fired from his last two jobs.

Executive who worked for five different companies in the last ten years.

Executive who dropped out from corporate life to run an organic farm in northern Wisconsin.

Woman whose children are grown and has just earned an M.B.A. degree.

Hospital chaplain who wants to get into business and strikes you as a natural leader.

Woman with a liberal arts degree who has been an elementary-school district superintendent.

Woman with a liberal arts degree and no business experience who wants to be your gofer and will study the business.

Woman executive with appropriate experience.

Job Stability

You hardly would be surprised that corporations seek stability in their executives. Inability or unwillingness of an executive to commit to a corporation's goals and philosophy causes that company a great deal of lost time, effort, and money that have been invested in him. The executive who has worked for five companies in the last ten years receives the worst rating of all candidates. Disqualified by 20 percent top executives and 16 percent middle, such a candidate is viewed as just one step ahead of the sheriff. Another 70 percent top executives and 67 percent middle rate this candidate as very poor to below average. This is because he represents the ultimate in instability.

This type of executive cannot develop shared interest in company objectives and is unable to see his job to completion. Such instability cannot be productive for the corporation or, over the long haul, the individual's own career.

Executives who have been fired are evaluated cautiously. Those having been fired from their last two jobs were either disqualified or rated as very poor by three out of four of both level executives. That's to be expected. The pattern is ominous. But some circumstances surrounding an executive's firing deserve special consideration. The executive who was fired from his last job is ranked as very poor to below average by roughly 50 percent of both level executives. They believe such a candidate has many odds to overcome. No matter how good an executive is, once he's been fired, the qustion always springs up: "What's wrong with him?"

As America's median population moves to the thirty-to-forty age bracket, the so-called midlife crisis is receiving increasing attention. Along with these crises come possible midlife career alterations. It is probable these changes are contemplated by more executives than we know about. This is because many think about such changes, but don't talk or do anything about them. That's wise. Careful consideration before changing careers is well advised.

Among journalists, for example, there is a common feeling that once a reporter leaves the lofty academic-type realms of newspapers and newsrooms to be tainted by writing for politicians or corporations, he never can return to his old snarling effectiveness in the newsroom. Executives abandoning corporate life for avocational pursuits with the thought that they always can come back are subjecting themselves to the same perils.

The executive who dropped out from corporate life to run an organic farm is not a good risk, according to executives. Though only a slight 6 percent of top executives disqualify this candidate, he is rated as poor to below average by over 50 percent of both level executives. Such a person is likely to be viewed as confused, dissonant with self, and a likely waste of time. Reorienting him is generally considered an unpromising chore.

In viewing outsiders trying to break into the business world, executives offer confused views. The female candidate whose children are grown and who has just completed an M.B.A. is rated by 30 percent top executives and 26 percent middle as above average. A forty-year-old man with no business experience, having just received an M.B.A., probably would not get as favorable consideration. Another 32 percent of both level executives rank this woman as an average candidate. Despite no business experience and her late career start, she is viewed as a potential contributor. That's fine. As a housewife she probably has administered numerous tasks that qualify her for initiating a business career.

When you look at the hospital chaplain who wants to get into business and impresses his interviewer as a natural leader, he gets minimal consideration. This poor fellow is rated by roughly 50 percent of both level executives as very poor or below average. He is disqualified outright by 14 percent of all executives.

You might be inclined to charge these executives with reverse discrimination. But when you look at the woman who has been an elementary-school district superintendent for ten years, you'll see that her rating is surprisingly similar to that of the chaplain's. She is disqualified by 13 percent of top executives; rated very poor to below average by 58 percent top executives and 52 percent middle.

What nonsense! These two candidates with experience in leadership and administration are viewed even less favorably than candidates dripping in gold, hairy-faced, and wearing scuffed shoes (as you'll see in our findings on personal appearance). A woman who has supervised a school district has demonstrated considerable administrative prowess. A few pertinent seminars and short courses could easily make her into an excellent managerial prospect. She knows budgets and people, makes decisions, has a public

Table 6
Ratings for Background other than Education

Candidate:	TOP EXECUTIVES						
	1 (%)	2 (%)	3 (%)	4 (%)	5 (%)	6 (%)	7 (%)
Fired from last job	1.6	16.6	33.3	37.6	9.0	1.6	0.4
Fired from last two jobs	29.7	48.2	18.2	3.3	0.6	0.0	0.0
Five jobs in last 10 years	20.4	44.4	25.8	6.5	2.5	0.4	0.0
Dropped out to run organic farm in northern Wisconsin	6.2	25.0	30.6	23.4	10.9	3.5	0.4
Woman with grown children/M.B.A.	0.8	4.9	18.7	32.0	29.6	9.9	4.1
Hospital chaplain who wants business and seems a natural leader	13.5	26.8	28.0	21.9	8.2	1.0	0.6
Woman with liberal arts degree/elementary-school district superintendent	13.1	28.6	29.5	16.4	10.4	1.4	0.6
Woman with liberal arts degree/wants to study business	16.4	34.1	26.1	15.8	5.7	0.6	1.4
Woman exec with appropriate experience	0.4	0.6	1.0	11.3	18.7	25.3	42.7

constituency to please, has an advanced degree and a professional orientation to her work. Still, such a candidate will have considerable difficulty in breaking the ice. To her long list of talents, she must add formidable salesmanship and tenacity that will persuade rigid, traditional executives that she can do the job.

If these experienced professionals will have trouble breaking into corporate life, what must it be like for an earnest but inexperienced individual? He will have even more difficulty. Executives give their highest disqualify-

Candidate:	MIDDLE MANAGERS						
	1 (%)	2 (%)	3 (%)	4 (%)	5 (%)	6 (%)	7 (%)
Fired from last job	1.2	19.5	31.3	35.9	10.4	1.1	0.5
Fired from last two jobs	30.4	44.5	19.6	4.8	0.5	0.2	0.0
Five jobs in last 10 years	15.7	45.6	21.7	12.2	3.5	1.1	0.2
Dropped out to run organic farm in northern Wisconsin	7.6	27.3	25.2	24.1	11.3	2.7	1.8
Woman with grown children/M.B.A.	2.1	6.7	17.3	31.6	26.3	10.9	5.1
Hospital chaplain who wants business and seems a natural leader	14.0	25.1	24.4	24.9	8.5	2.5	0.7
Woman with liberal arts degree/elementary-school district superintendent	12.2	29.8	22.0	21.3	11.5	1.1	2.1
Woman with liberal arts degree/wants to study business	14.6	31.4	23.3	19.2	7.2	2.3	1.9
Woman exec with appropriate experience	0.7	0.4	1.4	8.7	23.5	22.4	42.9

ing score to the woman with the liberal arts degree and no business experience willing to be a gofer and study the business. She is disqualified outright by 16 percent top executives and 15 percent middle; rated very poor to below average by 60 percent top and 55 percent middle. Fewer than one in six of both levels rate her as average. At least in dealing with these executives she has a chance to prove herself as a quick learner with high integrity. These may not seem like good odds, but as the cliché goes, it only takes one. One job, that is, as long as it's the right one.

Executives are not hesitant to hire women with adequate training and experience. In fact, they are *eager* to hire women who are properly qualified. The highest excellent candidate score goes to the woman executive with appropriate experience. A woman with the right experience achieves a rating of excellent from 43 percent of both level executives and above average to very good by over 40 percent of both level executives. Women like she have an excellent chance of making it big in corporate life. They are likely to get hired when young, and will qualify themselves further for advancement as they grow older.

Contacts: What They Do and Don't Do

Everybody's heard them: complaints that candidates lose jobs to those with connections in the corporation. Perhaps this argument offers quiet solace to the losing contestants. They feel better moaning, "The guy who got the job has a friend of a friend," or "His father's friend got him the job," or some other sob story. Nobody says this never happens. And nepotism itself often works well. Look at Malcolm Forbes of *Forbes*. Look at Sam Johnson of Johnson's Wax. Look at Amory Houghton of Corning Glass. Look at a lot of companies. But to most of competitive corporate America, talent and drive are valued far beyond connections. In fact, results from this study indicate that dependence on contacts has become a downright dowdy approach to job searching. It's largely frowned on by managers at both levels.

When we asked executives to rate candidates within the range of 1 to 7, their responses indicate that while some contacts are most beneficial in job searches, others can act more as a handicap. In some cases, contacts are established or attempted in unwarranted, largely juvenile fashion. Overall, such connections are ineffective. The specific responses of these executives to particular contact types are outlined in Table 7.

The highest disqualifying score is awarded by executives to the frumpy, insecure, tactless "son of an ex-college roommate who just graduated from your alma mater with a C+ in sociology." This is reassuring to hardworking candidates of more integrity. Out and out disqualified by 9 percent top executives and 7 percent middle, this student is rated as very poor or below average by 72 percent of all executives. Less than 1 percent of executives indicate that they might give special consideration to this son of a friend. Zounds! Cronyism is dead in large corporations.

Nor will sheer flattery likely lead to established contacts or celestial suites in executive heaven. Asked to rate a candidate "who called you at home one night, and told you he admired you and wanted to work for you," a moderate majority of executives responded with some disdain. While over 50 percent of both level executives rate this candidate from disqualified to below

Table 7
Contact Ratings

An executive recommended by:	TOP EXECUTIVES						
	1 (%)	2 (%)	3 (%)	4 (%)	5 (%)	6 (%)	7 (%)
Company search firm	0.2	0.4	4.7	29.1	37.0	21.9	6.7
Company employment agency	0.2	0.6	14.4	50.6	22.5	9.1	2.6
Company personnel department	0.0	1.6	5.1	30.9	38.8	19.3	5.3
Son of college room-mate; C+ in sociology from alma mater	8.6	35.8	36.0	15.9	3.1	0.6	0.0
Cold call at home; he admires you and wants to work for you	4.5	18.0	31.6	33.8	7.5	3.6	1.0
An executive recommended by:	MIDDLE MANAGERS						
	1 (%)	2 (%)	3 (%)	4 (%)	5 (%)	6 (%)	7 (%)
Company search firm	0.0	0.4	4.3	31.5	38.4	19.2	6.2
Company employment agency	0.0	1.4	12.3	52.8	24.4	6.6	2.5
Company personnel department	0.0	0.7	8.2	34.8	33.0	18.8	4.4
Son of college room-mate; C+ in sociology from alma mater	7.3	32.1	33.9	20.6	4.4	1.4	0.4
Cold call at home; he admires you and wants to work for you	4.6	16.7	33.6	33.6	8.7	2.1	0.7

average, 34 percent of both rate him average. Among these 34 percent there is still room for redemption for souls like this. They need it.

Getting attention is often advised as a competitive tool by various job counselors and questionable self-help books. But these often fail to discriminate properly between admirable attention-getting devices and those of the circus variety. Such antics might work well in competing for a role in the afternoon soaps, but only a hopeless narcissist would hire such a dope. Yet even these extreme measures do not always freeze a candidate out from a placement.

Contacts in themselves are not a bad approach to promotion-seeking and job-hunting. Much like aggression and field selection, it's how you establish that contact and cultivate it that determines success or failure.

How much professional integrity is used in establishing contacts determines the degree to which they can work for or against you. A losing candidate once complained to me that he had lost a job to an old acquaintance of the man who interviewed him. He decided to make his charge known to the executive and called him on it. The executive unabashedly admitted that indeed the lucky newly hired executive was an old acquaintance. But he hastily pointed out that the acquaintance was made on a previous job opening (which he didn't get) where he managed to demonstrate a high degree of integrity and capability. Who can castigate a corporation for hiring a fellow who made such an impression that his performance is remembered years later?

Specialization has led to greater efficiency within corporate realms. Likewise, specialized contacts have become an effective tool for executive placement. Executives respond affirmatively to what might be thought of as professional contacts.

In all humility and glowing deep self-righteousness, I must report that credibility and influence are ascribed to executive search firms by executives. While 29 percent of top executives are the most impressed with the candidates sent to them through their company's executive search firm, another 37 percent top executives and 38 percent middle rate such candidates as above average.

Only the corporation's own personnel departments come close to the high ratings given to search firms. Since most executives are familiar with the difficulties encountered when trying to break through personnel-department screening, you can understand that those who do it successfully are clever maneuverers and possessed of good salesmanship. Twenty-five percent of top executives rate those who prevail on a personnel staffer to have the company give them a second look as very good to excellent candidates.

Knowing how to pick and establish good contacts says a lot about an executive's savvy and street smarts. Executives who don't appreciate the difference in degrees of specialization and professionalism between executive search firms and employment agencies exhibit naiveté. True search firms do a considerable amount of screening on both ends of the interviewing continuum. By rigorous qualifying of clients and candidates for each other, they save time for everyone involved. Corporations willing to pay high, noncontingent fees for big jobs insist on searching high and low for their prospect. Employment agencies simply don't facilitate that type of extensive search. They present only job seekers rather than executives who must be wooed from corporations where they currently excel. The screening habits and geographic limitations of employment agencies often lead corporations to executive search firms, where their search can be conducted by specialized professionals adept at working with reluctant candidates and top-level corporate leaders.

Personal Appearance and Conduct

Some corporations are shifting from staunch, conservative views on personal styles, workstyles, and even dress codes. Nonetheless, recruitment candidates will be wise to heed the oldest advice in dressing for interviews: It is always better to dress down than dress up. No matter how trendy corporations may appear to be, keep this in mind. When recruiting, corporations seek people who blend rather than contrast with their peers and the general corporate image.

To determine just how interview performance influences the outcome of these meetings, we asked executives to rate candidates on appearance and conduct during interviews. Their responses (presented in Table 8) indicate increased tolerance for levels of individuality, but only marginally so.

Executives capable of meeting requirements that qualify them for executive jobs in the first place shouldn't blow their opportunity by being unkempt or attired in outlandish garb. If Albert Einstein walked into an interview with scuffed shoes, he could get a job in some corporations. Any other genius also could overcome such acts of nonconformity and think up more of his own. But the odds are distinctly against most candidates who demonstrate sloppy grooming habits. A quarter of both level executives rate the candidate showing up on his interview with scuffed shoes as very poor. These corporations are looking for candidates who enhance their images, not tarnish them.

Facial hair is fine in some places. But the preference in conservative corporate America is for clean-shaven faces—but not heads, unless nature did it. Perhaps some men believe their sporting whiskers shield faces they don't think pretty. But this won't fly. Even if a person's face isn't particularly pretty, he should try pretending. Though tolerance is shown by the clear majority of executives (55 percent) who rate a candidate with a beard as average, it is clear that there is little enthusiasm for such personal style in their organizations. Candidates with mustaches fare only slightly better. Just under 60 percent of both level executives rate a mustachioed candidate as average.

The general conclusion to be drawn from these statistics is that anything that distracts from business at hand is negatively perceived. In the case of the male candidate wearing neck chains and bracelets, the same disfavor comes through. Thirty-nine percent top executives and 45 percent middle rate this candidate as average. Another 27 percent top executives and 24 percent middle rate him as below average. King Tut, dripping in jewels and

Table 8
Personal Image Ratings on Job Interview

Appearance/Behavior	TOP EXECUTIVES						
	1 (%)	2 (%)	3 (%)	4 (%)	5 (%)	6 (%)	7 (%)
Unpolished or scuffed shoes	4.0	25.7	37.7	27.5	3.8	1.0	0.2
Has a beard	0.0	3.6	18.4	53.9	14.0	5.6	4.6
Has a mustache	0.0	0.0	7.6	59.3	19.2	8.0	6.0
Wearing a bracelet or neck chain	2.4	14.0	27.3	39.3	10.6	3.4	3.0
Wearing a sheer blouse	8.5	33.5	28.1	23.2	4.2	1.2	1.4
Is 5 minutes late for interview	1.2	14.6	44.8	32.1	4.5	2.2	0.6
Is 15 minutes early for interview	0.6	2.8	9.3	41.5	29.2	11.1	5.5
Orders alcoholic beverage during interview	1.4	5.8	17.8	54.0	13.2	5.4	2.4
Asks reflective questions about your company during interview	0.2	0.4	3.4	15.0	37.2	30.7	13.1

gold, sailing down the Nile in a splendid barge, is fine; if he wants a job in a corporation, he'll have to get into something a little more conservative.

Women also have much to consider in dressing for interviews. Perhaps even more so than men. By way of nature and their conventional dress standards, women generally have a harder time looking professional. Hair gets in the way. Jewelry gets in the way. And depending on how faddishly a woman dresses, her clothes can get in the way. The principle of wearing clothes, jewelry, and hairdos that don't distract from business applies to women as well as men.

The female executive who wears a sheer blouse to her interview gets the rating we all expect her to get. Over 30 percent of both level executives rate her as a very poor candidate. Over 25 percent rate her as below average and

Appearance/Behavior	MIDDLE MANAGERS						
	1 (%)	2 (%)	3 (%)	4 (%)	5 (%)	6 (%)	7 (%)
Unpolished or scuffed shoes	3.9	24.4	37.4	28.3	4.3	1.1	0.7
Has a beard	0.7	2.5	13.9	56.0	15.1	7.4	4.3
Has a mustache	0.0	0.4	6.0	57.9	17.9	11.2	6.7
Wearing a bracelet or neck chain	1.8	11.3	23.7	45.0	11.3	4.9	3.1
Wearing a sheer blouse	7.8	31.4	26.5	24.7	6.0	2.5	1.1
Is 5 minutes late for interview	0.7	18.7	41.9	31.3	4.8	2.3	0.4
Is 15 minutes early for interview	0.5	2.3	8.9	43.0	28.0	11.6	5.7
Orders alcoholic beverage during interview	1.6	6.8	17.3	52.2	11.5	7.4	3.2
Asks reflective questions about your company during interview	0.0	0.5	3.0	16.4	43.6	24.0	12.5

roughly 25 percent rate her as average. Only a lecherous 3 percent of both level executives—with tongue in cheek, I'm sure—rate this candidate as excellent or very good.

Conduct on an Interview

Anyone who shows up late for an interview displays poor ability to plan and schedule. He is not likely to be capable of meeting deadlines and is likely to throw his coworkers off schedule. For these reasons, executives express little sympathy for a tardy applicant. Such performance fails to consider the interviewing executive's busy schedule—and the busier executives are, the more they resent tardiness. Sixty percent of executives rate our tardy candidate as below average or very poor. Just over 30 percent rate this individual as an average candidate.

Arriving early to an interview can't hurt. However, arriving too early can lead to slightly negative sentiments. The candidate who arrives at his interview fifteen minutes early is rated as very good to excellent by 17 percent of executives and this is favorable. Seventy-one percent rate him as average or above average. While being early is certainly preferable to being late, being too early might suggest that the candidate has little else to do or is overly eager. Arriving too early also might make the interviewing executive feel slightly pressured to rush his schedule to accommodate the early arrival. And that's a no-no.

As we learned from the Whitewater hard-charger who won an executive position during his luncheon interview, personal carriage and conduct do a lot to add to or detract from already academically established images. If an Albert Einstein shows up at a luncheon interview wearing five gold neck chains, a pearl pinky ring, scuffed shoes, a sheer shirt, and smells a little, he's likely to be told to take a bath and see a wardrobe consultant. If he has three martinis, gets drunk, and offends the interviewer, he's likely to be disqualified. If he orders a glass of wine and asks reflective questions about the company, he will be on his way to redeeming himself from character suicide through loud and obnoxious dress habits. Since this student wasn't Albert Einstein, but just a nice guy from the heartland, *all* aspects of his dress and conduct affected the final decision to hire him.

In considering personal image, there are a few important but sometimes misleading developments in corporate life that deserve mention. As I have tried to show, corporations are increasingly tolerant of social changes and how these changes will affect their organizations and executives. Because corporations are survivors before anything else, they adapt and adjust—even tolerate when they have to. They might tolerate divorce among their executives, even to some extent extramarital affairs and, in extreme cases, maybe the discovery of extramarital affairs. They might tolerate an Einstein getting drunk and drooling through lunch if he has what they really need in technical wizardry. But corporations are still what they have always been—ultraconservative institutions that depend heavily on conservative policy implementation for survival. They tolerate as much as society demands they tolerate. They tolerate what they must to recruit, promote, and keep suitable leadership candidates. Yet after all is said and done, they are made up of fairly rigid structures that are retained stubbornly because, for the most part, they work.

It needs to be emphasized that a large number of executives rated various candidates who typify certain dress codes, morality codes, and behavior codes as "average." This makes it very, very clear that in many of these cases, while a single attribute of a person may be considered as unfavorable, other more positive attributes can overcome it. Though corporations may not be entirely tolerant, it is good to know that almost no one is frozen out automatically from corporate life if he or she is at all qualified.

Section II
How Corporations Function

A man who is not afraid of the sea will soon be drowned, he said, for he will be going out on a day he shouldn't. But we do be afraid of the sea, and we do only be drownded now and again.

—JOHN MILLINGTON SYNGE

Section III
How Corporations Function

9

Niches and Goodies

When Dr. Gary Servos left Standard Oil of Indiana in 1979, it wasn't because he was unhappy with the company. In fact, even today he boasts of the efficiency of that company, despite its vast size and complexity.

Instead, what persuaded Gary to leave his job as division exploration manager at Standard's Northeastern Texas Division was a simple offer from a smaller oil company. The enticement included a higher salary. That was good. And the smaller company threw in some prime perquisites: stock, car, and various other financial appeasements. That certainly made the offer harder to resist. But the choicest morsel in this bag of carrots was added responsibility. Gary snatched it up quicker than you can say gusher.

Gary had liked his work with Standard Oil. He was satisfied that he was with a good company. He had an appetite for responsibility. He worked well with his subordinates and was one of the best in his field, a technical one. As specialists in his field went, there weren't many who could surpass him. In addition to being a congenial manager and able geologist, he, like all good executives, thrived on challenge. For Standard Oil that was great, but it was also the source of the trouble.

Gary wanted more responsibility than his corporation could offer him. He wasn't a young M.B.A. upstart just out from B-school. Nor was he an impatient idealist with a multitude of theories untried in the real business world. He was simply a long- and hardworking executive who had reached the point where he knew what he wanted from his career, and knew he wasn't getting it. It was inevitable for him, as it is for many other talented executives, that sooner or later the right offer would be made by the right company at the right time. How could he refuse?

The money was certainly nothing to sneeze at. Neither were the handsome perks that came with the offer. Yet the real lure for him resided in one phrase—"sole responsibility." He had directed a $75 million annual budget for Standard and could spend half of that without seeking approval from his bosses. In his new role as senior vice-president of exploration at TransOcean Oil Company, he would have fewer people working under him and would have a smaller budget. But he would enjoy greater responsibility; liberty to exercise his initiative on exploration; freedom from the ambiguous collaborations, compromises, and approvals that are characteristic of large corporations. He now would have sovereignty in his decisions and a freer hand in setting his own objectives. No longer would he have to put off ideas until the opportunity for collaboration with other executives resulted in some sort of compromise. He and his new employers shared a compatible business philosophy about how exploration should be done. They also convinced him that they were flexible, innovative, and willing to experiment with new procedures. He was rid of the rigidity that all large corporations must have to avoid chaos. In short, his challenges and plans to meet them would be made less complicated by not having to comply with bureaucratic networks and systems. For Gary, that was a breath of fresh air.

Executive Perquisites

As the Gary Servos story makes plain, perquisites are not the critical enticements that lure executives from one company to another, nor keep them locked in where they are. But they never hurt. No discussion of executive performance and motivation can be complete without consideration of what some think of as lavish perks that executives receive. While discussion of these packages always seems to generate a phenomenal amount of interest among business and nonbusiness people alike, some debunking is in order.

Corporations are not usually in a financial position to pour special rewards and benefits on all their executives just to keep them aboard. More often than not companies offer perks to executives as a form of incentive. In the past, many companies placed too much faith in the belief that awarding special privileges and monetary equivalents to their executives created loyalty. They since have learned better. True, normal perks are attractive compensation for all executives. But unusual perk packages are bestowed on a limited basis to those executives who face extremely arduous tasks or where the risks of their not succeeding are unusually high. They also are bestowed on executives of extraordinary accomplishments.

After all the talk and rumor about extravagant perks and extra benefits awarded to already highly paid executives, it may come as quite a surprise that these special favors are not given out as extensively as you have been led to believe by popular magazine and newspaper articles. Oh, they exist. Corporations distribute them to their leaders with considerable frequency. Offering benefits in addition to salary has two purposes. First, perks act as incentives to encourage competition for the positions of top corporate leadership among lower-ranking executives. Second, and most frequent, they are practical tools by which the organization allays inconveniences, financial and emotional hindrances that otherwise discourage executives from taking on vital challenges and new responsibilities.

Commonly, corporations have competed for executive loyalty through issuing and offering a random array of perks. However, these packages can do no more than merely discourage executives from succumbing to more attractive career opportunities offered by other corporations. Even the most appealing packages don't keep an unfulfilled or unhappy executive from departing. Joseph Bachelder, a New York attorney who negotiates executive contracts, claims such perks are ineffective in holding unhappy executives. In an April 8, 1981, *Chicago Tribune* interview, he stated: "Usually it [executive flight] has to do with executives' present superiors. More often than not the real reason is political, with the executive believing that opportunity for advancement and greater responsibility is important to his career. Compensation is secondary."

You've heard of the bounty executives receive from the corporate horn of plenty. But when we asked them to indicate which perks they actually receive, it becomes clear that these are not simply goodies that corporations bestow to pamper their executives. Instead, they are utilitarian tools to motivate executives and, in some cases, to make their jobs more palatable.

Table 9 summarizes the range and distribution of perquisites that the executives in this study receive.

As I've said, lavish perks are available to some executives but nowhere on the scale popularly believed. The vast majority of these spoils go to top executives. Among top executives, 31 percent report that they work forty-six to fifty hours per week; another 44 percent say that they put in fifty-one-to sixty-hour workweeks; 17 percent say that they work over sixty hours per week. In other words, one in every six top executives works over sixty hours a week; 60 percent work over fifty hours a week. Suddenly, these benefits don't seem so lavish. In short, they are earned.

Middle managers are running hard for the same benefits. Forty percent say they work forty-six to fifty hours a week; another 32 percent say they work fifty-one to sixty hours a week; 11 percent report that they work over sixty hours a week. They continue to aspire, perspire, and await their day in the sun.

How corporations determine which perks they will award their executives is reflective of what each one values in its individual executive roles. If you look at these perks individually, you can see how awarding them to executives serves the organization. Not all of these perks are awarded as blanket benefits to all executives at comparable levels. Many are distributed according to what the company needs to accomplish in its relationships with individual executives.

Table 9
Executive Perquisites

Item	Received by Top Executives (%)	Received by Middle Managers (%)
Company-paid country club membership	13.4	2.1
Company-paid city club membership	14.4	4.9
Company-paid automobile	48.0	20.7
Use of company-owned/-rented limousine	8.2	3.5
Stock purchase plan	59.8	49.9
Interest-free or low-interest loans to buy company stock	11.8	10.7
Loans to purchase new home	7.4	3.7
Company-paid brokerage fees when relocating	59.0	39.8
Company makes up loss on sale of home when relocating	27.4	21.5
All moving expenses paid when relocating	89.1	73.9
One or more company-paid business trips per year with spouse	31.8	13.1
Company finds suitable employment for spouse when relocating	0.6	1.6
Use of company-owned/-leased aircraft for business trips	23.5	15.1
Use of company-owned/-leased aircraft for personal trips	0.4	0.2
Company-paid estate/financial planning	13.8	1.8
Company-paid income tax preparation	12.0	0.7
Lodge and vacation facilities	10.7	8.9

Pretax Perquisites

The slightly higher percentage of both top (14 percent) and middle (5 percent) executives who receive city club memberships over the 13 percent top executives and 2 percent middle managers who receive country club memberships probably indicates nothing more than that city clubs charge lower initiation fees and dues than do country clubs. More important, both sets of numbers are low. They support previous reports from executives that their corporations are not overly concerned with how they spend their time off the job. This is not to say, however, that they don't use their clubs often for corporate business and fraternization.

Among all company-provided transportation, the company-paid automobile is the most commonly cited. That's to be expected. Companies frequently provide sales managers and other mobile executives with appropriate means of transportation. Providing cars for these executives is less expensive for companies in some cases than reimbursing executives for use of their own cars on business trips. The September 7, 1981, *U.S. News & World Report* states that numerous General Motors managers borrow company cars for personal use. But these managers are also required to provide the company with detailed evaluation reports on the cars they drive after they return them. This helps the company to judge and improve their products.

Many large oil companies are threatened with losing valuable field technical managers (like Gary Servos) to smaller, independent oil companies with more impressive perks. To counter this possible exodus of executives from company ranks, some companies issue company-paid autos for many executives down the corporate ladder. A car is useful on the executive's job and serves as a possible incentive for him to stay with his organization.

Company-owned or -rented limousines are only rarely issued to top executives, let alone middle managers. However, when these 8 percent top executives and 4 percent middle managers do have access to this luxurious means of transportation, you can assume that their immediate task includes high-profile functions requiring an enhanced image for their corporations.

When corporations offer perks such as club memberships or cars to their executives, they are essentially pretax rewards. The executives don't have to purchase them from their own income on which they already have paid taxes. They are a tax deduction to the company. Almost everybody has to have a car, so company-paid autos are a real bounty; for two-car families, even more so. As a rule, the higher placed an executive is within his organization, the more impressive and luxurious his company-paid car.

Corporate Stock

Easy access to corporate stock ownership is a logical perk. It serves the company well to make such stock purchases available to executives. Such veering toward capitalist involvement in the executive's job is a motivation factor affecting both productivity and loyalty. You can see that corporations don't bend over backwards to make such purchases available to many executives. While purchase rights are available on convenient terms, it usually is up to the executive to see his way through the purchase.

When President Reagan signed his tax bill in August 1981, he revived corporate and executive interest in stock options as an appealing and effective perk. The new tax laws allow executives to enjoy lower taxes after exercising stock options offered by their corporations. New conditions that enable executives to pay lower taxes on their stock options than they have in the past also encourage longer-term investment.

Executives have up to ten years to exercise their stock options. But even this is easier for executives than it has been in the seventeen years before Reagan's bill was signed. Executives now pay only 20 percent capital gains tax on their profit when selling their stocks. Prior to passage of this bill, executives not only had to come up with the money to exercise their options, but they also had to pay 50 percent tax on their paper profit at the time their corporations granted the options. But executives also have to hold on to their stock for two years after exercising their options to receive favorable capital gains tax treatment on them.

As is the case when companies offer numerous perks to executives, some corporations use issuance of such stock and stock options to lock them into the corporation. These and other benefits often are referred to as the golden handcuffs. Nonetheless, small companies are in a better position to appreciate the President's tax bill. Being smaller and capable of more rapid growth, these organizations often can offer their executives the same type of options at lower prices than in large corporations. This is simply because they usually are in fledgling stages. Being largely unproven and more risky ventures, their stock is given a lower value by the investing public. Executives interested in greater capital gains can be persuaded more easily to jump their large corporate ships for options offered at lower prices in those companies that are likely to see quicker growth at larger stock-price multiples.

Some companies have been innovative in attempting to counter competition's winnowing away of their executives through such enticing carrots. Standard Oil of Indiana, suffering extensive flight of middle managers from their Amoco field operations to smaller oil companies, notified these executives that in addition to receiving company autos, they also would be granted company stock. Standard's top executives, as always, would continue to receive stock options, but they were not eligible for receiving the company's gift of stock. This tactic is easy to understand. The organization's task is to hold on to fleeing middle managers in this all-important area of exploration. So this handsome perk was issued to discourage their departure for any number of enticing jobs with smaller, less bureaucratic oil companies. Only time will tell how successful the program is.

Company-Paid Financial Services

Few companies provide company-paid income-tax preparation. Since some corporations, such as RCA, have lost perfectly able CEOs and other executives after they have been found guilty of income tax evasion, perhaps this benefit should become mandatory.

Aside from saving executives costly accounting and tax preparation fees, such services also can spare executives from having to spend valuable energy, time, and thought—in some cases, worry—over their tax preparation. Absence of this yearly headache also might increase an executive's attention to corporate business.

Other financial services are sometimes offered by various corporations. The report by 14 percent top executives and 2 percent middle that they receive company-paid estate and financial planning is a low percentage. Like many others, this perk appears to be offered only to the most valued of executives within corporations.

Travel Perquisites

As we already have seen, corporations are hesitant to send executives flying all over the country when the job can be done effectively at home. Yet when extensive travel is called for, companies are willing to do what is necessary to make the degree of travel comply with corporate needs. While some companies agree to flying executives' spouses across the country with them, this hasn't become a popular method of facilitating travel. Only 32 percent top executives and 13 percent middle say their spouses are offered an annual free trip to ameliorate conditions of their travel. Most corporations view the presence of spouses or families on a business trip as more distracting than anything else. Long hours are required of executives while they travel and this could leave spouses feeling left out, bored, even resentful. Corporations are more likely to provide first-class accommodations for their executives who have to travel and leave it at that.

As air travel costs shoot skyward, it has become more in vogue for corporations to purchase their own aircraft to shuttle busy executives around.

This, too, is not a common practice. Only 24 percent top executives and 15 percent middle say that they have access to company owned/leased aircraft for business travel. Unless an executive is the chairman of the board or an extremely valued middle manager, he can dismiss any hopes of borrowing the company plane for the weekend. Only two (0.4 percent) top executives and one (0.2 percent) middle in our whole sample reported they have access to such luxurious accommodations for their personal use.

Relocation Perquisites

When executives become increasingly immobile, as they have from 1979 through at least 1982, corporations are faced with providing perks that sometimes border on the theatrical to encourage relocation. When there is a vital need to relocate an executive internally or to recruit one from the outside, anything short of the entire rank of senior executives doing somersaults to entice the relocation candidate may be in order. In such cases, few of these perks should be shocking. In the mortgage climate of the past few years, sale of existing homes and purchase of new ones are major discouragements for relocation among most executives. Corporations either must respond to these problems or fail to relocate the executive. The report of 59 percent top executives and 40 percent middle that their companies pay brokerage fees to sell their homes shows that this practice is coming to be the norm. The 27 percent top executives and 22 percent middle who say their companies will make up the difference in losses incurred in selling homes when relocating is further proof of their value to the company at their new location. Any company that won't pay all moving expenses for relocating an executive can't really need him at a new site too badly. Their failure to pick up these expenses is downright chintzy.

Only 0.6 percent top executives and 2 percent middle report that their companies are willing to facilitate job searches for spouses when they relocate. Obstacles encountered by executives from two-career families increasingly have restricted relocation for many of them. I think it is likely, however, that companies will begin to offer more assistance in job placement for spouses as an added inducement for hesitant executives to relocate. When a company goes this far, it demonstrates its faith that relocating the executive in question is critical to its well-being. More often than not, corporations are willing to link a spouse with job-search firms or agencies. At other times they provide the executive's spouse with an array of contacts in other companies in the same locale.

Perks that facilitate relocation are reported by the largest percentage of both level executives. These reports highlight the needs that corporations seek to fill most urgently. They underscore that the function of issuing such perks is more utilitarian than benevolent. Though perks often may seem extravagant, it is important to remember that they permit the meeting of real needs of the corporations.

Loans, Lodges, and Loyalty

Benefits bestowed on executives with the intention of keeping or winning their loyalty serve as an expression of corporate goodwill. Their payoff to the company is less tangible than for many perks I have discussed up to now.

Issuing loans to executives to facilitate easy purchase of new homes reported by 7 percent top executives and 4 percent middle can be viewed as a generous provision by corporate leaders. Interest-free or low-interest loans granted to executives so they might purchase company stock is also an attractive perk. This benefit is received by 12 percent top executives and 11 percent middle.

Providing lodge and vacation facilities (reported by 11 percent top executives and 9 percent middle) is another example of kindly corporate largesse. A perk like this one serves to make executives of huge corporations feel that they are part of a family.

The lengths to which an organization will go to keep a valued executive may be measured to some extent by its distribution of perks. Executives consequently assess their own value to their corporations by the perks they receive. By examining these packages in their own arbitrary way, they rightly or wrongly conclude what their status is within their companies. However, no corporation in this study offered the identical set of perks to all executives sharing the same office, division level, or even job function within the organization. Each distributes perks randomly according to what it needs from an executive and what it most values in him.

Executive Bonuses

While many perks are more than justified, paying bonuses to executives may or may not be as laudable or as effective. Bonuses are not perks in the sense I have been discussing them. Rather they are cash payments made to executives by their companies on either a judgment (discretionary) basis or in accordance with a strict formula. Both purport in most cases to be based on the degree to which an executive has helped his corporation achieve its annual profit objectives. But corporations are criticized increasingly for awarding bonuses to executives who have failed to meet *long-term* objectives. These complaints center on the notion that short-term profits are the primary interest of most executives because they lead to larger bonuses. By delaying needed investment in new-product development, technological advances, long-term projects, and even advertising, executives can milk a business to gain immediate profits for the corporation. These profits are reflected in their bonuses. Operating philosophies and decisions determined by myopic managements overly concerned with immediate return on investment are regarded as detriments to the long-term interest of corporations.

Remedies for corporate tendencies to reward such shortsightedness have been suggested by scores of theoreticians and Japanese businessmen. Ask an academician or Japanese businessman what's wrong with American business and they'll both point to the need for American managers to pay more attention to the long-term needs of their corporations. Ah so, we say. But *how so* is more what we mean. The numerous formulas suggested to corporate leaders have failed to eliminate the problems. The businesses of Japan currently thrive under the watchful eye of the Ministry of International Trade and Industry (MITI). This is her government agency that seeks to police, support, and nurture innovation in those businesses. But relevance is what counts, and what works in Japan doesn't necessarily work in America. In fact, what works in one American corporation could be disastrous for another. As a result, management consultants are kept gainfully employed designing incentive bonus plans for their varied and inquisitive clients.

American corporations tinker incessantly with their incentive compensation plans. Some companies already have begun to develop incentive plans for their executives that, at best, encourage decisions made with a longer future in mind; and which, at worst, simply discourage decisions that are focused totally on the near future.

Progressive companies award bonuses based on formulas that reward a percentage for immediate performance, a percentage for meeting long-term objectives or establishing long-term projects, and a percentage for meeting personal objectives. Executives have a great deal to say about what their objectives should be. They participate in setting the measurements for success or failure in meeting those objectives. The one thing that all astute management consultants recognize is that no one formula is likely to be the answer for all or even many corporations. The personality and unique characteristics of each corporation determine the workability of particular incentive bonus plans.

In case you're curious, the annual cash compensation (salary plus bonus, if any) received by the 1,016 executives who were willing to provide us with such information is tallied in Table 10. You may be surprised more executives aren't in higher brackets. As in the case of perquisites, much media attention has been focused on gargantuan salaries and bonuses of chief and senior executives of large companies. The distribution of income in the table is typical. Starting with the chief executive at the very top of a corporation's pyramid, moving down through the tiers—each one marked by a lower salary range—to the lower ranks of middle management where the incumbents are not eligible for bonuses, it doesn't require a steep decline at all before, say, the $40,000 level is reached.

People from outside corporate life may indeed find this astonishing. As one social worker said to me recently, "I thought everybody in business made a bundle." Actually, social workers, educators and government employees go to work right after they complete their educations at salaries that on average are comparable to corporate entry compensation figures. It is not until executives climb the corporate ladder that wider disparities become apparent. And that doesn't occur until they become eligible for bonuses. Bear in mind, too, that as they rise, the pyramid narrows with fewer occupants in each tier than in the one below. Consequently, lower paid executives constitute the bulk of the corporation army.

The large number of executives below $40,000 on this table are predominantly younger, with hopes of rising fast. The long hours they put in for their salary is proof again of how committed they are to their careers and corporations, and that they are willing to postpone some rewards today for greater gain tomorrow. Older executives in the below $40,000 category have settled into a career culmination mode and undoubtedly do not put in the longer hours their high-hopes younger colleagues do.

Authority and Technocracy

The problems corporations are experiencing in maintaining adequate leadership require more comprehensive measures than a scattershot distribution of goodies. As you have seen, perks can have some effect on persuading executives to relocate or take on risky assignments. Occasionally, offering such benefits even may persuade an otherwise departing executive to stay with his company. But this is not nearly enough.

In addition to normal problems of training suitable leaders, corporations forever are struggling to hold on to their best managers after they have been trained. Managers today are less controllable. For example, no matter how much their corporations may want to retain them, more of them resist relocation. Then, thinking their future shot in a company where they refused a transfer, they may join another in their locale. M.B.A. s are another example. Overly ambitious ones may find it difficult to wait it out within one corporation until they achieve the level of promotion they think they deserve. The result is that many of them jump from one company to another.

The greatest problem that corporations are having in retaining quality managers has to be their inability to distribute responsibility and authority in a fashion that keeps these executives suitably challenged and confident of

Table 10
Executives' Cash Compensation

Compensation Range*	No. of Executives
$20,000 and under	42
20,000–29,000	132
30,000–39,000	247
40,000–49,000	193
50,000–59,000	127
60,000–69,000	89
70,000–79,000	54
80,000–89,000	25
90,000–99,000	19
100,000–124,000	36
125,000–149,000	21
150,000–175,000	14
176,000–199,000	2
200,000–249,000	8
250,000–299,000	2
300,000–399,000	2
400,000–499,000	1
500,000 and over	2

*Received during 1979 for majority of executives; 1980 for remainder.

evolving, fulfilling careers. Most corporations still manage their affairs through the pyramid organization structure. The geometry of that pyramid dictates that more capable executives will be ruled in these management systems than will rule. There just is more room at the bottom than at the top. The more executives reject authoritarian management styles, the more the pyramid structure will create tension and conflict. What arises out of the conflict is partly good and partly not so good.

M.B.A. s demanding quick promotions and other pampering attentions has proved to be pesty. Then the dramatic growth of many corporations in recent years has brought other strains on their organizations. As if these weren't enough, another problem has wreaked havoc on the traditional forms of management. Technical specialists have done the same thing to corporate management policies that special-interest groups have done to the two-party political system in the United States. They have tested the ability of management systems to meet all of their specific needs.

Vocal technocrats always have existed to some extent, though not with the same strength they have today. The greatest impact of such technocratic presence and strength in corporations is that they have reduced autocratic management greatly. Technical managers have gained greater and broader control over their job functions in recent years. They now make major decisions on the job. They have a stronger voice in determining their own futures and those of their departments.

As corporations grow, as M.B.A. s clamor for more responsibility and advancement, and as technocrats take more control over their own functions, corporations have responded with survival measures and opened up their management structures. More participative or collaborative management is increasingly the fashion among most large corporations. It may not be called participative management as such, but the emphasis on meetings in today's corporate atmosphere shows that's what it is nonetheless.

Corporations seem to have adopted the notion that if you can't make people like being ruled, you can distribute enough authority among them to make them think they are rulers, too. That is the basic premise of a more egalitarian management attitude that is spreading within companies today. But egalitarian management structures are riddled with pros and cons. Such systems can produce greater efficiency in some cases, but just the opposite in others. Where they are efficient, they seem to be so for only short periods.

The greatest problems encountered in any egalitarian system center on the actual job of governing. By definition, in the attempt to establish egalitarian systems, most members of a management group well may be concerned with being equal. But in the real world, most is all that can be expected. *All* isn't in the cards. Since only *most* people are preoccupied with being equal, dominance will flow to the least acquiescent members of the group—those who do not share the same value for equality. For this reason, fully participative, egalitarian management remains an unattainable ideal.

As corporations merge, acquire, and diversify, they are visited with newer, broader needs and purposes. What must accompany any thoughts executives have about sought-after changes in organization is the realization that their corporations for the most part have evolved to meet these new challenges efficiently. However they might wish for the realignment of their management structures, bureaucracy—which has befuddled many an executive—*will be served* in order to organize people and tasks on a large scale.

Actually, when you think about it, the idea behind democracy is *representation*. We entrust authority to others who can act and make decisions on our behalf. We don't have to give up our voices and influence, but we have to let those in whom we have invested authority get on with the job—even when their actions and decisions don't vibrate fully with all our rumblings.

Organization and operating structures continue to evolve in the direction of less authoritarianism. That is all to the good. But there are those who are grandiose and grasping in seeking so-called autonomy. They reject the notion that authority is good and necessary. That is, until they have it. As Eric Hoffer has said, "Actually, there is no alienation that a little power will not cure."

Truly, the contemporary corporation does very well in the matter of autonomy—as most executives think of it. You will see how it has granted autonomy among its executives. You will see how it goes about solving the complex problems that accompany extensive, autonomous management in ever-enlarging management networks.

10

The Corporate Network

How individuals view corporate life depends very much on where they are located on the organization chart. Executives at subsidiary companies or divisions may hold different opinions about various roles and functions within the organization than do executives at the parent company. This is especially true when what is now a subsidiary has been acquired against its will by another company.

Most parent companies oversee their businesses by dividing them into subsidiary or division units. Generally, subsidiaries struggle for greater autonomy from the parent company than do divisions. Sometimes they are composed of executives who have fought hard to avoid takeover by stronger, larger corporations. Having failed, for a time they may maintain a slightly resentful relationship with the parent. These tiffs can be reflected in the views these executives have of the overall operations of their parent. Typically, the more autonomy a parent grants executives at subsidiary and division levels, the less resentment it generates from executives at these units.

The difference between divisions and subsidiaries is largely academic. In a legal sense, divisions are not separate corporations, whereas subsidiaries are, even though their stock is controlled or wholly owned by their parent companies. Creating divisions is simply a way a corporation (the parent company) *divides* itself into pieces. Divisions are merely separate group functions and/or product lines that can be run more efficiently by being broken into such units.

A division general manager is a "little president" responsible overall for the results and profits of his piece of the corporation's business. A division can be physically located as close as within corporate headquarters, or as far distant as the opposite end of the earth. A division of a subsidiary is, in reality, a division of a division. It is just a further breakdown into a yet smaller piece for the sake of efficiency and control.

Among top executives in this study:

12.2% are at parent companies (corporate headquarters).

61.2% are at divisions of parent companies.

22.7% are at subsidiaries.

3.9% are at divisions of subsidiaries.

Among middle managers:

9.5% are at parent companies.

66.7% are at divisions of parent companies.

21.0% are at subsidiaries.

2.8% are at divisions of subsidiaries.

Therefore, you will have ample opportunity to examine the nature of parent companies and how their policies and operations are felt by subsidiaries and divisions.

Parent Company Perspective

As I have said, executives at all management levels have achieved greater participation in numerous corporate matters. Corporations have granted much autonomy to all executives throughout their entire structures. However, various subsidiaries and divisions even may warrant special treatment at different times in their business cycles.

To determine parent-company perspective on autonomy for operating units, we asked executives at parent companies to rate the variations in autonomy they extend to their subsidiaries. Our question: "How much do your subsidiaries vary in their autonomy?" Their answers:

	Top Executives (%)	Middle Managers (%)
a great deal	16.1	11.3
a fair amount	37.1	30.2
some	35.5	41.5
a little	11.3	17.0

Only 11 percent top executives and 17 percent middle believe their organizations treat all subsidiaries alike. Somehow that seems reassuring. It isn't even desirable that all units receive the exact same policy and level of attention at all times. I view corporations that say they treat all of their subsidiaries and divisions identically with the same degree of mistrust as parents who say they treat all of their children alike. It's impossible; and even if it weren't, it isn't smart.

Most parent executives believe they treat all of their subsidiaries individually. Fifty-three percent top executives and 42 percent middle at headquarters think they respond to subsidiaries according to what those units need. Those turning a profit and operating smoothly on their own are left alone. Subsidiaries not cutting the mustard get "help" from their parent whether they want it or not.

As subsidiaries and divisions become more specialized, parent companies are compelled to accommodate their special needs. In so doing, they assure adequate levels of growth, competition, and innovation. As corporations grow through acquisition, parent companies function more as coordinators of specialized functions within their different subsidiaries and divisions. With this kind of involvement in special projects or temporary corporate endeavors, operating structures will change to accommodate such coordination to suit a specific unit need at a given time. Indeed, this has become the norm in the operations of today's complex corporation.

That norm is well demonstrated in this study. By adding up percentages of both levels of executives who report that their corporations extend autonomy to their subsidiaries with either some or fair amounts of variety, you can see that over seven out of ten think their organizations believe in treating special circumstances with special considerations. Throw in those who think such autonomy varies a great deal and the commitment to this practice is made even more clear.

For large and still growing corporations, such variety is exactly what the doctor ordered. As individual problems and situations arise among subsidiaries, appropriate care and feeding from parent offices is vital to the maintenance of these units as profitable centers. Such involvement nudges subsidiary performance toward the overall corporate objectives. This is not to deny, however, that sometimes this "involvement" truly becomes meddling and exacerbates problem situations instead of clearing them up.

With the same spirit that parent company offices choose to vary treatment of subsidiaries when need be, they generally elect to leave matters concerning divisions of their subsidiaries to the subsidiary executives. When we asked, "How are the divisions of your subsidiaries administered?" parent company executives reported:

	Top Executives (%)	Middle Managers (%)
All through parent office	6.5	0.0
Most through parent office	21.0	13.7
Most through subsidiary HQ	46.8	62.7
All through subsidiary HQ	12.9	17.6
No subsidiary or divisions	12.9	5.9

Assuming that subsidiary divisions are even more specialized in what they do than the subsidiaries are, it makes sense that only 28 percent top executives and 14 percent middle from parent offices report that most or all matters of divisions of subsidiaries are run through parent offices. Sixty percent top executives and 80 percent middle think most or all policy for divisions of subsidiaries is administered through subsidiary headquarters. Different perceptions of top executives and middle managers suggests that autonomy at divisions isn't as great as middle managers may think. However, these figures show that subsidiaries and their divisions are running their own show.

Parent-company tendencies to leave matters concerning divisions of subsidiaries up to subsidiary management underscores the function of executives at parent companies—and even those at subsidiaries—as coordinators rather than specialists. The higher executives are perched on the corporate ladder, that is, the closer they are to their CEO, the broader their scope of corporate activities and the less specialized they are likely to be. Executives at parent offices coordinate the efforts of executives at subsidiary offices. Executives at subsidiary offices coordinate efforts of executives at their division levels and so on down the line. Marshall McLuhan said it: "The higher an executive gets inside any big corporation, the sooner he drops out; because he has less and less to do with the operation."

Bureaucracy and Personality

After Gary Servos spent six or seven happy months with his new employer, his blissful autonomy was interrupted by the merger epidemic that strikes or saves so many small and middle-sized corporations. For him, the merger wasn't welcome. While happy with the freedom to express and act on his ideas in his new job as head of exploration, he had nowhere near enough time to realize the successes that he had hoped for. TransOcean was snatched up by Mobil Oil. Servos stayed on with Mobil-TransOcean during a six-month transition period. At the end of that period he had learned he never could work for a large company again. What's more, it was during that period that he came to appreciate the difference between a well-run large corporation and a thoroughly stifling one. "Standard Oil delegates so much more responsibility downward," he would say later. "At Mobil, you have to run to New York for approval on every little decision."

While he found the snafus and time-consuming compliance to be an aggravation he could do without, he also came to an important realization. In short, though he recognized the need for bureaucracy in the large corporation, he simply concluded it wasn't for him. For Servos and others like him too much restriction or protection from a parent company hinders imagination and efficiency within its units. Yet the freedom they look for is largely a matter of personality. Many executives are quite content within larger, more bureaucratic corporations.

Most people agree that autonomy is a virtue. For powerful parent companies, it also may be a token of goodwill. Who can deny that Alexander the Great simply might be Alexander what's-his-name had he not had the wisdom not only to grant autonomy to his conquered peoples, but actively to share and delight in their cultures and customs? Executives in autonomous subsidiaries and divisions might not love the CEOs of their companies, but they benefit from greater initiative and unhampered decision-making more than executives in more tightly controlled units.

Like all virtues, however, too much of a good thing can be fatal. Corporations that grant autonomy to motivate and provide their subsidiary and division executives with rewarding work roles are also responsible for controlling and coordinating those efforts. In fact, control and coordination are the most significant jobs of parent-company executives. They walk a fine line. In the main, they do so pretty well. As we'll see, autonomy and authority are not mutually exclusive, nor destined to operate at cross-purposes.

Subsidiary and Division Autonomy

Since no subsidiary or division can ever be wholly autonomous, the word must be clarified for its use in large corporations. At its best, autonomy means minimal supervision from parent executives who know little about the specialized nature of subsidiary or division businesses. But it cannot be so liberal that no financial controls are maintained, and no direction applied toward the grand corporate scheme. At its best, subsidiaries and divisions are free to make decisions that affect their own daily operations—with only minimal policy guidelines to follow through mainly informal communications. Subsidiaries and divisions value such freedom, and the ability to contribute their ideas when they and their parent companies are collaborating on subsidiary and division objectives.

At its worst, autonomy at the subsidiary and division level is chaotic and confusing. It stifles executives in these units and cramps their style—in conformance to a narrowly conceived corporate charter. Initiative and risk-taking are verboten. Subsidiary and division objectives are set from on high without a collaborative effort. Reporting procedures are announced and administered in an autocratic manner.

The effects and benefits of autonomy at subsidiaries and divisions are viewed differently among executives at all levels of corporations. Subsidiary and division executives are likely to think that liberal autonomy they have enjoyed over recent years has been beneficial to production and progress within their units. But executives at parent companies may be concerned that the parent lacks sufficient control of these units.

To determine how much autonomy parent offices actually grant their subsidiaries and divisions, we asked executives at parent offices, subsidiaries, and divisions to rate such levels of autonomy within their corporations. Specifically, we asked:

How much autonomy do subsidiaries/divisions have?

How much has autonomy changed for subsidiaries/divisions over the past ten years?

How much policy input do subsidiaries/divisions have regarding matters that affect the subsidiaries/divisions themselves?

Answers to these questions would be interesting by themselves. However, they also allow us to determine the extent to which subsidiary and division executives agree with their parent executives on the amount and nature of the autonomy their parent company affords them.

Parent companies symbolize the "boss man" to their subsidiaries and divisions. Yet executives at parent companies advocate autonomy for these units. The different nature of business operations within each of them tends to justify such autonomy. Varying concerns of subsidiaries and divisions require specific technical and marketing knowledge often not shared at the parent company. Since parent offices are limited in knowledge of how subsidiaries/divisions achieve their technical and specialized objectives, their roles are limited to setting standards. Involvement of parent companies in setting standards varies. Almost always, parent offices have the final word in establishing financial objectives. By receiving financial reports from their subsidiaries/divisions, they maintain control over them. But more "parental" companies also are active in setting administrative and management standards at the subsidiary/division level itself.

Executives think their organizations are strong believers that autonomous subsidiaries and divisions are more effectively managed. Seventy-nine percent of top executives at parent companies believe they extend a fair amount or a great deal of autonomy to their subsidiaries. Middle managers at parent offices are even more convinced their companies grant more than adequate levels of autonomy to these units. Ninety-two percent of these managers see their organizations as granting a fair amount or a great deal of autonomy to subsidiaries. While these numbers say that subsidiaries generally have considerable independence, they also indicate that middle managers at parent offices think their corporations grant more autonomy to them than they really do.

Parent top executives rated their policies on autonomy for their subsidiaries conservatively. You might expect they would report greater autonomy for their subsidiaries than really exists. But executives at subsidiary and division levels agree with them. In fact, top and middle executives at subsidiary and division units report in greater numbers than top executives at parent offices that their units benefit from a fair amount or a great deal of autonomy. They believe their units are enjoying a liberal autonomy that has become central in corporate rhetoric in recent years. This concurrence is remarkable and speaks well of corporate harmony. The report of 89 percent of top executives at both subsidiaries and divisions even makes the report of top executives (79 percent) at parent companies seem modest. Middle managers at both subsidiaries and divisions assert with only slightly less fervor that they are free to make decisions and implement policy as they see fit.

Changes in Autonomy

Executives at all levels within the corporation well may agree that autonomy is a fairly standard policy for treatment of subsidiaries and divisions. Executives at parent companies like to think they have responded to needs for autonomy among their units. However, executives at subsidiary and division units think differently. Ask executives at parent companies what's new in corporate policy for subsidiaries, and they'll say they're granting more autonomy to executives at subsidiaries and divisions. Ask executives at subsidiaries and divisions the same question, and they'll say they write and read more reports.

Responses to the question "How much has subsidiary/division autonomy changed over the last ten years?" are indicative of widely divergent views among executives about *newly established* patterns of autonomy at these units. Seventy-two percent parent top executives and 70 percent middle think that their organizations have increased autonomy for subsidiaries over the last ten years. They think advocating autonomy has not always been a popular practice in their corporations.

Ratings of changed autonomy from executives at subsidiaries and divisions themselves, however, are vastly different. Are these levels of autonomy really something new? Subsidiary executives (30 percent top and 33 percent middle) agree with their counterparts at parent offices that autonomy for their units has increased. The same ratio of top and middle managers at

Table 11
Subsidiary/Division Autonomy

	FROM TOP EXECUTIVES AT PARENTS, SUBSIDIARIES, AND DIVISIONS		
	Parent (%)	Subsidiary (%)	Division (%)
How much autonomy do subsidiaries or divisions have?			
a great deal or a fair amount	78.7	88.6	88.5
some	14.8	7.0	9.8
a little	6.6	4.4	1.6
How much has subsidiary/division autonomy changed over the last 10 years?			
much or somewhat more	72.1	30.0	41.6
stayed the same	19.7	30.0	26.2
much or somewhat less	8.2	40.0	32.2
How much policy input do subsidiaries/divisions have re: matters that affect the subsidiaries themselves?			
a great deal or a fair amount	71.0	79.2	77.7
some	25.8	18.0	16.3
a little	3.2	2.7	6.0

subsidiaries (30/33 percent) think levels of autonomy at their units has stayed the same over the last ten years. And an unhappy 40 percent top executives and 35 percent middle managers at these subsidiaries think autonomy has even decreased at their units.

Executives at divisions are slightly more optimistic about increased autonomy at their units. Roughly 42 percent division executives at both top and middle levels think autonomy has increased in their units. Twenty-six percent top executives and 30 percent middle think autonomy in their units has

	FROM MIDDLE MANAGERS AT PARENTS, SUBSIDIARIES AND DIVISIONS		
	Parent (%)	Subsidiary (%)	Division (%)
How much autonomy do subsidiaries or divisions have?			
a great deal or a fair amount	92.4	84.8	82.8
some	5.7	13.4	13.5
a little	1.9	1.8	3.7
How much has subsidiary/division autonomy changed over the last 10 years?			
much or somewhat more	69.8	32.8	42.6
stayed the same	28.3	32.7	29.5
much or somewhat less	1.9	34.6	27.9
How much policy input do subsidiaries/divisions have re: matters that affect the subsidiaries themselves?			
a great deal or a fair amount	81.2	76.8	72.3
some	15.1	19.6	21.9
a little	3.8	3.6	5.8

stayed the same over the last ten years. But some executives at division units also share the view that they are less independent than previously. Thirty-two percent top executives and 28 percent middle at divisions believe their units are less autonomous than they were ten years ago.

Of course, since some of the reports of decreased autonomy come from executives with subsidiaries and divisions that were small, independently owned companies ten years ago, we probably would have to agree with them. The fact is that imposing controls on any group of people is likely to meet with some resistance. Those who have not been as subject to them before will chafe under them even more.

As parent-company executives think their subsidiaries operate with a free hand, they also consider them welcome contributors when establishing policies that affect the units themselves. Seventy-one percent top executives and 81 percent middle at parent offices think each subsidiary benefits from a fair amount or a great deal of participation in policymaking likely to affect it. Again, however, middle managers are a little more optimistic than top executives about the degree of policymaking collaboration their corporations engage in with their units.

Reports from top executives at both subsidiaries and divisions show that parent top executives rate the degree of collaboration a bit lower. Seventy-nine percent of subsidiary top executives and 77 percent of subsidiary middle managers say their units have a great deal or fair amount of opportunity to partake in policymaking decisions that will affect their own units. Division executives (78 percent top and 72 percent middle) also are satisfied they are free to contribute to policies affecting their destiny.

Generally, executives at subsidiaries and divisions more than corroborate the healthy state of autonomy at corporate operating units. They support most parent executives' views that there are adequate levels of autonomy at and decision-making contributions from subsidiaries and divisions.

As much freedom as most executives have, however, some always want more. Significant departure in views concerning adequacy of autonomy arise when executives rate the increase or decrease of autonomy over the past ten years. As I mentioned, between 30 percent and 40 percent both top and middle executives at subsidiaries and divisions think their autonomy has decreased. While these numbers should give pause to parent executives beating their chests, they also indicate that roughly two out of three subsidiary/division executives believe their autonomy has increased or stayed the same. Given that they think it is high to begin with, matters could be a whole lot worse.

The General Mills Experience

One of the more negative effects of increased autonomy in most management groups is that the more of it that is extended, the more of it many executives think they ought to have. Many of them think they don't need supervision or control. And the more specialized they are, the harder it is for them in their parochial interest to understand the need for their compliance with broad corporate financial and growth objectives. Recent revisions in autonomy policies at General Mills provide a classic example. That company has experienced extensive growth in recent years through acquisition of various types of unrelated businesses. Most of the entrepreneurs who started these small businesses now function as subsidiary chiefs under the leadership of General Mills' executives at their Minneapolis headquarters. Bruce Atwater, chairman and chief executive, revealed the reasons for their shift from liberal autonomy in the treatment of their subsidiaries in the September 7, 1981, *Business Week.* "We were so hands-off for a while [the last 15 years] that we had little discussion with subsidiary heads concerning strategy and virtually no discussion of people development." Atwater saw extreme independence of subsidiary chiefs as bound to lead to eventual chaos for overall corporate performance.

You would be right to expect that subsidiary chiefs are critical of new controls applied to their daily routine. Most controls are financial in nature. While they might be viewed as moderate by many corporate leaders, these reforms aroused much concern among newly reined entrepreneurs at General Mills' numerous subsidiaries. Most of them expressed concern that the parent-office executives didn't understand their particular needs and problems. They worried that complying with financial controls issued from the parent office might hinder their own efficiency.

Resistance from General Mills subsidiary chiefs points to various problems that parent companies are likely to experience when altering policies. When such alterations are perceived by subsidiary executives to be related to levels of autonomy, these unit leaders often fail to empathize with the total corporate financial and growth objectives. Part of this problem resides in the autocratic management backgrounds of many of these entrepreneurs-turned-corporate-executives. They often are not acclimated to the more collaborative, team-oriented management styles of large corporations.

If indeed corporations are increasing autonomy for their subsidiaries and divisions, it is largely because of their own growth and expansion. As they merge and acquire they become less competent to guide their operating units through their technical activities. To repeat, their main job is to coordinate and control these units. Cooperation between subsidiary/division management and executives at the parent enhances the organization's ability to keep managers at all levels gratified with their work. Greater job satisfaction among executives inspires greater loyalty and enthusiasm for the enterprise as a whole.

Autonomy works to hasten subsidiary/division procedures needed to put decisions into action. Inability to act on decisions without cumbersome approval-seeking from sometimes distant or busy parent offices is a major complaint among many of these unit executives from large corporations. While some cumbersome procedures may be needed to minimize risk and safeguard against decisions based on faulty information, autonomy to make decisions that are specifically related to a unit's needs remains an essential ingredient to a corporation's thriving. Being able to manage this trade-off is what separates the winners from the losers.

11

House-to-House Communications

The growth of the American corporation has been dramatic. As it continues to grow and expand, so does the complexity of its information and communications systems. As its changes dictate expanded roles for its executives, it also enlarges the networks through which these executives communicate. The concept of work control is central to the corporation and determines its decision-making processes and how they are structured. Controlling the work efforts of executives requires effective communications among them.

Executive relationships among parent offices, subsidiaries, and divisions are marked by a struggle for autonomy and independence. Executives like to be on their own. They prefer not to have to run to anyone for approval, let alone to some distant and elevated executive who is not likely to appreciate the unique handicaps and snaggles they experience on their specialized jobs. As much as they like to be left alone to make their own decisions and set their objectives, they also are dependent on timely, pertinent information from their parent companies. In more complex and interdependent management structures, building and maintaining effective communications between parent companies and their subsidiaries and divisions are challenges worthy of the most careful attention and commitment.

To determine whether or not parent companies are building and maintaining good communications between themselves and their subsidiaries and divisions we asked executives to rate:

Adequacy of parent/subsidiary/division communications.

Overall quality of parent/subsidiary/division communications.

How much their organization has adopted new communications techniques.

Mixture of formal and informal communications between parent and subsidiaries/divisions.

How much the quality of communications between parent and subsidiaries/divisions has changed.

How much the quantity of communications between parent and subsidiaries/divisions has changed.

Their responses indicate that corporations manage to adapt to communications needs as they continually grow and change. Despite rapid and unexpected changes within their organizations, executives believe their organizations have made improvements in communications between parent, subsidiaries, and divisions.

Adequacy of Communications

Parent companies have put a lot of energy into establishing better relationships with their subsidiaries and divisions. The energy is well spent. While they can't claim total victory by any means, parent corporations have done a suitable job on communications with their operating units. Top executives in all three spheres report remarkably similar perceptions that communications between parent companies and their subsidiaries and divisions are adequate. Though corporations are not free of problems in inter-unit communications, they have managed to moderate the most nettlesome ones.

Sixty-nine percent parent top executives and 71 percent middle say communications between them and their subsidiaries are adequate. Only 5 percent parent top executives and 6 percent middle say such communications are more than adequate between themselves and their units. While these latter numbers are low, they probably reveal a negative bias. Undeniably, they call attention to the fact that over 90 percent of parent executives are aware of communications problems, many of which are extremely difficult to overcome. As executives within and between parent, subsidiary, and division offices become more interdependent, and chains of command become harder to trace because jobs increasingly overlap, good communications become frighteningly precarious.

According to executives at subsidiaries and divisions, perceptions of parent-company executives about the adequacy of inter-unit communications are right on target. In fact, the concurrence they share on this subject is striking. Sixty-nine percent subsidiary top executives and 71 percent middle are identical with parent executives' views about the adequacy of communications between their offices. Likewise, division executives (69 percent top and 67 percent middle) constitute a virtual match with their counterparts in these other units. Such responses let us know that despite complexities and changes in management structures and styles, corporations are able to exchange necessary information adequately.

Table 12
House-to-House Communications

	TOP EXECUTIVES		
	Parent (%)	Subsidiary (%)	Division (%)
Rate adequacy of parent and subsidiary/division communications			
more than adequate	4.9	16.8	22.8
adequate	68.9	69.9	69.1
less than adequate	26.2	13.3	8.1
Rate overall quality of communication between parent and subsidiary/division			
good or excellent	24.2	51.3	54.4
adequate	50.0	31.9	34.2
low or very poor	25.8	16.8	11.4
How much has organization adopted new communications techniques?			
a fair amount or a great deal	37.1	48.7	35.1
somewhat	33.9	24.8	33.9
little	29.0	26.5	30.9
Rate mix of formal and informal communication between parent and subsidiary/division			
more to mostly formal	14.5	23.0	33.9
about equal	41.9	41.6	37.5
more to mostly informal	43.6	35.4	28.7
How has *quality* of communication changed between parent and subsidiary/division over recent years?			
somewhat or greatly improved	72.1	52.2	65.5

	MIDDLE MANAGERS		
	Parent (%)	Subsidiary (%)	Division (%)
Rate adequacy of parent and subsidiary/division communications			
more than adequate	5.8	15.9	17.3
adequate	71.2	70.8	66.9
less than adequate	23.1	13.3	15.7
Rate overall quality of communication between parent and subsidiary/division			
good or excellent	28.3	38.6	50.8
adequate	47.2	45.0	31.2
low or very poor	24.6	16.6	18.0
How much has organization adopted new communications techniques?			
a fair amount or a great deal	27.5	48.6	41.9
somewhat	49.0	29.2	30.7
little	23.5	22.1	27.5
Rate mix of formal and informal communication between parent and subsidiary/division			
more to mostly formal	9.6	38.9	31.7
about equal	40.4	33.6	37.9
more to mostly informal	50.0	27.4	30.4
How has *quality* of communication changed between parent and subsidiary/division over recent years?			
somewhat or greatly improved	61.5	46.4	64.5

Table 12 (cont'd)

no change	14.8	38.1	25.2
somewhat or greatly reduced	13.1	9.8	9.3

How has *quantity* of communication changed between parent and subsidiary/ division over recent years?

somewhat or greatly increased	77.0	61.0	62.5
no change	18.0	31.9	28.0
somewhat or greatly reduced	4.9	7.1	9.5

Few executives think communications between units are all they can be. Most know there is much room for improvement. Among those rating communications as more than adequate, most come from subsidiaries and divisions. Seventeen percent top executives at subsidiaries and 23 percent at divisions say communications between their units and parent executives are at this high level of sufficiency. When compared to those of parent executives, these figures lead me to conclude that parent companies feel short-changed on information. On the other hand, subsidiaries and divisions already feel overburdened with what they have to provide. Further evidence of parents having unsatisfied appetites for information can be seen in 26 percent of their top executives believing inter-unit communications are *less* than adequate. In contrast, 13 percent, or half, their counterparts at subsidiaries, and 8 percent at divisions feel this way.

The important matter to keep in mind centers on the word *adequate*. This word should not be viewed negatively. Adequate is adequate! The job is getting done. Perfectionists always will be with us. They're destined to be dissatisfied, no matter what. But when two-way communication in the most complex of settings can be achieved at a level where 70 percent of the executives involved consider it adequate, then the corporation need not offer any apologies.

Overall Quality of Communications

In rating overall quality of communications, executives at subsidiaries and divisions make clear they are more satisfied with the state of information flow between units than are parent-company executives. At parents, only 24 percent of top executives consider such quality to be good or excellent. But at subsidiaries, double that number, or 51 percent, give it high marks; at divisions, 54 percent do.

no change	32.8	46.4	26.0
somewhat or greatly reduced	5.8	7.2	9.5

**How has *quantity* of communication
changed between parent and subsidiary/
division over recent years?**

somewhat or greatly increased	73.1	59.9	59.0
no change	23.1	33.9	32.6
somewhat or greatly reduced	3.8	6.3	8.4

Twenty-six percent parent top executives and 25 percent middle think the quality of inter-unit communications is low or very poor. At subsidiaries, 17 percent of both levels rate it this way. At divisions, those percentages are, respectively, 11 percent and 18 percent. These latter figures are parallel to our findings on the adequacy of inter-unit communications.

Communications Technology

The extent of change and experimentation with communications techniques varies widely among organizations. While many companies encourage informal communications as much as possible to facilitate timeliness in decision making, they also seek ways to make sure such decisions are based on the latest information. Most large corporations dependent on speedy transmittal of information from one unit to another have employed direct computer lines and other sophisticated gadgetry. Many organizations use word processors and other computerized and electronic media for efficient communications between offices.

The ways in which corporations have dabbled in altered communications techniques presents some fascinating issues. For instance, subsidiaries report the greatest level of newly adopted communications techniques. Forty-nine percent of both top and middle executives say their subsidiaries have adopted a fair amount or great deal of new communications techniques. Thirty-five percent division top executives and 42 percent middle also report adopting a fair amount or a great deal of new communications methods.

On the other hand, parent-office executives report the least employment of new techniques for transmitting information. Thirty-seven percent parent top executives and 28 percent middle say their companies have adopted a fair amount or a great deal of new communications methods. Another 34 percent parent top executives and 49 percent middle think their companies have adopted *some* new techniques for communicating between units.

While it is surprising that a parent—the nerve center and focal point of the entire enterprise—would lag behind its operating units in communications technology, perhaps it shouldn't be. Subsidiaries are autonomous, and as such are free to experiment. In addition, they are expected to be producing in their specialized businesses. It behooves them to direct and control those businesses in the most efficient and progressive way possible. Hence, they would be more inclined to turn to productivity-enhancing technologies.

In its broad coordinating, policy-setting, and overview functions, a parent company is not required to be as flexible and fast-paced as its subsidiaries and divisions that face the marketplace directly and daily. Accordingly, the parent company has the luxury of relying on more traditional approaches and procedures in managing its far-flung, diversified empire.

It seems possible to me that one reason parent companies are more dissatisfied with the adequacy and quality of communications between them and their operating units is that they have trouble with the information they are sent. It does not arrive in a form they find palatable. Or they insist that it be served up in a manner beneath the competence levels of their reporting units. It is unlikely these subsidiary or division executives will let such occasions pass without expressing at least a small measure of irritation or rebellion.

Formal and Informal Communications

In spite of all the worthwhile technical advances in communications, what gets things done in a corporation is the proper mixture of formal and informal communications. The more preparation needed for formal presentations, the more pomp required for messages to be relayed between subsidiary or division offices and parent, the greater the chance for delay and confusion. Rigid, formal communications requirements often can stifle the otherwise simple art of exchanging ideas and information.

All large corporations have a mixture of both formal and informal communications. Companies that acknowledge only limited informal communications within their organizations are nonetheless victims and beneficiaries of informal networks that operate at all levels within the ranks of management.

Formal communications devices are used as an efficient and thorough means of apprising executives. Through memos, reports, presentations, slide and graphic displays, and scheduled meetings, information is methodically distributed among relevant executives. Executives everywhere complain about the frequency with which they must engage in and exchange memos and reports. They complain especially about meetings. But corporations depend on formal communications to provide the most pertinent information concerning current business to executives most in need of it. Formal communications reach the most executives with the least complication, confusion, and energy.

On the other hand, informal communications traverse unstructured, snaky networks that are randomly formed among the managements of all corporations. Information is made up, lost, stolen, ignored, withheld, embellished, played up, sped up, played down, slowed down, sold, bartered, and subjected to at least a thousand other treatments based on the frailties, strengths, and interests of all executives who interact in the name of management.

Because these patterns of informal communications are so common, significant, and hold such fascination, industrial sociologists have studied them for decades. What these sociologists called informal communications gave way to the more popular "hidden agendas." They are the result of cooperative or uncooperative relations among various groups within a company. Naturally, these agendas aren't always consonant with corporate objectives. However, many times they are.

The best-known vehicles for hidden agendas are the numerous cliques that exist in companies. In his book, *Men Who Manage*, Melville Dalton describes five types found most frequently in corporations:

Vertical symbiotic clique—arises when a top executive covers for some subordinates, defending their performance to those critical of it. In exchange, subordinates provide information concerning real or rumored threats to the top executive, relay current conditions, and advise on how to deal with troublemakers outside the clique.

Vertical parasitic clique—arises when a favored subordinate is linked to a top executive by kinship or friendship. Arouses resentment of subordinate's associates, who then keep secrets from him to hinder his ability to provide favors for the top executive. Result is often strife in top executive's department.

Horizontal defensive clique—arises when executives of same rank are threatened by a development such as an ominous reorganization, the hiring of a feared top executive, or the installation of a new control procedure. Clique disbands when threat is defeated or adjusted to.

Horizontal aggressive clique—arises in attempt to inspire rather than resist change. Examples might include fighting for bigger budgets, curtailing the expansion of a staff group, or getting somebody promoted who will help the clique.

Random clique—arises with friendship and social interests held in common as the basis for grouping. These associations are accidental and defy classification by executive rank, duties, or department. Members indulge in unguarded talk about people and events within company, but learn few secrets because of their loyalties to more crucial functional cliques.

I have gone to some length and properly can be criticized for being dramatic in describing the darker side of informal communications. However, my purpose has been to show that information can undergo changes that do not serve a corporation's need, no matter how clearly or formally that need may have been presented. In asking executives to give us their views on informal communications, we defined them as phone calls, unscheduled conversations, grapevine, and the like. It is in response to this more traditional and benign understanding of informal communications that they gave us their answers. It is also in this sense that I will address my comments on the subject in this and the next chapter.

Though formal communications are vital to distributing information, informal communications often are more effective in stimulating responses and generating ideas. Therefore, most parent companies steer clear of overdependence on formal communications to get their ideas across. Only a third of the executives at divisions say communications between their offices and parent offices are more or mostly formal.

Less than half of executives at parent offices (42 percent top and 40 percent middle) and subsidiaries (42 percent top and 34 percent middle) believe they employ an equal mixture of formal and informal communications for sending and receiving information. Only 15 percent parent top executives and 10% middle think their organizations rely on more to mostly formal communications in dealing with subsidiaries or divisions. Quite a few more subsidiary executives think so than parent executives. Division executives are divided almost equally into thirds over whether their exchanges with parents are formal, informal, or evenly mixed.

Changes in Quality of Communications

Most executives agree that quality of communications has improved in their organizations over recent years. Seventy-two percent parent, 52 percent subsidiary, and 66 percent division top executives think these improvements have been significant. Middle managers at these offices corroborate their beliefs. Sixty-two percent of them at parents, 46 percent at subsidiaries, and 65 percent at divisions rate quality of communications in their offices as somewhat or greatly improved.

While one-fourth of both level executives at divisions think there has been no change at all in communications quality between them and parents, there is wide disparity between middle and top executives at parent offices. Thirty-three percent parent middle managers say that the quality of communications between their offices and operating units is unchanged. That's more than double the 15 percent parent top executives who say there has been no change in such quality. Clearly, the top executives believe there has been greater improvement. Middle managers at subsidiaries are also less exuberant about the extent of communications quality improvements that have occurred over recent years. While only 38 percent of their top executives think there has been no change in communication quality between them and their parent, 46 percent of their middle managers report quality in communication has not improved.

Generally, executives from parent companies think their organizations have done a better job at improving quality of communications between themselves and their operating units than executives in these units do. But again there is no need for poor-mouthing. Actually, what is impressive is this: with the exception of 13 percent of top executives at parent companies, fewer than one in ten executives at both levels at all units think the quality of communications they exchange has deteriorated.

Changes in Quantity of Communications

While quality of communications in corporations has improved, quantity of communications has increased more. The executive suite is awash with paper. What executive doesn't complain about receiving long and tedious memoranda? But when pressed, what executive won't say that these communications are necessary to keep him and his bosses informed about issues critical to their daily business? As corporations have become more financial-control oriented because of expanding size and diversity, executives get swamped more with telexes, memos, financial data, and reports of all kinds.

Seventy-seven percent parent top executives and 73 percent middle say that quantity of communications has increased somewhat or greatly. Roughly 60 percent subsidiary top and middle executives agree. Sixty-three percent division top and 59 percent middle believe that such quantity has somewhat or greatly increased between them and their parents. So while on one hand parent-company executives may complain about thrashing around in a sea of white, then gripe about the inadequate communications they get, the operating-unit executives aren't all that thrilled with their lot, either. They believe their parents don't know what they want in the way of information, but whatever it is, they want too much of it. Not only is providing it distracting to their main efforts, they suspect it isn't properly understood or used when received.

12

In-House Communications

You have seen that, while not entirely successful, corporate headquarters have put much energy into improving communications between their offices and those of subsidiaries and divisions. Despite parent preference for formal communications between themselves and their subsidiaries and divisions, informal communications remain a valuable and unavoidable means of spreading the business word.

Good communications among executives *within* each of these units, however, might be expected to be easier to accomplish than communication between units. But executives in these units share different types of relationships. As with siblings, interactions between executives within offices reflect varying degrees of loyalty, competition, cooperation, and, at times, intense conflict. These relationships determine the unique priorities of the hidden agendas within each of these offices.

Despite organizational complexities, varying priorities, personal discord, and professional conflicts, smooth communications between executives must be maintained within each corporate unit. Such a flow of information is necessary to achieve corporate objectives. If this does not occur, individuals within the organization are likely to suffer as much as the corporation as a whole.

To determine the nature of communications between executives within parent offices, subsidiaries, and divisions, we asked executives:

How they evaluate the overall quality of communications within their unit.

If they have adequate communications with relevant others in their unit to get their job done.

What the mixture of formal and informal communications is within their unit.

How quality of communication within their unit has changed over recent years.

How quantity of communication within their unit has changed over recent years.

Their responses are summarized in Table 13.

Parent Companies

Executives at parent companies believe quality of communications within their offices has improved somewhat or greatly within recent years. However, their level of belief in improvement is lowest among all units. Nonetheless, their figures are impressive when you consider the growth and diversification their companies have been experiencing. Fewer middle managers than top executives perceive such improvements. Most middle managers (42 percent) think there has been no change in communications quality within their offices. Fewer than a third of top executives report communications quality has not changed within their offices.

While some companies busily have nurtured their relationships with their subsidiaries and divisions, they have neglected the home front. But even in these companies, severe communications breakdowns are rarely, if ever, tolerated. Fewer than one in five top and middle executives says quality of communications within his offices has somewhat or greatly diminished.

Communications problems are most grave when they interfere with completion of daily routines. How executives working together relate to each other makes all the difference to success or failure. If communications between them are good, they can overcome deficiencies and obstructions that occur when something has gone wrong in the overall communications network.

At parent companies, these basic communications are adequate. Fewer than one in three top executives considers the overall quality of his communication to be good or excellent. Fewer than one in six middle managers thinks so. Sixty-two percent top and middle executives say such communications between themselves and relevant others to get their job done are adequate. That's all to the good. However, as specific roles and functions for executives expand and diversify, basic communications between close-working executives can suffer. Twenty-one percent top executives and 27 percent middle say communications between themselves and relevant others to get the job done are less than adequate. This indicates limited access for them in their companies and is cause for concern.

Parent-company executives depend on markedly more informal communications among themselves than between themselves and their subsidiar-

Table 13
In-House Communications

	TOP EXECUTIVES		
	Parent (%)	Subsidiary (%)	Division (%)
How would you evaluate the overall quality of communications within your unit?			
good or excellent	29.0	49.6	55.7
adequate	43.5	30.1	29.6
low or very poor	27.4	20.3	14.6
Do you have adequate communication with relevant others within your unit to get job done?			
more than adequate	16.1	22.1	27.7
adequate	62.9	64.6	65.5
less than adequate	21.0	13.3	6.8
What is mix of formal/informal communications within unit?			
more or mostly formal	1.6	5.3	5.3
about equal	29.0	35.4	34.3
more or mostly informal	69.4	59.3	60.4
How has *quality* of communications changed within recent years?			
somewhat or greatly improved	52.5	57.5	71.2
no change	31.1	29.2	22.2
somewhat or greatly reduced	16.4	13.3	6.7
Within unit, how has *quantity* of communications changed over recent years?			
somewhat or greatly increased	65.0	61.0	68.7
no change	26.7	32.7	23.1
somewhat or greatly reduced	8.4	6.2	8.3

	MIDDLE MANAGERS		
	Parent (%)	Subsidiary (%)	Division (%)
How would you evaluate the overall quality of communications within your unit?			
good or excellent	15.4	42.0	46.9
adequate	55.8	33.0	32.0
low or very poor	28.8	25.0	21.0
Do you have adequate communication with relevant others within your unit to get job done?			
more than adequate	11.5	16.1	26.3
adequate	61.5	66.1	62.2
less than adequate	26.9	17.9	11.5
What is mix of formal/informal communications within unit?			
more or mostly formal	4.0	12.5	8.0
about equal	30.0	31.3	31.0
more or mostly informal	66.0	56.3	61.0
How has *quality* of communications changed within recent years?			
somewhat or greatly improved	38.4	53.5	66.6
no change	42.3	32.1	22.6
somewhat or greatly reduced	19.2	14.3	10.8
Within unit, how has *quantity* of communications changed over recent years?			
somewhat or greatly increased	52.0	66.1	63.3
no change	36.0	25.9	28.9
somewhat or greatly reduced	12.0	8.0	7.9

ies and divisions. The necessity of issuing policy statements, collecting information, publishing financial reports, coordinating projects, and maintaining communications, not only with their operating units but with shareholders and organizations outside the corporation as well, are all functions that explain this dichotomy.

Only 2 percent top executives and 4 percent middle at parents believe they communicate among themselves in a more or mostly formal way. Thirty percent top and middle consider the mixture of formal and informal to be equal. Seventy percent top and 66 percent middle think their manner of communications is more or mostly informal.

Parent companies have done a better job of improving communications between themselves and subsidiaries than improving those within their own offices. Yet, they have managed to keep information running smoothly enough among themselves to avoid catastrophe. For the most part they have met their immediate needs for effective communications, and put off further improvements until new urgencies arise. Part of the reason for not addressing such communications problems can be attributed to the sheer volume of communications needed to achieve the barest objectives. Overwhelmingly, executives at parent offices agree that if quality of communications hasn't increased that much, quantity has. Sixty-five percent top executives and 52 percent middle say they are sending out and receiving more information than in the past.

As corporations try new management structures, and especially as they turn more to temporary, ad hoc groups such as task forces to deal with special projects, better communications are needed. As chains of command become more amorphous in matrix-type organizations where functions overlap, executives increasingly share in decisions and are forced to cultivate the art of communication. Executives now commonly report to more than one superior. Skillful communications are the lubricant of these delicate relationships where friction can flare up quickly.

Subsidiaries and Divisions

Subsidiaries and divisions have done a good job of improving communications within their offices. Top executives at both of these units (58 percent subsidiaries and 71 percent divisions) think communications quality has somewhat or greatly improved within their offices over recent years. Middle managers in these offices tend to agree. Fifty-four percent at subsidiaries and 67 percent at divisions report significant improvement in their quality of communications.

Despite these rave reviews, over 60 percent of all executives in both subsidiaries and divisions communicate with relevant others in their offices just enough to get their jobs done. As you have seen before, these figures concur strikingly with those at parent offices. But unlike parents, these units have done a slightly better job of establishing basic communications between executives working closely together. You can see that among top executives (16 percent parents; 22 percent subsidiaries; 28 percent divisions) more-than-adequate communications between relevant others to get the job done are greater in subsidiaries and divisions. By the same token, reports of inadequate communications between relevant others are less among top executives in subsidiaries and divisions (21 percent parents; 13 percent subsidiaries; 7 percent divisions).

The dominance of informality in communications at subsidiaries and divisions is well documented. Like the almost 70 percent who report more or mostly informal communications to be standard among executives within parent offices, these units report significantly greater preference for informal communications in-house than what they engage in with their parents. Roughly 60 percent top executives at subsidiaries and divisions say communications are more or mostly informal within their offices. About 35 percent top executives at subsidiaries and divisions say their offices maintain an equal mixture of formal and informal communications. Middle managers from both types of units support these perceptions of formal and informal mixture in communications in their offices. While divisions are less formal in intraoffice communications than are subsidiaries, parent companies are less formal than both.

Improving the quality of communications is likely to have been hampered in subsidiary and division offices in much the same fashion that it has been in parent offices. Executives from both subsidiaries and divisions share the convictions of parent executives that quantity of communications has increased. Top executives in all three categories (65 percent parent; 61 percent subsidiary; 69 percent division) think there has been some or a great increase in the quantity of communications within their offices. Only a third of subsidiary top executives and just under a fourth of division top executives think there has been no change in quantity of communications. Middle managers at subsidiary and division offices agree quantity of communications has increased within their offices over recent years.

In thinking about the differences between parent companies and their subsidiaries and divisions, we often conjure up pictures of specific atmospheres more than anything else. We imagine parent companies as places of plush furnishings, thick carpets, and a consuming silence as thick as the carpeting. We don't expect executives in these offices to talk a lot among themselves. Instead, we see them swimming in a sea of white—sending and receiving an endless string of memos. When we turn to subsidiaries and divisions, however, the scene becomes busier. We imagine bare-tiled floors and desks made of metal rather than fine oak. Our images portray more bustle, more noisy collaborations between executives directly engaged in keeping that all-important customer satisfied. Responses from executives support some of these images, but not all. For example, parent companies are less prone to formal communications within their offices, but insist on them from their subsidiaries and divisions.

No matter what the style of communications—formal or informal—it must foster flexibility and efficiency if it's going to work. Coordination demands that prevail more and more in parent companies have required better relationships between parent executives and those in subsidiaries and divisions. Overall, these high survival-oriented parent companies comply with these demands with impressive skill and speed. However, the concentration of energies they have devoted to improving relations between themselves and their units has led to less impressive communications within their own shops.

13

Bosses and Work Relations

Some corporations encourage their executives to collaborate extensively with higher-ups to reach decisions. Others expect them to deliberate alone and come to their decisions independently. Still others make use of decision-making collaborations and processes as a kind of training ground for subordinates.

To determine general patterns in decision making and establish how executives interact with higher executives, we asked them to rate the following aspects of their relationships with their bosses:

Will your boss call meetings of all direct-reporting subordinates for discussion on major decisions?

Does your boss make major decisions on a one-to-one basis with his subordinates?

Do you and your boss share information essential to the business that is not shared with your department peers?

Do your boss and at least one of your department peers share information essential to the business that is not shared with the rest of you?

Is your boss too slow in responding to your recommendations?

Are you free to exchange operating information with your peers in other functions without approval from your boss?

The more highly placed an executive is on the organization chart, the more removed he is likely to be from technical problems and details. He also is likely to be barely aware or totally ignorant of how his decisions are felt lower down the management line. For this reason, his collaboration with subordinates is imperative.

It is true that many executives prefer to make decisions alone. But decision **123**

Table 14
Relationships with Higher Executives

	TOP EXECUTIVES			
	Always or Usually (%)	Sometimes (%)	Seldom (%)	Never (%)
Will your boss call meetings of all direct-reporting subordinates for discussion on major issues?	52.0	30.1	14.7	2.9
Does your boss make major decisions on a one-to-one basis with his subordinates?	47.7	40.5	8.8	1.4
Do you and your boss share essential business information not shared with department peers?	18.3	46.9	24.4	7.7
Do your boss and at least one department peer share essential business information not shared with rest of you?	11.2	45.2	26.9	9.4
Is your boss too slow in responding to your recommendations?	8.2	21.3	48.1	22.1
Are you free to exchange operating information with your peers in other functions without approval of boss?	92.8	5.3	1.0	0.4

"Don't Know" responses not included.

making in solitude is all but unworkable. As you'll see later on in this section in a case involving a board of directors, it can be all but fatal to a corporation. Whether executives like to admit it or not, decisions are almost always the result of collaboration with one or more superiors or one or more subordinates.

Collaboration inspires camaraderie. At the same time, such meetings of minds reflect and affect the office culture. Since informal communications play a large part in how things get done in a corporation, and since manage-

	MIDDLE MANAGERS			
	Always or Usually (%)	Sometimes (%)	Seldom (%)	Never (%)
Will your boss call meetings of all direct-reporting subordinates for discussion on major issues?	47.6	27.9	18.6	5.4
Does your boss make major decisions on a one-to-one basis with his subordinates?	51.4	37.3	8.8	1.6
Do you and your boss share essential business information not shared with department peers?	25.3	43.9	20.6	7.2
Do your boss and at least one department peer share essential business information not shared with rest of you?	15.3	44.7	24.1	9.0
Is your boss too slow in responding to your recommendations?	11.9	32.0	43.8	11.3
Are you free to exchange operating information with your peers in other functions without approval of boss?	86.3	9.3	3.3	0.9

"Don't Know" responses not included.

ment styles have become less authoritarian, collaboration is the evolved means of reaching decisions.

Group discussions among subordinates are effective for bosses trying to collect information or generate ideas before a final decision is made. For example, 82 percent top executives and 76 percent middle say their bosses always, usually, or sometimes call meetings of all direct-reporting subordinates for *discussion* on major decisions.

Group discussions usually result in generation of more ideas than can be used. After bosses have narrowed down the ideas generated in group discussion, they typically engage in a further analysis of pros and cons to reach their most desirable options. However, it is common that a more technical, detailed discussion of issues related to the decision will be held on a one-to-one basis with a subordinate most qualified to deal with the matter at hand. Just under 90 percent top and middle executives claim their bosses always, usually, or sometimes confer with subordinates on a one-to-one basis to *make* decisions.

Collaboration between a boss and subordinates, common as it is, may lead to hoarding of information essential to the business. Many executives take pride in being privy to information that their boss does not share with peers in their department who also report to him. They also believe, however, that their boss occasionally excludes them from information that is shared with others. Ordinarily, they choose to believe they are not excluded from information as much as their peers are.

Forty-five percent of top executives say their bosses sometimes exclude them from information that is shared with peers. These figures indicate that top executives have a healthy perspective on the need for intimate sharing of information in one-to-one collaborations. Only a grandiose 18 percent top executives think their bosses always or usually share information with them that is shared with no one else. And an even fewer suspicious 11 percent think their bosses always or usually share information with others that is not shared with them.

One in four middle managers thinks his boss always or usually shares information with him that is not shared with peers. One in six thinks his boss always or usually shares information with others that is not shared with him. Among middle managers, random one-on-one collaboration to exchange information is largely understood. Forty-four percent report that their bosses sometimes share information with them that is not shared with peers and 45 percent think these same bosses sometimes share information with others that is not shared with them.

While executives understand, and in some cases even welcome, exclusive sharing of information between their bosses and themselves or peers, such patterns of information exchange can disintegrate into an overly fierce, harmful, competitive situation between executives. However, such occurrence is relatively rare and is more a subject for journalistic fancy.

How peace—in fact, cooperation—is maintained while executives struggle among themselves to achieve status and dominance in their departments is mostly attributable to interdependence of their jobs. As executives gather information independently, their interdependent functions encourage them to share such information, when applicable and important, to get their jobs done. The overwhelming majority of executives are free to exchange information for job-related functions and projects as they see fit. Ninety-three percent top executives and 86 percent middle say they may do so with their peers in other functions without approval from their bosses. This random, unstructured passing of information underscores that informal communications are essential to organizational effectiveness.

After all this collaborating and dispersing of information is completed, executives like to have their recommendations considered seriously and quickly by their bosses. Speedy response to recommendations is interpreted by executives as another indication of how well they are competing with peers. If a boss acts quickly on the advice of one particular executive, that executive is secure in the knowledge that his contribution is significant and appreciated. He feels himself in a superior competitive position against his peers. The response time from superiors is surprisingly satisfactory to executives. Seventy percent top executives and 55 percent middle say their bosses are never or seldom too slow in responding to their recommendations.

I doubt that the bosses to top executives (often parent, subsidiary, or division presidents) are actually faster in decision response times than top executives are to middle managers. Rather, I suspect top executives are a bit more patient in waiting for answers to their recommendations. Call it mellowing, experience, or simply knowledge of the way things work, top executives will be less demanding on their bosses in this way than their subordinates are on them.

Generally, executives convince us of relatively healthy relationships between themselves and their bosses. When considering the levels of competition and struggle that are likely to bias their opinions in such matters as exclusion of information and speed in responding to their recommendations, it is clear that information flows between them and their bosses satisfactorily to get the job done.

Autonomy and Participation

When you think about autonomy in large corporations, or any large organization for that matter, you have to wonder to what degree it truly exists. The fact is that large, complex corporate structures beg for control. While executives clamor for more independence, autonomy, and responsibility, corporations are faced with the trade-off of controlling executive efforts without diluting motivation and feelings of participation. If too much control diminishes participation and even stifles leadership, this can lead the largest and most successful corporations down Bankruptcy Lane. However, the larger a company is, the more vulnerable it is to turmoil at the hands of a pure egalitarian management system.

Companies usually manage to control executives' efforts without making such control so apparent as to suffocate good spirits and producers. So in large corporations, the questions are: Is *autonomy* a shibboleth? Does it merely give comfort to executives without being real? How do corporations maintain control without shattering beliefs in autonomy among executives?

Balancing control and freedom is something of an art. Good bosses extend autonomy to subordinates while checks are provided by collaborating on subordinates' objectives, then measuring their performance against them. Executives in divisions and subsidiaries usually have operating autonomy (decentralization), but are subject to parent-company financial controls (centralization). Under such systems of control, most executives consider themselves to have adequate autonomy. Operating autonomy has increased within the corporation but so has centralized financial control. This artful balance leaves executives satisfied in the main that they are in charge of their functions.

We asked executives to indicate:

If their authority generally matches their responsibility.

If it should.

If their opinions are sought by their bosses as often as they would like.

If they have a voice in initiating new products or services.

If they should.

If they have customer contact.

If they should.

If they have a voice in setting objectives for their own area of responsibility.

Both top and middle executives overwhelmingly are satisfied with their match-up of authority and responsibility. Also, most of them are satisfied with how often their bosses seek their counsel. Sixty-four percent top executives and 55 percent middle are pleased with the frequency their bosses ask them for opinions. Twenty-six percent top executives and 35 percent middle believe their bosses ask for their opinions depending on circumstances. They admit, however, that there are times they are not consulted when they would like to be.

Most executives report they are active in developing new products and services. Since innovation is paramount in the corporate world, and those involved in development of new products are most valuable to their organizations, you can understand their commitment to this area. Eighty-seven percent top executives and 81 percent middle claim they have a voice in initiating new products or services.

Related to new products and services is customer contact. This is another means whereby executives have an opportunity to increase their value to their corporations. Eighty-one percent top executives and 69 percent middle

Table 15
How Executives View Their Autonomy

	TOP EXECUTIVES			MIDDLE MANAGERS		
	Yes (%)	Varies (%)	No (%)	Yes (%)	Varies (%)	No (%)
Does your authority generally match your responsibility?	87.5		12.5	81.0		19.0
Should it?	100.0		0.0	99.2		0.8
Are your opinions sought by boss as often as you would like?	64.7	25.9	9.4	55.1	35.4	9.5
Do you have a voice in initiating new products or services?	88.6		11.4	80.6		19.4
Should you?	100.0		0.0	100.0		0.0
Do you have contact with company's customers?	80.7		19.3	69.0		31.0
Should you?	100.0		0.0	98.0		2.0
Do you have a voice in setting objectives for your area of responsibility?	93.4	5.7	1.0	87.7	10.9	1.4

are satisfied they can and should become involved meaningfully in meeting their customers' needs.

The few executives (1 percent at both levels) who don't have a voice in setting their own objectives are in trouble. Further, the 6 percent top executives and 11 percent middle who say that their views on objectives for their own areas of responsibility are welcome only on varied occasions are standing on a shaky career base. Nine out of ten executives have strong voices when setting objectives that affect their own responsibilities. Executives who are forced to try to meet objectives set without their say are courting failure. No executive can experience individual growth without having some determination of his own objectives. He is frozen out from what his corporation values and is limited in his ability to compete with peers.

You can see that in all of these categories, executives function freely enough to justify their feelings of autonomy. While parent companies use the reins of finance and policy as control measures, executives strongly believe they have the freedom to act and contribute within broad guidelines.

Competition Between Executives

In the complex, more matrixlike structures that increasingly are employed in large corporations, it is more difficult to determine where final authority lies. These structures, created to provide flexibility and the ability to cope with problems that overlap traditional functions, have affected attitudes of competition and cooperation between executives. Wanting to know current attitudes of executives toward competition, cooperation, and career advancement, we asked them:

Do you believe:

Your job offers limited potential for advancement?

You are a candidate for your boss's job when he vacates it or retires?

Peers who also report to your boss are candidates for his job?

Do you consider:

Yourself in competition with department peers?

Yourself in cooperation with department peers?

Do you and department peers collectively consider your function to be in competition with other functions in your division or company?

Their responses suggest that competition may not be what you expect among executives in large, diverse corporations. They are outlined in Table 16.

Competition is what individuals choose to make of it. Only 56 percent top executives and 49 percent middle feel unlimited possibilities for their own advancement within their organizations. Twenty-six percent top executives and 29 percent middle say they are not in the running for future advancements. Does that seem a bit disheartening? It shouldn't. Executives who see themselves as being as far as they will go may be at peace with themselves while others—some realistically, some unrealistically—thrash around trying to get ahead. It also is possible that they are expressing a lack of comprehen-

Table 16
Executive Views on Competition and Cooperation

	TOP EXECUTIVES			MIDDLE MANAGERS		
	Yes (%)	Uncertain (%)	No (%)	Yes (%)	Uncertain (%)	No (%)
Do you feel your job offers limited potential for advancement?	26.0	17.4	56.4	28.9	22.2	48.9
Do you believe yourself to be a candidate for your boss's job when he vacates it or retires?	41.3	21.9	36.8	46.6	18.8	35.1
Are peers who also report to your boss candidates for his job?	55.0	24.2	20.8	42.7	24.1	33.2
	Always or Usually (%)	Some-times (%)	Never (%)	Always or Usually (%)	Some-times (%)	Never (%)
Do you consider yourself in competition with department peers?	19.5	45.1	23.2	20.6	41.4	26.2
Do you consider yourself in cooperation with department peers?	80.8	7.4	1.4	84.2	4.4	0.7
Do you and department peers collectively consider your function to be in competition with other functions in your division or company?	19.9	43.3	25.0	16.4	44.1	28.5

"No Peers" responses not included.

sion of the newer management structures within which they work. As chains of command become harder to define, it also becomes harder to know what one aspires to. Then, too, some companies are so adept in the way they move executives around that those executives can't determine if their latest move constitutes a promotion.

If executives think there is room at the top in their companies, such advancement is not necessarily through their bosses' jobs. Forty-one percent top executives and 47 percent middle believe they are contenders for their bosses' jobs should their seniors retire. But over a third of top and middle executives say they are out of the race when it comes to being considered for their bosses' jobs. In betting on who shall inherit the boss's job, most top executives are more optimistic for their peers than themselves. Forty-one percent see themselves as candidates, but fifty-five percent see their peers as candidates. Middle managers nurture higher hopes.

These figures allow you to peek behind the corporate veil and penetrate executive bravado. Though half of these executives perceive future advancement for themselves in their organizations, this is hardly overwhelming. More top executives believe their peers are more likely to take their bosses' places than they are. While reports from them are likely to be realistic, since the higher the rank in the pyramid management structure, the fewer positions there are to rise to, these statistics still reflect diminished anticipation for their futures. To be sure, the circle of executives who rate themselves likely for advancement and likely to win their boss's job will contain those individuals who ultimately grasp the brass ring.

Though the thrill of the game fizzles for many executives when they come to rate their own career expectations, that fizzle becomes even more faint when they define their competitive situation with their peers. A battle-scarred 20 percent top executives and 21 percent middle think they are always in competition with their peers. A wise 45 percent top executives and 41 percent middle think they are sometimes in competition with peers. But a naive 23 percent top executives and 26 percent middle actually believe they are never in competition with peers! These executives choose to see their relationships with peers as cooperative. That's fine. As matrix management obscures chains of command and the delineation of power figures, executives are forced to cooperate with each other as they work in overlapping groups. But I am a traditional believer that competition looms large in spurring executives to greater achievement. Do you remember Carnegie's analogy of managers to horses who either win or lose races? True, he is a man of history. However, things have not changed as much as many do-gooder organization theorists would have us believe.

The report of 81 percent top executives and 84 percent middle who see themselves always or usually in cooperation with department peers simply verifies that the predominant form of executive interaction is cooperation. But while corporations gain cooperation by inspiring appreciation for their broad objectives, this does not dim the prize of conquest for large numbers of executives. I come into contact daily with major corporations where competition is fierce between executives. I believe many executives who report a total sense of cooperation with their peers think they can go no farther up the corporate ladder. They opt to "cool it" since the race for them is over.

Probably the most realistic perceptions of competition are expressed by 43 percent top executives and 44 percent middle who say sometimes the functions of themselves and their department peers are in competition with those of others in their divisions or companies. As with political parties, this is the situation that allows for a cooperative or team spirit, the purpose of which is to unify so that you can beat the hell out of those bastards across the aisle.

Relations with Subordinates

You have seen that most executives believe they have good relationships with their superiors. Though some of them may complain occasionally about gaps in communications or response times from superiors, they generally think they work in a positive setting. While roughly one-fourth believe their advancement opportunities are limited, that leaves three-fourths who don't know or aren't sure. In addition, 41 percent top executives and 47 percent middle consider themselves candidates for their bosses' jobs.

Executives learn how to manage by observing their bosses. Superiors often are role models. At the least, they influence how subordinates will manage their own subordinates. After providing us with information on the nature of their relationships with their superiors, we asked executives for the same regarding subordinates.

We asked them:

Do you call meetings with all your subordinates for discussion on major decisions?

Do you make major decisions without consulting all of your subordinates present in meetings?

Do you make major decisions on a one-to-one basis with your subordinates?

Do you make major decisions without consulting your subordinates at all?

Do you think subordinates are too impatient for your responses to their recommendations?

Do you share information essential to the business with certain of your subordinates but not with others?

Do you accept on faith the competence of a subordinate in your company with whom you have never worked?

Do you believe subordinates should circumvent the chain of command?

What type of authority do you have concerning hiring and firing your subordinates?

Their responses indicate that executives treat their subordinates in the same ways (good and bad) their bosses treat them. It is clear, however, they consider their subordinates to be more fortunate than they. That is, these executives think they're better managers than their bosses.

Whether or not they like to collect information and exchange ideas through formal meetings, these executives—like their bosses—apparently think such sessions are necessary. Sixty-nine percent top executives and 65 percent middle say they always or usually call meetings with subordinates for discussion on major decisions. Only 52 percent top executives and 48% middle report that their *bosses* always or usually call meetings for discussion on major decisions. In other words, they claim to be more faithful to this necessary practice than their bosses are.

Seventy-three percent of both level executives report they sometimes make major decisions without consulting all their direct subordinates present in a meeting. I'm sure these executives see these occasions when they make decisions without including their subordinates as necessary and consistent. But their subordinates probably see them as arbitrary and variable. This means they engage in self-deception to justify actions they want to take and yet continue to think of themselves as good managers.

Their self-deception carries over to making decisions on a one-to-one basis. Thirty-seven percent top executives and 42 percent middle always or usually make decisions on a one-to-one basis with their subordinates. On the other hand, 48 percent top executives and 51 percent middle say their bosses make decisions this way. Given that collaboration with all subordinates is viewed by these executives as the "good" way to reach decisions, they see themselves departing from this ideal less than their bosses. Sixty-two percent top executives and 55 percent middle say they *sometimes* make major decisions in one-to-one collaborations with subordinates. As with beauty, "sometimes" is in the eye of the beholder. To me as a boss, it may be infrequent, but to you as a subordinate, it may be excessive. "Sometimes" gives me a lot of leeway to engage in behavior which I may not think is "ordinarily" right, but which is "required in this situation." This is also how I can think myself a collaborative or participative boss, but in fact truly be authoritarian and arbitrary. It is just one more way I can escape the realization that you see me the same way I see my boss.

Though it is a fact that many executives may not like to collaborate (57 percent top executives and 64 percent middle say they *sometimes* make major decisions without consulting their subordinates at all), you have seen that such collaborations usually are unavoidable. The higher executives sit in the corporate pyramid, the more their primary function centers on coordination of activities and information. Top executives have the least specialized jobs in their organizations. Therefore, they ultimately are dependent on collaboration with more specialized subordinates. Their favored form of reaching decisions is in meetings with subordinates. Decision making in isolation is more popular among middle managers. They can afford this isolation more while top executives increasingly are dependent on views and information from subordinates to make decisions.

Still, more specialized middle managers are forced to consult with yet more specialized subordinates. Only 6 percent of middle managers say they always or usually make decisions without consulting subordinates at all. This is only a few more middle managers than the 1 percent top executives who say they usually or always make their decisions alone. Isolation in decision making at any executive level is not practiced habitually or considered safe by most executives.

Yet, as I've said, when we asked middle managers to outline their basic patterns for making decisions, their responses indicated an inclination toward solitude. Though they want to be included in their bosses' deliberations, they still prefer to make *their* decisions alone. In other words, they don't include their subordinates in the way they want their bosses to include them. If collaboration is required, however, middle managers would prefer to consult with their subordinates rather than their bosses. Making decisions on a one-to-one basis with their bosses is clearly the least preferable method of arriving at decisions. This latter point is also true of top executives. Decision-making forms and preferences are outlined as follows:

Decision-Making Forms and Preferences

	TOP EXECUTIVES			MIDDLE MANAGERS		
	Most Frequent (%)	Less Frequent (%)	Least Frequent (%)	Most Frequent (%)	Less Frequent (%)	Least Frequent (%)
Alone	38.6	29.5	31.8	48.5	23.9	27.6
Meetings with subordinates	56.5	21.0	22.5	38.0	27.2	34.8
One-to-one with boss	16.8	38.6	44.6	28.5	38.1	33.4

Table 17
Relationships with Subordinates

	TOP EXECUTIVES			MIDDLE MANAGERS		
	Always or Usually (%)	Some-times (%)	Never (%)	Always or Usually (%)	Some-times (%)	Never (%)
Do you call meetings with subordinates to discuss major decisions?	68.7	29.2	1.9	65.4	30.8	3.6
Do you make major decisions without consulting all your direct subordinates present at meetings?	10.9	73.6	15.3	13.9	73.4	12.3
Do you make major decisions on a one-to-one basis with your subordinates?	37.1	61.9	1.0	41.5	54.7	3.6
Do you make major decisions without consulting your subordinates at all?	1.2	56.8	41.9	5.8	64.1	29.9
Do you think subordinates are too impatient for your responses to their recommendations?	1.6	59.1	34.2	2.4	59.6	30.2
Do you share essential business information with certain of your subordinates but not with others?	17.7	65.8	16.5	13.8	55.5	29.7
Do you accept on faith the competence of a subordinate with whom you have never worked?	18.9	42.1	35.2	17.9	38.2	41.0

	TOP EXECUTIVES			MIDDLE MANAGERS		
	Always or Usually (%)	Some-times (%)	Never (%)	Always or Usually (%)	Some-times (%)	Never (%)
Do you believe sub-ordinates should circumvent chain of command?	2.0	54.1	43.6	1.8	51.9	45.1

	Sole (%)	Joint (%)	Collec-tive (%)	No (%)	Sole (%)	Joint (%)	Collec-tive (%)	No (%)
What type of authority do you have in hiring and firing your subordinates?	44.8	52.2	2.5	0.4	33.5	57.7	5.9	2.9

"Don't Know" responses not included.

Executives resent the eager demands for decisions made upon them by their subordinates. Fifty-nine percent top executives and 60 percent middle think their subordinates sometimes are too impatient for their responses to recommendations. Yet they respond to those pressures nonetheless. They act, it seems, out of some some sense of coercion. They feel they must. You will remember that 70 percent top executives and 55 percent middle consider their bosses seldom or never are too slow in responding to their recommendations. The system values a fast pace and speed in decision making, and those who cannot comply are likely to encounter problems with both subordinates and bosses.

Executives report they are more likely to have secrets with various subordinates than their bosses are. Sixty-six percent top executives and 56 percent middle say they sometimes share information essential to the business with certain subordinates but not others. This percentage is considerably higher than the 45 percent of both level executives who think their bosses sometimes exclude them from information shared with their peers. They are guilty of greater sins than their bosses when it comes to random distribution of information to favorites. Or so they believe.

This pattern of communications is reflective of a pecking order in a corporation. Acquiring privileged information and distributing it to favored subordinates is one way status is assigned among executives. While most executives are aware that information is distributed in this fashion, they are likely to believe they are more privy to what's on their bosses' minds than they really are. They know their bosses have secrets, but think they are more apt to exclude their peers than themselves from such information.

On decisions for which they are responsible, executives strongly dislike being called upon to collaborate one-on-one with their bosses. They feel they are acting like their bosses' straight men. But then they meddle in their subordinates' decision making. What they do is very human. They usually want and expect from their bosses what they won't give to their subordinates. And they almost never realize it. A friend who is a contender for the CEO spot in one of the nation's major banks has told me he learns much more from his subordinates than his boss. What he may not realize is that many of his subordinates feel the same way about him.

Subordinates are faced with the task of proving themselves to their bosses. Once they have proved their competence, they begin to be trusted and confided in. Executives say they definitely wait for such proof of competence from their subordinates. Seventy-seven percent top executives are "from Missouri." Never or only sometimes do they accept on faith the competence of subordinates with whom they have never worked.

Even though these subordinates might be individuals who have worked elsewhere in the company, their new bosses like to feel them out. They have to be shown a sense of cooperation, commitment, and integrity in the subordinates before they take them seriously. You can't blame these bosses. After all, it's their necks on the line.

Despite the various points of conflict likely to arise in their work situations, executives exhibit adequate levels of trust for subordinates. Fifty-four percent of top executives and 52 percent of middle think it sometimes is necessary for subordinates to circumvent the chain of command. An insecure and unrealistic 44 percent of both level executives think such circumvention is never permissible. These notions are more unworkable than ever in today's interdependent management structures. As executives increasingly arrive at joint decisions, and superiors act more as coordinators than sole decision makers, circumvention becomes more necessary as unanticipated problems arise. The fact is that the chain of command in corporations increasingly is difficult to define. While an executive might have formal authority over decisions that require the knowledge of various subordinates, in reality problems are addressed and solved together. A subordinate's intimate knowledge gives him greater expertise. Collaboration is essential between him and his boss. To get the information he needs to defend a position he cares about—and from which the corporation may benefit—a subordinate occasionally will need to go around his boss.

Now and then subordinates might misuse the freedom to circumvent their superiors. Subordinates who are simply trying to show off or feather their own nests by extreme politicking are more than likely to get their comeuppance. Secure bosses rarely worry about such trite manipulations. They just give these clumsy types enough rope to hang themselves.

The amorphous way that responsibility is carried out in corporations is reflected in executives' observations that most of them don't have the power to hire and fire independently. While a significant 45 percent top executives claim to have sole power over such hiring and firing, 52 percent say they arrive at these decisions jointly with peers or superiors. Middle managers have even less authority to decide such matters alone. While only 34 percent of middle managers say they decide who they will hire and fire, 58 percent collaborate on who comes and goes.

14

Corporate Functioning

Executives have expressed views of their relationships with subordinates, peers, and superiors as being complicated with conflict, competition, and covert collaborations. The impression one cannot avoid is that executives are more charitable in rating their own performances and perhaps even their subordinates' performances over that of their bosses.

Unquestionably, executives are demanding of their bosses. But they are even more demanding of their organizations. We asked executives to evaluate their corporations' functioning by indicating if they strongly agree, merely agree, are uncertain of, disagree, or strongly disagree with the following:

The department for which you have responsibility operates efficiently.

The group or function for which your boss has responsibility operates efficiently.

Your parent company operates efficiently.

Meetings are too much a "way of life" within your company.

Throughout your company, too many people have too little discretionary authority.

Getting promoted in your company is largely due to time-in-grade.

Influence in having things go your way in your company is largely due to time-in-grade.

Formal controls within the corporation are necessary to curb corruption.

High Rating of Self

The overwhelming conviction of executives is that their corporations function well despite technical and random communications problems. This underscores their responses discussed on prior pages. Top executives are only slightly more positive than middle managers. Both believe strongly that their corporations are in good hands.

Ninety percent top executives and 87 percent middle hold firm convictions that their own departments, those for which they are directly responsible, are running efficiently. When these executives rated their bosses' performances, they were not as generous; in rating their parent-company efficiency, they were even less so. Seventy-three percent top executives and 74 percent middle say that groups or functions for which their bosses have responsibility run smoothly and efficiently. Thirteen percent of both levels expressed uncertainty about whether their bosses are doing a good job of running their departments or not. Only 5 percent of both levels had such hesitations about themselves.

It's a bit humorous, eh? At least if one can lighten up and not take himself so seriously.

These executives have failed to rate their own performances objectively, but we can get a glimpse from their ratings of their bosses' performances how their own subordinates would rate them. They're not alone. As with my banker friend, most of us believe we're better than our bosses. Both top and middle executives think this way. When it comes to evaluating our own job performances we're all a little self-serving.

That theme is borne out repeatedly. Executives simply think they do not make the same errors that their bosses do. And even if they do, there's a good chance they will consider their errors as somehow justified. Even though executives share the same problems in many cases, they often show little insight into their bosses' trade-offs. Though they sometimes themselves confess the same sins of omission and commission that their bosses do, they claim their lapses are due to unusual circumstances. They lack empathy for their bosses, who ordinarily face problems and decisions of greater magnitude. Meanwhile, they glamorize their own performances. So it goes on down the corporate ladder.

As executives are hard on their immediate bosses, so are they critical of their parent companies. An old attitude prevails—"Boy, if only I were in charge!"—even though it is clear that if they were, they would do many of the same things that they criticize. These attitudes don't negate positive findings that I discussed earlier on autonomy and communications. Such executives are merely saying there is much room for improvement at the top, and if they were there, they would make a big difference. This they believe in their heart of hearts. They staunchly partake in ritual griping about the

Table 18
Corporate Functioning

	TOP EXECUTIVES			MIDDLE MANAGERS		
	Strongly Agree/ Agree (%)	Uncertain (%)	Disagree/ Strongly Disagree (%)	Strongly Agree/ Agree (%)	Uncertain (%)	Disagree/ Strongly Disagree (%)
Your department operates efficiently	90.1	4.5	5.5	86.9	5.6	7.4
Your boss's group or function operates efficiently	73.2	13.3	13.5	74.4	13.4	12.3
Your parent company operates efficiently	67.3	22.9	9.8	64.4	23.6	12.0
Meetings are too much a "way of life" in your company	27.7	16.2	56.1	30.0	15.9	54.2
Throughout company too many people have too little discretionary authority	16.7	22.5	60.8	25.8	28.0	46.2
Promotion is largely due to time-in-grade	6.5	9.4	84.1	10.2	11.5	78.3
Influence is largely due to time-in-grade	11.7	13.3	75.0	11.1	18.0	70.9
Formal internal controls are necessary to curb corruption	51.2	17.0	31.8	56.2	20.6	23.1

power figure. Their gripes are harmless and inevitable. Sixty-seven percent top executives and 64 percent middle agreeing their parent companies operate efficiently wouldn't seem shabby at all were it not for their giving themselves efficiency ratings of 90 percent and 87 percent. That leaves roughly a third of them who disagree or are uncertain that their parent companies are efficient.

No Policy Complaints

While executives criticize overall efficiency of parent companies and performance of superiors, they do not blame any particular policy for lack of efficiency. For example, when asked to indicate whether or not meetings are too much a way of life in their companies, only 30 percent top executives and 16 percent middle responded affirmatively. Executives always complain about the time they spend in meetings, meetings, meetings, but they agree that while such meetings are oppressive, they are necessary. Fifty-six percent top executives and 54 percent middle strongly disagree that meetings are too much a way of life in their companies.

Nor do the bulk of executives think authority is too tightly centered among select executives in their companies. Earlier findings indicated that most executives are satisfied with their own ratio of authority/responsibility. Here, 61 percent top executives and 46 percent middle strongly disagree or disagree that not enough discretionary authority is distributed among the ranks. In short, most executives believe that a proper degree of authority goes with their jobs.

Twenty-three percent top executives and 28 percent middle are uncertain about whether or not too many people in their companies have too little discretionary authority. These are most likely executives perplexed by the layers of managers who need to be consulted before decisions can be made. Middle managers especially are aiming for authority commensurate with their ambitions. One in four believes there is too little discretionary authority spread throughout his organization. But among top executives who already feel fewer controls and already are working with suitable formal authority, fewer than one in five believes that too many executives have too little authority. As job roles become increasingly interdependent, levels of authority—even for top executives—become diluted. If authority is hazy at the top, you can imagine how difficult it is to define at middle- and junior-management levels.

Time-in-Grade

Executives aren't all that unhappy either about how they gain favor for their ideas or how they get promoted. Though the way that people acquire authority is dependent on ambiguous and random characteristics of the executives themselves, few of them protest. Since concentrated levels of authority lie at the very top of the corporate pyramid, executives who get themselves promoted will experience the authority they crave. As you have seen in Section I, promotions are awarded based on combinations of personal characteristics. They include having acquired the proper specialized background, then applying it to a corporation's mission.

Those who get promoted are assertive. They are active and imaginative on the job. They are not promoted simply because they've been on the job for umpteen years. Eighty-four percent top executives and 78 percent middle express disagreement with the notion that time-in-grade (in effect, seniority) leads to promotion. Some people sit in a hole in the wall in their organization for thirty years. If they fail to make their value to the organization known, they'll keep sitting in that same hole until it's time to collect their gold watch.

Even among top executives, there are constant struggles to see whose pet project is supported with efforts and dollars. But some executives are more aggressive and persuasive than others. They consistently get their way regarding corporate matters. They are proof for those who say that seniority has nothing to do with who wins and who loses corporate struggles. Seventy-five percent top executives and 71 percent middle strongly disagree that time-in-grade is important for executives in having things go their way.

These figures I have been citing are quite high. Their message is that while people like to moan and complain about their jobs and corporations, overall they are pleased with them. They find considerable security and room for growth; successful executives continue to identify strongly with their corporations.

Most executives believe controls within the corporation are necessary. Fifty-one percent top executives and 56 percent middle agree such controls are needed to curb corruption—or at least indiscretion. Their thinking is that the size and complexity of their management structures is an invitation for unchecked indiscretions or outright dishonesty available to a random few.

In the main, executives express satisfaction with their jobs and relationships with their corporations. While they have judged their superiors and parent companies fairly harshly, they also have expressed overall views that their companies function with adequate efficiency, despite the conflicts and struggles within. Conflicts exist beyond those of middle managers and senior executives; of vice-presidents and their chief executive officers. Struggles exist all the way up and into the boardrooms of most corporations and these tensions to a great extent determine one way that management functions within any organization. Yet like the relationship between private citizens and members of Congress, differences between views and interests of management and the board are hard to recognize and hard to resolve once they are recognized.

My final analysis of how executives judge the functional efficiency of their corporations focuses on their views of their boards of directors.

15

The Board of Directors

In the popular film *Network*, Howard Beale, the maniacally idealistic newscaster, aroused the wrath of the influential station owner. He was summoned to headquarters to receive a shocking reeducation on the balance of worldwide economy. The meeting between the hopeless idealist and the chairman of the board took place in the corporation boardroom. Aside from the vastness of the room, a great deal of dark jade-green is what comes to mind. I'm not suggesting that the exercise of power that occurs behind the heavy oak double doors is jaded, to be sure, but jade-green is the color that I remember. This room was the perfect place for such a clash between mad idealism and the harsh, cruel, cold, calculating facts of life and reason in the corporate sphere.

You may perceive a board of directors as sycophants. Or you may think of them simply as a group of individuals with more responsibilities than time or energy to handle them. Boards have received a lot of criticism in recent years for failure to address their responsibilities. Vocal persons from various quarters have asked for or demanded significant reforms within the boardrooms of America's corporations. Business analysts, B-school professors, and corporate statesmen argue among themselves over which turns to take. They try to determine which board reforms are best to assure responsible decisions and involvement of these directors, and which ones won't work at all.

Boards of directors across the country already have changed a great deal to comply with many of these demands. They quickly responded to suggestions from the Securities and Exchange Commission, making numerous efforts to demonstrate their responsible intent.

Since the numerous suits against directors of Penn Central following the company's sudden bankruptcy in the late sixties, similar suits have, with little hesitation, been addressed to directors of other boards. In 1979, an investment firm filed suit against Edwin Land and Polaroid for failing to alert investors to the company's earning setbacks incurred that year.

Throughout the United States, boards that fail to exercise their fiduciary responsibilities to shareholders are not exempt from harsh public criticism and bad press. In addition, they face the specter of having severe legal action taken against them. Large fines and jail sentences are not unheard of.

Many boards have been increased in size to facilitate adequate, in-depth discussion of complex issues that spring up in complex organizations. By and large, corporations have succeeded in gaining objective management opinion by bringing in outsiders to serve as directors. (When I first drafted this sentence, I accidentally wrote "oustiders." Often, that's what they do— oust!) Boards also usually have a few major stockholders as directors. In addition, corporations are complying with modernday demands that representatives of academic or social groups be placed on their boards. Seeking equal social representation, these corporations are opening their boardrooms increasingly to women and minorities. General Motors was one of the first corporations to appoint a black to their board of directors. They did so in the person of Leon Sullivan, minister and civic leader in Philadelphia. Sometimes these women and minorities have been labeled tokens. I disagree. They usually are strong individuals in their own right. Increasingly, boards are naming women and minority members of highly capable backgrounds. Their contributions can be significant.

Seeking Broad Representation

The appointments of former Congresswoman Barbara Jordan to the board of Texas Commerce Bancshares and former Commerce Secretary Juanita Kreps to the boards of AT&T, Citicorp, and J. C. Penney have won public approval. So have the appointments of college presidents Martha Peterson (Beloit) and Matina Horner (Radcliffe) to the boards of Exxon and Time, respectively. Contributions of women like Julia Walsh, on the boards of Esmark and Pitney Bowes; Mary Head, on the boards of Household International and Butler Manufacturing; Catherine Cleary, on the boards of AT&T, General Motors, and Dart & Kraft; and Jewel LaFontant, on the boards of Equitable Life, Bendix, and TransWorld, are well documented by people connected to these companies with whom I have talked. Gasps were heard from the old guard when Douglas Fraser, president of the United Auto Workers Union, was named to the board of Chrysler. A close friend who is one of the most admired labor relations executives in the country was aghast when I told him I was in favor of it. That nearly ended our long relationship. Fraser is a startling symbol in board reform.

While adding outsiders to boards is thought to be mandatory to achieve objectivity, breadth, and representation of social interests, the addition can increase tensions. The 1979 suit brought against Beatrice Foods by its own director and former president of its Samsonite group is an example of how and what can happen when outsiders start brawls. This was a case where outside board members tried independently to select Beatrice's new chief executive officer and chairman after the retirement of Wallace Rasmussen. The move was led by outsider Durward Varner and was dependent on the votes of eight other outsiders and two insiders. The maneuvering between the antagonists made Patton vs. Rommel look like a schoolyard skirmish. After a countergroup of nine inside directors and two outsiders successfully thwarted the independent attempt to put former deputy chairman Richard Voell in the chairman's seat, the inside committee elected James Dutt chairman and CEO, and in so doing averted what Beatrice executives regard as a terrifying management coup by outside directors. Today, Beatrice is humming under Dutt, and Voell is president of Rockefeller Center, Inc., not exactly a shabby organization! Events like this show the resilience of corporations and the top executives who run them.

Actually such corporate takeover attempts by ambitious outside directors are rare. Though some Beatrice executives may point to the incident as a reason to be cautious about outside board members, most still would agree the presence of outsiders on boards provides perspective in decision making and policy at the highest levels. However, some critics maintain that outside representation is not enough. Though many boards are more responsible to their shareholders and publics, they say the ability of some boards to make accurate and responsible decisions is still limited. The reforms being made provide guarantees of representation from a greater cross section of public concerns, yet the political nature of decision making in the boardroom may limit the benefits of these well-intentioned reforms.

In the January–February 1981 issue of the *Harvard Business Review*, Leslie Levy, a Harvard B-school researcher, describes the problems in boardroom decision making at many corporations. The board of directors in a case she cites consists of members with different backgrounds that comply with new demands for varied representation. But, faced with approving or rejecting an acquisition strongly urged by their newly appointed CEO, the board is still manipulated into making a bad decision.

Details surrounding the acquisition were presented by the CEO at a formal gathering the evening before the directors met. However, the vote for approval was not taken until after discussion between the CEO and the directors themselves the next morning. The well-prepared CEO, who had provided information about the acquisition through the mails over a week before the meeting, answered all questions raised concerning his favored acquisition. After managing to allay a few concerns mentioned by the directors, the CEO urged approval and got it. Later, after the acquisition proved disastrous, all directors and supporting managers who had worked with the CEO on the acquisition reported negative feelings about it from the start.

The problem was clearly of a political nature. Unlike the wise Japanese executives who negotiate via much conversation and expert listening, these directors and managers simply approached the acquisition in a question-and-answer format. While Japanese executives familiarize themselves with all aspects surrounding business issues through talking and listening, then talking and listening some more until their backsides are flat and numb, these directors were more concerned with not offending their chief executive officer. They even had failed to relay their misgivings to each other. Levy's final conclusion? These sophisticated, smart directors were unable to discuss the issues they were responsible for discussing. They had not learned how to work together.

After considering the inability of the board to work as a team, the only other check on the CEO was in the hands of his managers. But these managers also had failed to voice their doubts concerning the acquisition, even though they were more familiar with the problems likely to be incurred by the acquisition than the directors could hope to be. This is not surprising. Managers who curry favor with their chief executives for the sake of their careers can't be counted on to challenge them. So they simply go along.

This case shows how an ambitious CEO can set up his board to get what he wants. While concerned directors wrung their hands instead of discouraging their new CEO, managers within the company simply abdicated their responsibility. The directors sought to avoid being obstructionists to the CEO. They wanted to voice support of his good performance to date. They worried that rejection of his proposal might arouse his wrath and resignation. By skillfully navigating these political waters, the CEO managed to avoid the serious debate that his proposed acquisition merited.

Tough Hombres

With so much pressure on corporate boards of directors to carry out their responsibilities with greater care and awareness for public concerns, the previously cozy relationships between CEOs and their boards are slowly disappearing. With a certain satisfaction, Washington lawyer Roderick Hills, former chairman of the Securities and Exchange Commission and now director on three company boards, defends these board changes in the October 6, 1980, *U.S. News & World Report.* "Presidents are getting fired all over the place. Directors now have real obligations and liabilities." More critics are insisting that the chairman of the board and the president of the corporation be two different people.

The chief financial officer of a multinational, multibillion sales company headquartered in the East told me over dinner recently why he insisted that he sit on the company's board. "I've gotta be on the board. As CFO, my integrity and reputation are at stake on how this company manages its assets.

As a board member, I have even more obligations and responsibilities—with legal ramifications. I sit on that board, with the authority it carries, so that if the old man is wrong, *I can shoot him down!*"

Boards *are* acting with greater harshness and urgency regarding treatment of CEOs. When Edgar Griffiths became chief executive of RCA in 1976, the board charged him with making sure that long-range strategic plans were developed for each of the company's operations. By 1981, Griffiths had failed to comply with those directions. Further, he had acquired a reputation for bullying the board into approving his recommendations in last-minute decision-making presentations (much as described in Leslie Levy's case study). Griffiths had become known as an irascible SOB who indiscriminately hired and fired top executives and other key personnel. He also had a propensity for leaking news of internal affairs. He so drastically failed to comply with the board's desire for long-range planning that one source revealed in the February 9, 1981, *Business Week* that at RCA "long range planning meant 'what are we going to do after lunch.'" Griffiths was forced to offer his resignation. His story isn't unusual nowadays and especially not at RCA. Thornton Bradshaw, the chief executive named to follow Griffiths, is the corporation's fourth CEO in six years. Every chief executive before him was forced out by the board of directors.

Board Performance Approval

Beginning at the CEO level and working on down through top and middle management ranks, you might expect some confusion and mixed reviews from executives over the performance of their boards of directors. To determine what they think of their directors, we asked them to rate how strong their boards are in exercising their responsibilities. Their overall response indicates their boards achieve their objectives adequately. I actually was surprised to find that 62 percent top executives and 60 percent middle perceive their boards to be exercising their responsibilities with moderate strength. Over one third—37 percent of both level executives—think their boards are very strong at meeting their responsibilities to the organization.

After all the consternation and allegations, it seems that most boards of directors have conceded to demands for "board reform." These reforms are evident in that boards now take their roles much more seriously than they did just a decade ago.

Section III
How Corporations Succeed and Fail

You can't build a reputation on what you're going
to do.
—HENRY FORD

We have forty million reasons for failure,
but not a single excuse.
—RUDYARD KIPLING

16

Social Responsibility Successes

Boomtown, U.S.A. There were thousands of such small industrial settings throughout the country not more than sixty years ago. In most cases, these historic settings didn't stir up pretty pictures. The lore that sprang up within them gave wing to the belief that business and nature, profit and goodness, ambition and wholesomeness were incompatible. That same belief persists among many social critics today.

In historic settings where profit-oriented business grew, people simply accepted that their town and children would suffer bad social effects. They expected that their wages from jobs brought to their communities by industry simply would have to compensate for their loss of touch with nature, goodness, and a well-built social order. Job seekers descended onto their towns, populations grew more rapidly than their social systems could handle, and strains were put on social services until they often broke down. The results were bad housing, shortages of goods, crime and overcrowding. The more people accepted these conditions as inevitable in the wake of profit and progress, the more businesses were inclined to agree.

Community members simply resigned themselves to their losses and disadvantages. They reacted to their plight like Europeans coping with taxes of land barons and out-of-touch royalty. In commerce, it was only the most benevolent businessmen who took it upon themselves to protect and contribute to the welfare of local citizens.

People devoted to both town and commerce were unaware that their two sets of interests eventually would arouse enough strife to test the workability of democratically governed, capitalistic, economic systems. Bitter, dramatic tales were told concerning the events surrounding business leaders and their followers. Generally, they were portrayed as shady misanthropes interested solely in profit who didn't give a whit about the welfare of citizens or their own employees. Private citizens often were described as hapless social victims, hungry in the streets and their hovels. They frequently endangered their lives merely by stepping into the factory or mill.

Such were the chronicles of despairing members of society, alone in their individual battles to overcome the obstacles presented by huge (small by today's standards) money-worshipping businesses. They were just about the only literary exposure non-business Americans had to the world of commerce in those days. Many of the stories were true. But true as they were, the other side of the story was seldom told or written.

For the most part, business leaders felt little need to explain their problems, motives, and circumstances to society. So the two groups remained bitter enemies. The bitterness between social and business groups evolved into labor disputes, unionism, labor agreements, environmental protection legislation, occupational hazard regulations, antitrust laws, price control legislation, et cetera, et cetera, et cetera. Citizen action groups constantly pressured government agencies to help them keep irresponsible, uncaring businesses under control. Amazingly, it's only in recent times the two groups have begun to realize that they can pursue common goals.

It wasn't until long after both wars that people began to understand better how to push the buttons of their government. And push them they did! The revolts of the sixties in many ways were superficial. Hardly a year has gone by since then without a "name" leader of that decade proving by his or her actions to have been bogus. Yet in other ways, those were creative times for our country. The events of those years brought to light the responsibility that all major institutions have to their various constituencies. Despite President Reagan telling us (I agree with him) that many social programs were created with warm hearts but unclear heads, we'll never forget the lessons of the sixties.

On the other hand, it is dirty pool to suggest that most companies routinely ignored their social responsibilities as a matter of intent. Having undergone growing pains of their own, corporations have been hard pressed to deal with numerous matters (including survival) throughout their life cycles. Much like individuals who survive childhood and adolescence to acquire perspective on how they fit into the world, corporations now seem in a similar developmental period.

Many corporations still are possessed of perspectives that render them totally unrelated to their communities. For them, it's as if the world were a jigsaw puzzle, and their existence simply confined to one piece in the puzzle, having no relation to or dependence on any other of its pieces. Pathetically, their executives suffer from tunnel vision. Achievements and objectives directly concerning issues and affairs of business alone are all they can see. The consequence is spoiling. They are nearly blind to the effects of their organizations' parasitism.

The Main Question

In all fairness, corporations are concerned with numerous priorities at one time. They are compelled to address several social, economic, government, and personnel challenges simultaneously. It is idealistic babble to expect sweeping success in all efforts. But much progress already is apparent in the long-neglected area of corporate responsibility to social needs. For this, corporations deserve our praise. The main question facing a corporation here is not should it be socially responsible. Rather, it is *what is its place in the world?* How does it connect? How is it already engaged? What is the larger view of its mundane efforts that are "there" willy-nilly right now? I submit that most executives have not given serious thought to this question.

Slowly, corporations have become more educated about public sentiments. In the interest of occupying positions in society as good citizens, corporate leaders are wise to attempt compliance with widely held views of social responsibility. Regarding the most obvious expectations directed at them, corporations say they are eager to meet the needs of society, government, and their employees.

However, stated goals often are not supported sufficiently with action to see them through. Failure to act on rhetoric, failure to strive for expressed goals, is not necessarily gross avoidance of corporate responsibilities; it can be understood better as faintheartedness or latent disinterest.

When *Productivity Newsletter* publisher Norman Bodek toured a plant of a New England company, he discovered in conversations with employees that management supported quality in production in its rhetoric but catered to very different priorities in its actions. In his September 1981 issue, Bodek reports on this type of shortcoming. After seeing several large signs instructing employees to TAKE PRIDE IN YOUR WORK, WE MAKE A QUALITY PRODUCT, DO IT RIGHT THE FIRST TIME, Bodek was surprised to learn from an employee that management failed to support the pursuit of quality. After one woman had placed a reject tag on a defective item, the tag was removed by her supervisor, who lectured her on the way things are done to achieve high standards of quality. "We are paid for production," he said. "The quality control people will take care of that at the end of the line."

Bodek's story is a good illustration of how corporations both succeed and fail at their goals. I'm sure you've noticed with some frequency that when corporations truly want to see a goal through, there's no stopping them. They usually achieve it with flying colors. But when companies commit to goals for reasons other than heartfelt resolve and interest, they fall grossly short of their proclaimed intentions.

A CEO may feel urged to join in with other corporate leaders, sharing an interest in some cause or faddish issue. Wanting to be appreciated for his views, no matter of what stripe—economic, government, social, personnel—he asks his public relations department to issue press releases that state how committed his company is to resolving the issue at hand. In cases like this, when the company's achievements are measured against its expressed interests, it is easy to see what's important to its executives and what isn't. Typically, the "hot issue" takes a back seat to more routine priorities.

No company leader would say that his company isn't committed to quality products. Indeed, all companies claim to be committed to quality. But many companies actually will be more interested in volume production than quality. So they will talk quality and produce a tawdry line.

Overly Harsh Judgment

It isn't cricket to be overly harsh in judging corporate behavior where social responsibility is concerned. After all, individuals rarely meet all the social responsibilities they might be expected to assume. And where an individual is laggard, it's easy to know where to point a finger. The shunning of corporate action in certain social endeavors is acceptable in many cases. No one should expect corporations to be saddled with conquering all the problems of their complex communities, and certainly not single-handedly. But the size and power of corporations endow them with resources and a come-hither look that always catches society's hungry eye.

If corporations should not be judged too harshly for their failure to cure most of the ills plaguing contemporary society, they definitely can be upbraided for failing to contribute to such cures when they are being stared in the face by them. The size and complexity of corporations make it difficult to locate their sources of apathy. They cannot be identified with merely one or even several individuals in a company. This gives executives an easy out from accountability where social action is concerned. They just look at each other and shrug their shoulders when such subjects come up. That corporate shoulder-shrugging—the sign of puzzlement—is proof that the real problem with social involvement in corporations is not action itself, but attitude. It's not one of getting corporations to *become* involved. It's getting them to realize they already are.

And since they are . . . there might be a better way. . . .

A corporation that fails to recognize itself as a member of its community lays itself open to the same danger as an executive who fails to identify with his corporate or office community. That danger is failure—pure and simple—from lack of engagement. This is ineffectiveness owing to a lack of comprehension. It is the "My Lord, I had no idea" syndrome.

Before corporations, institutions, or individuals genuinely can be helpful in social and community problems, they must have an adequate understanding of their own part in the overall fabric of society. Common experience teaches that there is no such thing as being a little bit pregnant. When you're there, you're there. It's just a matter of knowing when the baby's due and delivering it under the best of circumstances. Likewise, a corporation cannot deny it is already part of its world. Its task is to get down to business in determining what it has to contribute and gain by becoming alive in its social milieu. Ignorance is not an option.

Having said all that, I also must say corporate engagement in social responsibility is bound to result in degrees of success and failure. The extent to which companies fail or succeed is determined by their unique approaches and attitudes regarding social matters. They may be well intentioned and stupid and fail. They may be hard and smart and succeed. But to do the latter, they can never be truly cynical.

Levi Strauss, a Model

Historically, social attitudes have varied widely among corporations. Those of each corporation generally are keyed by its top leaders. The differences between, say, Control Data and McDonald's or Levi Strauss set them as far apart from each other as Alaska and Timbuktu. Founders of these companies —and executives who have followed—established and nourished attitudes and perceptions of how they fit into and coexist with their local communities and society at large.

The degree to which corporations choose to engage themselves in social concerns is readily perceived by outsiders, stockholders, and employees. Generally, corporate philosophy and sentiments on the subject are passed on quickly and absorbed by their executives.

Astute publicity-oriented corporations are quick to focus much attention on their good deeds. Some would have us think they are charitable organizations rather than profit makers. This perception usually enhances their reception in most communities. McDonald's franchises, for example, often are involved in an array of social-improvement campaigns that include fire prevention, bicycle safety, or litter clean-up. These activities provide several two-way benefits for McDonald's and the communities where they have restaurants.

No one can challenge the value of the community interests of companies like McDonald's. On the other hand, Levi Strauss is a classic example of a company with a history of staunch commitment to social and employee welfare. Ever since Levi Strauss started his blue jean company during the 1850s gold rush, the company has set an example of seemingly selfless involvement with social needs. His descendants carried out his charitable programs long after he died. After the 1906 earthquake destroyed the Levi

Strauss facilities and most of San Francisco, the company took out ads in the city's papers notifying employees that salaries would be continued until further notice.

The company is described in the almanac *Everybody's Business* this way: "Beyond offering a reliable product in a shaky world, Levi Strauss has become widely known for assuming responsibility for the well-being of their employees and of the communities in which they have a presence. And they do this with a minimum of fanfare."

To this day, Levi Strauss maintains social programs that keep pace with profit growth. A 33 percent profit increase in 1979 led to a doubling of its charitable contributions. Levi Strauss's twenty-two-person staff Foundation with its community-affairs committee is one of the largest of its kind in American business. It alone is a testimonial to the company's social commitment. Company chairman (since retired) Walter Haas, Jr., adds his own in the September 21, 1981, *Fortune:* "When we went public in 1971, we told investors right in the prospectus that we had strong convictions about our social responsibilities." In the November 1981 issue of *San Francisco* magazine, he says: "A lot of people feel the way Milton Friedman does—that the only responsibility a corporation has is to make money. I disagree with him completely."

The programs addressed in Levi Strauss's 1980 charitable contributions of $9.6 million (3.1 percent of pretax earnings) include a wide assortment of social problems and groups. By encouraging employees in sixty-five communities where Levi Strauss plants are located to direct company attention to needy programs within each community, the company has managed to diversify its charity involvement widely. Donations have been made to finance programs for handicapped children in Benton, Arkansas, as well as to fund welfare services for battered women in Memphis, San Antonio, and Hobbs, New Mexico.

A *San Francisco* article, "Levi's Laundry," reports foundation director Ira Hirschfield's refreshing view: "We're particularly interested in supporting activities that catalyze employee involvement." The article's author, Roger Rapoport, explains how this works:

Community Involvement Teams composed of employees have been started in all company towns with company funds. Workers give time to such causes as child care, nutrition programs for the elderly, and prevention of spouse abuse.

The company also makes direct cash contributions to any non-profit organization served by a volunteer from Levi who has worked with the organization for a year. And the foundation will match every employee dollar contributed to a college with a two dollar gift. "We don't apply political criteria to these donations," says foundation director Hirschfield. "The employees tell us what they think is important. We gave some money to Planned Parenthood last year. If a Levi worker got on the board of a non-profit anti-abortion group, we'd send them money, too."

Thus Levi's work force directs the company's reinvestment in its own communities, and the company benefits from improved loyalty and productivity. The end results are a better product, higher sales, and more profits to share in every plant's home town.

Obviously, not all companies have the same resolve where social responsibility is concerned. However, more corporations are becoming enlightened to the need to be engaged in their community problems. At least by voice and print, they express anything from fair to avid interest in fulfilling their obligations to society.

Success or failure of corporations to contribute funds and efforts to social needs can be viewed and judged on the basis of several factors. Internal awareness is one measure of a corporation's success. By increasing awareness and educating executives about community problems and how they can assist in alleviating some social ills, a company achieves the kind of success that in the early stages is the most important. Even by themselves, proclamations of interest and concern heighten awareness for both the community and the corporate executives.

However, after corporate leaders proclaim their interests and concern, how they back their words with action becomes the most important success. As do individuals, corporations often pay lip service to faddish issues that have been deemed by media or other opinion shapers to be of current significance.

Meeting Society's Needs

Marshall McLuhan was right. We live in a global village. Communications, commerce, and transportation constantly shrink the world. As they do, corporations face the consequences of their actions as they affect communities all across the globe. As long as corporations fail to recognize their responsibilities in their local communities, they can't be counted on for an ounce of insight on their place in the worldwide community. It seems that only the most progressive corporations have accepted the challenge of being engaged in their world instead of just being *attached* to it.

Most executives impart attitudes about corporate responsibility that spring directly or indirectly from their leaders. Corporations reputed to put heavy emphasis on playing responsible roles in their communities are those that have top executives who take pride in their commitment to social well-being. Corporations that fail to acknowledge and address social matters usually have top executives who make clear by either loud voice or total silence that such are irrelevant to their priorities.

To determine corporate attitudes and behavior regarding certain forms of social engagement, we asked executives: "How important is this activity for your corporation? How often does your corporation do this?"

Being aware of the public's image of the corporation.

Contributing funds to community facilities.

Providing goods and services for society's needs and wants.

Creating jobs.

Asking these questions above allows us not only to assess corporate rhetoric, but achievement as well. How corporations achieve a measure of success in these areas of social engagement is summarized in Table 19, page 161.

Perceived Corporate Image

Corporations profess their need to project a positive image in their communities. In this day and age, any company that doesn't appreciate the need to make itself felt as a contributing member of its community would have to be devoid of public sentiment and oblivious to community opinion. But *wanting* to project a positive image and succeeding at it are two different matters. Therefore, it is critical for a corporation to know what its image to the public is as opposed to what it hopes it is. On this score, there is no lack of sense of mission. Overwhelmingly, executives are mobilized for understanding how their corporations are perceived within their communities. This sense of being on alert extends to both levels of management. Sixty-four percent top executives and 66 percent middle think their companies place very much or most importance on awareness of the public's image of their corporations. Approximately another 25 percent of executives say this is of fair importance to their companies. Further, roughly 55 percent of all executives say their corporations generally or virtually always know how they are perceived by their publics. Such knowledge allows a corporation to take action on that image to make sure it conforms to its wishes.

Some companies enjoy favorable images by accidental means. For example, by being a baker, the National Biscuit Company brings pleasure to its neighbors' olfactory senses. In Nabisco's company history, *Out of the Cracker Barrel,* we are told:

When the wind was right, seamen and stevedores coming off the North River docks could sniff appetizing smells of Vanilla Wafers and Marshmallow Fancies. On other days the aroma of Animal Crackers and Fig Newton Cakes contrasted sharply with the smells emanating from taverns along Ninth Avenue. "An air of innocence," one writer put it, "clings to the National Biscuit Company, as it must to any business where grown men concern themselves with a ginger snap named ZuZu."

Table 19
How Corporations Succeed at Social Responsibility

	DEGREE OF IMPORTANCE				
	No (%)	Little (%)	Fair (%)	Very (%)	Most (%)
Top Executives					
Being aware of public's image of corporation	1.2	8.0	26.3	41.6	22.4
	Rarely/ Never	**Some- times**	**Fre- quently**	**Gener- ally**	**Virtually always**
Achieved	3.6	21.7	19.1	35.4	19.5
Contributing funds to community facilities	4.6	25.3	38.2	21.6	6.9
Achieved	9.4	28.3	26.5	21.0	11.0
Providing goods and services for society's needs and wants	2.4	14.6	30.2	32.5	15.4
Achieved	3.8	20.4	23.0	35.3	12.4
Creating jobs	5.4	29.3	36.9	18.9	6.8
Achieved	6.2	32.5	30.1	20.3	7.4

	DEGREE OF IMPORTANCE				
	No (%)	Little (%)	Fair (%)	Very (%)	Most (%)
Middle Managers					
Being aware of public's image of corporation	0.5	10.3	21.8	41.0	25.0
	Rarely/ Never	**Some- times**	**Fre- quently**	**Gener- ally**	**Virtually always**
Achieved	4.5	20.3	19.3	31.4	23.0
Contributing funds to community facilities	5.5	26.1	35.7	21.6	5.4
Achieved	12.2	29.0	24.4	19.7	8.8
Providing goods and services for society's needs and wants	2.1	11.1	29.7	34.2	17.0
Achieved	3.8	19.9	22.4	32.7	14.9
Creating jobs	6.4	26.6	39.9	19.6	4.6
Achieved	8.9	33.5	28.1	21.0	5.0

"Not Applicable" responses not included.

Corporate Giving

By opening their pocketbooks, corporations have met some of their social responsibilities. While making contributions to special community projects may be among a corporation's easiest and most self-serving practices, the value of its contributions at the community level is undeniable. In the September 21, 1981, *Fortune*, Lee Smith writes, "Few corporations engage in philanthropy because others need money." He backs up his opinion by pointing to such examples as railroad sponsorship of YMCA hostels that provided places for their employees to sleep, donations made by a firm to an Olympic swimming team where a client's son was in training, or the classic example of the standard write-off of donations as business expenses.

There can't be any doubt that giving to hospitals likely to care for employees during an emergency, B-schools where companies are likely to recruit, or any other well-directed activity is beneficial to corporations as well as to the groups these funds support. In light of the noninvolvement of many companies in community problems, this activity is a step forward.

Executives rate their companies as being moderately committed to making such contributions. Twenty-nine percent top executives and 27 percent middle think their companies are very much or most interested in making contributions to community facilities. Another 38 percent top executives and 36 percent middle say such activities are of fair importance to their organizations. Therefore, 65 percent of both levels of management say their companies are from fairly to most interested in making contributions. Clearly, these figures underscore the willingness of corporations to offer financial support to community projects.

When it comes to putting their money where their mouths are, corporations exceed their expressed interest. Thirty-two percent of top executives say their companies virtually always or generally meet their commitment to contribute. Another 27 percent of top executives say their companies frequently back up their statements of interest with money. Middle managers share the same beliefs as top management. Twenty-nine percent claim their companies virtually always or generally make contributions that back up their expressed interests, and another 24 percent believe their companies usually make contribution to community facilities.

Corporations that are interested in supporting social programs with donations do so with extensive commitment and eagerness. As you have seen from the example set by Levi Strauss, when social needs are among a corporation's top priorities, it hastens to make contributions that exceed its own financial payback. Smith describes four types of corporate givers:

Stand-up Conservatives—Extremely conservative, these donors select self-serving activities for their contribution targets. More than any other group, they make contributing funds a business in itself. They scrutinize, narrow their options, and insist on directing a percentage of their contribution toward activities that advance their own interests directly or indirectly.

Tough Liberals—Companies such as Levi Strauss, Hershey, and McDonald's are tough, liberal donors. They avidly seek programs through which to funnel donations, but investigate their philosophies and effectiveness before pouring in dollars.

Parvenu Patrons—Rather than funneling all contributions into one or just a handful of programs, some companies have found a way to decentralize them. They allow their executives at operations around the country to distribute their monies to various organizations. This enhances their image among wider audiences. Interpace Corporation previously channeled funds into United Way programs, but now is distributing them through their individual plant allocations. By funding art shows and sculpture exhibits, the company hopes to convey commitment to quality and stay in the good graces of Wall Street creditors who are on museum boards.

Enlightened Educators—Large corporations who are dependent on well-educated executives increasingly steer their giving to academic institutions where they believe those dollars will be used most appropriately to their interests. A General Motors contribution to Harvard years ago may have sent anthropology students off to the outer limits of Africa to study apes. Today, GM's donations are placed directly with Harvard's B-school, a hall of learning the company believes more in line with its own purposes.

Providing Goods and Services

Corporations that express interest in social activities and prove it by backing up their statements with action can be considered successful. But in some cases, the level of proclaimed interest belies the narrow perceptions of corporate leaders and executives of how their functions relate to and help society. As I've said, these executives fail to see their place as a part of the communities in which they exist. Nowhere is this more apparent than when executives rate the extent to which their organizations provide goods and services for society's needs and wants, and create jobs.

If a hard-nosed businessman wants to scuttle "social responsibility types" —to whom he wouldn't give air in a jug—he can do so effectively and legitimately with one barrage. That is: "Business creates jobs. Business produces goods and services for society's needs and wants. That's enough. Get lost!" This may or may not be a narrow view. It depends on how much he's thought it through. Further, it has the ring of honesty. I can live with it and respect the man.

It is in facing his argument that social-responsibility advocates are most vulnerable. Well, they need not fear it. Apparently, corporations don't see these two areas as critical to their mission. They are given only lukewarm commitment by executives. Forty-eight percent top executives and 51 percent middle think providing goods and services for society's needs and wants is either very important or among their organization's highest goals. Only half! Tell me, what company can survive without doing so? This is the core activity of a business. The only possible explanation for the responses to this question is that this function is accomplished unwittingly by executives and their corporations. Without this, there's nothing else, even in the absence of competition. When competition is fierce, the very goal of business centers on a company's providing such goods and services better than anyone else.

Forty-eight percent of both level executives say their companies generally or virtually always provide their consumers with what they need. Twenty-three percent of both level executives say their companies frequently meet these needs. This makes most companies as successful as they care to be. Actually 71 percent general satisfaction among corporations' consumers is not a bad record. Just imagine what they could do with a sense of purpose.

One organization with such purpose is the Bank of America, headquartered in San Francisco. It is our nation's largest bank. You might expect that almost all its income is earned through financing the businesses of large corporations. While corporate banking is indeed important, producing goods and services for society's needs and wants—BankAmerica style—is shown in its long history of being totally and extensively involved with small and individual consumers. Responding to special needs of members of its community, this bank developed services for various special groups. It has set them up for non-English-speaking people, the physically handicapped, students, and the elderly—to meet their unique banking requirements. In so doing, the bank may not add directly to its coffers, but it generates a great deal of community goodwill. BankAmerica's article of faith is that providing services to the bank's customers often involves more than simply financial considerations.

Creating Jobs

Executives think that creating jobs is of either very little or fair importance. One-third believe their companies regard creating jobs as either of no or very little importance. Just over one-third say their companies place a fair amount of importance on creating jobs. One-fourth think their companies believe this activity is of very much or most importance to their companies. As with providing goods and services, the attitudes of executives are matched by achievement of their goals. The executives who see this activity as of no or little importance fairly match objectives and performance.

I grant you that a problem may exist for some executives answering this question because of the word *creating*. They rightfully believe it is not the responsibility of a company to *invent* jobs that don't exist—make-work, in other words. But if a company starts a new business, builds a new plant, opens a new office, or just expands because of increased sales volume, it certainly creates new jobs.

The large number of executives who responded to this question and the one on providing goods and services with the opinion that these activities are not of great importance show that they are not reflective on the role and impact of business in the world. Nor are they cognizant of what their own companies need to survive. So when it comes to social responsibility, they aren't even aware of the good their companies are doing. Consequently, they aren't in a position to claim or enjoy the sound purposes they fulfill. That hard-nosed businessman actually has a sense of social responsibility. But these unreflective executives do not.

Minneapolis-based Control Data Corporation is an example of a company showing hard-nosedness and imagination in producing goods and services for society's needs and wants, and in creating jobs. Its accomplishment in numerous such projects is based on a corporate philosophy expressed by chief executive William Norris: "The major needs of society are profitable business opportunities." Odd as it may seem, this sentiment makes a company such as Control Data a model for corporations meeting most social responsibilities. Self-serving and profit interest don't hinder achievement in social concerns for companies. What is necessary is frighteningly simple: that corporations learn to appreciate themselves for producing quality goods and services essential to a healthy, well-run society.

Control Data's urban revitalization program has successfully placed plants in numerous poverty areas throughout the United States. After instituting training and various service programs such as day care centers to assist local residents with personal needs, the company has hired local residents for their plants. Such programs provide entry to a life of enjoyable, beneficial employment for an entire community of disadvantaged persons. Moreover, the program works for the benefit of Control Data. The company properly derives sheer pleasure from achieving laudable objectives. While helping to eliminate poverty, the company has trained and employed workers at plants marked by low rates of absenteeism, tardiness, and turnover. CDC's success stories, which I will be describing over the next few pages, are in contrast to the experience of most corporations.

17

Social Responsibility
Failures

To determine corporate attitudes and behavior toward additional forms of social engagement, we again asked executives: "How important is this for your corporation? How often does your corporation do this?"

Advancing the technological sophistication of society.

Articulating company needs to the public.

Educating the public on the free enterprise system.

Improving the quality of life for members of society.

Making life less burdensome for the poor in society.

As we have seen, corporations have had a measure of success in the matter of social responsibility. However, though many corporations spend much energy on social matters, they often fail to maintain an image of themselves as a part of a larger world than business itself. This means either that their definition of the world is too big, or their definition of business is too small.

Executive responses to the issues above are summarized in Table 20.

Advancing the Technological Sophistication of Society

The technological advancement of corporations is tantamount to the technological advancement of society. Corporate executives might not know that, and it's evident that in some cases even society doesn't. Technology is a bugaboo, to be shunned by timid, fearful citizens who, remembering the extensive changes brought about by the industrial revolution, are frightened that even more changes will emerge from the technological revolution.

The numerous, common charges made against technology by resisters of change and some intellectual elitists are summed up by Samuel C. Florman in his short, lively book *The Existential Pleasures of Engineering:*

Technology—out of human control; will spoil our lives.

Technology—will lead us to tedious work and degrade us.

Technology—creates elitists of technocrats, and disenfranchises the masses.

Technology—forces us to consume things we really don't want.

Technology—cuts us off from the natural world.

Technology—leads to diversions that destroy our sense of being.

Florman imaginatively defends the art of technocrats against these charges. His main arguments are that (1) technology is an activity, not a force to be controlled; (2) technology advances average citizens rather than subjugates them; (3) urban life itself has already removed us from nature; and (4) we are already a nation of people who want too many things. The first two deal with what he considers misconceptions about technology. The latter two, he says, are maladies for which technology should not be blamed.

Florman's words properly may arouse some sympathy for misjudged, underestimated technocrats. But they do not defend the value of technology in modern life nearly as well as technological achievers do with their actions. In this respect, Control Data is a shining example. This company puts numerous technological advancements to work for the clear, observable betterment of society.

Control Data is a computer company; a good one. The November 30, 1981, *Business Week* features this company in an article entitled "Control Data beats the industry." The article states, "In a year when most mainframe computer makers—including IBM, NCR, Sperry and Honeywell—have seen slower sales growth and declining earnings, Control Data Corporation is racking up continuing gains."

By directing computer applications to specific social problems, CDC benefits more social groups than would any number of contributions or other acts of charity. For example, through its PLATO computer-based education programs, personalized basic education is offered to children while vocational education is made available to teen-agers ready to join the work force. The program offers patient, highly individualized learning processes to those with varied educational needs.

Computerized health care programs are distributed by Control Data to underprivileged communities where citizens might not have easy access to medical facilities. These programs emphasize preventive health care measures. The company has implemented various computer-based research pro-

Table 20
How Corporations Fail in Social Responsibility

	DEGREE OF IMPORTANCE				
	No (%)	Little (%)	Fair (%)	Very (%)	Most (%)
Top Executives Advancing the technological sophistication of society	10.7	32.1	28.0	14.2	4.7
	Rarely/ Never	**Some- times**	**Fre- quently**	**Gener- ally**	**Virtually always**
Achieved	20.4	32.3	18.8	13.2	4.2
Articulating its needs to the public	9.7	36.7	27.8	17.1	3.6
Achieved	22.0	38.9	20.4	9.6	3.6
Educating the public on the free enterprise system	10.7	36.9	23.5	17.6	6.3
Achieved	28.2	36.3	14.1	11.1	4.8
Improving the quality of life for members of society	9.3	34.3	34.3	11.3	2.4
Achieved	22.5	34.9	21.1	10.6	2.4
Making life less burdensome for the poor in society	18.4	42.9	23.3	4.2	1.0
Achieved	34.4	35.4	14.3	3.8	1.4

"Not Applicable" responses not included.

grams to facilitate urban renewal and rural development programs. In these circumstances, the company achieves rigorous profit objectives, engineers and technicians gain professional fulfilment, and sophisticated technology is spread through a society that stands to benefit from its applications.

Computer-related business is only one of the legion of sources of rapid technological advancement in this country. Yet most companies still do not consider themselves as directly or even indirectly dependent upon or involved with technological advancements. Fewer than one in five of all executives says his company places very much or most importance on advancing the technological sophistication of society. As far as achievement goes, just over half of all executives assert their companies never or rarely provide or contribute to such advances.

Nonetheless, American life-patterns change constantly, rapidly. The everyday technical life of any one family in the United States is not likely to

	DEGREE OF IMPORTANCE				
	No (%)	Little (%)	Fair (%)	Very (%)	Most (%)
Middle Managers Advancing the technological sophistication of society	12.3	26.8	27.0	13.1	3.6
	Rarely/ Never	**Some- times**	**Fre- quently**	**Gener- ally**	**Almost always**
Achieved	19.8	31.5	16.9	11.2	2.8
Articulating its needs to the public	9.0	37.1	27.6	14.5	3.8
Achieved	24.2	36.3	16.5	11.5	3.1
Educating the public on the free enterprise system	14.3	32.1	22.5	16.2	5.5
Achieved	31.8	29.5	15.0	9.6	4.1
Improving the quality of life for members of society	14.3	28.5	31.2	11.8	2.9
Achieved	23.2	36.3	15.6	10.8	1.8
Making life less burdensome for the poor in society	22.4	35.8	21.5	6.0	0.7
Achieved	34.4	32.8	11.2	6.1	0.4

"Not Applicable" responses not included.

be the same as it was just ten years ago, unless that family has made strenuous efforts to avoid advancements. Corporations responsible for introducing new home convenience devices such as Moped, new fuels, home computers, new communications methods, and even new timesaving food conveniences, are all bringing technological sophistication into homes as well as workplaces. These changes alter life and work habits and, therefore, the life patterns of most Americans.

Any housewife knows the advantages of preparing technologically developed frozen dinners in her technologically developed microwave oven. The five to ten minutes required to do this, compared to the one to two hours for a meal from scratch, provides a dramatic saving of her time and effort. Executives who work on the development of new products or modifications of old ones are bringing technological advancement to society. Their limited awareness of the necessity and ends of their labors invites the charge that businesses are only means-oriented, lacking an understanding of their link-ups with society.

The computer industry is one of the most technologically advanced on a worldwide basis. It is from this industry that changes in our everyday lives are being felt most dramatically. An article in the August 8, 1981, *Business Week* says that expectations for our nation's resurgence in technology are said to be most likely to take place within this industry. "Some executives predict that by 1990, the U.S. will surpass Japan and Germany in the race to automate and will thus maintain the U.S. lead in industrial productivity." Some of these developments are expected to have major impacts on the style and environment of factory life in America. The assembly line won't remain the problem-ridden collection of tedious tasks that frustrate today's workers. "U.S. companies are on the edge of achieving a dream: manufacturing enterprises where push-button factories and executive suites, no matter how physically remote, become parts of the same integrated, computerized entity."

Industries aside from those that are computer-based also are increasingly in a position to affect the lives of all Americans with their technologies. A February 4, 1981, *Wall Street Journal* article says: "By the end of this decade, and certainly in the 1990s, the free world may require less than half of the oil it uses today." Aside from substituting for the 50 million barrels of oil per day currently consumed in the free world with diluted-gasoline mixtures, natural gas, nuclear energy, and various forms of coal, specific technologies are expected to reduce energy use. These include new coal technologies and advances in refinery technologies capable of producing lighter fuel products.

The fact is that most industries, whether they deal in industrial products or even services, are likely—directly or indirectly—to bring the benefits of advanced technology to society. What remains puzzling is that this occurs without corporations' seeing it as a significant part of their mission. Their failure is not performance as much as perception.

Educating the Public

Though companies want to maintain positive images in their communities, they are much too reticent when it comes to voicing their requirements to those communities. Only 21 percent top executives and 18 percent middle say their companies put very much or most importance on articulating their needs to society. Few companies perform well at this task. Only 13 percent top executives and 15 percent middle say their companies generally or virtually always make their needs clear to the public.

Yet when the time comes for price increases and other unpopular action to be taken, executives at most corporations can't understand why the public isn't more sympathetic to their problems; why citizens can't appreciate their difficulties. Twenty-eight percent top and middle executives say their companies place fair importance on articulating their needs to the public. This figure indicates that corporations committed to having the public become aware of what *they* need to function successfully aren't nonexistent. But such endeavors to contribute to two-way understanding with society are paltry.

Corporations have much to gain by educating the public on business matters. In his *Landmarks of Tomorrow*, Peter Drucker says: "Education must teach responsible citizenship. It must fit a man to rule himself and to take responsible initiative for his society." It is a corporation's responsibility to see that citizens are educated to understand its business problems and conditions. As public sectors and corporate communities share in the same problems, and as members of these two groups become aware of their interdependence, it is essential that they add to each other's understanding.

Some corporate leaders recognize the need for corporations to encourage better understanding, at the community level, of their problems and of business economics. But they are few. Only 24 percent top executives and 22 percent middle think their companies place very much or most importance on educating the public on the free enterprise system. Another 24 percent top executives and 23 percent middle assert their companies place a fair amount of importance on educating the public about how free enterprise works.

Some executives not only encourage educating the public about the business system of our country, but believe that neglecting such education is dangerous. In the Lee Smith *Fortune* article I mentioned earlier, Edward Littlejohn, vice-president of public affairs for Pfizer, ventures that some businesses donate to charities as a kind of apology for their profits. In fact, he believes some corporations turn their backs on the free enterprise system. He refers to the hesitance of one corporation to contribute to a study of capitalism, wishing to avoid involvement in "controversial ideology." The interests of business and communities alike are natural linkups to the free market system. To support its commitment to educating the public and executives about the free enterprise system, Pfizer directs $2 million a year to organizations such as the American Enterprise Institute and the Institute of Educational Affairs.

Newspaper columnists like to call AEI "the Washington-based conservative think-tank." IEA was founded by former Treasury Secretary William E. Simon and social thinker Irving Kristol. Among its most important functions is funding "journalistic and academic projects that do not share the 'adversary' ethos that, in IEA's view, disposes modern culture to condemn the society, including the economic system, that sustains it."

Bank of America also supports increased efforts to educate the public about our free enterprise system. In 1980, the bank channeled $120,000 to the California State University and Colleges Foundation for an economic literacy project. The bank also is involved in the local Junior Achievement program. In 1979, the bank sponsored forty JA companies. One hundred fifty of its employees volunteered to guide students through phases of forming and operating a business. JA activities long have acquainted young people with the workings and problems of business in the free enterprise system.

Another West Coast company—Atlantic Richfield—deserves praise for its recent advertising campaign. It is designed to educate citizens to the trade-offs they face on environmental issues. This company's literate, intelligent message, centered on the theme "There are no easy answers," makes clear that simple black-white/good-bad decisions are not available to us. At the same time the campaign conveys ARCO's eagerness to enter into dialogue with the public. It also is instrumental in defending the company's stake in the environment, from which the overwhelming bulk of its income is derived.

Quality of Life

Executives do not see their companies as taking part in improving the quality of life for society at large. Only 14 percent top executives and 15 percent middle think their companies place very much or most importance on this activity. Thirty-four percent top executives and 31 percent middle say their companies place a fair amount of importance on improving quality of life for society. That leaves over a third of all executives who say their companies have no responsibility to improve the quality of life for society. Of course, we have seen how corporations through their products and services improve our lives every day. Thank goodness they do. However, it's obvious that their executives don't see their corporate activities this way.

Perspective on the Poor

The final and gravest area where corporations are irresponsible is in their perspective on the poor. Only 5 percent top executives and 7 percent middle think their organizations place very much or most importance on making life less burdensome for the poor in society. Another 23 percent top executives and 22 percent middle say their companies place fair amounts of importance on helping the disadvantaged in their communities.

Granted, there are not many companies with the charitable orientation of Levi Strauss or Hershey. There are even fewer with the imagination or interest to combine their own profit functions with the amelioration of social ills. Corporations hold a strong position in most communities. Their failure to be resourceful in creating economic opportunity and a can-do spirit in their communities can be interpreted as nothing less than negligence.

Community assistance for the poor is appreciated more and is of greater long-term benefit when it is in the form of education and training rather than simply contributions. Money helps. But holding noses and giving handouts won't work. Among corporations that choose to address the problems of society, education is often an effective means of assistance. For example, Bank of America recently paid salaries, benefits, and expenses of forty-nine officers who were part of a full-time program to train and advise community, government, and other nonprofit agencies. During 1980, the cost to the bank for this alone was $780,000. Other educational programs in which the bank engaged include achievement award programs, public school and training assistance programs, and funding of schools to enable purchase of computers and other equipment as aids for better education.

Control Data has initiated programs that carry needed services to remote regions and entire poor communities. The company's Rosebud health care program carries quality health care to six thousand Sioux Indians on the Rosebud Reservation in South Dakota. Control Data's mobile clinic circulates among ten communities. In addition to developing training programs for paramedics from within the communities, CDC provides immunization programs against childhood diseases, and prenatal and infant care education for Rosebud residents.

Despite the plain benefits that corporations stand to gain in dealing with and within healthy communities, they staunchly seem to resist any meaningful interaction with them. Their policies seem to be summed up in "We'll take care of our problems; let society take care of its own." Despite the resources of corporations to act effectively in solving problems, they're letting us know that little help is on the way.

All that has been needed for many corporations to become engaged in their surroundings is a catalyst. Control Data has been active in organizing various venture corporations that address specific social needs. Control Data's City Venture Corporation combines efforts of various professional and religious organizations and eight corporations. Learning from past urban failures, they have harnessed resources anew within communities to revitalize decaying inner cities and build new ones. President Reagan's concept of enterprise zones in our older cities also sounds promising as a catalyst.

Corporate attitudes on social engagement indicate that executives don't share a sense of connectedness with the outside world. They assume that their profit-oriented activities have almost nothing to do with the noncorporate realms of society, even though logic and various marketing disciplines defy such notions. Executives further assume that if their activities and problems have nothing to do with the noncorporate world, then the problems and dilemmas of the noncorporate world have nothing to do with their roles and functions.

Perhaps the most harmful aspect of executives' compartmentalized thinking where social matters are concerned is that it keeps them from being aware of and exulting in the enormous good corporations perform for society in their everyday activities. In this way, they disown a kinship with society that already exists.

18

Personnel Successes

In 1970, NBC aired a special documentary on the Coca-Cola Company. The narrator of the special labeled Coca-Cola—employment king of the South —as a perpetrator of gross neglect of less-favored employees. He referred specifically to the treatment of migrant workers in their Minute Maid orange groves. Executives at Coke hemmed and hawed, bowed their reddened faces, shuffled their feet a bit, and murmured that some time before, they had embarked on a plan that would change all that.

Coca-Cola is a big company that does things in a big way. The company *had* embarked on a plan that would change things for their migrant workers. In fact, so drastic were Coca-Cola's planned changes that migrant workers in Florida orange groves were about to experience levels of self-determination and improved working conditions unknown to such workers anywhere else in the United States. Over a ten-year period, Coca-Cola would help their migrant workers create, maintain, and nurture their own thriving community.

In 1977, nine years after Coca-Cola's experiment in improved working conditions for their agricultural employees began, 40 percent of their migrant work force had become stabilized, permanent workers of the company. The company had invested large sums in refining living conditions for these laborers, provided specific fringe benefits and seniority rights for permanent employees, assisted in the development of various community services (child development, dental and medical centers), and maintained numerous educational programs (consumer, voter, and legal-rights education) for workers. The payoff to the company was greater worker productivity; their pickers now box 21 percent more than any other migrant workers in the world.

Coca-Cola made changes in the treatment and handling of personnel that most corporations have had to address with all employees, from top executives to hourly workers. The circumstances that led this company to over- **175** haul the unsatisfactory working conditions of their migrant laborers were not different in principle from those of other corporations seeking to improve conditions for their workers. The key objective for Coca-Cola in such reform was stabilizing the work force. By providing conditions to keep migrant workers working steadily in their fields, Coke hoped to reduce processing expenses accompanying the thousands of migrant workers who dropped in and out of their employ. All corporations are faced with the same personnel challenges: people seek to enjoy their work, to achieve greater fulfilment on the job. To reduce turnover and compete effectively for quality workers, corporations have had to improve work conditions.

The major tests for most corporations are in providing workers with more participative production systems, developing tomorrow's leaders from incoming young managers, and making all employees feel that they belong. In addition, corporations increasingly will be called on to offer equal opportunity for achievement through employment for minorities. Pressures from government regulatory and special interest groups will have varying effects on corporations as each rises to meet the need for personnel reform in its own unique fashion.

To determine how effectively corporations respond to their personnel's needs, we asked executives to rate how important the following activities are to their corporations. In follow-up, we asked how often their corporations engage in these activities.

Providing a "feeling of belonging" for:

—top executives

—middle managers

—clerical staff

—first-line supervisors (foremen)

—hourly workers

Encouraging a collaborative management style as opposed to an authoritarian one.

Creating an atmosphere of openness to new ideas by top management.

Matching up executives' positions and personality traits.

Gaining maximum performance from newly recruited executives.

Rewarding superior achievers.

Helping executives broaden their skills.

Responses from executives indicate that corporations perform well in responding to needs of their employees. Whereas corporations often fail to meet their responsibilities in addressing social issues, they mostly succeed in dealing with their personnel. The responses are outlined in Table 21.

The Feeling of Belonging

Coca-Cola's efforts to improve life for its Minute Maid migrant workers may not have been a top priority in overall corporate strategy. No matter. They generated a feeling of belonging among previously neglected pickers. Most significant is that their migrant workers now share some of the fringe benefits and seniority privileges of other company employees.

In rating the degree to which companies make employees feel valued—providing a sense of belonging—executives make clear they pamper their top and middle executives more than they do other employees. Ninety-three percent top executives and 88 percent middle say their companies place anywhere from fair to most importance on stimulating such feelings among top executives themselves. Seventy-eight percent top executives and 74 percent middle say their companies frequently to virtually always achieve these goals. Commitment to making other employees feel they belong decreases gradually with each rung down the corporate ladder. Ninety percent top executives and 82 percent middle say their companies place fair to most importance on making middle managers feel they belong; 75 percent top executives and 60 percent middle say their companies deliver on these goals. Seventy-seven percent top executives and 74 percent middle think their companies place fair to most importance on making hourly workers feel they belong; 57 percent top executives and 50 percent middle say their companies achieve these goals.

Companies clearly pamper according to what is most valuable to them. Top executives and middle managers are the best taken care of. They are made to feel at home and a vital part of the company. But management is the voice of a company, and it is to management we have addressed our questions. Their answers naturally reflect their biases. While they can be expected to give themselves special treatment in the way Congress votes its own raises, they show that corporations go to considerable effort to provide their masses with the same sense of belonging.

How a company goes about achieving a sense of belonging for all employees is dependent on the conviction it has of employees being a kind of family. Kimberly-Clark is regarded by its community and employees as a company that cares about them. Chief executive Darwin Smith declares in K-C's annual report that one of the company's five-year objectives is to support the requirement for management to have genuine respect and concern for all the people in the company. The company stresses this attitude as an overall component in its management style.

Table 21
How Corporations Succeed in Personnel Relations

	DEGREE OF IMPORTANCE				
	No (%)	Little (%)	Fair (%)	Very (%)	Most (%)
Top Executives Providing a "feeling of belonging" for: Top executives	0.6	6.1	24.5	48.6	19.8
	Rarely/ Never	Some- times	Fre- quently	Gener- ally	Virtually always
Achieved	3.2	18.8	20.4	40.1	17.2
Middle managers	1.6	8.2	28.4	48.2	13.3
Achieved	4.7	20.0	27.1	38.1	9.9
Clerical	2.4	20.2	38.4	30.0	8.6
Achieved	8.3	32.6	28.5	24.3	5.9
First line	1.8	11.8	34.1	40.4	10.4
Achieved	4.6	26.9	29.9	31.3	5.7
Hourly workers	2.2	18.9	32.7	33.9	9.9
Achieved	7.3	33.7	26.4	25.6	4.6
Encouraging collaborative vs. authoritarian management style	2.2	12.6	28.5	43.5	12.8
Achieved	6.5	20.8	27.4	35.5	9.3
Creating an atmosphere of openness to new ideas by top management	0.4	6.5	19.2	52.4	21.1
Achieved	3.8	16.4	23.8	41.6	14.1
Matching up executives' posi- tions and personality traits	4.8	20.4	33.7	32.1	5.9
Achieved	12.8	27.9	26.9	24.8	4.2
Gaining maximum performance from newly recruited executives	0.4	3.2	27.6	54.2	11.2
Achieved	1.6	13.1	33.7	40.4	7.8
Rewarding superior achievers	0.8	3.9	22.2	51.4	21.3
Achieved	3.0	16.0	21.6	38.6	20.4
Helping executives broaden their skills	3.0	10.4	32.5	40.0	13.2
Achieved	5.8	28.4	28.0	29.2	7.9

"Not Applicable" responses not included.

	DEGREE OF IMPORTANCE				
	No (%)	Little (%)	Fair (%)	Very (%)	Most (%)

Middle Managers
Providing a "feeling
of belonging" for:

	No (%) / Rarely/Never	Little (%) / Sometimes	Fair (%) / Frequently	Very (%) / Generally	Most (%) / Virtually always
Top executives	0.7	7.6	30.2	42.8	14.7
Achieved	1.8	19.4	22.6	38.9	12.8
Middle managers	2.3	15.0	37.7	33.9	10.4
Achieved	5.5	33.3	25.6	28.4	6.3
Clerical	5.1	25.0	36.3	24.9	6.5
Achieved	12.5	41.2	21.4	20.0	2.5
First line	3.5	16.6	40.4	28.9	8.3
Achieved	8.0	36.9	25.4	23.9	3.2
Hourly workers	6.7	16.6	38.3	26.8	8.8
Achieved	10.4	36.4	24.0	22.4	3.7
Encouraging collaborative vs. authoritarian management style	3.4	17.5	34.0	36.9	6.2
Achieved	9.0	31.3	25.3	26.9	5.1
Creating an atmosphere of openness to new ideas by top management	1.6	12.7	27.3	41.8	15.0
Achieved	6.7	27.2	23.9	31.4	9.2
Matching up executives' positions and personality traits	4.5	22.5	40.1	26.0	4.1
Achieved	13.8	32.9	26.3	20.0	3.2
Gaining maximum performance from newly recruited executives	0.9	6.8	31.6	48.0	8.2
Achieved	2.9	22.8	27.2	36.2	6.3
Rewarding superior achievers	2.5	10.6	29.2	44.4	12.0
Achieved	5.9	29.6	20.6	33.2	9.6
Helping executives broaden their skills	1.8	14.7	36.4	38.7	7.6
Achieved	6.5	31.0	31.2	24.6	5.5

"Not Applicable" responses not included.

Collaborative Management

Through increasing collaborative or participative management programs, large corporations may achieve this sense of belonging for many of their employees. In a July 5, 1981, article, *The New York Times* describes a new enthusiasm for work among employees at General Motors' Buick plant in Flint, Michigan. Assembly-line workers, who now share in making "decisions on adjusting machine settings, rejecting faulty raw materials and moving machinery," have found new enjoyment in their work, and are more enthusiastic for quality than they were under previous quota production methods. The added expense of training employees and shifting to a participative program has been noted by GM. But the company expects this expense will be offset by fewer worker grievances, better quality in production, less absenteeism, less scrap after production, and more productivity in the long run.

Fifty-six percent top executives and 43 percent middle claim their companies place very much or most importance on encouraging collaborative management styles rather than authoritarian ones. Add to that the just under 30 percent top and 34 percent middle who rate it of fair importance and you can see that this is an issue in management style that gets much attention. More importantly, almost three-fourths top and well over half of middle say their corporations *practice* collaborative management frequently, generally, or virtually always.

Actually, most companies have little choice when it comes to supporting participative management. Especially large companies are compelled to distribute power and authority. Aggregating all decision-making authority around one or two top executives simply slows action and guarantees that much good information will be ignored. The concept of participative management is one that has evolved to meet the needs of larger companies with more interdependent work groups. Most participative management systems, such as the one at the Buick unit, are still in experimental stages. Most often they are viewed skeptically by old-time authoritarian managers. Lloyd Reuss, vice-president of Buick and a worker-participation enthusiast, told *The New York Times* that he detected tepid interest for his project from heads of other GM units.

At its plant in Goldsboro, North Carolina, R. G. Barry Corporation has implemented participative management with conviction. Corporate leaders there believe this management style is not just a slogan. Collaboration in the workplace has benefited both employees and profits at this footwear manufacturer. Executives' descriptions of the shift to collaborative management appear in Norman Bodek's *Productivity Newsletter* in the September 1981 issue. Workers' piece-rate pay system was changed to hourly rates. Later, they even went on salary. Time clocks came off the walls. Quality-control supervisors became obsolete. Employees were called associates and reorganized into teams of six to ten people. According to Barry executives, these changes have been responsible for increased production, increased and renewed employee interest in their work, absenteeism falling to 2 percent, and an annual employee turnover of 10 percent in an industry where, according to Bodek, 100 percent is common.

The Barry shift to collaborative management was not implemented without struggles, this despite chief executive Gordon Zacks's seeming to have participative management in his blood. His father ran the company via MBWA: management by wandering around. That is, wandering around the plant talking to employees, collecting their ideas, and putting them to use. Zacks the younger still encountered difficulties in pulling off the shift in management style. After clarifying his purpose, scope, and objectives with an operating management team, he convinced them to join him in decentralizing the organization. In reorganizing, Zacks says he and his team found that the company's traditional management approach sharply contrasted with the new philosophy: "We had been saying that people are our most important asset, that we must trust people, that the individual on the job knows the job better than anyone else, that people want to do a good job, and that people desire additional responsibility." But Zacks believed the company's more authoritarian management structures restricted initiative, allowed for little trust in subordinate opinions, and rarely succeeded in making all employees feel important.

Barry's restructured associate team led to 300 people producing 21,000 pairs of foam-soled slippers per day, rather than 300 people producing 16,000 pairs of slippers per day two years before the change. Plant manager Jim Daughtry thinks money has less to do with employee enthusiasm than does personal satisfaction in a job well done. Christmas bonuses awarded to employees are based on seniority rather than production rates, so in that case there surely is no financial incentive. Instead, Daughtry feels that openness to opinions and views of employees makes them feel that they are a key part of their individual teams. "In this building we don't have one trained industrial engineer, we have 585 industrial engineers." Employees are encouraged to come up with new ideas to increase and improve production during bi-weekly hour-long team meetings.

Executives in our study agree with Daughtry's notion that atmospheres that encourage open exchange of ideas also encourage greater productivity and problem solving. Seventy-four percent top executives and 57 percent middle say their companies place very much or most importance on creating open atmospheres in their offices. Rhetoric is greater than achievement, however. Fifty-six percent top executives and 41 percent middle say their companies generally or virtually always achieve conditions conducive to idea generation.

Free access of informal communication is the single most important factor in helping participative management styles to succeed. That's ironic because as much as informal communications may serve to involve employees and generate ideas, they also present arenas for confusion and greater conflict. R. G. Barry is a fine example of an effective collaborative management. But it should be emphasized that its experimental plant is staffed by only three hundred employees. As I have mentioned, larger corporations attempting to operate under similar management styles are more likely to be troubled by internal struggles and inter-office communications problems. Even at little R. G. Barry, collaborative management and problem solving is checked by controls. Senior executives reserve the right for final decision-making while encouraging employees to make their contributions freely and openly. Whether talking about Buick, which is big, or Barry, which is small, participative, more egalitarian management still must deal with the knotty problems of governing.

Executive Selection

Companies usually don't go to great lengths to match up positions with the personality traits of their executives. Roughly a third of top and middle executives say their companies place very much or most importance on this kind of activity. Thirty-four percent top executives and 40 percent middle say their companies assign it fair importance. This paternalistic activity, where corporations frequently turn to professional psychologists or psychological testing for help, is highly overrated. It doesn't work. The rate of predicting executive success through such procedures is not impressive. Senior executives making promotion, job-assignment, and recruitment decisions are well advised to trust their own judgment. They won't always be right, but then nobody is.

It also needs to be pointed out that the overzealous attempt to fit jobs and temperaments may be appropriate for middle managers with limited potential, but works against the development of top-caliber executives on whom a corporation will depend down the road. Contrary to the best intentions, it may only serve to shelter executives from hostile or incompatible situations that good leaders eventually have to deal with. This type of activity actually fosters a kind of executive who can't deliver what modernday corporations require. Leadership in corporations today demands broadly able, flexible, agile individuals. Protecting executives from unfavorable or incompatible work environments prevents them from learning to adjust and work around problems.

Corporations seem to be aware of this. It might seem kind of them to profess that they pay special care to the temperamental needs and sensitivities of their executives, but overall they fall short of their rhetoric. Twenty-nine percent top executives and 23 percent middle say their companies work hard at this. Another 27 percent top executives and 26 percent middle say their companies frequently attempt to match up executives and their positions. These responses come from executives who say their companies maintain fair concern with attempting such harmony. These corporations are more sanguine and hopeful about executives' meeting new job, career, and reporting relationship challenges.

Few executives rise to the top without having to work within at least one unfavorable reporting relationship. Executives who weather diversity well and overcome difficulties in their varied assignments are the likeliest candidates for promotions. Those who succumb to their personality likes and dislikes and require a lot of pampering and special attention are not top leadership material. Actually, one of the benefits of bureaucracy that gets ignored, but is essential for larger corporations, is that it takes advantage of an individual's talents while minimizing his quirks and foibles. Such a lovely device creates personal freedom every bit as much as it hinders it. As a result, corporations needn't be overly zealous about peering into their executives' psyches.

Gaining Maximum Performance

Ability to adapt to a company style and atmosphere is among the most essential characteristics corporations look for in an executive when recruiting. Such adaptability is critical to executives who want to excel in a company. In starting out, executives have to learn a company's inner workings, strategies, and objectives. They also have to prove their worth fast. Any newly recruited executive is on trial. By the same token, well-managed corporations are prepared to do their part from day one to assure their gaining maximum performance from a newly recruited executive.

It is clear those who say gaining top performance from new executives is most important to them are not very successful in achievement—at least not to the degree that they claim they covet it. Sixty-five percent top executives and 56 percent middle say their companies place very much or most importance on gaining the maximum performance from newly recruited executives. However, only 48 percent top executives and 43 percent middle claim generally or virtually always get the most from new recruits.

Another 28 percent top executives and 32 percent middle say their companies place only fair importance on getting the most from executives the minute they walk through the door. But this is fascinating. Of this group who say their companies put only fair importance on maximizing performance of newly recruited executives, the top overachieve (34 percent) and the middle approach (27 percent) their objectives. Many companies like to sound tough and aggressive in order to present a challenge to ambitious executives. They crack the whip from the very beginning! But as is apparent, this is not particularly effective. On the other hand, companies that are more sanguine about gaining maximum performance offer adjustment time for incoming executives to prepare for the problems they were brought in to solve. While the high achievement numbers for such corporations come partially from the spillback of corporations that set higher goals and fail at them, we can assume these more sanguine firms come pretty close to their goals of placing fair importance on getting the most out of newly recruited executives.

Companies of the 4 percent top executives and 8 percent middle who perceive little or no corporate commitment to gaining maximum performance from incoming executives are likely to be paternalistic. By making minimum demands on new executives up front, these corporations may make entrance into the organization more pleasant. But executives generally thrive more from some pressure and demands on them than from more leisurely entrance. Fifteen percent of their top executives and 25 percent middle think their companies never or rarely succeed in getting the most from new executives. Ask not, get not.

Corporations that shelter executives from demanding initiation into their management are likely to get shortchanged. If the management groups or teams that new executives are to work with don't take the time to introduce them to their tasks and convey their expectations, this becomes the visible part of the iceberg symbolizing an unpreparedness to expect and benefit from a newcomer's best effort.

Rewarding Superior Achievers

Once executives have overcome entry obstacles and proven themselves to be valuable additions, corporations compete fiercely for their loyalty. Executive loyalty is hard to come by. Corporations are quick to seek measures to keep executives happily in the fold. As we saw in the discussion on perquisites, to be effective those rewards must include psychic as well as economic benefits.

Seventy-three percent top executives and 56 percent middle think their companies place very much or most importance on rewarding superior achievers. The difference between perceptions of top and middle executives is easy to understand. Organizations value their top executives most of all. Senior executives are rewarded with higher promotions and enjoy greater status. They are recipients of more perquisites, larger bonuses, and higher salaries than middle managers. Of course, these top executives aren't shy. They're the first to call themselves superior achievers, and by definition, that's what they are. Middle managers are likely to see themselves as superior achievers, too. But since they have achieved less in their careers—partially because they haven't lived or labored as long—they don't get the credits, promotions, perks, bonuses, or salaries that top executives do. When it comes to judging performance on these goals, these divided perceptions persist. Middle managers feel a little neglected.

No matter how much companies like to reward their superior achievers, they're not always good at it. Fifty-nine percent top executives and 43 percent middle say their companies generally or virtually always reward outstanding managers. That's a gap, but it occurs mostly in the "very much importance" category. For those corporations that place most importance on this activity, their performance is excellent.

Twenty-two percent top executives' corporations place fair importance on rewarding their best executives, and seem to meet their goals. But that's deceptive. Some of this achievement is spillback from those companies that placed very much importance on rewarding their superior achievers, but fail. This activity is one of the few where those who profess to give it the most importance actually achieve their goals. If "it" is important enough, truly important, then the goal will be met. If it isn't important, but is merely *said* to be important, the "goodness" or "rightness" of the goal is enough to give comfort in the absence of its achievement.

Finally, 5 percent top executives and 13 percent middle say their companies place little or no importance on rewarding superior achievers in their organizations. Further, 19 percent top executives and 35 percent middle claim their companies never or only sometimes reward their superior achievers. These executives are either working in poorly managed operations at their companies or are particularly sour about the treatment they believe they have received unjustly.

Broadening Skills

Corporations succeed at broadening the skills of their executives. However, as you'll see in the next chapter, they do not succeed at preparing their executives for general management responsibilities. It is important to keep in mind that an executive can broaden and deepen his skills in his main discipline or function for years without ever moving outside it. It is not until he or she tries new functions that an executive can begin to assess his or her appropriateness for and interest in possible general management assignments.

Eighty-six percent top executives and 90 percent middle believe their corporations place fair, very much, or most importance on this activity. Sixty-five percent top and 62 percent middle believe their corporations achieve their goals in these categories. While two-thirds achievement is satisfactory, and makes clear that corporations are good at bringing their executives along in their disciplines, it is likely this success will spawn too many specialists and not enough generalists.

Hiring and Training Minorities

In recent years, social pressures have mounted for corporations to hire minorities. These pressures derive from the belief that corporate America is responsible for obliterating the lack of opportunity for minorities to enter the mainstream of business life. There can be no question that corporations should provide opportunity for qualified minorities to enter their ranks. In actual practice, however, corporations accept little pro-active responsibility for recruiting minorities into their operations whether qualified or not. Executives convey some increased sensitivity to the need to induct minority members into business circles, but such indoctrination is not of major concern to their companies. Further, corporations are more willing to recruit qualified minorities into their ranks than to hire unqualified minorities. Table 22 shows that the most vocal, demanding groups have made corporations open their doors to them more than to groups who have been passive.

Hiring women is rated as very to most important to corporations by 47 percent of their top and 38 percent middle executives. Thirty-five percent top executives and 43 percent middle say their companies place fair importance on hiring women. These latter companies that proclaim moderate interest in hiring women are the ones that come closest to achieving their goals. Thirty-three percent of their top executives and 35 percent of middle managers say their companies frequently hire women. Only 34 percent top executives and 31 percent middle offer that their companies generally or virtually always hire women.

We already have had ample opportunity to see that corporations generally are eager to hire women when they are well qualified. Women with M.B.A.'s are welcomed to the ranks of most corporations. But like all groups, women without appropriate backgrounds will have a hard time finding a suitable or challenging position in most corporations.

Some critics may point the finger disparagingly at the companies that aren't willing to give much time and money to train women for senior management positions. A third of top executives and a fourth of middle claim their companies place very much or most importance on such training for women. Also, about a third of both top and middle say their companies place fair importance on training women. So I can't agree with these critics. Senior management rank is hard to achieve for the most skilled and committed executives. Given women's recent entry in significant numbers to business careers, corporations are demonstrating tremendous dedication, as shown by these figures, in making way for them at the top by training.

Some companies are intensely interested in creating opportunities for women and put the needed energies into training them for management jobs. Seventeen percent top executives and 13 percent middle think their companies generally or virtually always train women for senior management jobs. Another 22 percent top executives and 25 percent middle say that their companies frequently train women for senior executive positions within their organizations. I repeat, these figures are impressive.

Blacks rank second to women in corporate hiring and training of minorities. Thirty-eight percent top executives and 32 percent middle believe their companies are very or most interested in hiring blacks. Another 37 percent top executives and 41 percent middle say their companies are fairly interested in recruiting blacks. Once again it is the corporations that claim only moderate interest in the task—in this case, hiring blacks—that come closest to meeting their stated goals. Twenty-seven percent top executives and 28 percent middle say their companies frequently hire qualified blacks for management. Twenty-six percent top executives and 24 percent middle say their companies generally or virtually always hire blacks. Corporate commitment to train blacks for senior management is less than for women. That commitment is even less for the other minorities.

Enthusiasm for hiring Hispanics is expressed by 28 percent top executives and 23 percent middle managers. Thirty-five percent top executives and 37 percent middle managers say their companies are fairly interested in hiring Hispanics. The achievement level of their corporations, while not impressive, shows that progress is being made.

The three minority groups that receive the highest ratings are those that have been clamoring for equal opportunities in employment for years. While corporations have few or no hesitations in hiring minority members who are qualified, the greatest obstacles in providing suitable employment for them center on their lack of suitable education and experience.

Some corporations may feel compelled by social pressures or government regulations to place minority members within their ranks whether they are qualified or not. Many of these companies may try to train minorities to work successfully on their management teams. But by and large, hiring minorities without suitable backgrounds places both the corporation and the minority member at a disadvantage. Whether it is of assistance to hire unqualified minorities for management jobs is questionable. Minorities entering corporate life with inadequate training are not able to compete, and are therefore in danger of failing in their endeavors. Such failures are a waste of time and money for corporations, and a waste of time and possibly self-esteem for minority members. Such failures also are likely to result in failure patterns for individuals who constantly take on challenges with which they are ill equipped to deal.

Table 22
How Corporations Succeed at Hiring and Training Minorities

	DEGREE OF IMPORTANCE				
	No (%)	Little (%)	Fair (%)	Very (%)	Most (%)
Top Executives					
Hiring Women	2.8	12.5	34.5	38.4	8.9
	Rarely/ Never	Some-times	Fre-quently	Gener-ally	Virtually always
Achieved	6.6	23.4	32.9	28.7	5.2
Training Women for senior management	7.3	23.0	33.1	26.9	4.8
Achieved	16.8	38.9	21.6	13.8	3.2
Hiring Blacks	4.3	17.4	36.5	30.6	7.7
Achieved	12.5	30.4	26.8	20.7	5.6
Training Blacks for senior management	8.1	29.2	31.0	20.6	5.2
Achieved	30.0	30.6	20.2	10.2	2.6
Hiring Hispanics	5.3	25.5	35.4	23.5	4.7
Achieved	17.7	33.9	24.3	13.5	4.4
Training Hispanics for senior management	12.9	34.2	25.0	15.9	3.4
Achieved	35.5	29.7	14.8	8.2	2.0
Hiring Orientals	10.2	31.3	30.5	16.7	3.6
Achieved	22.0	35.5	19.8	10.8	3.0
Training Orientals for senior management	20.6	36.5	20.4	8.5	2.0
Achieved	45.7	26.3	8.8	5.4	1.2
Hiring American Indians	12.5	30.6	27.0	16.5	3.0
Achieved	29.7	31.5	15.0	8.8	2.6
Training American Indians for senior management	24.4	36.3	15.7	7.9	1.8
Achieved	54.4	19.0	6.0	5.0	0.8

"Not Applicable" responses not included.

	DEGREE OF IMPORTANCE				
	No (%)	Little (%)	Fair (%)	Very (%)	Most (%)
Middle Managers					
Hiring Women	2.2	11.9	42.8	32.0	5.8
	Rarely/ Never	Some- times	Fre- quently	Gener- ally	Virtually always
Achieved	6.5	22.3	34.8	25.4	5.6
Training Women for senior management	7.0	23.7	36.2	23.1	2.3
Achieved	19.2	35.4	24.6	11.8	1.8
Hiring Blacks	3.6	8.3	41.3	26.9	5.0
Achieved	11.5	31.4	28.1	20.2	3.8
Training Blacks for senior management	9.0	30.3	35.9	14.6	2.2
Achieved	26.5	37.0	17.4	9.1	1.6
Hiring Hispanics	7.9	24.8	36.8	20.3	2.7
Achieved	19.2	33.5	21.7	15.6	2.5
Training Hispanics for senior management	13.9	33.6	30.7	10.6	1.1
Achieved	34.0	34.5	13.2	6.5	1.1
Hiring Orientals	10.6	27.6	34.2	16.0	1.8
Achieved	23.0	35.4	17.7	12.3	1.8
Training Orientals for senior management	21.4	36.0	22.3	8.5	0.4
Achieved	43.5	31.9	8.0	4.3	0.9
Hiring American Indians	13.2	29.1	30.0	14.6	1.8
Achieved	43.5	31.9	8.0	4.3	0.9
Training American Indians for senior management	24.1	36.3	18.2	7.7	0.4
Achieved	53.0	23.5	5.6	3.6	0.7

"Not Applicable" responses not included.

The views that executives express are not necessarily indications that their corporations are resistant to hiring minorities. They simply mean that companies prefer not to hire minorities merely to hire them. Corporate refusal to hire minorities just to appease them, to provide racial or ethnic compensating balances—in essence to patronize them via placement in jobs they aren't qualified to fill—is a better survival policy for both corporations and individuals who might fall into minority groups. Unless people are trained to compete within the corporate environment they aren't likely to succeed there. Moreover, it is true that well-qualified minorities have advantages over equally qualified nonminority individuals in certain cases.

Policies of funding minority education to equip individuals with the competitive edge that will see them through successful careers are far more beneficial to disadvantaged groups. Bristol-Myers' Clairol Inc. initiated a policy years ago by which they issued scholarships to women returning to school. Numerous organizations have offered scholarships to women who wish to major in business. Ford scholarships long have supported minority individuals seeking otherwise unaffordable educations. These programs have provided assistance that counts to minority groups who prove themselves to be capable and eager to achieve needed education.

Even more helpful to minority efforts in overcoming disadvantages are programs such as Control Data's computer-based education projects mentioned earlier. Through several programs conducted in conjunction with various other companies, city programs, and educational institutions, Control Data has been able to introduce education to disadvantaged youths and adults to aid in their eventual entry into the job market.

Through youth programs, Control Data's projects assure better learning facilities that can help disadvantaged children who may require specialized attention to overcome learning handicaps. For example, through use of Control Data's PLATO computer education program, non-English-speaking students can learn at their own pace. They can do this rather than suffer poor grades because of their inability to comprehend at the pace of fellow students. At the same time, the children are provided with education to help them learn English without interfering with other studies. Through Control Data's Fair Break Program, adults are educated via computer to catch up on or acquire skills that will assure their entry into the job market.

No matter where you stand on the debate as to how far corporations should go out of their way to hire women and minorities, no more striking symbol of corporate achievement in this respect exists than in the performance of Exxon—our nation's largest company—begun by "big bad John D" and standing at the fore of the "big bad oil business."

As a percentage of its total American work force, Exxon, in the decade between 1969–1979 doubled its women and minority members. By 1979, minorities represented 16 percent of all employees; women 23 percent. This company hired 11,153 people in 1979. Of these, 19 percent were minorities; 41 percent women.

19
Personnel Failures

Surprisingly, few corporations enthusiastically seek to inform employees about what their primary strategies are. Still others claim high goals in this area but then fail to back their intentions with appropriate action. Forty-two percent top executives and 37 percent middle offer that their companies place very much or most importance on articulating corporate strategies to employees. Another 34 percent top executives and 35 percent middle say their companies place a fair amount of importance on having their strategies understood by employees. Twenty-three percent top executives and 27 percent middle say their companies place no or very little importance on articulating corporate strategies to employees.

Corporations that fail to inform their employees about what they are committed to achieving over a long- or short-range period of time cannot hope to provide employees with a sense of belonging in their organizations. Moreover, employees who work in the dark about why they're doing what they're doing cannot enjoy satisfaction on their jobs. One of the major benefits of more participative management systems, where employees are likely to be more thoroughly versed on corporate strategies, is that employees thrive on their sense of contribution to final, broad goals.

As much as corporate leaders talk about apprising their employees of overall strategies, they rarely succeed. Only 30 percent top executives and 26 percent middle can boast that their companies generally or virtually always succeed in spreading the corporate word about their purposes. Twenty-two percent top executives and 24 percent middle say their companies frequently succeed in achieving this goal. Such executives represent companies that either arbitrarily address the need to share information with employees on what they consider key issues, or habitually make fainthearted efforts in this direction.

Team-member attitudes are valued in today's corporations. Yet corporate leaders fail drastically in encouraging the kind of participation that leads to **191** victory. They seek loyalty from employees, devotion to the job, low absentee rates, low turnover rates—all without putting out an effort to arouse team spirit. No wonder many employees long for new coaches.

Building Morale

Corporations just barely eke by in their morale-building efforts. Fifty-eight percent top executives and 48 percent middle think their corporations place very much or most importance on developing high corporate spirit. Thirty percent top executives and 34 percent middle say their companies place only a fair amount of importance on building such morale among executives. Forty-two percent top executives and 30 percent middle say their companies generally or virtually always succeed in building morale for executives. Twenty-six percent of both level executives say their companies frequently achieve suitable levels of morale among executives. These executives are from companies that are at least equipped with attitudes to address the problems of building morale. Once top management knows of its need to build such a spirit, it can attempt methods to meet it. Some companies do quite well at it.

Some companies are of the firm conviction that conflict and intense levels of competition are a must for high productivity. They care little about the morale needs of their executives. Thirty-two percent top executives and 44 percent middle claim their companies never or only sometimes engage in morale-building among their executives. Macho managements that fail to recognize the need for warmth and high spirits in corporate corridors will suffer negative effects not only among executives, but downward among all their employees.

Morale is not a kind of thing you can put your finger on easily. But somehow it is identifiable in most corporations. Where morale is high, energetic performance is apparent, general overtones of excellence prevail, and pleasure in a job well done is its own reward. Where morale is low, tension, negativism, lack of care and proprietary sense all run rampant. Only the cynic seeks an out from the responsibility of building morale by saying it's akin to motherhood and apple pie. Morale building starts at the top. If corporate leaders don't bother themselves with enhancing the morale of their executives, executives won't be able to build it among themselves or their subordinates. Corporations that make the mistake of thinking that paychecks are all they owe their employees will be losers in the end.

I never cease to be amazed at the lack of curiosity top management typically has about what's on its people's minds. By participating in this study, certain companies at least have shown they have an interest in gaining such knowledge. Even at that, their record on building morale is not

Table 23
How Corporations Fail in Personnel Relations

	DEGREE OF IMPORTANCE				
	No (%)	Little (%)	Fair (%)	Very (%)	Most (%)
Top Executives					
Articulating corporate strategies to all employees	3.1	20.0	34.0	31.8	10.6
	Rarely/ Never	Some- times	Fre- quently	Gener- ally	Virtually always
Achieved	12.8	34.8	21.5	23.1	7.3
Building morale of executives	1.8	10.6	29.5	42.9	15.0
Achieved	5.7	25.9	25.7	33.1	9.3
Helping executives attain self-actualization	7.8	22.7	30.4	29.0	4.6
Achieved	18.5	31.7	23.0	17.7	4.1
Preparing executives for general management responsibilities	2.4	10.7	29.4	43.7	13.4
Achieved	5.2	25.9	30.5	31.3	6.8

	DEGREE OF IMPORTANCE				
	No (%)	Little (%)	Fair (%)	Very (%)	Most (%)
Middle Managers					
Articulating corporate strategies to all employees	4.6	22.3	35.4	27.6	9.4
	Rarely/ Never	Some- times	Fre- quently	Gener- ally	Virtually always
Achieved	16.7	33.0	23.6	20.2	5.9
Building morale of executives	3.5	12.7	34.3	37.7	10.6
Achieved	9.9	33.9	25.5	24.5	5.1
Helping executives attain self-actualization	5.7	24.1	37.0	25.5	4.3
Achieved	17.1	37.1	23.0	15.8	3.4
Preparing executives for general management responsibilities	1.4	18.6	30.4	40.5	8.1
Achieved	8.2	33.9	24.1	27.8	5.1

"Not Applicable" responses not included.

impressive. Imagine, then, what the group spirit must be like in many corporations.

Self-Actualization

The term *self-actualization* has a fair measure of currency among both the general population and business executives. But, as with morale, understanding what it means to corporations and executives is a little like trying to pin custard pie to the wall. The term was invented by the late psychologist Abraham Maslow. Though the question we asked executives just as easily could have used the terms *self-fulfilment* or *self-realization*, we chose self-actualization because of the popularity of Maslow's work and the rest he earned from fellow behavioral scientists.

While our questionnaire generally does not define terms, it is our belief that in answering the question pertaining to self-actualization, executives give us some idea of their sense of personal and emotional fulfilment on the job. We also learn something about corporations' perspectives on the notion of personal development. Do they feel committed to help their executives achieve it? Or is this an area in which they should not concern themselves?

Though Peter Drucker's concern was for another topic altogether when he wrote *The Effective Executive*, it is in that book that he came up with what I consider the best definition of self-actualization for an executive. He says the effective executive is one who has learned how to make his *strengths* productive. What could be more rewarding, personally satisfying? My own view is that whatever self-actualization is, it is up to the individual executive to take the responsibility for attaining it as he defines it for himself. The corporation needs what the executive has to offer in the way of ability and experience. It is up to that executive to seek ways to put his ability and experience to use.

Despite the difficulties one might presume in interpreting executive responses to this question for lack of clear definition, executives weren't chary about it. One thousand fifty-four executives, or 97 percent of our sample, answered it. Sixty-four percent top executives and 67 percent middle claim their companies place fair, very much, or most importance on this activity. Forty-five percent top and 42 percent middle believe their corporations achieve their goals in these categories. So, while two-thirds think that corporations place value on self-actualization for their executives, fewer than half take measures to help their executives attain it satisfactorily. The exception to this relatively poor performance can be seen in the small number of companies who are *most* committed to self-actualization. They seem to know what they want in this regard, and make sure they get it.

Preparation for General Management

For a corporation to ensure its future, it has to prepare its younger, high-potential executives to run its various businesses. No matter how successful or dominant a company has been in its markets, for it to remain and grow as a vital force, it must provide for orderly succession of its top management.

The dictum is that management comes and goes, but the company remains forever. In order to pass the baton without breaking stride, a company has to be able to select winners for key spots at the top: executives who have shown breadth of perspective and the ability to manage all the disciplines necessary to running a business. In the best set of circumstances, this means a corporation can call upon younger executives (usually somewhere in their forties) who, though not expert in all these disciplines, are competent at supervising finance, manufacturing, marketing (including sales), and personnel.

"Who's News" is a daily column in *The Wall Street Journal* that announces key executive appointments—vice-president and above—in the nation's major corporations. Sometimes I think the column should be named "Who's Sacking Whom" because it often begins with who got the ax. In the last few years particularly, top executives have been turning over like managers of baseball teams at the end of each season.

Corporations aren't very good at preparing members of their ranks to handle the top jobs. This is symbolized most dramatically when chairmen and presidents are sent packing, but it also is true that corporations have enormous difficulty in staffing key profit-and-loss (general management) positions at the vice-presidential level.

You will remember I pointed out in Chapter 7 that the general-management function is the one that senior executives look to most when considering young executives for promotion. I said this is as it should be; that people who have shown the ability to manage smaller businesses successfully are most likely to be able to do the same on a larger and higher scale.

While parent companies would like to tap these young general managers, they have fewer to call upon all the time because they increasingly organize their businesses in functional ways. That is, corporations in greater numbers develop executives who become better and better at less and less. In short, they develop specialists: finance specialists, marketing specialists, manufacturing specialists, and personnel specialists. When these specialists get to the top, they are bewildered (though they can't admit it) at the trade-offs they face in running an entire business. They simply aren't prepared for broad issues and making decisions that affect a wide array of businesses, locations, and people.

The people who manage corporations are aware of their shortcomings in this respect. Fifty-seven percent top executives and 49 percent middle believe their companies place very much or most importance on preparing executives for general management. Roughly another 30 percent of both levels say their companies give this activity fair importance. While these figures aren't great in expressing the proper amount of commitment to what counts, they're not bad. But performance is. Fewer than 40 percent of both top and middle levels of management indicate that their companies generally or virtually always prepare their executives for general management. Less than a third of both levels can claim their companies even frequently prepare executives to run their businesses successfully.

20

Economic Successes

Traditionally, the role most ascribed to the American corporation is its function in our society as the ultimate symbol and engine of capitalism. The pros and cons of this pervasive function—and of capitalism itself—are discussed and hotly debated by critics from numerous sectors. Some of these critics even come from within the corporate community.

As corporations respond to their critics and address these debates, they find themselves hard pressed to explain away the contradictions of capitalism and their place in it. Capitalism is a system that inevitably leads to two kinds of results. It must be admitted that one of these is greed. But the other—growing out of innovation and development—is progress. As an incurable defender of the corporation, I am led by this state of affairs to play with the great credo of Socrates and say that the *untainted* life is not worth living. Accordingly, I do not grieve for critics who harp on the inability of capitalistic systems to redistribute wealth effectively. Ironically, many of them are primary beneficiaries of the capitalistic system. Disparity between their views and those of the free-market soldiers is likely to exist forever.

In the fall 1976 issue of *The Public Interest*, Ernest van den Haag notes the irony of capitalism's being taken to task by its critics. He argues that one of the greatest effects capitalism has had is the reduction of poverty of stricken populations. Though capitalism does not completely eradicate poverty, it has shrunk poor populations to a minority. "As long as they were a majority, or at least a plurality," van den Haag asserts, "the poor themselves accepted their condition as natural. So did everybody else. But the poor have become a minority, and rather than separate and different, they feel isolated and passed by." The final outcome—that wealth produces guilt feelings in the rich and resentment among the poor—is among the strongest, most frequent sources of the anticapitalistic spirit that flows through America's intellectual and even economic community.

I'm a believer that by being unfettered economically, corporations are most capable of meeting their main responsibilities to all of their constituencies. By surviving, then thriving, they provide society an abundance of jobs, goods, and services, and work with (sometimes in spite of) government agencies to perpetuate social stability.

Undeniably, corporations not only strive for success intellectually, but at the gut level as well. Often they act instinctively, much like the animals that were used to describe them at the beginning of this book. Their sheer size, breadth, and power often lead them to ambiguous, intricate relationships with their various constituencies. The benefits and difficulties arising out of those relationships are sometimes hard to distinguish and are likely to leave combatants and colleagues wondering whether they should laugh or cry.

We have seen that corporations have difficulty in defining and meeting some of their responsibilities to society. In response to blatant demands, some corporations perceive that they have extensive obligations to alleviate society's ills. But even without intending to, or directing attention to solving these problems, most corporations—by virtue of being part of the same social fabric—become unwitting partners in easing the burdens that their communities bear.

Because of this obfuscated relationship that has evolved between the public sector and corporate leaders, consternation has become more common in recent years regarding the role corporations play in our economic system. There can be no question that there are several contradictions within capitalism. But these derive from elements that are essentially unavoidable within most economic systems. Socialistic systems have evolved with more contradictions than those of capitalism. President Reagan has pointed out with considerable justification that socialistic countries have done an inferior job of remedying the social ills that they castigate capitalistic systems for causing and perpetuating. And it was Winston Churchill who pointed out, "The inherent vice of capitalism is the unequal sharing of blessings; the inherent virtue of socialism is the equal sharing of miseries."

The spirit of anticapitalism can prevail only in an overall self-indulgent and self-deluding society. But if one will examine how capitalism works in the corporate arena, he will see that the reality of its checks and balances renders it more or less constantly progressive—even if not fail-safe—against faux pas, scandals, and assorted catastrophes. Since freedom as a concept is difficult to define, and beyond what is workable here, let me say simply that *freedom to compete* is ultimately the most valued liberty within the capitalistic system. That value alone monitors the motivations, choices, and inevitable courses of corporate leaders in their everyday work.

Like individuals, corporations are free to compete for commercial success. Through such a market system, corporations are independent and able to direct their human and material resources toward unlimited economic achievements. At the same time, individuals in society are free to direct their energies toward independent achievements irrespective of those sought by large corporations. Neurosurgeons, taxidermists, and quarterbacks are but three examples. They may function at their crafts despite the pervasiveness of corporations that more or less direct the life paths of most Americans.

The free-market system is a complex structure of checks and balances which ultimately results in progress for all nimble corporations and the societies in which they operate. Through exposure to these checks and balances, companies are compelled to respond sooner or later—and granted, at times it is later—to the facts of economic life, to meet the needs of their various constituencies that make up society itself.

To determine corporations' commitment and effectiveness in carrying out their economic role, we asked executives to indicate the importance and frequency of their corporations' engaging in these activities:

Driving competitors out of business.

Surviving as a distinct corporate entity.

Avoiding being acquired.

Producing high-quality goods and services.

Increasing annual sales volume.

Increasing before-tax profits.

Managing financial controls.

Increasing return on assets.

Fulfilling capital commitment objectives.

Retaining board members who are not members of management.

Providing income for stockholders.

Providing incentive compensation for executives.

Having good union relations.

Having good information flow necessary to decision making.

Their responses are outlined in Table 24.

Corporate Competition

John D. Rockefeller held the conviction that he was born to be rich. In 1870, he entered a phase of business marked by his enthusiasm for competition. By that time, he already had multiplied the proceeds of a modest loan he received from his father at 10 percent interest. (His father later justified his own profiteering ways: "I like to cheat my boys every chance I get. I want to make 'em sharp.")

John D. negotiated a deal with the Lake Shore Railroad to give him a

Table 24
How Corporations Succeed in Economic Activities

	DEGREE OF IMPORTANCE				
	No (%)	Little (%)	Fair (%)	Very (%)	Most (%)
Top Executives Driving competitors out of business	25.8	43.1	16.5	5.3	1.8
	Rarely/ Never	Some- times	Fre- quently	Gener- ally	Virtually always
Achieved	56.7	27.1	4.2	2.2	1.2
Surviving as distinct corporate entity	0.8	2.6	7.7	31.8	52.1
Achieved	2.8	2.8	8.6	17.7	54.0
Avoiding being acquired	5.7	3.7	5.5	28.4	37.3
Achieved	21.7	5.7	1.8	6.3	28.2
Producing products/services of high quality	0.0	1.2	8.6	29.0	61.0
Achieved	0.6	5.9	15.3	42.6	35.4
Increasing annual sales volume	0.0	0.8	7.1	34.9	56.9
Achieved	0.0	2.9	13.0	30.5	53.2
Increasing before-tax profit	0.0	0.0	1.8	19.4	78.8
Achieved	0.0	5.1	15.3	36.1	43.4
Managing financial controls	0.0	0.4	4.9	33.2	61.3
Achieved	0.0	2.0	10.7	36.1	51.1
Increasing return on assets	0.0	1.2	4.1	22.0	72.0
Achieved	0.8	8.6	17.3	38.7	33.8
Fulfilling capital commitment objectives	0.2	3.0	19.4	49.6	25.9
Achieved	0.8	8.9	23.8	43.3	21.2
Retaining board members who are not members of management	2.6	4.0	21.0	42.9	15.9
Achieved	2.2	4.8	13.6	32.2	33.8
Providing income for stockholders	0.8	2.8	8.9	29.8	42.9
Achieved	0.8	4.4	10.3	27.6	41.9

	DEGREE OF IMPORTANCE				
	No (%)	Little (%)	Fair (%)	Very (%)	Most (%)
Middle Managers					
Driving competitors out of business	24.1	43.3	17.1	5.6	2.2
	Rarely/ Never	**Some- times**	**Fre- quently**	**Gener- ally**	**Virtually always**
Achieved	54.5	28.2	5.2	1.4	1.1
Surviving as distinct corporate entity	1.6	1.8	8.3	34.3	47.6
Achieved	2.0	5.6	9.4	19.5	47.9
Avoiding being acquired	6.6	6.4	7.0	27.0	31.5
Achieved	23.1	8.3	2.7	6.1	24.5
Producing products/services of high quality	0.0	0.9	8.0	30.3	59.0
Achieved	0.2	7.0	16.9	37.8	36.4
Increasing annual sales volume	0.2	0.9	3.6	31.2	63.6
Achieved	0.0	4.5	13.6	29.6	52.2
Increasing before-tax profit	0.0	0.4	3.0	22.1	73.5
Achieved	0.2	7.5	18.5	37.8	34.9
Managing financial controls	0.2	1.1	6.0	35.7	56.7
Achieved	0.4	3.0	11.9	39.3	44.8
Increasing return on assets	0.0	1.1	4.8	27.8	64.2
Achieved	0.4	11.5	18.3	37.1	30.6
Fulfilling capital commitment objectives	0.0	2.0	17.6	50.8	26.0
Achieved	1.1	8.6	23.2	41.9	21.0
Retaining board members who are not members of management	2.2	6.4	22.9	38.9	9.7
Achieved	4.1	8.3	14.8	29.6	23.1
Providing income for stockholders	1.2	4.1	10.2	28.6	39.8
Achieved	1.8	4.9	12.7	25.3	39.1

Table 24 (cont'd)

	DEGREE OF IMPORTANCE				
	No (%)	Little (%)	Fair (%)	Very (%)	Most (%)
Top Executives					
Driving competitors out of business	25.8	43.1	16.5	5.3	1.8
	Rarely/ Never	Some- times	Fre- quently	Gener- ally	Virtually always
Providing incentive compen- sation for executives	0.6	4.3	24.9	47.9	21.9
Achieved	1.8	13.9	17.1	29.4	37.3
Having good union relations	0.6	1.8	25.4	53.0	11.8
Achieved	0.8	8.1	20.4	52.4	10.7
Having information flow for decision making	0.2	2.9	19.4	56.5	20.8
Achieved	1.0	15.9	26.0	44.3	12.4

"Not Applicable" responses not included.

secret rebate for oil he shipped from Cleveland to the East Coast. For this, he guaranteed the railroad a daily shipment of sixty tank cars of oil. As his business grew, other railroads were inspired to invent a more sophisticated rebate scheme that would involve the largest refiners in New Jersey's major refining centers. Their shipping rates would go up, but the refineries would benefit through rebates and additional kickbacks. The smaller refiners were not included. They paid full price for shipping. Ever the opportunist, Rockefeller decided that this practice would rid him of pesty competition. He offered the smaller refiners the option to collapse into his business, or go bankrupt. His brother, Frank, was one such competitor who resisted his offer. Frank went broke.

These small potatoes weren't enough for Rockefeller's appetite. He later gobbled up independent refiners in New York, Philadelphia, and Pittsburgh. Eventually he controlled 95 percent of the nation's oil. He bribed legislators and eventually drove all his competitors out of business. He bought oil fields across the country and also moved into foreign markets.

The outcome of Rockefeller's special style of competition was the establishment of antitrust laws in several states. A Supreme Court decision during Teddy Roosevelt's administration declared Rockefeller's Standard Oil to be

	DEGREE OF IMPORTANCE				
	No (%)	Little (%)	Fair (%)	Very (%)	Most (%)
Middle Managers					
Driving competitors out of business	24.1	43.3	17.1	5.6	2.2
	Rarely/ Never	Some- times	Fre- quently	Gener- ally	Virtually always
Providing incentive compen- sation for executives	2.3	13.3	28.7	38.9	13.4
Achieved	7.4	23.6	14.9	29.5	20.5
Having good union relations	1.6	3.0	25.6	46.5	14.1
Achieved	2.0	9.7	23.1	44.4	11.8
Having information flow for decision making	0.2	5.3	21.8	55.2	16.8
Achieved	1.6	19.9	27.5	41.0	9.4

"Not Applicable" responses not included.

an illegal monopoly. He had engaged in unfair trade, and had in fact denied others the right to compete. Rockefeller's combine was dissolved into thirty-four separate companies. The makeup of competition in America has been changing ever since.

Part of the mystique of capitalism that enshrouds the American corporate image concerns its hellish, warring ways of competition. Walk into any thriving corporation and you will find competition operating throughout. In addition, competition abounds between companies vying in the same markets. Corporations welcome competition for various reasons that are implicit rather than explicit. One to one, if you asked executives if they'd like to wipe out their competition from the market—obliterate them from the entire business community altogether—some might give rousing support for the idea. But by no means all.

To be sure, corporations don't entertain such notions as corporate philosophies, and companies who successfully compete often like the idea of stiff and sturdy adversaries. If executives identify with their companies, if they take enough pride in their product or service, they are likely to receive their competition with grace. Competition is challenge. Corporations and their executives thrive on challenges.

So you can see that today's corporations view competition in a markedly different way from John D. Rockefeller. It is through competition that technological innovations are encouraged and fostered. Through the desire to outdo and out-achieve each other, companies stimulate innovation and product or service development. The ultimate result for corporations individually, and for society as a whole, is progress through vigorous competition. Society and corporations grow and flourish through such contests between corporations.

Only 7 percent top executives and 8 percent middle believe their companies place very much or most importance on driving competitors out of business. Companies that spend their energies on such matters are likely to end up on the endangered species list themselves. Creativity rather than pure competitive energies are more beneficial to thriving corporations who serve technologically progressive and expanding markets. Strategic rather than tactical approaches have slowly proved to be the preferred means of competition for modern corporations. Today, companies are required more than ever to compete in imaginative, well-thought-out maneuvers that result in increased profits. For them, business isn't war after all. It's a game to be engaged in with sound ideas and careful, though sometimes hurried, decisions.

Even among companies who would like to drive their competitors out of business, little energy is directed toward this nonproductive goal. While 7 percent top executives and 8 percent middle assert their companies would like to drive their competitors out of business, only 3 percent say their companies are generally or virtually always successful at it. Most likely, the competition drive themselves out of business or succumb to takeover by acquisition or merger.

Early American business was speckled across the board with one clever entrepreneur after another. The likes of Rockefeller's avaricious schemes were inevitable in newborn industries that were evolving a competitive game. By the time Standard Oil was forced to split into thirty-four companies, Rockefeller had retired, though he lived to be 97 years old. His own Standard Oil of New Jersey (now Exxon) was then run by his handpicked fellow entrepreneur and previously bitter enemy, John D. Archbold. Even Archbold's successor, Walter Teagle, was the son of an early Pennsylvania oilman who had shared in Rockefeller's deal-making ventures. If these men weren't shining examples to today's businessmen in the ways of handling and addressing competition, they certainly were artful at creating something from nothing. It is that spirit that marks the likelihood of success for even today's entrepreneurs.

Business history is filled with the stories of clever and innovative businessmen who managed to turn rather humble business concepts into grand corporate complexes. Who would have guessed that Procter & Gamble's knowledge of candle- and soap-making would lead this company to become the largest manufacturer of household products? When C. W. Post first marketed "Elijah's Manna" (today known as Post Toasties) and "Monk's Brew" (Postum) using strong advertising campaigns to promote his products, no one was likely to envision this enterprise as the precursor of giant General Foods.

The trail from entrepreneur to successful marketer to major corporation to conglomerate almost seems too straight to be credible. But that succession is the general pattern for numerous businesses.

The Horatio Alger Tradition

Whether Horatio Alger knew it or not, he was teaching the value of competition to all the little boys who read his rags-to-riches stories. The fact is that at the turn of the century, when his books were so popular, there were almost as many entrepreneurial opportunities available in every American town as there were people. Those who chose risk over security and obstacles over safety were as rare then as they are now. Entrepreneurs today are as valued a part of the overall economic and corporate system as ever. They are a strain of businessmen with the temperament and belief in themselves to see their ideas and dreams through to fruition.

Fellow spirits are venture capitalists—individuals who financially back fledgling businesses. New-breed entrepreneurs in their own right, they enter into risky ventures. They realize their own business success by finding and recognizing the gifted individuals who promise entrepreneurial success. According to most venture capitalists, these talents largely come down to personality. Tommy Davis, partner of California's Mayfield Fund, likes to steer away from entrepreneurs who have "built-in filters that eliminate the boos and amplify the hurrahs—those who aren't likely to recognize when they're in trouble."

Self-confidence that enables an executive to tolerate uncertainty is the trademark of a promising entrepreneur. The "I'm going to do well, no matter what" attitude rather than the "I'm the big cheese" self-sop is more serviceable in the rough going ahead. Such tenacity and do-or-die determination are characteristic of all successful entrepreneurs. Entrepreneurial situations require grit and, usually, backgrounds devoid of pampering or pedigree. These people have something to prove!

Concerning the social implications of successful entrepreneurialism, Patrick Lyles, former Harvard professor and principal of the Charles River Partnership, tells a cute story. It appears in the August 3, 1981, *Forbes*, and details the obstacles facing a success-bound Yalie, barred by social conventions from the joys (and terrors) of entrepreneurship: "A friend of that Yale grad had not gone to college, but instead bought a second hand dump truck and went into business for himself." The Yalie complained: "It dawned on me that I could never buy a second hand dump truck . . . I was with XYZ Corp., the largest producer of this and that in the world." In short, this kind of go-for-the-jugular behavior was beneath his polite conventions. Kevin Landry, of T.A. Associates, told *Forbes:* "If you still think that entrepreneurship is something you can learn at Harvard Business School, forget it. Entrepreneurs seem to be born, not made."

The *Forbes* article argues convincingly that there certainly is more than enough room and need for the Horatio Alger story to be retold in today's American business community. "Pension funds, corporations and individuals are pouring unprecedented millions into venture capital deals." And most venture capitalists scrutinize the individual a lot more thoroughly than they scrutinize their ideas. "Good ideas are a dime a dozen," says William Stevens, founder of Triad Systems. The rare, practical, gutsy individual who can turn those ideas into realities is far more critical to venture capitalists.

After an individual has won funding for his idea and created a viable business from nearly nothing, he or she is going to want to maintain that business as a distinct corporate entity on its own. Generally, he or she hangs on to such an autonomous existence as long as it is feasible. In a time of merger and acquisition, such autonomy is dearly prized when it is feasible. Over 80 percent of all executives claim their companies place very much or most importance on surviving as distinct corporate entities. The commitment to this autonomy, self-sufficiency, and identity is borne out in their achievement. The majority of companies manage to avoid bankruptcy or takeover by conglomerates and fast-growing companies. Roughly 70 percent of executives say their companies have been successful (generally or virtually always) in standing alone.

It should be kept in mind there is a difference between surviving as a distinct corporate entity and avoiding being acquired. While a company may indeed have the financial resources to remain freestanding, this does not automatically ensure its being able to fend off unwanted, powerful suitors. How successful corporations are in this respect is dealt with momentarily.

Companies with growing needs and inadequate funds to meet them have no choice but to join hands with other corporations to realize their goals. Eight percent of all executives assert their companies place only fair importance on surviving as distinct entities. Nine percent say their companies frequently avoid takeover or merger with other companies. These executives may be with companies that are not likely to be independent much longer, or are with divisions or subsidiaries that have been acquired in recent times. They may be aware of financial need or economic vulnerability that makes them likely candidates for acquisition or merger in the near future. One might even guess that the few executives who report little or no importance placed on maintaining such independence (3 percent top and middle) represent companies who definitely want to be acquired.

Avoiding Acquisition

Merging with another company to acquire additional financing and strength is an everyday occurrence. Companies may not welcome their new sponsors with open arms, but worse things could happen. Among them is the threat of an especially unfriendly acquisition. Acquisition can be either a bane or a benefit for companies. The attitude toward such takeover depends largely on their operating values and how compatible they are with the acquiring corporation. When in need of capital for growth, many companies actually seek acquisition by others who promise them adequate levels of autonomy.

Sixty-six percent top executives and 59 percent middle believe their companies place very much or most importance on avoiding acquisition. But their rhetoric outstrips their performance by a wide margin. In other words, they voice an abhorrence to being acquired, but don't seem so resourceful in combating it in practice. About one-third indicate their corporations are generally or virtually always able to ward off suitors. I take this to mean that even if their corporations have not been acquired, many believe they are vulnerable to such acquisition.

Ambivalence to being acquired is understandable. Free-standing companies well may benefit from the good name and management expertise of a larger, acquiring corporation. They also may bask in the security that their high degree of specialization guarantees autonomy under their new corporate rule. However, even the most specialized of acquired companies are subject to financial controls and management coordination from parent companies. It's hard to make anyone enjoy being ruled, and these companies are no different. No matter how autonomous they turn out to be, and how many benefits they gain from their new parent companies, independence is hard to relinquish, and is worth fighting for in most cases.

As valuable as operating independence is, and as much as executives within corporate entities like to cling to their freedom, the fact is that such acquisition and merger merely represents an aspect of evolving corporate life in the free market system. Overall, the benefits must outweigh the negatives for the markets that these companies serve. The magnitude and frequency of mergers and acquisitions have grown out of the need for corporations to service their specialized markets in as competitive a way as possible over the long term.

Producing Goods and Services

The primary objective of any corporation is to provide goods and services for society. Despite less than impressive understanding of this by executives, such provisions in fact form the bulk of corporate life. As I mentioned, the job is getting done unwittingly. Roughly 90 percent of all executives report that their companies place very much or most importance on producing products or services of high quality. The perception executives have of their place in society becomes dramatically clear here. Earlier, when asked to rate the degree of importance of "*providing* goods and services for society's wants and needs," executives reported much lower commitment than shown in these scores. But when we asked them how their companies view *producing* high-quality goods and services, their responses zoomed sky high. The questions seem essentially the same, but they aren't.

The difference in the responses to these questions again documents the lack of connectedness executives have to the world outside of business. Producing is seen in technical and mechanical terms. Production can mean generating things without regard for the consumer, whereas providing means connectedness with the consumer. Companies and executives may like to say and believe they produce "the best," but everyday experiences of the consuming public show they often fall short of this goal.

My argument is not that corporations do a poor job of delivering goods and services to their markets—which is to say, society. Rather, it is that their lack of a sense of connectedness with their consumers renders them less effective than they could be. Overall, corporations do well in producing and providing goods and services. Obviously, the job is getting done. Such activity is the only way that companies can realize the profits that make them successful. It is their primary function.

IBM's recent breakthrough into the personal computer market is only one example of how companies constantly seek to improve their products to outdo their competition. In an August 31, 1981, article, *The Wall Street Journal* suggests IBM's model seems better suited than that of its competitors to handle bigger tasks. Not only has IBM managed to pull all its mighty resources together to produce a highly effective and competitive personal computer, but the company also innovatively has employed different marketing (providing) tactics for its new product. In the fall of 1981, organizations like Computerland and Sears began selling these highly efficient computers in Chicago, Dallas, and Boston. IBM's presence in the personal computer market is expected to have several beneficial effects for consumers and distributors alike. Sears' chairman Edward Telling thinks IBM will enhance sales because "IBM has a strong product offering but also is a company with a reputation for standing behind their product." Computerland president Ed Faber says that IBM's entry into the personal computer market will enhance credibility of personal computers and that "will create more demand."

Increasing Sales Volume

Increasing annual sales volume is the most commonsense, generally under-stood goal that corporations set for themselves. It is an effort that requires more than merely fattening up the company sales staff. In attempting to increase total sales volume, companies engage in unavoidable risk. They have to expand their markets, develop new products, or alter their marketing strategies for existing products. All of these actions involve risk.

When a company sets out aggressively to increase sales volume, it must do a lot more than the obvious. To achieve significant volume increases, companies (1) maintain adequate knowledge of the needs of existing mar-kets, (2) identify new and developing markets, (3) play a part in developing those markets, and (4) finance the research and development technology to meet the needs of those changing markets.

Charles of the Ritz is a company with an admirable record in defining, creating, and satisfying markets. However, it is not content to rest on its laurels. In an August 20, 1981, article, *The Wall Street Journal* reports this company continues to define and develop a critical portion of its perfume market. For two and a half years, Charles of the Ritz searched for the kind of woman who resists past products from competitors such as Charlie (for the carefree woman), Jontue (for the romantic), Aviance (for the housewife), or Enjoli (for working mothers). With this time devoted to research and experimentation with 250 scents, Charles succeeded again. Today's woman has been seeking adventure, passion, and Senchal—the company's newest fragrance. As I write this, I don't know that the company will achieve its hoped-for sales increase from this new fragrance. But the $750,000 invested in research that led to the identification of a new market and the develop-ment of this product is an example of risky corporate effort to increase sales volume.

Ninety-two percent top executives and 95 percent middle say their com-panies place very much or most importance on increasing annual sales volume. Companies that include this effort among their highest goals are not assured automatically of overcoming risks that accompany these activities. Achieving increased volume in a fluctuating market is a challenge for any company. Eighty-four percent top executives and 82 percent middle claim their companies actually achieve increasing total annual sales volume. This is certainly an impressive majority. But the unsuccessful few are likely to be candidates for financial problems or acquisition.

Increasing Before-Tax Profit

Increasing before-tax profit often is a more formidable task than increasing sales volume. If a corporation succeeds at the latter by incurring exorbitant costs in advertising, manufacturing, or packaging a product, it still is likely to lose in the end. Therefore, increasing profit is generally a more brainy, sophisticated endeavor. Companies today are more interested in increasing profits than in boosting sales for sales' sake. Ninety-eight percent top executives and 96 percent middle assert their companies place very much or most importance on increasing their before-tax profits. Companies achieve such feats largely through financial controls. How effectively they can control costs in manufacturing, marketing, and personnel also contributes to their success in increasing profits. How resourcefully they manage their own cash, investments, costs, and debt influences to what extent they are likely to enjoy success in such goals. The high degree of corporate interest in this activity explains the current corporate interest in financial executives I referred to in Chapter 7.

It is clear that the subject of profits has everybody's attention. Yet performance, while successful overall, is not as impressive as you might expect. There is a wide gap between what top- and middle-level executives claim is among their highest goals and what they achieve. As a rule, however, profit growth is at satisfactory levels for most corporations. Eighty percent top executives and 73 percent middle say their companies are generally or virtually always successful in increasing before-tax profit.

Executives are not the only ones interested in profits. Wage concessions that have been made in the past two years due to a slack economy show that profits are everybody's business. It was pioneering labor leader Samuel Gompers himself who said, "The worst crime against working people is a company which fails to operate at a profit."

Managing Financial Controls

By astute management of financial controls, companies can add to their financial success. Such measures as budgeting, financial planning, and keeping costs low can offset poor sales or profit years to the extent that unsophisticated investors will hardly notice in the newly issued, gleaming annual report. For most companies, managing financial controls well is a difficult task. It is in this area that financial executives have earned their praise as valued resources in most corporations. For example, one question companies face is whether or not to invest in the company's own future by spending dollars on costly new buildings, equipment, or product research and development, where the return might not be as great as you and I get from, say,

Treasury bills. During high inflation, staying liquid with cash often is preferable to relying on long-range, fixed lower-return investments. But then the business itself can't be built without investment. These kinds of trade-offs are what companies have to resolve.

Earlier I commented that well-managed companies are known for their chief executives' being "Johnny One-Notes." Ben Heineman, Northwest Industries' brilliant chief executive, hammers away constantly at his executives about sophisticated management of financial controls. NWI is a company that has enjoyed uncommonly rapid growth partially through a sophisticated system of allocation and control of its capital and assets. NWI has managed to increase its earnings per share (of common stock) to $5.03 in 1980 from $.53 in 1968. The company also has more than doubled its after-tax return on average total capital. Up from 5.4 percent in 1968, the company in 1980 earned 12.2 percent after-tax on the average dollar of total capital employed.

Corporations can enhance their financial resources long-term through several means. Two of the most important ones are (1) increasing annual return on assets and (2) fulfilling capital commitment objectives. A brief discussion of each follows.

Increasing Return on Assets

Companies today are devoted to increasing the productivity of their total assets. For our purposes, this should be understood as being virtually the same as increasing return on total capital employed. Return on assets has become the single most important measure of a corporation's financial success. Corporate "ROA" is the lingo that gets the attention of all astute executives, sophisticated investors, and acquiring companies on the prowl. A company's assets are everything it owns—property and equipment, and all its capital—no matter how employed or invested. The ROA percent figure is arrived at by dividing a corporation's after-tax profit by its total assets. If a company's assets are $100 million, and its after-tax profits are $8 million, its ROA is 8 percent.

Proof of ROA being a key component in corporate rhetoric can be seen in the 94 percent top executives and 92 percent middle who say their companies place very much or most importance on getting the most productivity out of their assets. Achievement is a mixed bag, however. Companies placing *most* importance on increasing their ROA fail dismally. Because of this, when looking at Table 24 it appears more companies are generally successful at increasing such return than strive to be. But this is not the case. While it is probable that companies placing very much importance on this activity achieve or come close to their goals, the excessive achievement figure here comes from the large spillback of companies seeking *always* to be successful at increasing their return, but failing at it. Incidentally, this is the same pattern that occurred in corporate striving to increase before-tax profits.

A high ROA figure, say 15 percent, is impressive indeed, but not if it is achieved for only one year. The mark of a truly successful company is being able to achieve a good return on assets year after year. What makes such a record a good one is that it assures investors and employees that top management is not only smart with its capital, but is thinking long-range. It means the company is not just milking the business to achieve a high return this year, but is investing capital in new business to make sure the ROA figure will remain high five, ten, fifteen years from now. You will note that several companies participating in this study and described in Appendix B show a high return on total capital employed, compared with their competitors, averaged over five years. This means their ROA and profitability are consistently high and that they are well managed.

Dart Industries and Kraft were merged in 1980. Both of these were excellent companies in their own right. Combined, their annual sales volume was just under $10 billion. As a means of conveying their goals to their shareholders, chairman John Richman and president Warren Batts reproduced, on the cover of the Dart & Kraft 1980 annual report, a copy of a memo they sent to all their operating unit heads under the title "Performance Objectives." In part, it reads: "We have established the long-term goal of being consistently among the best performing of our principal competitors. In today's inflationary economy, this means we must achieve 15 percent annual earnings growth and return on total capital of 15 percent. Our pro forma results for the past five years were certainly above average, and we believe we can achieve these goals."

That's laying it on the line for the world to see. Now they have to deliver!

Fulfilling Capital Commitment Objectives

Failure to provide adequately for long-term stability and growth has come to be recognized as a major shortcoming among many American corporations. These are the shortsighted, opportunistic companies I alluded to in my discussion of ROA. No one denies the risk of spending on new business. A company might decide to invest heavily in development and marketing of a new product, for example. The product may look to be one of considerable potential according to all market studies and other carefully collected data. But, in the real market the product may flop disastrously. However, the difference between Scott Paper, once the packaged paper products leader in this country, and Procter & Gamble, now the leader, is the latter's relentless spending on new plants, equipment, new product development, and advertising.

By directing a proportionate amount of revenues on a yearly basis into its own future, a company assures its steady and constant growth. One company that does this particularly well, and is admired, is Intel, the developer of the tiny computer "brain" in 1971. Since then, this little company in "Silicon Valley," California, has developed twenty highly innovative products. Their sales soon will be $1 billion annually. Intel's innovative excellence can be attributed to the company's policy of putting up to 10 percent of all revenue into research and development annually. Consequently, the company has managed to hold a lead position in developing and improving the technology of microprocessors. Until the recession of 1981, this company also had an uninterrupted string of high profit-margin years. One of the most successful investment fund managers I know thinks of Intel as the new IBM.

Pressure is mounting for American corporations to increase their capital commitment objectives. They must build or rebuild plants; invest in more productive equipment. Increasingly, they have to pour more money into R and D—if not to keep up with American business competitors, to keep up with the more technologically advanced foreign suppliers to world markets. Companies hear the complaints directed at them for failing to put the money needed into their long-term growth. But because of the inflated economy over the last ten to fifteen years, many companies have backed down on serious capital commitment objectives.

Most American business leaders realize their responsibility to see capital commitments through to completion. Just over three-fourths of all executives think their companies place very much to most importance on meeting capital commitment objectives. Naturally, some corporations are squeamish about risk, or intimidated by complex economic problems, and fail to live up to their commitments. Almost wishing for government protection through agencies such as Japan's MITI, they often cringe at the hazards they face by spending on business expansion. Yet even without such protection, an impressive 65 percent top executives and 63 percent middle claim their companies achieve their investment commitments.

Nonmanagement Boards

"Find out what that damn board wants. And, Bobby, please get those guys to swear [their support] in blood whenever you do something."

This quote isn't from the soap opera *Dallas*. These are the words that Amfac, Inc.'s Harry Walker used to advise Robert Pfeiffer on his entry to the chief executive's position at Alexander & Baldwin in Honolulu. If those words sound a little ominous, they should. Operating like RCA's board of directors, the board at Alexander & Baldwin has changed chief executives five times since 1970. What's more, according to Kathryn Christensen in her article of August 20, 1981 in *The Wall Street Journal*, the board has "bought or established—then sold or closed—five companies" since 1960.

The company's instability over the last ten years reflects so erratic a relationship between its executives and board of directors that A&B has become infamous. The *WSJ* article quoted a Honolulu businessman who heard the chanting of a Hare Krishna group outside his office window, and quipped, "The A&B board must be meeting again." After the company loudly initiated an $86 million acquisition in 1979, then abruptly backed out of the deal, Alexander & Baldwin has lost credibility. They are the subject of all this turmoil not only because of the changing social, economic, political, and labor climates in Hawaii, but also because of the board's continuing inability to find satisfaction with the direction of management in the changing climate.

It is important for executives of a given corporation to retain members of the board of directors who are not from their ranks. Such board members provide objectivity more likely to assure success in the long run. True, there often is clashing between board members and the corporate executives. Each faction represents a different point of view. Executives are more intimately involved with the corporation's operations and needs than are boards of directors. Yet the objectivity and fresh point of view brought into the major decision making of companies by outside board members are beneficial for executives, their companies, and society at large.

Adding nonmanagement members to the board is a new issue for some companies. While they may realize the benefits of this practice, many companies are divided in their opinions about how many outsiders should sit on their boards, and whether these outsiders should come from nonbusiness sectors or other corporations.

Fifty-nine percent top executives and 49 percent middle believe their companies place very much or most importance on retaining members of the board who are not executives of the company. These reports reflect management's hesitation, rather than its outright resistance, to the retention of outsiders on their boards. This is shown by 66 percent top executives and 53 percent middle stating that their companies generally or virtually always add members to their boards who are not executives from their own ranks. The fascinating figure is the small number of executives who say their companies give this activity the most importance. However, over double that number claim their companies virtually always add outside directors. This demonstrates knuckling under to pressure from critics for fair representation on corporate boards. Whereas companies that place only fair importance on other activities tend to meet or approach their goals, on this one they underachieve markedly.

Providing Income for Stockholders

While corporations must take the long view in managing their businesses, they are not exempt from having to perform well in the present. There is no chief executive who, facing his board and stockholders, thinks for one moment that he needn't give careful attention to short-term successes.

A typical example of concern with near-term success can be seen in the premium corporations place on providing income for stockholders. Seventy-three percent top executives and 68 percent middle assert that their companies place very much to most importance on providing income for stockholders. From one standpoint, it can be argued that stockholders cause undue attention to short-term measures. They want growth of their investment dollars in the near future. Few are willing to wait five to ten years for the returns they seek.

However, this popular argument can be misleading. There are legions of investment analysts—working for the major investment banks, commercial bank trust departments, insurance companies, stockbrokerages, research firms, and investment publications—whose job is to turn a gimlet eye on corporate managements. That is, they constantly analyze corporate financial statements and relentlessly query top managements on their plans and reasons for taking the actions they do. The purpose of this intense analysis is to provide a basis of financial reporting to investors, whether they be individual brokerage customers or large-fund professional investors (such as pension funds).

If a corporation is solely committed to the short-term and takes actions that make its profits look good this year, but likely to suffer next, there are any number of analysts who are well paid to blare this to the public. The result of this—if the view is shared by enough analysts—is that the share price of the company stock will plummet. So it is either the unsophisticated or exceedingly nimble investor who seeks short-term results from a company at the expense of its tomorrow. The former is likely to get caught holding the bag. The latter usually gets out before the company's blemishes are brought to public view.

A company best takes care of today by having planned for it long ago. And the company that does so also does best by its stockholders. Sixty-nine percent top executives and 64 percent middle claim their companies generally or virtually always provide them with suitable income on their investment.

Incentive Compensation for Executives

Companies such as CBS, Crown Zellerbach, and Shell Oil are strongly committed to providing their executives with incentive compensation. In addition to a base salary, their executives receive a bonus once they reach a certain level on the corporate ladder. This is usually upper-middle management.

These companies are, by far, in the majority. A fourth of all top executives say providing incentive compensation is fairly important to their companies. Almost half consider this very important. Almost another quarter place it among their companies' highest goals. That leaves only 5 percent top executives whose companies believe providing incentive compensation for their executives is of no or very little importance. One such company is Carnation.

This doesn't mean Carnation executives are paid less. On the contrary, they are well paid and the company is very successful; a leader in most of its markets both here and abroad. The Carnation philosophy on executive pay is straightforward: An executive with a particular set of abilities and experience is paid what a well-defined job is worth to the company. It is up to the executive to live up to the responsibilities of the job.

While a Carnation is in the smallest of minorities, other companies that profess commitment to providing incentive compensation don't always deliver the goods. While a quarter of top executives believe their companies give this a fair amount of importance, 17 percent live up to their goals. While 48 percent claim it is very important, 29 percent make good on their goals. On the other hand, more companies always provide their executives with incentive compensation than claim making such awards to be among their highest goals.

At the conclusion of Chapter 9, I said that progressive companies award incentive bonuses based on formulas that reward a percentage for immediate performance, a percentage for meeting long-term corporate objectives, and a percentage for meeting personal objectives. Such companies are committed to the belief that the incentive carrot is a way to achieve their own performance objectives, both short and long range. In companies like Esmark, CBS, PepsiCo, and Phibro-Salomon, a top executive can more than equal his base salary in incentive compensation by meeting high objectives set in collaboration with his superiors. If he does not meet them, he may get next to nothing in bonuses.

The figures from executives in which there is a wide discrepancy between rhetoric and performance indicate those who aren't pleased with the incentive compensation they receive, or companies which have a haphazard or misunderstood policy of making incentive awards. In the case where more companies make incentive awards than claim to be highly committed to the

practice, such compensation in some of those companies will be fairly automatic rather than truly incentive. That is, executive performance standards
are easy enough to achieve that so-called incentive compensation is not
actually at risk.

Union Relations

While companies place impressive energies into improving and maintaining
productive relationships between themselves and their executives, they also
are charged with maintaining good relations with hourly, clerical, and other
kinds of support-staff employees. No matter what rank employees hold
within a corporation, they all represent a particular value to their companies.
It cannot be questioned that replacing top executives and middle managers
is inconvenient and expensive to corporations in terms of time, energy, and
money. However, it is just as costly to replace employees on a wider basis.

The importance of maintaining healthy relations with employees and
their unions is important to executives and their corporations. Sixty-five
percent top executives and 61 percent middle claim their companies place
very much or most importance on having good union relations. Companies
are loath to waste valuable production time over bitter invective, lengthy
negotiations, and strikes. Moreover, this is another area where corporate
managements are able to back up their intentions with action. Sixty-three
percent top executives and 56 percent middle say their companies generally
or virtually always achieve success in maintaining good relations with unions.

On the other hand, recent efforts at conciliation have been coming from
unions. As an uncertain economy imposes hardships all around the globe,
management and employees join efforts to ward off catastrophic effects. The
October 10, 1981, *U.S. News & World Report* documents the current willingness of employees in several large corporations to accept cutbacks in pay
and benefits to avoid possible reduction in employment. Some of these
compromises have reached surprising proportions. For example, General
Motors employees in a ball-bearing plant in Clark, New Jersey, agreed to
buy the facility to keep it from closing. Pan American World Airways, Inc.
workers, as well as laborers at several other ailing airlines, have agreed to or
are considering taking a 10 percent cut in wages. Employees at a Firestone
plant agreed to accept a one dollar per hour cut in pay to keep their plant
operating.

The New York Times always has been friendly and supportive of organized
labor. Yet in a November 5, 1981, editorial, it gave voice to the sentiment
that unions need to back off on wage demands to help fight inflation. Says
the *Times*, "Thus, if labor is determined to war on interest rates, the task

ahead is clear. Wages are still the major cost of running a business. If wage pressures could be restrained in the months ahead, inflation would drop—and so would interest rates." Both management and labor are finally realizing that they are working for very similar goals. Economies sick enough to threaten survival of plants and businesses across the country can be no better for employees than for the corporations that suffer large losses.

Flow of Information

The figures on corporate communication intentions and accomplishments bear out the findings I discussed in Section II. There, while considering inter- and intraunit communications, I pointed out that while not ideal, the flow of information was adequate to get the job done.

Seventy-seven percent top executives and 72 percent middle think their companies place very much or most importance on having good information on which to base decisions. Even though companies fall short of these goals, as seen in only 57 percent top and 50 percent middle claiming their companies reach them, 26 percent top and 28 percent middle state their companies frequently achieve good information-flow. My impression is those 'frequent" times occur when such communications are essential. That is, the necessary information is received by executives when they need to make critical decisions. Therefore these percentages add up to a flow that, while not all one might hope for, is indeed workable.

21

Economic Failures

There are eight major economic activities at which corporations fail. All of these impinge on expansion and innovation. To determine specific corporate attitudes and performance in these areas, we asked executives to indicate their degree of importance and how often their companies reached their goals in relation to them:

Making acquisitions.

Planning for the long-range.

Adapting to changing markets.

Expanding into and creating new markets.

Developing new products and services.

Marketing new products.

Expanding international business.

Staying abreast of technology.

Their responses are tallied in Table 25.

Making Acquisitions

Companies that fail to plan acquisitions carefully often end up with serious financial problems. Acquisitions are major turning points for both corporations involved in a deal. For highly diversified corporations like Alco Standard, Signal Companies, Beatrice Foods, and General Mills, acquisitions are a common but well-planned way of life and growth. For others, they can be an awful mismatch that may lead to the ultimate undoing of both parties.

Table 25
How Corporations Fail in Economic Activities

	DEGREE OF IMPORTANCE				
	No (%)	Little (%)	Fair (%)	Very (%)	Most (%)
Top Executives					
Making acquisitions	2.7	7.8	21.2	38.8	27.8
	Rarely/ Never	Some- times	Fre- quently	Gener- ally	Virtually always
Achieved	8.1	34.9	32.1	9.1	14.0
Planning long range	0.0	5.7	15.7	37.6	40.9
Achieved	2.0	15.1	21.4	23.7	37.5
Adapting to changing market demands	0.2	1.8	15.6	51.8	30.5
Achieved	0.8	19.6	26.9	37.2	15.4
Expanding into and creating new markets	0.6	5.3	21.5	41.7	30.3
Achieved	3.3	32.0	25.7	27.5	11.2
Developing new products/services	0.2	5.1	17.3	41.0	34.7
Achieved	1.0	27.3	26.5	29.5	13.9
Marketing new products/services	0.4	6.5	22.6	50.5	18.3
Achieved	2.6	29.8	28.6	28.0	9.1
Expanding international business	3.1	15.5	27.8	34.8	14.5
Achieved	9.4	32.1	17.9	25.8	10.0
Staying abreast of state of the art of technology	0.0	1.6	15.7	47.3	34.2
Achieved	0.6	14.4	23.9	40.0	20.1

"Not Applicable" responses not included.

Accordingly, mergers and acquisitions aren't always a sure way to success. Acquisitions made on the basis of faulty, inadequate information or wishful thinking lead to disaster. Such bad moves are made frequently. Still, the urge to merge seems impossible to suppress for many companies, even when they have to make gargantuan loans at exorbitant interest rates to see their acquisitions through.

	DEGREE OF IMPORTANCE				
	No (%)	Little (%)	Fair (%)	Very (%)	Most (%)
Middle Managers					
Making acquisitions	5.2	10.0	23.7	37.6	19.6
	Rarely/ Never	Some- times	Fre- quently	Gener- ally	Virtually always
Achieved	13.0	32.3	32.5	8.9	9.6
Planning long range	0.4	3.2	13.6	42.0	40.4
Achieved	2.1	14.1	15.4	28.8	38.7
Adapting to changing market demands	0.4	1.9	14.5	53.1	29.7
Achieved	1.4	17.4	27.9	35.3	17.4
Expanding into and creating new markets	0.4	8.0	20.2	39.8	30.2
Achieved	4.8	31.4	25.1	27.4	9.5
Developing new products/services	0.2	5.5	18.5	42.6	30.6
Achieved	4.5	24.6	24.6	29.1	14.1
Marketing new products/services	0.0	7.6	22.2	51.3	17.5
Achieved	3.7	30.1	27.8	27.5	9.4
Expanding international business	4.8	11.6	29.0	32.7	10.7
Achieved	8.7	29.1	20.9	21.6	7.3
Staying abreast of state of the art of technology	0.2	4.6	14.5	44.3	33.9
Achieved	2.5	18.4	20.0	37.0	19.5

"Not Applicable" responses not included.

Some companies, like Consolidated Foods, are so dependent on successful acquisitions for economic growth that their entire reputations are built around their history of acquiring. In the case of Con Foods, it is said that "they'll buy you today and sell you tomorrow." But for more strategic companies, such as Chesebrough-Pond's, successful production and marketing of a diversity of products is a profitable art form. In fourteen years as chief executive of Chesebrough, Ralph Ward has maintained a conservative, methodical approach to one acquisition after another. This has resulted in an uncommon success story of growth through imaginative, careful, profitable diversification by acquisition.

Sixty-seven percent top executives and 57 percent middle state their companies place very much or most importance on making acquisitions. However, the element of risk in making these acquisitions, and the problem of raising sufficient funds to finance them, make success in this activity inordinately difficult for many companies to achieve. To be successful in making acquisitions, companies have to have a stomach for taking strangers into their house, paying premium prices, and wooing the prospective acquisition management 'til hell won't have it. And that is just the beginning of a working partnership that has yet to throw off problems that never fully can be anticipated. There are up-front givens for any corporation that is going to see an acquisition through, then make a success of it. Numerous companies say they want to acquire because it is stylish to do so. But doing so with distinction is a feat that takes moxie and tenacity. While 67 percent of top executives say their companies place great importance on making acquisitions, only 23 percent can claim their companies generally or virtually always succeed in making such acquisitions. Middle managers report comparable failures.

Long-Range Planning

Corporations improve their profitability by making sound economic decisions. After considering conflicting priorities, unknown economic hazards, and the constant changes in the marketplace, corporations fairly well manage to make decisions to assure their survival. But there is one area where all but the most progressive companies fail in their decision making. While companies that claim to be most committed to long-range planning actually do well at this, the majority of corporations are unable to prepare themselves innovatively and technologically for the future needs and demands of society.

This failure results from inattentiveness to future opportunities rather than inability to address them. Consistently, corporate leaders are tempted to put off investment in the corporate and market future in favor of seemingly more pressing and immediate needs. Criticism from academic theoreticians and European and Japanese business executives has helped to bring about a new awareness among American businessmen of the need to take the longer view.

Thirty-eight percent top executives and 42 percent middle believe their companies place very much importance on tending to long-range planning.

These executives likely represent companies eager to respond to popular criticisms from the outside for being shortsighted. Sixteen percent top executives and 14 percent middle say their companies place fair importance on long-range planning. These are likely to be executives who readily understand their need to address the future in planning, but feel limited in their ability to respond to future needs as thoroughly, perhaps, as need be. They suggest an attitude more in the direction of: "Sure, we know we need to worry about the future. But we also know we'll have more problems in meeting future market needs and future competition if we first don't overcome our existing problems; those that will pop up next year." Concern for short-term needs is legitimate. Unanticipated problems always arise in business, no matter how carefully a company does its planning.

The 21 percent top executives and 15 percent middle who believe their corporations frequently succeed in long-range planning are partially a spillback from companies that place very much importance on planning for the future but fail to live up to their goals. Only 24 percent top executives and 29 percent middle say their companies generally make good on long-range planning. These reports make clear that companies undeniably are aware of their need to direct creative energies toward future opportunities. Most make some attempt to be more farsighted. But many don't. They are companies that choose to ignore future needs altogether, and eventually lose out to their competitors in the marketplace.

No force has encouraged the attentions of today's corporations to be focused more intently on addressing future market needs than competition from outside the American business community. Oddly enough, foreign manufacturers appear to have been more sensitive to the needs and wants of the American consumer in recent years than American ones. Consumers have let their preferences be known. As foreign manufacturers continue to make inroads to the American consumer, American corporations are slowly realigning their energies and priorities to regain lost ground.

Adapting to Changing Markets

Industries that cater to fragmented but strong existing markets have no choice but to keep in touch with their markets in order to compete. For example, the food industry is compelled to keep up with market wants to replace its waning products with new ones that may or may not be replicated by competitors. There are probably few corporations that see as short a life for new products as food and other packaged-goods manufacturers do. Even when products have long life within existing markets, such as Procter & Gamble's Crisco or 3M's Scotch tape, manufacturers maintain their best competitive stance by hovering constantly over their markets.

Corporations are required to keep up with and adapt to changing markets, but don't do as well at this as they should. Eighty-two percent top executives and 83 percent middle think their companies place very much or most importance on adapting to changing markets. But only 53 percent top and middle executives think their companies generally or virtually always succeed at this. As often has been the case in these success-and-failure discussions, companies placing only fair importance on the matter at hand—in this case adapting to changing markets—do better at meeting their goals than their more ambitious brethren.

Success or failure in adapting to changing markets is influenced by how many dollars a company is willing to spend on new products and divining unknown markets. As much as successful adaptation is a goal of long-range market planning, it is at the same time a function of technological excellence and risk taking. As companies adapt to changing markets, they spur innovation. Two primary requirements to achieve success in adapting to changing markets are (1) determination to expand into new markets and (2) financial commitment to develop new products and services for these markets.

Expanding into and Creating New Markets

Do you remember the large sum Charles of the Ritz had to invest just to find out what an already existing market is looking for? The expense and risk involved in expanding into new markets is considerably larger than what it costs to maintain a market. The most common way that companies manage to diversify into other markets is through acquisition. That also happens to be the "safest" way—if there is a safe way—to expand. As I mentioned, Chesebrough's Ralph Ward has overcome tough odds by acquiring several new product lines, then expanding them. Yet despite his long-standing track record of successful entry into new markets, he still admits to getting squeamish whenever Chesebrough does so.

Consequently, he stresses the importance of overcoming fears in the face of risk. In the September 28, 1981, *Forbes* he says, "Sometimes you can't admit you're scared. You just keep going until you get it right."

Some companies have little interest either in starting a new product from scratch or acquiring. A case that illustrates this is written up by Robert Levy in an article entitled "Innovate or Replicate?" in the June 1980 issue of *Dun's Review*. Levy says that Airwick Industries, a U.S. holding of Switzerland's Ciba-Geigy, has filed suit against Sterling Drug's Lehn & Fink division for pirating their product Carpet Fresh. Airwick invested two years and $16 million in research and development, advertising, and promotion. It created a market where none had existed with its product that housewives pour onto their carpets, then vacuum. Lehn & Fink concluded that this product and market looked promising. In six months, its copy of the product Love My Carpet was on the market.

The suit is still pending. It might never have been brought except for the public statements of Lehn & Fink's new products director, Steven Lapham. In 1979, he said in a speech before executives at an American Marketing Association conference that L&F's marketing philosophy was to "replicate rather than innovate. Someone else has gone and done your homework for you. They have taken the risk and the time, and spent the dollars." He detailed his former ridicule of and doubt in Airwick's product idea in early market-testing stages. "The whole idea had to be wrong. What housewife in her right mind would sprinkle white powder onto her carpet before vacuuming?" When Lapham's words were published in an *Advertising Age* editorial, Airwick decided to use the report as partial basis for its patent-infringement suit against L&F.

We shouldn't be too hard on Sterling for the errors of one of its divisions. That's the risk of autonomy. Besides, the company has done a magnificent job with Bayer aspirin, Lysol, and d-Con over the years. While many companies claim not to rely on a "me, too" marketing philosophy, performance data is not impressive. Seventy-two percent top executives and 70 percent middle offer that their companies place very much to most importance on expanding into or creating new markets. But fewer than 40 percent of all executives say their companies generally or virtually always succeed at breaking such new ground.

Though Sterling's Lapham got himself and his company into a legal tangle, he expressed many executives' reasons for resistance to venturing into new markets. The risk and expense for most companies is usually more frightening than encouraging. Companies may want to break into new areas, but the overwhelming risks they face discourage all but the most determined.

Developing and Marketing New Products and Services

When discussing social responsibility, I pointed out that only about half of all executives believe their corporations place very much or most importance on *providing* goods and services for society's wants and needs. But in the last chapter on corporate economic successes, I indicated that executives give their companies high marks on *producing* high-quality goods and services.

I further offered my belief that the discrepancy in these figures was a result of executives' lacking a sense of connectedness with the world outside their business; a loss of touch with and perception of the end-user or consumer. Producing is seen in technical or mechanistic terms. But providing requires contact outside the producing sphere.

My belief in this regard seems to be borne out in the figures having to do with the expansion into and creation of new markets by corporations—just discussed—and the development and marketing of new products and services. Except for those companies who place only fair importance on these activities, corporate performance is dismal when measured against its rhetoric. And in this case, the producing level of companies—as seen in the development of new products and services—almost has come down to the providing level—as seen in the marketing of new products and services.

Seventy-six percent top executives and 73 percent middle claim their corporations place very much or most importance on developing new products or services. Forty-two percent of both meet their goals. Sixty-nine percent of both level executives think their corporations place very much or most importance on marketing new products or services. Thirty-seven percent of both meet their goals. If you ask any marketing vice-president how successful his company has been in introducing new products, unless he is the exception, he'll tell you his organization's record in this area is way below what he seeks.

Expanding International Business

Most businessmen staunchly maintain that major corporations have no choice but to broaden their international markets. Still, for corporations with little experience in this area, risks and problems are sizable. In addition to normal business expenses, the expansion of international markets also involves overcoming cultural barriers and dealing with significant communication and public-policy gaps.

International business is a sophisticated and appealing concept to many corporations. Companies such as Coca-Cola, McDonald's, Caterpillar, and General Motors, whose products have a universal demand, have refined their expertise in international business. There is strong support for involvement and growth in international business communities from several banking and government agencies in this country. Services from the World Bank, Export-Import Bank, and various government international and export agencies offer extensive advisory and financial services to companies interested in expanding their international markets. Moreover, when done well, international business can spell great profit to a corporation.

Despite such services and profit enticements, companies are cautious in the international marketplace. Only 49 percent top executives and 43 percent middle believe their companies place very much or most importance on expanding their international markets. Moreover, only a moderate number achieve their objectives. Roughly a third of both level executives say their companies generally or virtually always succeed in overseas expansion.

Staying Abreast of Technology

While I believe corporations are more comfortable with the producing side of their businesses, this by no means implies that they have kept abreast of the state of the art of technology relevant to their businesses. The reason for this is easy to understand. It's horribly expensive. But not to do so curtails innovation, and that, in the end, is far more costly to a company. It is precisely in this area that many companies are tempted to take the short view.

Despite the dependency on technological advances for a vital competitive edge, corporations stumble at developing and artfully using the technological and research talents within their ranks. Few companies are like 3M, giving a relatively free hand to research, putting impressive backing into major technology projects. However, there's no shortage of rhetoric on this score. Eighty-two percent top executives and 78 percent middle assert that their companies place very much to most importance on staying abreast of technology. But only 60 percent top executives and 57 percent middle claim their companies generally or virtually always reach their goals of technological advancement.

As has been the case repeatedly in this study, companies that place fair importance on keeping abreast of technology generally match their goals. Such moderate commitment to technology may reflect a corporation's concerns for problems it is likely to encounter when it has little previous technological sophistication to fall back on. A poll published by *The Wall Street Journal* on September 9, 1981, states that despite the many companies climbing "aboard the high-technology bandwagon, most of them don't have the slightest idea how to manage their technology efforts effectively."

Management consultants Booz, Allen & Hamilton recently conducted a technology survey among twelve of the largest corporations in the United States. Results of their survey show that executives generally are aware of their need for enhanced technology for productivity, growth, and new-market development. It is management of technology, rather than awareness of the need for it, that seems to be the major problem in American companies.

The Wall Street Journal article names B. F. Goodrich as an unusually enlightened company when it comes to managing technology. Perhaps the most productive aspect of Goodrich's technological philosophy is its regard for technology as a capital asset. With the "capital asset" attitude toward technology, companies are encouraged to manage technology in a truly professional manner. At AccuRay Corporation, a quality performer in managing technology, investment in technology is clearly tied to achieving specific market goals. The company uses sales volume to determine whether it is putting too much or too little into research and development. As does

3M, AccuRay encourages the all-out efforts of its staff scientists. Hewlett-Packard is a sophisticated technology company that has grown rapidly. Donald Hammond, director of H-P's physical electronics lab, says, "We encourage our people to take about ten percent of their time for under-the-bench projects." Progressive, technology-dependent companies establish close working relationships between technical people and other executives. The benefits of such relationships are apparent and unlimited. This is because most executives eventually have to make some sort of business decision based on technological research, no matter how little they understand it. Frequently, executives barely understand the circumstances and information around which they make such decisions.

22

Government Relations— Successes and Failures

The relationship most corporations have with government is marked by antagonism. We often hear business complain that government burdens it with excessive regulations to the detriment of profit growth. Large corporations, especially, complain that government acts ineffectively to create an environment conducive to growth and profit. Without a counterpart to Japan's government agency (MITI) which oversees, supports, and nurtures innovation among businesses, American corporations see themselves left alone to finance their own innovation, but badgered to conform to harmful regulations created by unknowing bureaucrats.

While companies consistently point the finger at government for failing to support their efforts for profit and innovation, they fail to acknowledge the ironic relationship that business leaders have had with government agencies ever since Franklin Roosevelt's administration. In reality, these two vital groups—business and government—are the strangest bedfellows.

In his book *The Phaeton Ride*, historian Forrest McDonald describes FDR's conviction that, in 1933, the American economy was suffering from (1) overproduction, (2) destructive competition, and (3) a complete lack of planning. McDonald says:

> To rectify these supposed ills, every industry was requested to draw up "codes of fair practice," along the lines of a "blanket code" drawn up by the President, the objects being to fix uniform prices, wages, and working conditions, and to integrate each industry through its trade association, into what was in effect a single whole. When each code was adopted and approved by the President, it took on the force of law. Within a year five hundred codes had been adopted, some 23 million workers were under them, and more than 4 million had been re-absorbed into industry.

In McDonald's opinion, this was the beginning of a partnership between business and federal government in which government became industry's biggest consumer and its regulator. Many business leaders, while losing **229** much of their initiative, found the relationship comforting in some ways and downright financially advantageous in others. McDonald continues:

> Partly by accident, partly by design, the federal government's policies made possible the "wheeler-dealer"—the politically oriented businessman who makes enormous fortunes and gains great prestige and power by going into partnership with government, by exploiting special influence or inside information, or by turning to personal advantage programs that are designed for purposes of general welfare. Ironically, however, it was in precisely this area that it first began to be apparent that the Americans had fixed themselves to a course that could end in paralysis.

It is obvious that business is not blameless for its oft-lamented predicament of overregulation. No less stalwart a champion of conservative politics and free enterprise than Barry Goldwater himself has called attention to this. Recently, the senator chided business for its dependence on and coziness with Washington.

To gain insight into current relationships between government and corporations, we asked executives to rate the levels of importance and frequency with which their companies are engaged in the following:

Working to limit state and federal regulation of business.

Working cooperatively with government and regulatory agencies.

Reorganizing production to reduce energy needs.

Complying with environmental regulations.

Paying their share of corporate taxes to government.

Legally reducing their share of corporate taxes.

Responses from executives show passive corporate resistance in meeting unfavorable requirements placed upon them by government regulatory agencies. Untangling the relationship between business and government, even with a pro-market-forces administration like President Reagan's, will take a long time. Radical change of this relationship with its approach-avoidance qualities surely will not happen overnight, or even within the term of this administration.

Limiting Regulation

Business says that government growth needs to be checked. Government says that business growth needs to be controlled and regulated. Under President Reagan, business leaders are currently enjoying a sympathetic leadership in Washington; one that is likely to ease up on the costly, time-consuming regulations with which corporations are compelled to comply.

Table 26
How Corporations Fail in Government Relations

	DEGREE OF IMPORTANCE				
	No (%)	Little (%)	Fair (%)	Very (%)	Most (%)
Top Executives Working to limit state and federal government regulation of business	1.0	9.8	23.1	42.2	19.7
	Rarely/ Never	Some- times	Fre- quently	Gener- ally	Virtually always
Achieved	6.2	22.7	21.5	29.9	14.7

	DEGREE OF IMPORTANCE				
	No (%)	Little (%)	Fair (%)	Very (%)	Most (%)
Middle Managers Working to limit state and federal government regulation of business	1.3	10.8	23.9	41.7	16.5
	Rarely/ Never	Some- times	Fre- quently	Gener- ally	Almost always
Achieved	6.8	25.0	20.0	27.2	15.1

"Not Applicable" responses not included.

Corporations resent having to comply with government regulations, especially since government has failed to regulate itself. As a result of the tremendous proliferation of government agencies, corporations end up in confused attempts to meet overlapping regulations from various agencies operating autonomously. The federal agencies with which corporations must deal most are:

Environmental Protection Agency

Food and Drug Administration

Occupational Safety and Health Administration

Equal Employment Opportunity Commission

National Highway Traffic Administration

Federal Trade Commission

Federal Communications Commission
Consumer Product Safety Commission
Securities and Exchange Commission

As I said, the resistance is passive, deriving to some extent from a sense of powerlessness, justified or not. Corporations seldom counter government interference in business. Aside from an occasional suit from one business or another concerning what is deemed to be unfair or illegal regulation, companies largely comply with such regulation. Sixty-two percent top executives and 58 percent middle say their companies place very much to most importance on limiting state and federal government regulations. But most find it difficult to take time and money to fight. Only 45 percent top executives and 42 percent middle can claim their companies generally or virtually always limit such state and federal government regulations in their businesses.

The extent to which corporations passively accept regulation is evident in the fact that fighting it is the only failure that is reported by executives in their government relations. Failure at other government/business relations is more likely to be costly and even dangerous for their survival. So they comply with regulations, even if they do so with resentment.

While the rhetoric and stated purposes of regulatory agencies sound impressive, worthy, and deserving of citizen support, they, like those of corporations, can be overblown. Government executives are as prone to power seeking as corporate ones and as skilled (if not more so) in protecting —and whenever possible, enlarging—their turf.

The Reagan administration seems to be acting on its belief that this is so, and offers promise to corporations that think many regulatory agencies have gone too far. A case in point is the Occupational Safety and Health Administration (OSHA). The October 21, 1981, edition of *The Washington Post* reports that OSHA chief Thorne Auchter has halved the number of federal monitors who check on state OSHA programs. In addition, he is proposing to reduce the number of inspectors each state must employ before it can win final certification from the feds.

The *Post* article shows the contrast between the Carter and Reagan administrations: "In the last year of the Carter administration, OSHA said that 1,683 health inspectors were needed in the 22 states and two territories that have chosen to supervise their own OSHA programs. This year, OSHA says only 499 inspectors will be required in the same states. In Virginia, for example, the Carter administration required 125 inspectors, the Reagan administration 71; in Maryland, Carter required 73, Reagan 42."

Anyone who has had any real contact with corporations, and maintains any but the most jaundiced views of corporate conscience, has been aware that OSHA inspectors—tripping all over each other—have thought up some of the hokiest demands imaginable for corporations in the name of safety. The Reagan staff reductions will force the remaining inspectors to be spread more thinly, kept constructively busy, and realistic in carrying out their responsibilities.

Cooperating with Government

In many relationships between government and business, the historic philosophy that "one hand washes the other" still applies. But in most cases, corporations succumb only with reluctance to work cooperatively with government agencies. While both Washington and business leaders are busy seeking change in levels of regulation and in many federal laws, reformers from both groups still are confronted with the problem of exactly how business/government relationships should change, and what forms these changes should take.

The adversarial role between these two groups continues. Government agencies probe, tax, regulate, and penalize for failure to comply. Businesses try as they can to minimize government impact on their affairs. But many suffer mixed emotions, because among their markets Uncle Sam is a big customer. The most dramatic examples of this are corporations that serve specialized industrial markets, but are also defense contractors. United Technologies, Litton Industries, Lockheed, and Chrysler are cases in point. I mention Lockheed and Chrysler in particular because the federal government kept them from bankruptcy.

The way corporations have minimized the impact of government interference in their industries is by simply cooperating and complying (though, as I've said, at times passively and resentfully) with regulations from government agencies. Sixty-four percent top executives and 58 percent middle say their companies seek to work cooperatively with government agencies as a rule. And, likely to pay hefty penalty fees for failure to do so, these corporations manage to meet such goals of cooperation. Sixty-four percent top executives and 59 percent middle say that their companies are generally or virtually always successful in linking hands with government agencies.

Reducing Energy Needs

Some energy regulations have most likely provided a benefit for corporations. Companies that were required to make energy-saving revisions in their production systems have certainly ended up saving money and enhancing revenues in the long run. In fact, years ago when such energy conserva-

Table 27
How Corporations Succeed in Government Relations

	DEGREE OF IMPORTANCE				
	No (%)	Little (%)	Fair (%)	Very (%)	Most (%)
Top Executives Working cooperatively with government and regulatory agencies	0.6	6.3	28.2	50.1	14.0
	Rarely/ Never	**Some- times**	**Fre- quently**	**Gener- ally**	**Virtually always**
Achieved	1.0	12.1	21.8	40.1	23.8
Reorganizing production to reduce energy needs	1.6	5.3	19.6	45.7	23.1
Achieved	2.8	14.1	20.4	40.3	17.3
Complying with environmental regulations	1.0	2.2	18.0	48.4	25.7
Achieved	1.6	3.4	13.3	42.5	34.3
Paying its share of taxes to governments	4.5	9.7	34.2	41.5	7.9
Achieved	1.4	4.6	15.5	25.3	51.0
Legally reducing its share of taxes to governments	0.4	3.4	16.3	53.8	23.4
Achieved	1.8	9.2	15.2	39.0	31.0

"Not Applicable" responses not included.

tion regulations were begun, this may have been the first time some companies were forced to turn investment dollars far forward. This function now
is recognized by many corporations as a means of getting more out of fixed
assets. Sixty-nine percent top executives and 64 percent middle believe their
companies place very much or most importance on reorganizing production
to reduce energy needs.

Most succeed fairly well, too. Fifty-eight percent top executives and 54
percent middle think their companies generally or virtually always manage
to reduce production energy needs. Not only do these companies avoid
possible penalty fees, but they also improve their own opportunity for
greater profits.

	DEGREE OF IMPORTANCE				
	No (%)	Little (%)	Fair (%)	Very (%)	Most (%)
Middle Managers Working cooperatively with government and regulatory agencies	0.5	7.7	29.2	43.4	14.7
	Rarely/ Never	Some- times	Fre- quently	Gener- ally	Virtually always
Achieved	2.0	14.2	20.3	34.9	24.1
Reorganizing production to reduce energy needs	1.4	6.6	21.0	40.3	23.2
Achieved	2.9	15.4	20.0	33.6	20.4
Complying with environmental regulations	0.7	3.2	20.5	47.0	19.9
Achieved	0.5	3.6	17.3	37.4	32.2
Paying its share of taxes to governments	3.2	7.0	35.1	42.7	8.6
Achieved	0.7	3.6	14.4	27.1	49.9
Legally reducing its share of taxes to governments	0.4	2.5	20.4	52.7	18.9
Achieved	1.3	9.3	19.1	35.7	29.0

"Not Applicable" responses not included.

Environmental Regulations

Corporate responsibility regarding the environment apart from energy has become a confused issue in recent years. Environmentalists, placing greatest priorities on conserving natural sites, reducing pollution, and restricting handling and creation of nondegradable wastes, charge that American corporations have been bad actors in maintaining livability in our urban and even rural environments. On the other hand, corporations say it is possible to be too concerned with the environment. They believe that overconcern with some of these issues only serves to hinder progress; that such hindrances ultimately hurt society more than they help.

Industry has found an ally, if not a friend, in Anne Gorsuch, the Reagan-appointed administrator of the Environmental Protection Agency. She is sympathetic to its point of view. Recently, she was asked, "How would you revise clean-air rules to allow more industrial expansion?" Her reply, published in the October 19, 1981, *U.S. News & World Report:*

A lot can be done through administrative changes. For example, currently the federal government sets air-quality standards for each of several pollutants and then tells states, "You figure out a plan to meet those standards."

But we go through that process in such excruciating detail. The plan is submitted by a state. Then every change to these plans has to be submitted by the state to the federal government. We have approximately 1,000 proposed changes in the system at any one time. We simply must streamline the process to reduce this paperwork and the delays and confusion it causes for government and industry planners. For example, it now takes almost two years to get a permit to discharge waste water.

The New York Times is unhappy with Anne Gorsuch's administrative changes. In a November 7, 1981, editorial, it points out she plans to cut EPA's work force from 11,400 to 8,300; the cost of enforcing the Clean Air Act by 31 percent; EPA research budget in half and operational spending in 1983 to $975 million. The latter figure is just 60 percent of what the agency will spend in 1981.

The *Times* doesn't like it that Mrs. Gorsuch says that's all she needs to do the job. It concludes its editorial with: "The exact nature of environmental regulation may be debatable. The need for a strong Environmental Protection Agency is not. When Congress instructs the agency to do more work, Mrs. Gorsuch contributes more to skepticism than sense by insisting that she needs fewer people to do it."

This naive editorial writer doesn't realize it has ever been thus—that in organizational matters, less is frequently more. But he needn't worry. So long as the EPA is in a position to pass and implement regulations and charge fines to corporations who fail to comply with its regulations, corporations will make efforts to comply.

Moreover, no one will find Anne Gorsuch an administrator who will allow the EPA to be abused. Seventy-four percent top executives and 67 percent middle claim their companies place very much or most importance on complying with environmental regulations. Apparently, hefty fines prompt corporations to overachieve concerning their goals in meeting environmental regulations. Seventy-seven percent top executives and 70 percent middle boast that their companies generally or virtually always meet their goals in complying with environmental regulations.

Share of Taxes

Corporations long have complained that the more governments tax them, the less money they have to invest in their own futures. That complaint is certainly valid. But recent changes in tax regulations made by the Reagan administration provide corporations opportunities to prove the value of lower corporate taxes. It remains to be seen whether companies will apply their saved tax dollars to expanding their enterprises or safely place them into other investment alternatives. New, liberalized depreciation codes should encourage business to make greater capital investment.

No matter what government does, however, corporations cannot be expected to *enjoy* paying taxes. As with individual citizens, this activity is often viewed as a necessary evil. Forty-nine percent top executives and 51 percent middle say their companies place very much or most importance on paying their share of taxes. The critical word here is *share*. Every corporation *must* pay what it owes in taxes or it also pays a big fine and its executives go to jail. This means half of executives believe their corporations are highly committed to paying the amount of taxes determined by law. The other half believe that their companies think this share is pegged too high and are not enthusiastic about meeting what they consider inflated requirements. And from the other side, when three out of four executives say their companies generally or virtually always succeed in paying their share of taxes, this means that one in four thinks that, on occasion, their corporations don't pay enough.

Few companies will say openly that they don't like to pay taxes. If you ask tax managers within major corporations what their companies' tax philosophies are, they are likely to tell you that their companies resent paying taxes. But their CEOs would not express their corporate tax philosophies this way. Truly, there are any number of conservative companies who maintain the philosophy that their taxes contribute to national growth. They consider it their responsibility to pay their taxes. While they make every effort to reduce taxes through whatever legal means available, they do not go to extreme or questionable lengths to do so.

But other companies search high and low to find any loophole they can to claim deductions for themselves. Seventy-seven percent top executives and 72 percent middle say that their companies place very much or most importance on seeking legal ways to reduce their tax load. Seventy percent top and 65 percent middle claim they succeed. However, there are a lot of gray areas in matters of tax. How corporations interpret these gray areas reveals the perspective they maintain on payment of taxes. Many tax consultants believe that the corporate tax relief provided by the Reagan administration will stimulate greater investment and productivity in industry, and will result in the government's actually increasing its total tax receipts.

In 1975, two Fruehauf Corporation executives (chairman William Grace and president Robert Rowan) were found guilty of conspiring along with their company to evade paying over $12 million in excise taxes. The indictment in this case had been brought against the company and the two executives in 1970. Throughout the trial, these two executives held their jobs and Fruehauf paid their legal fees.

After the two were found guilty of designing a scheme to charge lower prices to their customers in order to pay less taxes on their sales (they made up the differences in price by charging for services normally provided for free), the two executives were granted an unsalaried leave of absence. Later, the board of directors was petitioned to allow them to return to their board positions, which had been held open. This measure was passed overwhelmingly. These executives, charged by most social critics as irresponsible, were treated more or less as heroes by their corporate peers.

The Fruehauf case is an extreme example of how far some companies may go to reduce their taxes. Grace and Rowan employed out-and-out deception.

Boy, at what price profit? There's a better way!

No company succeeds or fails in pure form. The highflyer always has the seeds of destruction floating in its crosswinds, while the mediocre performer may someday stumble to daylight. Likewise, to praise or castigate American industry as a whole on any issue is to place a halo over too many heads or tar too many with the same brush.

Never had this idea been made clearer to me than it was a couple of years ago by a senior officer of the Continental Illinois Bank. His bank just had been named one of the country's five best-managed firms by *Dun's Business Month.* After I congratulated him, he chortled, "If we're one of the best, God help the rest!" This executive isn't lacking pride in the bank, nor did he think it was undeserving of the award. Rather, he's blessed with a sense of humor and realizes that success and failure constantly flirt with each other.

Some corporations set their goals so high that they cannot possibly meet them. Yet if they achieve them partway, their accomplishments may outstrip those companies whose goals were met, but were much less ambitious to begin with. Who is to say unequivocally which group is more successful, at least long-term?

On the other hand, after reviewing the data covered in this section, I am left with one overriding impression. It is that those companies in which fair importance is placed on most activities and very much or most importance is placed on one or two activities in which the stated goals are met—that these companies are the most in harmony and likely to thrive over time. I admit that this is an article of faith, but I also think it probable that the "frequent" occasions on which these companies achieve the performance they seek coincide with the times when such performance is essential to corporate success. In other words, they get what they need when they need it.

Alfred Adler, the great Viennese physician and psychologist, advised his students in psychiatry that when dealing with their patients, they should "trust only movement." Adler taught them that attention given to their patients' rhetoric or good intentions would only prove distracting to their efforts to help them perform life's tasks. It was the doctor's job to show them what purpose the patient served by choosing certain evasive actions over constructive ones.

Corporate behavior can be looked at in the same way. Despite rhetoric and good intentions, corporations often engage in actions that serve purposes far afield from their stated goals. Those actions show their true goals, whether they themselves recognize them or not. Top managements make a mistake by sending out conflicting signals to their people, as they do when they say by their words that an activity is critical, but by their movement that it isn't. Such behavior gives rise to cynicism and assures nonperformance.

Any observer who wants to understand a corporation, of course, will listen to its words; but, more importantly, he will watch its feet.

Section IV
What Executives Are Like

To know one's self is, above all, to know what one lacks. It is to measure one's self against truth, and not the other way around.

—FLANNERY O'CONNOR

23

The Corporation Executive

Before you can become an executive, you have to have a clear idea of what one is. Where do executives come from? Where are they going? What are their attitudes? What are their doubts? How do they live? What are their families like, and what changes do they face at home? How are they educated? How old are they? When did they start planning their careers? How did they get their start? What career hurdles do female executives face? These are some of the questions you must ask and answer before you can know (1) if you want to become an executive, (2) if your chances for success in the corporate world are good, and (3) what you must do to qualify yourself for that world, if you choose to enter it.

If you find yourself unable to answer many of these questions at this point, be assured you're not alone. Despite the impact of their decisions on our lives, executives of large corporations are shadowy figures to most Americans. Many don't know them, and have at best only vague images of what they should look and act like. Unwittingly, we stereotype them in ways that arouse our suspicions or envy, or both. We conjure up thoughts of men in three-piece gray suits and guess at what they're like. We can't even begin to guess about who they are because their identities are well concealed (though not intentionally) by their corporations. And we're just now getting used to the idea of women occupying lofty positions in the executive suite.

Who Is That Masked Man?

Men and women who are executives make decisions that affect lives and events in a society that barely knows they exist. How many citizens could name five major leaders of corporations today? Even if we throw in Lee Iacocca to make it easier, I'll wager 95 percent of the American population **243** can't name four more. Executives remain masked behind their corporate logos, still creatures to be guessed about and stereotyped by the society in which they function.

I have tried to bring into focus that hazy picture most people have of corporate executives. As you have seen throughout this book, these are highly energetic and motivated individuals. You know they generally share similar values with their corporations, and that the most successful executives identify closely with their companies. But unless you're one yourself, you may know little about the kind of lives they've lived, the personal choices they've made, how those choices were arrived at, or what priorities they were based on.

While we perceive executives as financially motivated and aggressive, we have little concept of the foundation for those motivations. Do these leaders come from prosperous families? Do they marry well-to-do, socially elite wives? And despite their tedious schedules and excessive work hours, do they have happy marriages?

Wanting to learn more about what kinds of people executives are, we got them to tell us about some of their personal choices and backgrounds. The resulting profiles in this and the following chapters not only provide a better understanding of what executives are like, but also make clearer the kind of person corporations hire. If you are in the position of wanting to be hired by a corporation, possessing such information can do nothing but work in your favor. If you aspire to be an executive, this section will show you what successful executives are like and what you must do mentally and physically to prepare to be one.

A General Profile

Corporations are traditional institutions. You only have to look at the makeup of their executives to see this. While executives may have impressive titles and seem to be blessed with superhuman energies, they are just plain folks when it comes to their personal statistics. Examining top executives first, 32 percent are between the ages of thirty-one and forty; 42 percent between forty-one and fifty; 21 percent between fifty-one and sixty. They're very much committed to marriage: 87 percent are married; 5 percent are divorced and remarried; 4 percent are simply divorced; not quite 1 percent are widowed. That leaves only 4 percent who are single (never married). Even the popular belief that executives must be Paul Bunyan types to get ahead goes by the board. More top executives (56 percent) are under six feet in height than over (44 percent). One-fourth weigh 165 pounds or less; three-fourths weigh more. Given their breakdown on height, this latter number does suggest that their diets aren't plain!

Middle managers have most of the same characteristics except that a few more are still single and, as you know well by now, they are younger. Forty percent are between thirty-one and forty years old. They eagerly are anticipating promotions within the next ten to fifteen years of their careers. By the time they are forty they already will be a fairly weeded-out group. The most promising of them already will be launched on impressive careers. While 32 percent of top executives are between the ages of thirty-one and forty, most of them are closer to forty than thirty, and are among the brightest of their peers. Their relatively early promotions into top executive ranks signal promising futures. In contrast, 19 percent of middle managers are between the ages of fifty-one and sixty and have missed their chance. Most will never reach management's top tiers. They are career managers and no longer direct the bulk of their energies toward winning major promotions.

While most executives describe themselves as being of average physical dimensions, such features have little to do with the success they have earned for themselves. Average though they may be in this respect, you will see that in personality characteristics they are anything but average. Through their commitment, energy, discipline, and ability, they have managed to win their place and destiny in society.

Family Educational Background

In 1955, W. Lloyd Warner and James Abegglen published a top-quality study entitled *Big Business Leaders in America.* Their study revealed that executives of large corporations in this country between 1900 and 1950 were *not* predominantly individuals who developed their business acumen at the dinner table or inherited business opportunities from their fathers. Only 18 percent were sons of college graduates; 38 percent were sons of men without a high school diploma.

The big news from Warner and Abegglen centered on the fact that business success seemed to increase for men whose fathers were not executives or owners of large businesses. Indeed, at that point in history, the number of executives who were sons of big business owners had decreased. Opportunity was available to anyone with the ambition to achieve. Said the authors, "Rather than closing in on men of low birth, holding them to the positions into which they were born, our social system continues to make it possible for men from all levels to move into elite positions in commerce and industry."

In 1955 that was a valuable lesson, and one that most Americans could believe in easily in the midst of smooth prosperity. Reacting to that message today, however, you might be inclined to say, "Well, fine . . . but the sons and daughters of business executives from a generation ago by now have gone to college and are today's business executives." Our study shows that this is not true. Today's business executives are much the same kind of pioneering spirits that the last generation's executives were. True, they are more educated than their predecessors: 8 out of 10 top executives and 7 out of 10 middle have college degrees; 6 out of 10 of Warner and Abegglen's executives (surveyed in 1952) had college educations. But a significant majority of contemporary executives achieved their success through independent endeavors. Few of them had the benefit of family contacts through mothers or fathers who were business executives.

Even when executives come from privileged families, this is hardly a guarantee everything goes smoothly for them. An amusing example of this appeared in *The Boston Globe* on November 8, 1981. This issue tells the story of William Osgood Taylor II taking over as chief executive of Affiliated Publications, owner of the *Globe*. He is the fourth member of his family to be head of the enterprise founded by his great-grandfather, General Charles H. Taylor, over a hundred years ago.

This new head of the company had joined the family business earlier than he'd planned, in 1956. As the paper describes it, "He had wanted to go to business school, but the Harvard Graduate School of Business Administration rejected his application and, in his own words, he 'dropped the idea and decided to go to work.' " I'm impressed with Harvard's independence, if not its judgment. The School obviously misjudged an excellent prospective business leader. On the other hand, when you come from the family that has the biggest public voice and clout in Boston, and can't get into Harvard, that's proof enough that connections alone provide no surefire royal road to the top.

More than anything, the personal stories of executives support the Horatio Alger tradition that hard work, determination, and aggression are the major determinants that lead to successful careers. Those who have leaned comfortably on the notion that the majority of successful business leaders today enjoy their status because of privileged access to information, opportunity, or education can kiss that dreamy cop-out good-bye.

The educational levels of the parents of the executives in our study are indicated in Table 28.

Our study shows that opportunity goes to the most determined competitors. Executives had to work hard, sometimes against considerable odds, to get where they are today. Most successful executives are not born elitists, but rather are farsighted, aggressive individuals with the courage to act on their long-range plans and carefully made choices early on in their lives.

Most executives are markedly more educated than either of their parents. Fifty percent top executives and 53 percent middle have mothers with only a high school diploma. The fathers of forty-three percent top executives and 42 percent middle have no more than a high school education. Twenty-three

Table 28
Parents' Highest Level of Education

Mother's Education	TOP EXECUTIVES (%)	MIDDLE MANAGERS (%)
Elementary	23.0	18.2
High School	49.7	52.6
Some college	13.8	15.4
Bachelor's degree	11.0	11.2
Master's	2.4	2.3
L.L.B. or J.D.	0.0	0.2
Doctorate or M.D.	0.2	0.2

Father's Education	TOP EXECUTIVES (%)	MIDDLE MANAGERS (%)
Elementary	25.7	21.6
High School	43.1	42.2
Some college	12.5	17.2
Bachelor's degree	12.2	12.1
Master's	2.9	2.8
L.L.B. or J.D.	1.2	1.2
Doctorate or M.D.	2.4	2.8

percent top executives and 18 percent middle have mothers with only an elementary-school education; 26 percent top and 22 percent middle have fathers with the same educational achievement.

The number of executives with college-educated parents is surprisingly small. Only 11 percent of both level executives have mothers with college degrees. Fourteen percent top executives and 15 percent middle have mothers with some college education, but no degree. Their fathers are rarely more educated than their mothers. Thirteen percent top executives and 17 percent middle have fathers with some college. Twelve percent of both levels have fathers with a college degree.

Family Professional Background

Many executives in Warner and Abegglen's study reported that they were from nonexecutive parents. Some said their fathers worked as laborers, farmers, or clerks. But most of these executives' fathers were white-collar workers. Many executives studied by Warner and Abegglen reported they were motivated toward success more to avoid despairing futures in the types of jobs held by their fathers and/or older brothers. "As a kid, I had the idea of getting out, of getting away from the steel mill," is the way one executive put it.

Some executives described distant relationships with their parents, especially their fathers. "My parents were divorced when I was about sixteen. I never did get along with him [his father]. . . . I generally took advice from my mother. I avoided my father as much as possible."

If today's executives don't share the childhood discontent that some prior executives had, many of them share the same economic and family occupational backgrounds. Most executives today do not come from families in which the mothers or even fathers held corporate executive positions.

Family Members Who Are Executives

	TOP EXECUTIVES (%)	MIDDLE MANAGERS (%)
Mothers who were corporate executives	1.6	1.1
Fathers who were corporate executives	26.0	21.5
Siblings who are corporate executives	20.7	20.6

Only 2 percent top executives and 1 percent middle said their mothers were corporate executives. Of course, that comes as no surprise. But when asked if their fathers were corporate executives, only 26 percent top executives and 22 percent middle said yes. In other words, the majority of these executives were not reared for business.

Neither do they seem to have responded to family pressures encouraging their success. When asked if they have any siblings who hold corporate executive positions, executives again indicated that they do not come from business-oriented families. Only 21 percent top and middle executives say they have siblings holding corporate executive positions.

As was true of Warner and Abegglen's executives, ours show themselves to be a vital, dynamic group of individuals who have been energetic and imaginative in breaking through social boundaries. Their career ambitions were not typical in their families, and perhaps, in many cases, even in their communities. To escape distasteful careers represented by their fathers' lines of work, or simply to enact step-by-step an oft-repeated dream, they invested in greater educations and steered themselves toward professions with which their families were unfamiliar.

You can see that more than anything else, these are individuals who have moved, as Warner and Abegglen put it, "the longest social distances." Their current social and professional positions are remote from and perhaps even unfathomable to their parents and most of their childhood peers. After executives leave the social milieu to which they were born, they routinely enter and leave a multitude of social levels and surroundings until they have achieved the level of success where they finally come to rest.

24

Education of
Executives

From the time Americans first began to shift from agricultural to industrial life patterns, education came to be seen as an essential exercise designed to secure our futures. Even today, few people anticipate college educations for their children primarily for intellectual stimulation, but rather to assure their economic well-being. The valued sheepskin is won, however, only by those who are willing to make the considerable sacrifices necessary to overcome financial hurdles and other obstacles. Such sacrifices cannot be underplayed. They are formidable enough to prevent the majority of Americans from receiving college degrees. As valuable as most Americans have come to see such degrees, only a surprising few are able to earn them. In his compilation of statistics which he calls The *"Average American" Book*, Barry Tarshis maintains, "Overall average educational level throughout the country keeps rising every decade." But he says this after reporting that 50 percent of all Americans who enter college don't finish. A low 19 percent of American men and 11 percent of American women manage to receive degrees.

Of those few who complete a college education, many aim their educated energies toward business careers. By and large, executives are a highly educated group. What's more important, they are living proof of the kind of social mobility and economic advancement that Horatio Alger's stories of aspiration are all about.

In his *Landmarks of Tomorrow* (published in 1957), Peter Drucker asserted: "An abundant and increasing supply of highly educated people has become the absolute prerequisite of social and economic development in our world . . . it is rapidly becoming a condition of national survival." When Drucker discussed the scale of the education explosion in society, he was referring to the increase in the number of people with high school educations. He predicted that the day was near when "practically every working American will be a high school graduate." As a nation, we have come close to that threshold. High school degrees are the norm rather than the exception.

Adults are educated with more specialized and general programs than ever before. But not everyone takes advantage of these forms of education. There can be no question that education has an increasingly valuable place in our society. But only the most motivated of individuals seek such opportunities. When they do, the benefits of that education are generally funneled directly back into the system that inspired it. More than any other institution, the corporation is the direct beneficiary of a highly educated society.

Among executives in our study, highest educational attainment breaks down this way:

	TOP EXECUTIVES (%)	MIDDLE MANAGERS (%)
High school	99.0	98.6
With college degree	81.1	73.0
With some college	14.7	20.4
No college	4.2	6.7

The great majority of executives in our study attended college, and most of them majored in technical or business areas. Eighty-one percent top executives and 73 percent middle graduated from college. Fifteen percent top executives and 20 percent middle attended college, but did not receive degrees. Once again, the absence of absolute rules in the business world is made apparent in that 4 percent top executives and 7 percent middle did not attend college at all.

Types of Degrees

Despite the discouragement college students hear from the business community about earning a bachelor of arts or liberal arts degree, executives themselves were not all trained for business. Thirty-four percent top executives and 31 percent middle say they received a B.A. That is a much lower percentage of executives with B.A. degrees compared to B.S. degrees than in Warner and Abegglen's 1955 study. Today, corporations lean toward more specialized areas and degrees. Fifteen to twenty-five years ago, when most of these executives were completing their educations, most corporations were not as dependent on as highly educated and specialized business executives. General backgrounds were more welcome in corporations. The ranks of such generalists are being thinned now by the infusion of executives hired on the basis of their particular area of study, and by the specialized training which the corporations themselves are giving their young recruits. As I have said, this results in executives who are not properly developed to assume general management responsibilities later on.

Type of College Degree	TOP EXECUTIVES (%)	MIDDLE MANAGERS (%)
B.A.	34.0	31.0
B.S.	61.8	64.5
Two-year degree	4.3	4.5

Though less marked in the past, there never was any question about the preference corporations have for scientific, technical, engineering, or accounting majors as executives. These are majors that ordinarily carry the B.S. distinction. Warner and Abegglen's study contained a randomly selected sample of 505 executives who had graduated from college. These 505 had earned 596 degrees. Of them, 232 had received a B.S. degree; 211 had received a B.A. degree. Sixty-eight others had received specialized degrees: 9 bachelor of business and 59 bachelor of law. Seventy-two had received master's and doctoral degrees. Thirteen weren't classifiable. Our executives completed specialized and graduate training with even greater frequency, and both top and middle executives preferred the bachelor of science over the more general bachelor of arts degree by a margin of about two to one.

It still stands that where there is a will, there is a way. Some of these executives have proven that to be true. Four percent top executives and 5 percent middle have managed to climb to their positions with a two-year Associate of Arts degree. Four percent top executives and 7 percent middle have reached their level of success despite the fact that they did not attend college at all. And an ever so slight, but impressive, 1 percent of both level executives managed to compete successfully without even graduating from high school. They have overcome overwhelming odds.

The lack of formal education of these resourceful executives is likely to affect both their personal relationships with their peers and their management roles with subordinates. Those who have managed to make it to the top ranks especially may be sensitive to the educational differences between themselves and their peers. For some executives, the fact that they don't quite match their peers educationally may cause them to establish closer working relationships with subordinates. They may be more "down to earth" or "folksy" in their management style.

Whatever the working relationship between these executives and their peers and subordinates, the fact that such executives exist is remarkable. Their presence makes clear that while strong educational preferences always have existed in the corporation (and appear to be increasingly the norm), there are no absolute rules which ensure that such-and-such a preparation will spell instant success for an executive or which doom to failure a candidate lacking a college degree.

Advanced Education and Specialization

Many executives conclude that undergraduate training is not enough. Advanced education and specialization is judged by them to increase their competence and advancement potential. Thirty-five percent top executives and 28 percent middle received a degree from a master's program or some other professional university program. About a fifth of top executives and a fourth of middle managers have taken some courses toward a master's but did not complete the degree.

Executives with Master's or Professional Degree

	TOP EXECUTIVES (%)	MIDDLE MANAGERS (%)
With master's degree	35.4	27.8
Nonmatriculating or some courses	22.5	24.3
No master's degree or courses	42.2	48.0

Through continuing education, executives add to their knowledge. Such further education and training enables them to compete more effectively and do their jobs better. Executives receiving advanced education are brought abreast of current developments in their areas of concentration and in business generally. Further, they are better prepared to take on new tasks within their companies.

Still, as valuable as the M.B.A. itself has become in corporate life, it definitely is not the be-all, end-all ingredient that guarantees a successful career. It offers no assurance that corporations will carry you off to their top executive suites. This is true even though some companies have a reputation for snapping up M.B.A. s as they file out the schoolroom door. Keep in mind that many such companies chew them up and spit them out as quickly, too.

Forty-two percent top executives and 48 percent middle received no education at all toward a master's degree. Their success defies the M.B.A. faddishness of many corporations. Their experience and accomplishments won them promotions with more regularity than many M.B.A. executives are destined to realize in their careers.

Individuals intent on a business career who go on for a master's degree are fairly sure about their direction. Today it is increasingly popular to go on for such an advanced degree directly out of undergraduate school. But many executives who get work experience first, then go back to school, will claim this is a more enriching sequence.

Type of Master's or Professional Degree

	TOP EXECUTIVES	MIDDLE MANAGERS
	(%)	(%)
Business	63.5	65.7
Engineering	11.7	8.6
Law	8.8	5.7
Social sciences	3.6	3.8
Other	12.4	16.2

No matter how or in what sequence they earn them, most holders of master's or professional degrees are specialized in their business interests. Far and away the most common type of master's degree earned by ambitious executives is in business. Roughly 65 percent of all executives who earned a master's degree did so in business. It is by earning such a degree, incidentally, that many liberal arts majors have found redemption. A distant second is in engineering. Only 12 percent top executives and 9 percent middle earned them in engineering. It isn't in every company that engineers are likely to rise to top executive positions. But technical degrees are becoming more valuable and necessary in today's business climate. Executives who combine technical backgrounds and the ability to understand broad corporate problems are in an excellent position to rise to the top.

Social sciences have become more appreciated in some companies. The human resources function is an expanding field in most corporations, and can most directly draw upon education received in these fields. However, be forewarned that the social sciences are not an area of concentration that usually places an executive in a position for promotion to the top. They most often lead the person into staff positions. The limitations of advisory roles are well known, and executives most ambitious for general management rarely invest their energies in them. Only 4 percent of both top and middle executives have master's degrees in social sciences.

Areas of Concentration

For executives who received their master's degrees in business or engineering, these areas of concentration generally determined the direction they took within their companies. Many of them were Indians learning to be chiefs while they worked for their degrees. By specializing in management, they hoped to round out their abilities to direct the work efforts of others who were perhaps more specialized than they, but less effective in leadership roles. Thirty-six percent of all executives concentrated on management while getting their master's degrees.

Field of Concentration for Master's or Professional Program

	TOP EXECUTIVES (%)	MIDDLE MANAGERS (%)
Finance	12.8	17.1
Accounting	5.3	6.7
Marketing	7.5	12.4
Organizational behavior	5.3	3.8
Management	36.8	35.2
Others	32.3	24.8

Actually, M.B.A. program curricula are quite similar no matter what the area of concentration. A few electives enable degree recipients to claim themselves more competent in one area or another, but the basic education still has been fairly general and applied to all students. However, concentration in one or another is thought to be more valuable to some corporations than it is to others. The predominant trend in recent years has been for students to seek out that sliver of specialization in the area of finance. As corporations have sought increasingly to maximize profits through sophisticated financial control and strategy, executives eagerly have competed for jobs in corporate finance. Thirteen percent top executives and 17 percent middle concentrated in finance while working toward their master's. In past days, it was marketing that was viewed as the sure road to success. Eight percent top executives and 12 percent middle concentrated on marketing as their master's major. I expect a revival of this specialization.

The corporate world changes constantly. Executives who fail to adapt and change with it grow stale and fall behind. This has not meant, however, that they must seek yet more education. Few executives choose to become so specialized in their functional area that they pursue formal education beyond master's degrees. Twenty-one percent top executives and 17 percent middle have post-master's degrees. Eight percent top executives and 10 percent middle have taken courses toward a post-master's degree. The majority (71 percent top and 73 percent middle) have taken no courses toward post-master's degrees.

Executives Who Attended a Post-Master's Program

	TOP EXECUTIVES	MIDDLE MANAGERS
	(%)	(%)
With post-master's degree	20.6	16.5
Courses toward post-master's degree—no degree received	8.1	10.1
No post-master's courses or degree	71.3	73.4

Of executives with post-master's degrees, 50 percent top executives and 44 percent middle have earned a Ph.D. Eleven percent middle have an M.D. I assume most of these are corporate medical directors. Only in a very few companies, such as those engaged in making pharmaceuticals, is an M.D. likely to rise to a top executive position. Most executives with professional degrees are lawyers. Thirty-six percent top executives and 33 percent middle hold an L.L.B. or J.D. Doctors and lawyers are both in highly specialized fields. This specialization is likely to keep them from ever occupying chief-executive-officer positions within most companies.

Type of Post-Master's Degree

	TOP EXECUTIVES (%)	MIDDLE MANAGERS (%)
Ph.D.	50.0	44.4
M.D.	0.0	11.1
L.L.B. or J.D.	35.7	33.3
Other	14.3	11.1

Prestige Degrees

In Chapter 1, I pointed out that the impact of so-called prestige degrees on a young job candidate's chances for getting hired is overrated. Judging from the distribution of schools where the executives in this study did their academic work, the same can be said for the impact of prestige degrees on executive advancement. This is shown to be true in all three levels of studies: (1) bachelor's, (2) master's or professional, and (3) post-master's. Obviously a degree from a prestige school seldom hurts. All kinds of capable executives have one! However, a person need not consider himself at a disadvantage if he is not in possession of one.

In her book *Making Good,* Jane Adams includes an interview she conducted with George Green, president of New Yorker Magazine, Inc. Green is the ripe old age of forty-two and a graduate of Yale. He offers his view on what being a Yale graduate means in business: "People say the old boy network helps, whether it's Yale or the right clubs or the right connections, but I don't think there's much of a network today among my generation. I think it's a total meritocracy and that a blue tie [a Yale tie] isn't worth a damn if you're no good."

By comparing the executives in this study with those surveyed by Warner and Abegglen in 1952, it is apparent that today's group are more educated. Inexorably, education has become available to more people. This highly educated cross section of America exemplifies the ultimate payout in a capitalistic society. It is a group Peter Drucker described in his *Landmarks of Tomorrow* as "a new class which is neither capitalist nor worker, but

Table 29
School Ratings

	TOP EXECUTIVES	MIDDLE MANAGERS
Bachelor's Studies	(%)	(%)
Ivy League	4.0	4.5
Other prestigious private	20.0	17.6
Prestigious state	33.2	30.8
Other state	21.5	23.3
Other private	19.3	22.3
Other	2.0	1.5
	TOP EXECUTIVES	**MIDDLE MANAGERS**
Master's/Professional Studies	(%)	(%)
Ivy League	8.6	6.4
Other prestigious private	25.0	24.5
Prestigious state	28.6	31.8
Other state	17.9	11.8
Other private	18.6	24.5
Other	1.4	0.9
	TOP EXECUTIVES	**MIDDLE MANAGERS**
Post-Master's Studies	(%)	(%)
Ivy League	14.3	0.0
Other prestigious private	21.4	23.5
Prestigious state	25.0	47.1
Other state	21.4	11.8
Other private	17.9	11.8
Other	0.0	5.9

which is rapidly becoming dominant in all industrially developing countries: the employed middle class of professional managers and professional specialists." These are executives who came largely from ordinary or, in some cases, even deprived social backgrounds. Through their educational achievements they gained access and entry to jobs and professions that eventually will lead to upward mobility in their social position.

25

Early Beginnings

While great shifts in American life patterns have been noted on many fronts, they certainly could not be deduced from any differences in career initiation between older top executives and younger middle managers. For the most part, both began their work careers at about the same ages. Six percent top executives and 4 percent middle first considered a business career between the ages of five and thirteen. Twenty-three percent top executives and 22 percent middle already realized they wanted business careers between fourteen and seventeen years of age. Roughly 44 percent of both top and middle realized they wanted business careers when they were between ages eighteen and twenty-one. Nineteen percent of both levels of management didn't consider entering business as a career until they reached the twenty-two to twenty-five age range.

Age Executives First Considered a Business Career

	TOP EXECUTIVES (%)	MIDDLE MANAGERS (%)
5–13 years	6.0	3.9
14–17 years	23.2	22.3
18–21 years	43.3	44.3
22–25 years	19.0	18.8
26–30 years	5.2	7.4
31–70 years	3.6	4.2

The earlier involvement in business among somewhat greater numbers of top executives can be seen in the ages at which they and middle managers first began to work in corporations. Twelve percent of top executives held their first full-time corporation positions when they were between the ages of seventeen and twenty. Nine percent middle managers did so. Past this age range, top and middle executives even out on when in their young lives they went to work for corporations.

Age Executives First Began a Full-time Corporate Position

	TOP EXECUTIVES	MIDDLE MANAGERS
	(%)	(%)
12–16 years	0.8	0.2
17–20 years	11.6	8.6
21–25 years	55.2	55.9
26–30 years	18.2	19.3
31–40 years	10.3	12.5
41–70 years	3.0	3.9

Level of Education on Entering Business

Most executives enter their business careers with a bachelor's degree. Fifty-four percent top executives and 50 percent middle held a bachelor's degree when they got their first corporate job. That is admirable since many executives' family backgrounds did not facilitate a luxurious college career followed by leisurely entry into the corporate world. Nineteen percent top executives and 24 percent middle held their first corporate jobs while they had only some college credit toward a degree. Thirteen percent top executives and 17 percent middle, in fact, began their first corporate positions with only a high school diploma. Only 10 percent top executives and 8 percent middle held a master's degree or equivalent before they began their first full-time corporate job. Five percent top executives and 2 percent middle held a doctorate before taking their first jobs within a corporation.

	TOP EXECUTIVES	MIDDLE MANAGERS
	(%)	(%)
High School	13.3	16.5
Some college	18.8	23.9
Bachelor's	53.5	50.2
Master's or equivalent	9.6	7.8
Doctorate	4.7	1.6

The above figures suggest that in many ways executives in this study are not terribly different from executives in Warner and Abegglen's sample. While about half of executives at both top and middle management levels were able to receive a full college education before taking their first corporate jobs, a sizable proportion of these corporate leaders had to make extra effort to earn their degrees.

Students Who Worked Full Time

Some executives are likely to have held their first corporate jobs as summer fillers between school years. Others may have been forced to leave school for a time and reenter after holding full-time corporate positions. Some executives simply worked all the way through their bachelor's degree. Just over one-fourth of top and middle executives worked full time while earning degrees. Eleven percent top executives and 12 percent middle worked full time while completing their undergraduate education. Another 7 percent top executives and 4 percent middle worked full time while completing their master's degrees. Only 1 percent of top and middle executives earned a law degree while working full time. Still another 2 percent of top and middle managers worked full time while earning an engineering degree.

After obtaining a bachelor's degree, some executives think it necessary to earn an M.B.A. to enhance their careers. Many of these executives have carried through admirably on this. Some did so at great hardship; 8 percent top executives and 5 percent middle worked full time while earning their M.B.A. s

	TOP EXECUTIVES	MIDDLE MANAGERS
Degree received while working full time	**(%)**	**(%)**
Bachelor's	10.7	12.4
Master's	7.0	3.9
L.L.B. or J.D.	1.0	0.9
Engineering degree	1.7	1.6
M.B.A.	7.6	5.3
Other degree	2.3	2.3

Obviously, fulfilling the requirements to achieve the kind of corporate success they sought wasn't easy for many executives. Many already were possessed of the determination that leads to executive success at early ages. After completing their educations, however, getting themselves placed in a meaningful corporate position where growth and advancement are feasible became the crucial next step. This required strategies beyond the rudimentary educational demands. In this activity, it is likely that executives who received their degrees with substantial work backgrounds already behind them enjoyed considerable advantage over inexperienced graduates.

How They Got Started

Wanting to know how executives got started in their careers, we asked them: "When you took your first full-time job with a corporation, indicate the means by which you were introduced to that company." In answering this question, executives reaffirm that there is no single best way to avail oneself of corporate opportunities. Many of them (25 percent top executives and 19 percent middle) say they got their first jobs through college campus recruiters. Another 22 percent top executives and 21 percent middle say they came to their first jobs through arrangements of a relative or friend. But the overall most successful means used to initiate a career by both level executives (25 percent top executives and 30 percent middle) was contacting the company directly. These executives are testimonials to the truth that there's nothing like a little old-fashioned ingenuity, persistence, and aggressiveness for achieving career goals.

How Executives Got Their First Job

	TOP EXECUTIVES (%)	MIDDLE MANAGERS (%)
Employment agency	11.8	9.7
Executive search consultant	1.2	0.7
Campus recruiter	25.0	19.3
Responded to magazine or newspaper ad	7.9	11.1
Responded to radio or TV ad	0.2	0.4
Friend or relative arranged	22.2	21.3
Contacted company directly	24.8	30.1
Other	7.1	7.5

Resume Readiness

Most top executives feel secure about their futures with their current employers. Only 23 percent report that they have resumes prepared with their current job titles and descriptions indicated. In the main, these are not individuals in an age group or career position to be actively seeking employment elsewhere. Many top executives are beginning to anticipate their retirement, and moving to another company could be risky to their financial security. In most cases, top executives have put in enough time with their corporations to have developed a sense of loyalty to them and to identify with their philosophies. However, I know from my own business that many top executives are likely to prepare such an updated resume in the near future. They may be on shaky ground, or they may be eager to make a better life for themselves in a company offering more of what they seek in their careers.

With less time in harness, middle managers have not developed strong company loyalties. Consequently, they may be more willing to leave good jobs in good companies for what they consider still better opportunity. Youth is on the side of career risk-taking. There is less to lose. Thirty-three percent middle managers say they have resumes prepared that include descriptions of their current job titles and responsibilities. Moreover, even larger numbers of them than of top executives are likely to prepare such a resume in the near future. If they are good at what they do and have established a solid reputation among their coworkers, it is likely that executive recruiters will find them and lead them to the kinds of positions they seek.

26

The Role of Spouses

Look at them smiling
Like they knew one another
And they never would come down

Ten years singing right out loud;
I never looked, was anybody listening?
Then I fell out of a cloud;
Hit the ground and noticed something missing.

Moving through my changes as fast as I can
Trying to bring a balance to me and the man.
—CROSBY, STILLS, AND NASH

Warner and Abegglen concluded in their study that business executives generally marry at or near their social level at birth. Members of the social elite generally marry others of the elite; laborers generally marry other laborers' children. Their study reported the greatest intermixing of economic class among white-collar workers. Our study indicates that little has changed in that regard. As sociologist Peter Berger has said, "The lightning shafts of Cupid fall within rather rigidly defined class lines." Most of our executives come from family backgrounds where parents had minimal education and did not hold business executive positions. These executives, like executives before them, still tend to marry at their own social level. Relatively few of their wives are degreed or hold competitive professional positions. So, like executives of the 1920s and the 1950s, their social rise to higher-paid positions and more powerful, influential roles in their corporations and communities is a task encountered by both the executive and his or her spouse. As executives succeed, they take their spouses with them. Their success is with the help of their spouses or in spite of the lack of it.

No matter what sex the spouse may be, there are likely to be complications and problems in meeting the needs of executives as they attempt to climb their corporate ladders. Warner and Abegglen found that women tend to marry "up and out of their own levels more than the men, but the difference is not great." The psychological problems a woman may encounter in meeting her husband's professional and personal needs can be considerable. Feelings of inferiority and insecurity are inevitable as executive husbands grow in their jobs. Even when executives marry within their same social class, sacrifices demanded of spouses are often heavy. When the spouse is a man, and especially a man with a career of his own, reversals in roles at home and socially can be confusing and difficult to comply with.

Spouse selection can make all the difference in terms of advancement and opportunity for executives. How extensively spouses participate in assisting executives' successes varies in all situations. And as much as the extent of spouse support in advancement varies, so does the *means* of support that is important to each executive.

Borrowing from Warner and Abegglen's analysis, but modifying it somewhat, there are four primary roles available to executive spouses in offering assistance to their mates in their careers. A spouse can be a (1) wife/husband, parent, and homemaker, (2) participant in social affairs and activities, (3) listener/advisor to the executive in his/her career, or (4) sharer of professional interests with executive spouse while developing independent careers of his/her own. A spouse is not limited to any one of these. He or she may become involved in any of them at one time or another or concurrently.

How have spouses changed in thirty or more years? It shouldn't be too hard to guess. Warner and Abegglen's study led them to conclude: "The family-centered woman appears not infrequently, but the wife who is heavily engaged in civic affairs and the social life of the community is most frequent. The wife who is an active and valued consultant in business is rare. The career woman seldom appears."

Reports from our executives describing their spouses' educational and work status show that already much has changed. The family-oriented spouse is still a major part of the lives of most executives, but more spouses work outside their homes. Some even have careers of their own. Last but not least, more of these spouses are not wives, but husbands.

Wives of executives in days past learned that they played significant roles in furthering their husbands' careers. In recent years, husbands of corporate women have learned the same lesson. Generally, these husbands are corporate figures themselves, if not corporate executives. In their cases, a good understanding of the kind of support their executive wives need is more than likely easier to grasp than it may have been for family-oriented wives with no business background. This does not mean, however, that the alteration in roles for husbands of corporate women doesn't take getting used to.

The August 23, 1981, *Los Angeles Times* contained a feature on corporate women and their husbands. They were asked to describe the difficulties and needs of husband support in the wives' careers. Aside from the usual needs for shared responsibilities at home, most women and their husbands agreed that the most valuable assistance their spouses offer is in terms of meeting social responsibilities. One couple said that they alternate cooking and serving responsibilities depending on whose business associates are being entertained. "Of course I'll cook if she's entertaining," one helpful husband said. "If I'm entertaining, she cooks. We change roles naturally." His corporate wife underscored the need for her husband's support and assistance in such entertaining circumstances: "If I have to do the serving, the whole way the men perceive me will go down the drain."

Other women emphasized the need for their husbands to accompany them at corporate social events. "Wives come to these functions, and if you're there by yourself, everyone is uncomfortable. By bringing my husband, I alleviate the fears of some of the wives that I'm trying to get their husband." Women also expressed a concern that if their husbands didn't accompany them at these functions, coworkers and other business associates might wonder why they weren't there. Husbands' support makes the role of women in corporate life a lot easier. With it, women are spared having to, as one woman said, "make difficult decisions they might otherwise have to make, such as putting off a family."

While husbands may cheer for the financial assistance from their wives' corporate careers and may even feel less pressured in their own, they generally experience discomfort of one kind or another by offering the encouragement and support their wives may need. Bill Bendat, dean of counseling at Moorpark College and a licensed marriage and family counselor, says, "Men may have adjustment difficulties . . . role models for so many years have been traditional men who are the heads of their households. The symbols today are still not so liberated. We can see some, but they are not the majority." One husband expressed eagerness in supporting and assisting his wife in her career. But he admitted that his efforts are generally not without some cost to his own pride. "It can be a problem the way that men look at other men who appear to be in a secondary position to the wife."

The fact is that the jolts these men have been experiencing in recent years are of the same nature that many women have experienced for ages. Feeling as if one's being is of no or little consequence is a common—or at least occasional—complaint of executives' spouses, no matter of which sex.

Still, most executives depend on one kind of support or another from their spouses, and more often than not, they get it. Seventy-four percent top executives and 64 percent middle say their spouses always have been supportive of them in their careers. Middle managers, as we might expect after learning that more of their spouses work and have careers of their own, are slightly more independent of spouse support than are top executives. Sixteen percent of top executives and 21 percent middle say their spouses usually supported them in their career ambitions. Only 5 percent top executives and 6 percent middle say their spouses sometimes supported them. Just 3 percent top and 4 percent middle claim never to have received such support.

Middle managers who are getting less active support from their spouses also begrudge its absence a bit less. Top executives place more importance on receiving such support. Sixty-two percent top executives and 56 percent middle assert that support from their spouses has been very important in their career advancement. Twenty-five percent top executives and 28 percent middle say their spouses' support has been somewhat important to their career advancement. A highly independent 10 percent top executives and 13 percent middle say that support from their spouses has been of marginal importance to their success. How today's executives view their spouses' assistance and support in their careers indicates most of all how the roles of spouses have changed in the last thirty years. We learned those views by asking executives, using the four guidelines below, in what ways their spouses have helped their careers along.

Family-Centered Activities
> maintaining a well-run household
> relieving executives of household duties
> keeping children quiet while executives work at home

Social Affairs and Activities
> volunteer work related to the corporation
> dinners, parties, or other similar entertaining of business-related people
> socializing with other executives' spouses

Listener/Advisor
> moral support and encouragement
> willingness to relocate

Career Women
> financial support

Family-Centered Activities

As wives of executives and keepers of the hearth, women play the most traditional of roles. These functions can be fulfilling for many women, and are usually invaluable to their executive husbands. But executive marriages —like all marriages—are stressful for spouses whether they are men or women. Much has been made of the need for husbands to share household activities and chores with their executive and working wives. The greatest source of stress for husbands filling such roles is in weaning themselves of dependency on traditional work roles. However, compared to the countless stories about demeaned housewives, such male adjustments to shared family responsibilities take on less significance.

We often hear complaints from executives' wives concerning their family roles. They say they have put aside their own needs in caring for and feeding their husbands' careers. The physical workload of managing heavy chores around a house where the husband is scarcely present invites many gripes. The most perilous danger in the executive marriage where the wife's main responsibility is family centered is that she will grow apart from her husband, intellectually and emotionally.

The extent of her sense of alienation and how wide the gap becomes between her and her husband depends somewhat on her personality. While no woman enjoys putting her own needs aside to support those of another, many women find ways to compensate for their sacrifices by engaging in other activities as an outlet for their energies and creativity. Under the best possible circumstances, the family-centered woman places primary interest in their children, is supportive of her husband, and generally is adaptive to his career needs.

Warner and Abegglen described women who successfully fulfilled their roles as executive wives. They found that women varied from passive to forceful in their execution of family-related tasks, with satisfactory effects on both their own and their husbands' lives. But how they viewed their partnership with their husbands determined how they approached these roles. For example, a woman with drive and long-range plans for her own future might transfer her desires for achievement to the career of her husband. Such a woman is likely to be a dynamic force in her husband's career development.

Many women in Warner and Abegglen's study were not troubled at the idea of being viewed solely as sex objects. Their study described one wife who "views herself more as a sexual object, and she sees her husband as valuing her more because she is. . . . She tells her friends that not only is a woman's position interesting and satisfactory, but that for a woman who knows how, it is subtle and provides deep satisfaction. She is highly conscious of her female self, for life itself is founded on the basic sexual division." There is no question that today many women (happy homemakers or not) would cringe at that description. Still, the type of woman being described is not necessarily an intellectual invalid. Women who place a lot of value on their husbands' and their own positions and who think their present positions depend on their husbands' success are more often than not quite capable of standing on their own. Such a disposition and such attitudes create life patterns that can only support the achievement of an executive's career goals.

Most executives are very dependent on their spouses' involvement in family activities. The less turmoil executives have to put up with on the home front, the more energy they can focus on their jobs. Of all three family-centered activities, executives in our study valued their spouses' maintaining a well-run household the most. Seventy-six percent top executives and 66 percent middle claim their spouses have been supportive of their careers because of this activity.

Household duties are chores that every executive (male or female) is grateful to escape. Top executives escape more successfully than middle managers. Fifty percent top executives and 29 percent middle say their spouses actively support their careers through relieving them of household duties. True, top executives in any case might, more often than not, make enough in salary to afford a maid or cleaning service. However, as you have seen, younger middle managers are more supportive of their working wives and husbands. And if we can believe the popular press, shared household responsibility is actually getting to be fairly trendy among young executives.

Generally, executives have the traditional American family. Few have more than the appropriate two and a half children, and many are beyond child-rearing years. Twenty-nine percent top executives and 32 percent middle are living in empty nests, or never had children. Some of these middle managers are likely to be a bit older and have been passed up for promotion to senior positions. But just as many are likely to be middle managers who either have put off having children or plan not to have children. Middle managers tend to have more career-oriented spouses. Further, many of these ambitious executives are young. Eleven percent of the middle managers in the sample are twenty-five to thirty years old. Some simply have not yet started their families.

Seventeen percent top executives and 21 percent middle are parents with only one child still living at home. Thirty-three percent top and 27 percent middle have two children at home. The percentages decrease dramatically when we arrive at those executives who have more than three children at home. Sixteen percent top and 14 percent middle have three children still living with them. About 4 percent of both level executives have four children living at home while 1 percent top and 2 percent middle have five.

Children are presumably the responsibility of both parents. But some executives prefer that the bulk of that responsibility be carried out by their spouses. It is no doubt disturbing to social critics and perhaps even to the spouses themselves that 30 percent top executives and 21 percent middle note with appreciation that their spouses "keep the children quiet when they are working at home." Considering the heavy work schedules that executives keep away from home, I have to shake my head at this report. Spouses justifiably could complain, "They're your kids, too!" While a good many executives may be appreciative of their families' needs and of their presence and support, some obviously view their homelife disdainfully. Many spend excessive hours at the office, and travel extensively even when they may not need to, in order to avoid a less than happy home.

One case discussed by Warner and Abegglen outlined such executive discontent with homelife. The two authors conducted many of their interviews in the executives' homes, but on contacting one executive, he pleaded, "Couldn't it be somewhere else?" When the researchers asked, "Isn't she a part of the story?" his answer was, "Definitely not. I believe she would agree with me that the only way she has helped is by doing a good job of raising our three children so that I don't have to take time out to straighten out a bunch of brats." The executive said he spent the average of one night a week home for dinner. He explained that he had managed to keep his homelife completely apart from his business life. "My wife has never met my business associates' wives, and never will, if I can help it! I get a salary almost as much as Eisenhower and she can't even imagine half that!"

This particular man by no means portrays the typical executive. Still, his wife is successful in fulfilling her position as a helpful spouse and seems to her friends to be content with her role. She is described as a "passive, accepting person with few personal resources . . . highly dependent on others to give her life meaning and to shape her goals . . . accepts males on their terms, sees them as strong, controlling and dominating . . . a rather cheerful person who takes things pretty much as they come without letting herself become too upset about problems or people. . . . One of the most notable features of her personality is her lack of anxiety . . . she is not frightened or tense . . . while quickly responsive to people, has little insight into their more basic motivation." Because of a social background that apparently failed to equip this woman for a "full partnership in a success story," and the persistent isolation from the professional life of her husband, he complains, "It would be nice if she knew what to do to help."

This nebbishlike woman, only minimally effective, underscores the effects that a more positive dynamic spouse can have in an executive's career. For such women, adaptability to their husbands' career demands, successes, and upward mobility become almost second nature. And they garner a great deal more self-esteem in the process.

Social Activities

The number of executives who place importance on their spouses' involvement in doing volunteer work related to their corporations is minimal. Only 10 percent top executives and 8 percent middle cite this kind of activity as being valuable to their career advancement. The two most valuable tasks spouses can perform for their ambitious executive partners are (1) participation in dinners, parties, and other activities concerning business-related people and (2) associating and socializing with other executives' spouses.

Social activities are important, but less so for middle managers than for top executives. Many midlevel executives are not in jobs where their spouses need to focus social energies to give them support. In fact, it is conceivable that women executives are more likely to appreciate their spouses' social utility than are male executives. As was shown earlier, women executives who attend corporate social functions alone are more likely than men to fall prey to awkward situations among clients and business contacts.

Top executives place more emphasis on their spouses' ability to assist their careers through social activities. Fifty-four percent top executives as contrasted to 41 percent middle aver that their spouses have helped their careers along by attending or hosting dinners, parties, or other similar entertaining of business-related people. The differences between the two levels of management show that less emphasis will be placed on those activities in the future. However, as the younger middle managers rise in the hierarchy, for the sake of their careers they will need to engage in such activities more than they anticipate at this point.

Spouses' willingness or ability to socialize with other executives' spouses also is viewed as important but with the same distinctions by top and middle executives. Forty-three percent top executives and 34 percent middle say their spouses have boosted their careers in this way. Spouses' diplomacy and awareness of corporate functioning and etiquette are critical when they associate with spouses of other executives. Information shared between such spouses is subject to the defined guidelines of informal communication that is passed in every office. A February 1979 *Management World* article, "The Executive Marriage—in Sickness and in Wealth?" offers a good example of what I mean. It says, "Executives can be 'blacklisted' if their wives confide to other wives their concern over possible relocation." Wives who complain about their circumstances to other spouses may hurt their husbands' chances for promotion.

Listener/Advisor

Warner and Abegglen concluded, "A few women participate directly in helping their husbands solve their business problems . . . they do this by full discussion with him, by understanding his problems." Their study placed limited emphasis on the role of women's understanding and moral support as key factors in helping their husbands achieve success. Contemporary executive spouses act as advisors in much the same way that Warner and Abegglen described. *But they do so in greater numbers.* Moreover, their willingness or failure to offer this kind of support is far more appreciated or missed in today's corporate world. Executives appreciate this kind of support. It is cited as the most effective way that spouses assist their husbands or wives in executive career endeavors. A robust 87 percent top executives and 80 percent middle claim that their spouses assist them in their career advancement by offering moral support and encouragement.

By being supportive and encouraging, spouses reduce their own risks of becoming isolated from their executive mate's office problems and interests. They can prevent the gulf that so often is experienced by spouses who have disengaged themselves from their mates' professional lives.

Willingness to relocate is a trait most executives cherish dearly in their spouses. It also is among the most difficult kinds of assistance that spouses can offer. Whether spouses of executives are women (which they most commonly are) who are trying to establish their own careers or simply to sink roots in a community for their own and their children's sake, relocation can become dislocation. The physical and emotional stress of moving from one part of the country to another a number of times within the first ten or so years of her executive husband's career has left many an executive wife in total emotional disarray.

Promotions—often requiring relocation—are the primary objective of most executives. Consequently, they appreciate it when their spouses are willing to relocate, despite the personal hardships such moves may impose on their family and her work life. For this reason, the *Management World* article asserts, "some husbands and corporations may prefer and even encourage the stay-at-home role for the wife." Seventy percent top executives and 59 percent middle say their spouses have helped them achieve success by being willing to relocate when it was necessary.

Career Women

Spouses with careers may be more empathic. They can be helpful to executives because they understand better the corporate and professional problems their mates encounter on a daily basis. Moreover, most executives are likely to benefit at one time or another in their own careers (usually in their early years) from the financial support their spouses' careers provide. This kind of support is named by a fair number of executives as being a source of great assistance to their own career growth. Middle managers are somewhat more appreciative of such support than are top executives. Fifteen percent top executives and 20 percent middle state their spouses have helped them to grow in their careers by offering financial support.

Many middle managers with spouses who have careers of their own are grateful for their sharing the burden of financial obligations. They know they have a partner in their monetary goals. Middle managers who welcome financial support from spouses with careers of their own are most likely younger than others who prefer more traditional roles for their spouses.

Numerous middle-aged men have confessed considerable anguish in attempting to adjust to their spouses' sudden involvement in careers of their own. A November 9, 1981, article in *The Wall Street Journal* records the reactions of such men upon their wives' return to the work force. Executives report being stunned at the sudden lack of attention they receive from their spouses, now involved in their own jobs. One executive was hurt when he asked for his wife's opinion about a press kit he had spent hours preparing. When she responded that she hadn't made time to look at it, he had one more slight on which to base his resentment of her newly launched real estate career.

Other executives complain that after their wives found satisfying careers, personality characteristics emerged that they had never seen before. "Meticulous housekeepers become more tolerant of sloppiness. Easygoing mothers flare up over the children's balkiness or dawdling." Another executive expressed intimidation by his wife's newfound professional assurance and polish. "She is no longer the never-judging homemaker, but a forceful, critical intelligence." That change in attitude makes even a criticism for forgetting a task difficult to cope with. The executive complains about the "icy feeling of being weighed and found incompetent."

27

The Role of Marriage

Advancement for all executives, whether it is direct or indirect, conscious or subliminal, is affected by their involvement or lack of involvement in the marriage tradition. Especially for men, marriage is an indicator of stability to most corporations. As I pointed out in Chapter 6, most companies are increasingly tolerant of unmarried or divorced status when hiring young executives. Nonetheless, they are more traditionalist when considering single instead of married executives for promotions. For men seeking advancement within their corporations, having taken wedding vows is virtually a must. Most executives who are single, or have been married several times, face career handicaps.

The January 22, 1979, issue of *Industry Week* contains an article entitled "Wedding vows a career must?" In it, Dr. Bill T. Meyer, president of Rohrer, Hibler & Replogle, the highly respected industrial psychology firm, offers sound advice. He warns that for executives with lofty ambitions, the best time to divorce is early in life. The work and corporate functions of executives experiencing divorce early in their careers (for most in their early twenties) are minimally affected. But the higher an executive is on the corporate ladder, the more impact the trauma of divorce is likely to have on his business role.

Some executive recruiters note in the article how frequently the issue of marriage arises in the formulation of hiring and promotion decisions. One of them, Robert Smith, president of Johnson/Smith, Inc., a New York firm, cited a particular case. Responding to a client's suspicions regarding an impressive, intelligent, but single candidate, Smith checked him out with coworkers on his previous job. He discovered that the candidate had a reputation for "popping pills." Through further investigation, he learned these pills were vitamins. After all this reconnaissance, Smith concluded, "There was no evidence of the core issue: homosexuality. Thus, the man was hired. But if he had been homosexual, the outcome would have changed."

Concern for keeping homosexuals out of corporate offices (as you will see documented in Table 39) isn't the only reason that corporations are hesitant to hire more experienced single executives. The higher the position an executive holds, the more likely he is to have client contact and to be involved in social events. One executive interviewed for the *Industry Week* article suggested that single men at corporate social functions are the "odd men out." Most important for corporations preferring marriage for executives is their belief in the benefits of support on the home front. Spouse support is considered a "mental plus." They believe it adds to an executive's stability and enhances his effectiveness on the job.

Marriage for executives is a kind of unspoken expectation and generally is complied with. Many corporations expect their executives to possess personality characteristics that support strong marriages. They look with favor on executives who have the intelligence, stability, and self-confidence to create a positive family situation. For these companies, a successful marriage is indicative of a more balanced life. Ninety-one percent top executives and 84 percent middle are married. Only 4 percent top and 7 percent middle are divorced. Four percent top and 8 percent middle are single. Keep in mind that a good proportion of the latter statistic represents female executives.

Sex Differences

The importance of marriage takes on a different significance for female executives. The stigma of being single doesn't apply to women in the corporate world. Being divorced only enhances a woman's professional image. She is thought of as being more "worldly." In fact, the *Industry Week* article says, "single or divorced women enjoy a plus over married women." These women are more desirable to corporations because of their availability for a lot of travel, and especially relocation, without upsetting a family life or a spouse's executive career.

The importance of marriage and how it varies between the sexes is fascinating. In our study, 94 percent of all executives are male. Eighty-five percent of these men are married, 4 percent are remarried, and 5 percent are divorced. Five percent are single. Among 6 percent of female executives in both levels of management, 53 percent are married, 2 percent are remarried, and 18 percent are divorced. Twenty-eight percent of female executives are single.

These percentages clearly indicate the greater emphasis that corporations place on marriage for male executives than female. Moreover, males show by their behavior they believe strongly that marriage is good for their careers.

Marital Status of Male and Female Executives

FEMALE EXECUTIVES (TOP AND MIDDLE)		MALE EXECUTIVES (TOP AND MIDDLE)	
	(%)		(%)
17 single	27.9	49 single	4.8
32 married	52.5	865 married	85.4
1 remarried	1.6	45 remarried	4.4
11 divorced	18.0	49 divorced	4.8
0 widowed	0.0	5 widowed	0.5

While marital status affects the way executives are judged and evaluated, if only on an informal basis, the kind of marriage they have is even more important to their career growth. Spouses can play key roles in advancement in different ways for different executives.

Shifting Marriage Roles

Whom executives marry reveals a great deal about what they expect from their spouses in terms of support. An executive who marries a man or woman with a high school diploma and domestic interests obviously seeks support in child rearing and keeping a happy and comfortable home. He is not looking for counsel and discussion on his professional problems. An executive who marries a man or woman with an M.B.A. in accounting is seeking a more professional, peerlike relationship with that spouse, but must anticipate complications in family planning and maintaining a workable home front. Things get a little knotty, however, for executives who married seeking a traditional one-breadwinner family situation, but whose spouses have later embarked on their own careers. These shifts can be traumatic for both partners and sometimes even fatal to the marriage. Such marital situations are becoming increasingly common in the homelife of executives today.

It is difficult to determine what kind of marriage is the norm for executives. Media coverage would lead us to think that women are entering corporate executive ranks, leaving family management and child rearing to day-care centers, and expecting moral support for their careers from their husbands. Yet it is apparent that the number of women who enjoy high-ranking corporate executive positions is far from overwhelming. Only 2.5 percent of top executives are women. We read articles all the time that say more and more executive husbands have executive wives. The sheer quantity of such publications suggests that the average middle manager, at least, is a male with a wife rising fast in the corporate world. There is evidence for this in that 8.5 percent of middle managers are women. The phenomenon of two-executive families indeed is on the rise. But the trend is hardly of elephantine proportions. All executives are not married to spouses with M.B.A.'s. In fact, all executives are not even married to spouses with bachelor's degrees.

Ninety-one percent top executives and 84 percent middle managers are married or remarried. Only 30 percent top and 27 percent middle have spouses with a bachelor's degree. Only 4 percent top and 7 percent middle have spouses with a master's degree. Just 1 percent of both levels have spouses with a doctorate. That leaves over 60 percent of all executives who are not married or have spouses with less than a college degree. Roughly 30 percent of top and middle executives have spouses with some college, which leads to the conclusion that their spouses left college for marriage. Only 6 percent top and 10 percent middle say their spouses obtained their degrees after the executive was employed in a corporate position.

While significant shifts in marital traditions are under way, they do not apply yet to a majority of executives.

The younger middle managers report with slightly higher frequency than top executives that they are married to degreed spouses. This supports the notion they share more mutually professional interests with their spouses. Four percent more middle managers than top executives say their spouses finished their education after the executives entered corporate jobs. The natural consequence of higher education among spouses of middle managers is that they are more likely to have working spouses than are top executives. Their spouses are more likely to be attuned to recent social changes.

Among top executives, 21 percent say their spouses work full time, 17 percent part time. Fifteen percent of their spouses do not work, but plan to enter the job market. Almost half (47 percent) of all top executives have spouses who do not work at all, and don't plan to work outside the home at any point in the future. These latter executives and their spouses are traditionalists. They see themselves as the family breadwinners. Even when spouses of such traditionalists do work outside the home, much greater importance is placed by both on the husband's job.

Departure from traditional job roles within the marriage of some older top executives can lead to traumas in their personal and corporate lives. Frequently, they can't imagine the extensive alterations and anxiety they may experience when their spouses are involved in careers of their own. In the November 9, 1981, *The Wall Street Journal* article mentioned in the last chapter, one executive complained, "I kept thinking nothing was going to change when my wife said she was going to resume her career. I thought she'd always be just like before—supportive, adjusting to my needs." The article describes the considerable pain and confusion that a growing number of executives experience as 6.2 million women between the ages of thirty-five and forty-four start new careers or revive old ones.

The majority of executives, both top and middle, still consider their jobs as the most important ones within their family units. Top executives are a little more staunch about the supremacy of their jobs within their families than are middle managers. Seventy-eight percent top executives say their jobs are much more important than those of their spouses. Thirteen percent top executives say their jobs are somewhat more important. Only 8 percent top and 12 percent middle consider the importance of their spouses' jobs on a par with theirs.

Since top executives tend to see themselves as the key breadwinners within their households, they do not place much emphasis on their spouses' jobs in contemplating relocation. Five percent top executives say their spouses' employment situations will very strongly influence their own relocation decisions in the future. Eighteen percent top executives say their spouses' jobs either will strongly or somewhat influence future relocation decisions. Views that they are the primary professional figures within their families, however, lead the majority (77 percent) to say their spouses' jobs will have very little or no influence on their own future relocation decisions.

Middle Management Attitudes

It is evident that the younger middle managers are shifting in attitude from strong traditional roles of executive-breadwinner/spouse-homemaker marriages toward more equal participation in both professional and family-oriented responsibilities. This is in contrast to top executives, who tend to be more comfortable with the more traditional roles.

Middle managers report that more of their spouses share professional lives and responsibilities. Thirty-two percent middle managers (compared to 21 percent top executives) state their spouses hold full-time jobs. Twenty-one percent state their spouses work part time. Only 35 percent middle (compared to 47 percent top) say their spouses do not work and have no plans to enter the job market.

For the most part, middle managers are ambitious for their own careers. Twenty-two percent say their jobs are somewhat more important than those of their spouses. Sixty-four percent consider their jobs much more important than those of their spouses. Yet they make less in salary than top executives. That lower salary alone can make spouse financial assistance an appealing inconvenience. While the number of middle managers who are as supportive of their spouses' jobs as they are of their own rests at a meager 12 percent, they generally are increasingly open to this idea. Being younger and more adaptable to reform, they appear to offer less resistance than do top executives to sharing the professional limelight with their spouses.

At both levels of management it is likely many executives have spouses with current jobs that do not direct them in career paths. Rather, they simply are fulfilling in some way, or are a means of providing extra financial assistance.

Several factors affect an executive's attitude toward how extensively a spouses' employment should affect his own professional decisions. These often come to the fore when relocation is being considered. Salary differences are likely to be major factors in leading executives to place more, as much, or less importance on spouses' careers relative to their own. But concern for spouses' career development also can lead to executives' staying put. Corporations are being forced to deal with these kinds of shifting attitudes among more of their young stars. Demands for relocation are likely to be greater in the case of middle managers, yet they increasingly are resistant to relocation—often because of spouses' career considerations. This is true even though the vast majority of middle managers still view themselves as the primary breadwinners in their families.

The percentage of middle managers who say their spouses' current employment situation is likely to influence their own relocation decisions very strongly is higher than that of top executives, but not by a large margin. Seven percent of middle managers say their spouses' jobs will have such weighty affect on future decisions to relocate. On the other hand, 25 percent of middle managers say their spouses' jobs will strongly or somewhat influence their decisions to relocate. This suggests that shift in attitude I'm talking about. In this, middle managers have views quite different from those of top executives. And whereas 60 percent top executives say such consideration would have no influence on their relocation decisions, only 45 percent middle managers take this position.

Middle managers may feel less competitive in vying for promotions when they are helped financially by their spouses. It is quite possible that, between two married upward-bound executives, family financial goals might be met without either of them ever getting to the top. Younger middle managers also are likely to be more sympathetic to spouses' needs for job fulfilment than some older, more tradition-bound top executives. The effect of this kind of attitudinal change among middle managers poses some problems for corporations. They must be more sympathetic to two-career families. Some companies have begun to address these newly established needs by offering benefit options, leave-time for parental responsibilities, and, in some cases, flexible work schedules.

The desire some middle managers have to moderate their own career ambitions in favor of overall family needs is understandable. Generally, however, this shift in attitude represents a clashing of individual and corporate values. The liberality with which corporations cater to such personal requirements is less critical to executive advancement than is the resourcefulness executives show in working around their family concerns. Corporations may bend with the wind, but when it comes down to final decisions, those who get the plums and promotions are the ones who want them the most and make sacrifices to win them.

Executives can survive very well in the corporate world and still address their two-career family needs. But those who put their careers before anything else are the ones most likely to climb the corporate ladder quickly. Make no mistake about it: Despite what I have said about shifts in attitudes by middle managers, most of them are in this highly aggressive category. For example, along with the 45 percent who say their spouses' employment will have no influence on relocation, throw in 22 percent more who say it will have very little and you'll end up with two out of three young executives who have blood in their eyes when it comes to their careers. Undeniably, executives who care about maintaining well-balanced two-career families more than their own advancement can exist happily within the corporation. But those who seek promotion most aggressively are more likely to end up at the top.

28

Whither Goest, Woman?

Corporations do not put much energy into hiring women just to hire women. While top managements have been forced to recognize the waste of talent they encourage by not insisting on the hiring and promoting of women, they can't be faulted for their unwillingness to hire and train educationally unqualified women. Women who expect much and have little to give in return have rightly become a joke.

Women can organize and reorganize to talk about their inequalities in pay and opportunity all they want. Achievers among women, however, have been quick to discover that organizing and articulating do little beyond heightening awareness. There is no question that awareness regarding the problems that women face needs underscoring among men and women in the business world. But simply stating the fact that women are at a disadvantage doesn't bring them hirings and promotions in major corporations.

There *are* inequalities in corporate communities, along with unfair rules, methods, and biases that work against the achievement of women. There can be no argument about that. But the uncomfortable truth is that there are many unfairnesses in life. Those eager to seek out injustice can find plenty of it in nature—between males and females, if they seek it there, and, of course, between predator and prey.

Malthusian Harshness

Malthus had a similar view that respected the vital but sometimes cruel forces of inconvenient inequality when he proclaimed the wrongfulness of human interference in natural catastrophes of all sorts. The tribal Eskimos conducted a ceremony in which they simply turned out their elderly and infirm into the cold on a night determined as their time to go. In Malthus's view, they'd have been complying with the laws of nature.

The Eskimos' mores blessed their behavior with rectitude, so they suffered no guilt. But to us, they and Malthus propose approaches to life that are unconscionably cold and heartless. I certainly don't advocate hardcore, crusty Malthusian solutions to life's problems. But his views offer food for thought in considering the plight women face in achieving fulfilment in their careers. Disadvantaged individuals, like disadvantaged species, must either come to grips with their obstacles, overcome them, and be victorious, or be quelled by stronger forces. Women are by no means weak as a force. They have proved that constantly through their history of accomplishments, acknowledged and unacknowledged. As corporations come to realize the waste of talent they perpetuate in avoiding or ignoring the contributions of women, they are as perplexed about how to overcome inequalities of history as women are about how to make up for their historical disadvantages and limitations.

Of the executives in our study, 97.5 percent top and 91.5 percent middle are males. Executive positions filled by women in many corporations are scant, to be sure. But only in recent years have women embarked on corporate roles with suitable educational requirements and competitive work histories. In the August 24, 1974, *Saturday Review/World*, Clare Boothe Luce complained drearily, "Today there are no women in the Cabinet, no women in the Senate, no women governors, and only 16 women representatives. Our 4 women ambassadors serving abroad are in Barbados, Zambia, Togo, and Luxembourg." In that article, she cited three areas that had or would contribute to the achievement of greater opportunity for women. According to Luce, (1) the pill had emancipated women from involuntary motherhood, (2) government regulations and enforcement agencies would protect women's rights, and (3) greater availability of education to women would at least approach equalizing women's condition in the working world.

Oddly enough, Luce underestimated the most powerful of those three. About the opportunities for a woman with education to equal any man's, Luce further complained, "But as matters stand, her ambition is understandably dampened by the knowledge that even if she graduates at the top of her class, she will not find it easy to translate her well-earned degree into an upward mobility job."

In evaluating Luce's assessment of women's advantages and disadvantages today, not even ten years later, major flaws in her logic are apparent. First, while no one would deny that the pill has had a significant impact, government regulation has done little to advance women's ability to *succeed* in corporations. Second, ambition that is dampened before a candidate even starts out is not ambition but merely a wish. Finally, since women have begun to join the ranks of well-directed and competitive M.B.A. graduates, they have entered the management forces of corporations with impressive speed. In August 1981, the Labor Department reported that the number of women managers has more than doubled since 1969. The fact that in the makeup of our study only 2.5 percent top executives and 8.5 percent middle are women makes clear that they have not begun yet to reach more senior management jobs in any numbers. But their presence in middle management positions shows women are making steady, if somewhat slow, progress toward assuming corporate leadership positions.

Handicaps definitely exist for aspiring corporate women. Like all handicaps, they only can be overcome effectively by strategic planning and immeasurable determination. There is little question that women are well equipped to deal with managerial responsibilities. With all the juggling and maneuvering that women historically have done just to survive in a man's world, it would be difficult to question their versatility.

Versatility and Growth

Versatility is demonstrated every time a woman has to interrupt her career to facilitate her executive husband's relocation. However, companies increasingly are becoming sensitive to the career needs of spouses when relocating their executives. With ever more frequency, they establish extensive job-search facilities within their own offices to assist spouses in finding adequate job replacements. An article in *The New York Times* on August 30, 1981, listed several companies that now engage aggressively in helping spouses to find jobs at relocation sites. Westinghouse Electric uses the prestige of the corporation itself in assisting spouse job searches. Tony Martin, manager of the company's Career Center, says, "When the companies know these people are part of a major corporation and we can introduce them personally to the personnel director, it means far more than simply coming off the street." When Union Carbide transferred one man from New York City to company headquarters in Danbury, Connecticut, the company provided his spouse with personal referrals and a standing job offer within the corporation if she couldn't find a job. Such assistance is viewed as far more meaningful than previous lip service and sympathy to the needs of relocated spouses.

Some relocation agencies prepare women to change careers when they relocate and jobs within their fields are impossible to find. Flexibility in making such career changes is actually a potential benefit to a woman's career. As unfair and inconvenient as these necessary changes may be, they also demonstrate a woman's adaptability. Learning to focus attention on that versatility eventually can lead to career pluses for her, not to mention the personal enrichment and growth it provides whether appreciated at the moment of inconvenience or not. Most important in preparing women to attempt these changes is obliterating any undertones of resentment that they may express about the relocation. Joie Smith, vice-president of marketing and spouse counseling at Drake-Beam & Associates, career counselors in New York, says of such resentful undercurrents, "That hostility feeds on itself and the individual becomes less marketable."

There is no better example of female versatility in adapting to a new job than in the transition of Beverly Sills, diva, to Beverly Sills, general director, New York City Opera. In her short term as general director, she has managed to cut production costs, departmentalize backstage operations, increase efficiency, and move toward production for cable TV as a means of expanding sources of income. Beverly Sills has moved from being a specialist (and what a specialist!) to a generalist. She has shown she is a true business executive.

The innate capability of women to be executives actually never has been questioned, at least not by anyone with a jot of intelligence. Women's frustrations at their slow advancement are not due entirely to concern for their possessing needed skills. Rather they are caused by their failure to compete effectively for those positions to begin with, and to maintain them and grow within them once they are hired. In the January 12, 1981, *U.S. News & World Report*, noted career counselor Marilyn Moats Kennedy claims, "Both women and minorities tend to be Calvinists. They do not believe in team play, because they have never been part of—or seen themselves as part of—a team." The consequence is that women often fail to observe hidden agendas within their offices, fail to play politics, to inform themselves and use their power, and fail to delegate because "no one can do the job as well as they can." Kennedy is generalizing, of course. What she says does not apply to all women. But her point is well taken and deserves careful attention by any woman executive seeking to improve her performance. The behavior patterns she describes are directly opposite from those which assure survival in the corporate world. And without cooperative teamsmanship, no woman ever can expect to be promoted.

Other Options

Competition is a way of life within corporate corridors. And rising through the ranks is a time-consuming procedure. For example, on average, it takes an executive about twenty-five years to reach the ceiling-level position in his career. Later he may hold other jobs, but they will represent lateral rather than upward movement. Women who don't have a lot of time to achieve their career goals through the tedious succession of corporate promotions have some options available to them. Various springboards increasingly are available to women who are ambitious and sharp enough to take advantage of them.

Management consulting is an area that offers excellent experience to women within a fraction of the time it would take to acquire such knowledge in industry. Through management consultant positions, energetic and bright women increasingly are exposed to a variety of corporate operating styles, corporate problems and solutions, and a sizable mixture of strategic approaches in many industries.

These consulting positions have enabled several women to bypass the slow rise up some corporate ladders. Such positions give them instant visibility. An August 17, 1981, *Corporate Women* article says that after a few years as a management consultant, women are equipped with adept problem-solving skills, an ability to "think like top management does," and a few opportunities that offer the possibility of rapid ascent up the corporate ladder.

Many women still seek to establish their careers in fields that are pretty much dominated by women. "Seventy-eight percent of the Public Relations Student Society of America, a league of campus public relations groups, are women," says a September 11, 1981, article in *The New York Times*. Thirty-eight percent of the Society's membership were women in 1968. But areas that are dominated by women tend to be areas where unequal pay is most common. In a September 2, 1981, article *The Wall Street Journal* claims that "persistent placement of women in certain jobs accounts for much of the earnings gap between men and women." Various studies indicate that men continue to be paid between 40 percent and 50 percent more than women despite the influx of women workers in the job market over the past twenty years.

A Supreme Court decision issued in June 1981 allows women to sue companies for unequal pay and for failure to reevaluate their jobs compared to those of men. But controversy surrounds the comparable-value basis for job reevaluation, and women who bring suit against their companies virtually kill their chances for promotion in that company and perhaps others.

Trade-offs for Women

As with all social reforms, the process of equalizing women's roles in the corporate world has been cumbersome, but progress is apparent. Along with these positive developments come some negative effects in many executive women's lives. Vying for promotions requires women—just as it does men —to face priority trade-offs. For example, more women find that they often have to relocate to achieve promotions.

Matina Horner, president of Radcliffe, underscores this situation in the November 23, 1981, *U.S. News & World Report:* "Today, some women who pursued careers are saying that the price of success is too high. They are beginning to want to have children and deeper relationships. They viewed the career route as the primary source of their hopes and now are questioning that decision."

Horner isn't selling out on the women's movement at all. She's just calling attention to the trade-offs: "Young people today, who are seeking a more balanced life, are questioning the either/or choice—and that is good. It is a mistake to expect to get all one's rewards out of any one kettle of fish." This is indeed a big, big issue for women and causes them a great deal of anguish. What sociologists call "role conflict" is evident in many talented, ambitious women. In 1980, researchers at Stanford's Business School found that among 123 M.B.A. graduates, four times more women than men were experiencing stress.

Big business can and should help deal with this problem. Matina Horner offers some observations that give pause, and she leaves corporations with a challenge that is worth taking up: "Women now account for 51 percent of college graduates. That's a big investment society has made. These women should be able to raise children if they want to. There's a growing concern that it is our well-trained women who have opted not to have children, and that can have long-range consequences that are very important for American society. If a woman chooses to have a family, do not punish her for taking two or three years out from a career to do it; make it possible for her to return to her work."

Women are paving their way in the corporate world with adequate success. But in so doing, they, too, are having to make sacrifices that are characteristic of every executive. As a result, they are as deserving and entitled as are all executives to the rewards that go with those trade-offs.

The vastly enlarged role of women in corporate life is one of the two major changes that has occurred among executives in the thirty years between the Warner and Abegglen study and this one. The family-oriented spouse of thirty years ago was, of course, a wife. While she is still predominant, she is ever less so because many like her have gone outside the home for at least part-time employment of one kind or another, while large numbers of younger women are opting for professional careers, gaining the greater education involved, and postponing having children.

Such sea changes in women's behavior both reflect and contribute to like changes in their attitudes toward themselves, their careers, their lives in general, and in particular the men in their lives. As a result of this, men likewise have undergone change in behavior and attitude and will continue to do so. Whereas the spouse of an executive thirty years ago was automatically a woman, today, a spouse is often a man, even though the man himself is an executive.

Along with changes in male-female work relationships come changes in homemaking, family patterns and child rearing. The old adage holds: change the function and the structure will change; change the structure and the function will change. Our entire society is undergoing shifts in structure and function that are both cause and effect of the altered roles of women.

The second major change among executives, but not nearly so significant as the first, pertains to education. More of today's executives have completed college and post-graduate programs. Further, the educations they choose are more given to "hard" specialized studies than those of the "soft" liberal arts and humanities. Evidence for this is shown in their earning a much greater proportion of B.S. compared to B.A. degrees than a generation ago, along with more of them pursuing post-graduate studies in disciplines directly related to business.

As fascinating as the two broad changes that occurred among executives in the last thirty years is what has remained *unchanged*. The main elements of constancy among executives all cluster around social status and mobility. As was true of their predecessors of thirty years ago, today's executives predominantly are not from highly educated, wealthy, or business families. Today's executives might not say they want to avoid the "despairing futures" of their fathers, but they definitely seek "a better life" than that of their fathers and mothers.

As with the executives in the Warner and Abegglen study, executives in this one tended to marry at or near their own birth level as far as social status is concerned. Given their relatively modest backgrounds, it is as true of these as their generation-earlier counterparts that they have traveled the "longest social distances." Their having leaped over social boundaries demonstrates that where executive achievement is at issue, along with the economic and social rewards that accompany such achievement, the field of opportunity remains wide open.

You might be inclined to wonder where all the sons of businessmen have gone. Since most executives thirty years ago came from nonexecutive families, and that trend continues to the present, you might ask what our nation has done with the children who grew up hearing their fathers discuss business at the dinner table.

Indeed, many of them have gone into business careers. Some have prospered, even exceeding the accomplishments of their fathers. Others have matched them, while still others, not being as "hungry" or able as their forebears, have not done as well. But no matter what their level of achievement, with America enjoying an expanding population, a growing economy, and corporations that are burgeoning with a consequent swelling of management ranks in absolute numbers, executives who are children of executives remain a minority in the overall scheme of things.

Incidentally, these children of executives—made aware early on of the value corporations place on education—are more likely to boost their business careers by preparing for and attending "prestige" undergraduate colleges and universities. Thirty-two percent of the top executives in this study whose fathers were executives attended Ivy League or prestigious private schools. In contrast, 21 percent of top executives whose fathers were not executives attended such schools. Among middle managers, 33 percent whose fathers were executives attended Ivy League and prestigious private schools. Nineteen percent of those whose fathers were not executives attended such schools.

Many offspring of executives, of course, have chosen paths that took them away from corporate life. Some became doctors or educators. Others pursued the arts, while many studied law and joined legal aid services. Some became social workers, clergymen, or museum curators, while others undoubtedly were black sheep who ran off to Europe to live lives of concupiscence, or dropped out in some other way.

This undulating, enriching pattern shows how the corporation continues to function as our central institution for opening up society; for providing socioeconomic opportunity to would-be accomplishers who grow up on the wrong side of the tracks. At the same time, the well-off children whose parents grew up on the wrong side of the tracks are free to contemplate careers and contributions to society apart from overcoming their own economic adversity. It is particularly gratifying to note that today a more rightful share of these children are daughters, and that in a not-too-distant tomorrow a more rightful share of them will be sons and daughters of minority group parents.

Section V
How Executives Succeed

I'm taken by those who celebrate life by making
much of their own. It's a subtle altruism.

—The biographer in *Dubin's Lives*
by BERNARD MALAMUD

29

Women Executives

After one year in a personnel administrative capacity in General Electric's aerospace program, Janice Stockstill was tapped to recruit cryogenic engineers. That was in the early sixties when she didn't know what cryogenics was. She now wonders aloud at her fears. She took the recruiting job not knowing if she'd ever completely understand the functions of a cryogenic engineer. Until this promotion, she resourcefully had been playing her career by ear. A graduate of the University of Southern Mississippi with a B.S. degree in business, she first secured a secretarial job, then an administrative assistant position, before joining General Electric. Those two experiences left her with a strong conviction that she preferred professional work. "I wanted to do what the men were doing," she recalls.

In the early sixties there weren't many groups around to assist women in their job searches for professional status. There weren't even a lot of self-help books around to inform women about their disadvantages or inequities in the corporate community. Without a lot of hoopla and rhetoric about the snarls that confront women in the corporate world, Jan set out to find a job "doing what the men did." The activation manager at GE's aerospace program persuaded Jan it would be to her long-run benefit to take a $150-per-month cut in salary from her job as an administrative assistant to join the company's new program. She believed him and took the job.

Since then, her career has been a series of moves, transfers, and promotions. After a series of human-resources jobs at General Electric, Jan was promoted to the company's New York headquarters. By the time GE decided to relocate its headquarters to Connecticut (less than a dozen years after she joined the company), Jan had built up a great deal of broadening experience. Knowing she now was approaching a management level where her next job would be a key one in influencing the remainder of her career, and that she didn't want to spend the rest of her life in the Northeast, she sought to return home to the Gulf region.

A former boss and friend from GE had a couple of contacts he thought might help her out. After talking to a few people, he managed to have Jan considered for a position at Exxon in Houston. Since taking that first position with Exxon seven years ago, she has earned five promotions with this mammoth company. At GE, she had been identified as a "comer." By taking on the new job at Exxon, she had to learn to apply her abilities and skills to a new industry and prove herself all over again. The move itself provided the kind of increased exposure that spurs an executive's growth. She had moved from a people-intensive industry to a capital-intensive one and had to learn a new set of criteria for decision making.

In her new capacity at Exxon, Jan instituted long-range human-resources programs, concentrated on various executive development programs, conducted labor-relations studies, and articulated numerous company positions on human-resources issues. After a year, she was transferred to Exxon's Baytown, Texas, refinery—the largest refinery in the United States. Acting as department head of compensation and benefits, she began work on various special projects and designed negotiations proposals. "That move was a kind of test," she says. The company was seeking not only to develop her skills further, but also to gauge her abilities and determine her effectiveness and judgment in making independent decisions.

After moving up through another job, Jan was asked to go from Baytown to Exxon, U.S.A., in Houston. For one year she worked there as a corporate secretary—a plum of a job for which one to three executives each year are selected to gain exposure to broad corporate functions and management philosophies. She left that position with a rich new perspective and firsthand knowledge of how Exxon functioned from the top down. Clearly she was being groomed for top executive responsibilities.

That was 1979. Jan then was sent back to the Baytown refinery as employee relations manager, the position she now holds. In that capacity, she was in charge of all human-resources functions, including training, recruitment, and labor relations. She was chief negotiator in dealing with Baytown's four unions, and was a member of the Baytown refinery management committee. On that committee, she gained exposure to a wider array of corporate problems than those occurring in her human-resources department. She reported to the refinery's general manager. As I write this she now is anticipating her sixth promotion into another key human-resources position at Exxon, U.S.A. Jan is not a vice-president, but to hold the significant job she does in America's largest corporation is, at her age (early forties), a remarkable accomplishment. If you were to check the ages of the vice-presidents throughout all the operations of Exxon, you would find most were born during the twenties. She was born in the late thirties.

The manner and circumstances that surround Jan's rise up the corporate ladder are not unique—for women or men. She performed according to standard requirements for any executive hoping to acquire significant advancement within any corporation. Like many women today, she started her career amid confusion and uncertainty about exactly where she was headed. Though she had convictions about wanting to be a professional, she had little insight about which roads might lead most assuredly to success. She compensated for this handicap by taking advice and risks.

Given the opportunity to prove herself, she demonstrated that lack of direction in planning her career was just about the only handicap she had to overcome. She thinks she was just plain lucky in starting her career. Many successful executives are inclined to think they were lucky; that they were in the right place at the right time. But the function of luck in successful career planning is vague and even arguable in many cases. In Jan's case, she clearly set about her career with actions that left relatively little need for luck in the classic sense of the word. She grew and ascended the corporate ladder in ways that are essential to advancement for all executives.

Promoting Women Executives

In Section IV, you learned the makeup of executives in today's corporations. You noticed that for the most part they are males from lower-middle- to upper-class backgrounds. While few of these executives have been women, it is well known that women are entering corporations with increasing frequency. As more of them enter corporate management, they will win promotions in greater proportion than they do today.

Jan Stockstill points out that she felt fortunate in working for bosses who focused more attention on her capabilities and skills than on her gender. While there is little question that discrimination exists in corporations, the climate increasingly yields to advancement for women. The August 10, 1981, *Industry Week* heralds unlimited possibilities for women seeking corporate advancement today. "Path is Clear for Women to Move Up," one of its articles proclaims. The article says this is because of the more pragmatic educations being sought by women—their increasing tendency to study business rather than liberal arts. It also says, "For any young woman interested in attaining executive status, the time has never been better. It is so good that corporate recruiters from all over the country woo them."

Despite such expansive claims that women now are being embraced openly by corporations and aggressively pushed up the corporate ladder, there are many who disagree. They deny such avid interest on the part of corporations. Responses from executives in this study already have shown that corporations put no more emphasis on seeking women to hire than they do on avoiding hiring them. The survival orientation of corporations prompts executives simply to hire the best-qualified and most competitive, able candidates. The same applies to promotion policies.

We asked executives about promotion practices for women in their companies. We sought their reactions to these statements: As contrasted to male executives with equivalent qualifications, female executives in your corporation are likely to:

Advance faster.

Advance at the same rate.

Enter at a higher level.

Need greater sponsorship for promotion.

Have a lower risk of being fired.

Be more successful if they remain single.

Be at a disadvantage if they have children.

Their responses indicate it is the effective meeting of the competitive challenge, and not gender, that leads to promotions. To competent and gifted women in executive ranks, that is a positive position. No capable woman wants to be hired or promoted because she represents a "humanitarian" cause for her corporation.

Advancement for Women

Jan Stockstill is walking evidence of the potential for women to realize advancement in many corporations. While it certainly is true that some companies maintain Neanderthal policies in advancing women to top executive positions, more companies are aware they are wasting talent when they lock out women from key positions. Overall, women are experiencing fewer obstacles in seeking promotions.

For most executives, the chances of being promoted depend a lot on who is evaluating them for promotion. In this matter, women have a slightly more complex issue to deal with than do male executives. When executives rate their companies' practices about promoting women, real attitudes are hard to determine. For example, among middle managers, 63 percent say their companies are eager to promote women to top executive jobs. But only 50 percent say their companies are eager to promote women to middle management positions. This latter figure represents a hurdle for women seeking advancement in some companies. Middle managers first must promote women to middle management jobs before those women can be considered for jobs in top management. While middle managers are expansive in their perceptions about company policy regarding promotion of women to top management, they take a constrictive reading about how their companies want them to act in promoting women to the critical, launching, high-exposure middle management positions.

Conversely, top executives find it easier to envision women in middle management jobs than in top executive positions. Eighty-five percent top executives say their companies are eager to promote women to middle management positions, while only 68 percent claim they support moving women into top executive positions. Everybody agrees that women should be promoted—but somewhere else! Middle managers say, "Let top executives hire them for top executive jobs" (something they know can never happen without women first filling middle management positions). Top executives say, "Let the middle managers promote them to middle management jobs." In reality, the burden of promoting falls most logically to middle managers—who are less confident making unconventional choices. The task women face is persuading aspiring middle managers that they are able to perform splendidly in middle management positions.

Notions that women are recipients of easier promotions than men are widely disputed by executives. Forty percent top executives and 43 percent middle aver that women are not likely to advance faster than men with the same qualifications. In fact, 28 percent top and 29 percent middle say women are not even likely to be promoted at the same rate as their male executive counterparts. The report from 33 percent top and middle that women can be promoted at the same rate as their equally qualified male competitors, however, suggests that slowly opportunities for promotion of women are opening up.

Overwhelmingly, these figures make clear that there are no special considerations being directed toward women seeking executive careers. If women are given little extra consideration for being promoted, they are receiving even less consideration for entering at levels higher than equally qualified men. Fifty-two percent top executives and 54 percent middle say they somewhat or strongly disagree that such elevated entry positions are offered to women. Another one-fourth of both top and middle executives maintain no strong belief (i.e., are neutral) as to whether or not their companies offer higher entry-level positions to women than to men of equal qualifications.

Considering the data showing that women do not receive extra consideration for promotion and hiring, it is obvious that aspiring women will need more sponsorship for succeeding in their careers than do men. Thirty-four percent top executives and 36 percent middle assert that women do need greater sponsorship. One of Jan Stockstill's greatest aids in succeeding at her various jobs throughout her career, and in winning promotion after promotion, was the benefit of mentor relationships with all of her bosses. The mentor relationship can be valuable for any executive in his or her rise to top executive positions. It is through such relationships that learning executives gain the support and guidance that make them wise in the ways of their particular corporate world.

Table 30
Evaluation and Promotion of Female Executives

	TOP EXECUTIVES					
	Strongly Agree	Agree	Neutral	Disagree	Strongly Disagree	Don't Know/ Inapplicable
As contrasted to male executives with equivalent qualifications, female executives in your corporation are likely to:						
Advance faster	2.0	10.0	33.7	36.1	4.3	13.9
Advance at the same rate	1.0	31.6	25.1	26.3	1.8	14.1
Enter at a higher level	0.6	6.1	26.4	47.4	4.5	15.1
Need greater sponsorship for promotion	3.3	31.1	25.2	24.5	1.4	14.5
Have a lower risk of being fired	2.9	30.7	23.9	27.0	2.0	13.5
Be more successful if they remain single	0.6	10.2	30.7	36.0	4.5	18.0
Be at a disadvantage if they have children	0.6	19.0	27.8	31.7	4.1	16.8

Team participation is a significant area where many women seeking success in their corporations fall short. As team members, male executives more routinely and less hesitantly make their contributions to the various projects and functions that surround their jobs than do women. They seem more able to accept criticism without condemning themselves. On the other hand, women often have allowed their professional errors to damage their self-esteem. In her book *Wising Up*, Jo Foxworth says, "Top management is results-oriented and action prone. It expects you to get things done and that means doing a lot. That, in turn, means making mistakes." Acting as

	MIDDLE MANAGERS					
	Strongly Agree	**Agree**	**Neu-tral**	**Dis-agree**	**Strongly Disagree**	**Don't Know/ Inapplicable**
As contrasted to male executives with equi-valent qualifications, female executives in your corporation are likely to:						
Advance faster	0.9	9.0	31.7	37.9	5.5	15.0
Advance at the same rate	1.1	32.0	23.9	25.4	3.4	14.3
Enter at a higher level	0.4	5.5	24.7	46.6	7.8	15.2
Need greater sponsorship for promotion	1.8	33.7	21.3	25.9	1.8	15.5
Have a lower risk of being fired	1.8	24.7	24.6	30.9	2.7	15.4
Be more success-ful if they remain single	0.5	10.2	26.7	37.5	6.0	19.1
Be at a disad-vantage if they have children	0.7	16.4	25.4	34.1	4.9	18.4

male executives would—with a willingness to make mistakes or admit not understanding—is thought to be unpalatable by many women. In failing to tackle a job with the same attitude of risk taking that men do, they systematically, though unwittingly, keep themselves outside the team.

Some corporations maintain different stances on why they have women executives to begin with. Companies that seek to keep their quota of women on staff are less likely to fire women for poor performance. Moreover, you will remember from Chapter 4 that there are paternalistic companies that keep all or most mediocre executives on board simply as a matter of tradition.

It follows then that some companies tend to shelter the female executives within their ranks even more. Thirty-four percent top executives and 27 percent middle say their companies maintain practices whereby women are less likely to be fired than are men with the same qualifications.

There is only a small difference in perception between top and middle level executives regarding firing women, though their relative positions are roughly reversed on each side of this issue. This is borne out by 29 percent top executives and 34 percent middle managers who say they *disagree* with the notion that women stand less chance of getting fired than equally qualified men. Further, a fourth of both levels do not have a strong opinion on what their companies' practices are in this matter.

Marriage and Family

While there are those who say a woman with a family seeking executive advancement is operating with one hand tied behind her back, there are others who say that it doesn't matter if she has a family or not.

Forty-one percent top executives and 44 percent middle disagree with the statement that a woman is likely to be more successful if she remains single. That's a large share of executives who think marital status makes little difference to a woman interested in pursuing her executive career. That notion is supported by the fact that, as I mentioned in Chapter 6, executives typically *claim* marital status is insignificant to an executive's career. Yet almost all of them are married! Umm. Most executives also believe anyone who wants to make it to the top has to know what trade-offs he faces when he gets there. But a sizable number have no idea about how marriage or lack of it can affect a woman's career. Thirty-one percent top and 27 percent middle maintain neutrality in rating the level of aid or hindrance women might experience in being married. Another 18 percent top and 19 percent middle say they don't know what effect marriage has or that the question is not applicable to them.

Jan Stockstill married a couple of years ago. She described to me the likely impact her marriage will have on her career. While her husband is supportive of that career, and understanding of her professional problems, she is sure that being married eventually will bring about a limitation to her growth at Exxon. For example, she says, "I wouldn't be able to take a job at Exxon headquarters in New York. But I've decided that there is plenty of opportunity for me here, and I was willing to make the necessary trade-offs." She finds comfort in her marriage that justifies the trade-offs. "Women need the support that an understanding husband can offer," she suggests. But she is quick to point out she has no children: "I really take my hat off to women who have professional careers and are raising a family at the same time—that's a lot of work."

Unfortunately, all women aren't the TV-ad heroine who can bring home the bacon, fry it, pass out kisses, get the wash on the line, and be at work by five minutes to nine. Women executives are compelled to set priorities for the demands of home and work and gain the support of their families for their careers. If they can be successful at this, their difficulties on the home front will be minimized.

Thirty-six percent top executives and 39 percent middle think women are not necessarily at a disadvantage in getting promoted if they have children. As with male executives, women are expected to leave their family problems at home and perform objectively and professionally on the job. Since working women only recently have begun to crowd corporate offices, the degree of realism in this approach remains to be seen.

Age and Promotion

We asked executives at what ages and to what degree their corporations support promoting women executives. Their responses are summarized in Table 31.

Top executives, more than middle managers, believe their corporations support the promotion of women. For women entering the corporation through traditional channels, the middle management hurdle is a difficult obstacle to overcome. It does most women only minimal good to have the support of top executives when middle managers are the ones who award their subordinates promotions. It is middle managers who are the mentors and advisors to most women vying for higher rungs on the corporate ladder. Before anyone can be promoted by a top executive, he has to move up through middle management ranks.

Among top executives, 18 percent say their corporations offer strong or some support to promoting women between the ages of forty-six and fifty; 25 percent say their corporations offer the same to women between forty-one and forty-five; 35 percent say their companies do so with women between thirty-five and forty. All these numbers are higher than those from middle managers.

Possibly the greatest indicator of corporate practice regarding promotion of female executives, or lack of it, can be seen in the high percentage of both levels of management who persistently report they don't know what their corporate posture is on this issue or that it is not applicable to them. The real message here is that hordes of executives don't think about how much their companies support promoting women because they don't think their

Table 31
Age Preferences for the Promotion of Female Executives

	TOP EXECUTIVES					
	Strong Support	Some Support	Neu-tral	Some Op-position	Strong Op-position	Don't Know/ Inapplicable
In general, how much does your corporation support promoting female executives who are:						
Over 55 years	2.0	6.3	41.9	11.1	5.7	33.0
51–55	2.0	9.3	42.2	11.1	4.0	31.5
46–50	3.4	14.7	43.8	5.3	2.8	30.1
41–45	5.3	20.0	40.6	3.4	1.6	29.1
35–40	9.7	25.3	35.2	1.6	0.6	27.5
Under 35	10.5	24.4	33.5	4.0	0.8	26.9
At any age	8.7	29.6	31.0	5.6	1.4	23.8

	MIDDLE MANAGERS					
	Strong Support	Some Support	Neu-tral	Some Op-position	Strong Op-position	Don't Know/ Inapplicable
Over 55 years	1.6	4.4	34.0	9.9	9.2	40.9
51–55	1.6	5.0	34.9	10.6	7.6	40.2
46–50	2.3	7.6	39.8	8.2	3.9	38.2
41–45	3.2	14.9	37.1	5.7	2.3	36.9
35–40	7.1	23.1	30.2	3.4	1.6	34.5
Under 35	7.6	21.5	30.4	5.7	1.6	33.2
At any age	5.4	21.8	32.7	7.9	1.6	30.7

companies have a solid policy for promotion of females in the first place. The lack of commitment to promoting women can be attributed to attitudes and perceptions of women executives that don't meet the eye readily. It may be that some top executives are supportive in a flippant way about promoting women because they themselves do not deal often with specific decisions and cases concerning the promotion of women. Middle managers may be somewhat threatened by what they perceive as overeagerness by their corporations to promote women. They may fear that their positive performance will be overlooked in favor of those of women who may gain advancement to fill quotas and provide humanistic images of the corporations to the outside world.

30

Attitude: Mainspring to Success

The mark of a successful leader is an attitude of expectancy.
—ARNOLD GLASOW

One of the most important factors leading to Jan Stockstill's success is her attitude. It is the kind that requires she learn from failures and bad experiences. It is one that demands she not direct negative energy into feeling unfairly treated or generating a bad case of the "if onlys." Jan admits there have been times when she felt left out or obstructed, but she glides over the occurrences and persuades me she has mobilized her formidable energies for constructive efforts. In short, she has adopted growth-feeding rather than growth-blocking attitudes.

The choice to direct attention to something that can't be changed usually leads to a chip on one's shoulder. People who bear those chips are likely to get weighed down and become ineffective. In corporations, all the double-dares and defiances in the world won't inspire productive executives to waste time trying to knock that proverbial chip off of the shoulder of a pouting executive. Rather he is left alone to stew in his own juice.

Jan Stockstill elected to ignore the occasional unfair treatment she received throughout her career. Instead, she devoted herself to accomplishment that eventually won recognition and advancement. She mixed it up in corporate politics—the give-and-take of information and the ebb and flow of power and influence—in a forceful but not overbearing fashion. All executives, male or female, must follow the same procedure to overcome occasional career setbacks and missed opportunities.

The value of a good overall attitude is apparent every time a corporation reorganizes its management structure or suffers a cutback. When the economy goes through difficult periods, such situations arise in most corporations more often than many executives care to think about. For reasons of economics, or politics, or personality, many executives are fired from their jobs. Others are passed up for promotions and, if they are not aggressive about their careers, are eventually placed in lifetime middle-management jobs. Numerous individuals find solace for their failures and exclusions by reciting a common list of excuses that serve as decoys from self-awareness. Ultimately, this kind of self-deception only serves to protect failing executives from confronting the real core of their problem, which is within their own personal makeup. While other executives were kept on or promoted, the failing executive cannot confront the fact that he was let go or passed up.

To determine the impact of attitude on career advancement, we asked executives to rate the following characteristics:

Rebounding from adversity.

Overcoming a serious personal problem.

High expectations for your own achievements.

Aggressiveness.

Drive.

Positive thinking.

Optimism.

Perceptiveness about people.

Persuasiveness.

Idealism.

Their responses are tallied in Table 32.

Overcoming Problems

Upward-bound executives frequently are exposed to a wide array of problems and obstacles. Whether these problems are centered on conditions in the corporate, social, economic, or personal sphere, or reside in the personality of the executive, ability to remedy them quickly is imperative for achieving career success.

Adversity arises on the job in various forms and occurs frequently. Executives who spend endless hours hovering over and lamenting the source of problems before getting down to business solving them won't be considered for promotions. Solving problems quickly is the prescribed diet of the successful executive. Time itself is the effective executive's most precious commodity and speedy recovery from adversity is his mark. Eighty-three percent top executives and 79 percent middle claim that ability to rebound from adversity is important to their advancement.

Sometimes the problems that interfere with effective management reside within the executive himself. Executives may be told about their deficiencies in periodic reviews or, more beneficially, by mentors or bosses in informal

Table 32
Career Impact of Attitude

	TOP EXECUTIVES				
	Very Positive	**Somewhat Positive**	**Neutral**	**Somewhat Negative**	**Very Negative**
Rebounding from adversity	33.6	49.4	15.4	0.2	0.2
Overcoming a serious personal problem	6.3	30.2	56.3	2.0	0.2
High expectations for your own achievements	41.7	50.1	7.2	0.8	0.2
Aggressiveness	50.4	45.5	3.5	0.6	0.0
Drive	60.9	37.9	0.8	0.2	0.2
Positive thinking	49.0	46.5	4.1	0.2	0.0
Optimism	39.1	52.3	7.4	1.0	0.0
Perceptiveness about people	49.6	46.5	3.5	0.2	0.0
Persuasiveness	48.0	47.5	4.3	0.2	0.0
Idealism	8.6	41.6	39.3	9.4	0.6

"Don't Know" responses not included.

conversations. If the executive is concerned with broad-based achievement and performance, he or she will take the critique, ponder it carefully, and determine what he or she can do to remedy the problem. If the executive is fragile or of low self-esteem, he or she may not be able to make the best use of such criticisms. Such a person might seek ways to blame his or her critic rather than himself or herself for poor performance. Others may prefer to pout and feel singled out for unfair treatment. An executive who is told that subordinates have complained about not being able to communicate with him can grow by making efforts to increase his collaboration with them. He should do this rather than blaming the subordinates for being too incompetent to understand what he is telling them.

Personality quirks that show themselves in deficient management style, or otherwise contribute to poor performance, comprise one form of personal problem an executive needs to overcome to gain career progress. Another form is the personal problem that presents itself in one's private life. Reverses

	MIDDLE MANAGERS				
	Very Positive	Somewhat Positive	Neutral	Somewhat Negative	Very Negative
Rebounding from adversity	32.1	46.6	18.4	0.9	0.2
Overcoming a serious personal problem	10.8	27.1	52.5	3.0	0.9
High expectations for your own achievements	40.7	48.7	9.2	0.9	0.0
Aggressiveness	48.5	45.1	4.2	1.9	0.0
Drive	58.1	37.7	4.1	0.2	0.0
Positive thinking	50.2	43.2	5.7	0.5	0.0
Optimism	38.5	52.5	8.0	0.4	0.0
Perceptiveness about people	44.5	48.6	6.2	0.7	0.0
Persuasiveness	49.1	44.0	5.5	0.9	0.0
Idealism	10.6	38.7	39.5	9.4	0.7

"Don't Know" responses not included.

that may occur in an executive's life—or in the life of someone close to him—can throw him for a severe loss. Setbacks in health; a death; a terminal illness; a debilitating accident to a child; divorce; alcoholism; depression; suicide. These are difficulties that must be borne by most executives at some time in their lives. They often strike unexpectedly, and must be faced and overcome. Almost 40 percent of all executives believe that being able to overcome a serious personal problem has a positive impact on career progress.

High Expectations

Executives have high expectations for their own achievements. Ninety-two percent top and 89 percent middle believe high expectations for their own achievements have very much or somewhat positive impact on their career successes. This stands to reason. Wise men have known for a long time that if you can change a person's expectations you can change his behavior. However, although we know this, we do not always make proper use of such important wisdom in our daily lives.

Perhaps this is because we have been burned by leaders who have misused —or, at the very least, misunderstood—the powerful tool of inspiration. Unfortunately, inspiration has been used more often than not to manipulate others for self-serving ends rather than for their own fulfilment. The lesson from political life is clear: rash promises and the call to new hope among dispirited people lead to even greater depression and apathy when those promises go unfilled and those hopes are proved unjustified.

However, I think there are deeper reasons for our not being comfortable with the notion that by changing our expectations we can change our behavior. And I think the discomfort stems from knowing that this makes each of us responsible for the outcome of his life. It is always easier to blame others for some personal disappointment or problem rather than to see how our own negative attitude assured its occurrence.

At work, you can see this harmful principle operating daily. For example, a subordinate has an idea with real merit, but he is sure the boss won't like it, so he never presents it. Or even if he does, his presentation is so lacking in verve that the boss is hard pressed to take his attention away from his other duties to give the idea the consideration it deserves.

What purpose is served for the subordinate who has set up his failure with such low expectations and a consequent unenergetic performance? Is it that he can now comfort himself by blaming his "close-minded" boss for prohibiting what surely would have led to a stellar outcome? I think so.

To one extent or another, I believe we all trip ourselves up this way. Without being aware of it, we use low expectations to get ourselves off the hook. By assuming a lack of cooperation on the part of others, we assure their uncooperativeness and our nonparticipation in an activity in which we would be expected to make a contribution. In this round robin, we excuse ourselves from an activity where we question our ability to perform and save face by blaming someone else for thwarting our ambitions. What we hide from ourselves, of course, is our ambition to be the star and our fear that we will never make it.

How does one break this self-limiting cycle? How does one meet a challenge on positive ground? How does one adopt a positive view of what he is, what the circumstances are, and what he can accomplish? In short, how does one raise his expectations? By not being afraid of making a mistake. Courage to risk failure is what leads to success. Self-confidence comes by taking risks where the outcome is no more than the fruition of what you truly believe can be accomplished. And remember, even when you make a mistake, that doesn't mean you are one!

Green Grass, No Moss

Throughout Section I, I pointed out that executives take pride in seeing themselves and their corporations as aggressive entities. It follows that since corporations seek to approach the competition with aggressiveness and drive, aggressive executives will be the most valued. The object of the game is to compete fiercely but optimistically, and with perceptiveness about who your friends and enemies really are.

The terrain covered at fast pace by most executives requires that they have abundant aggressiveness and drive. These are valued traits. Ninety-six percent top executives and 94 percent middle say being aggressive is significant to their career advancement. Likewise, 99 percent top and 96 percent middle say that drive is necessary to keep them propelled toward career success.

Thinking positively inspires coworkers to adopt right attitudes and believe in themselves. It also is an aid in spotting, attracting, and utilizing good talent. Over 90 percent of all executives say they can advance their careers measurably by (1) thinking positively, (2) thinking optimistically, (3) being perceptive, and (4) being persuasive in dealing with their coworkers. While the first three seem fairly self-explanatory, let me devote some discussion to the fourth—persuasiveness—and its relationship to power.

The Power of Persuasion

Greater comfort hath no man than that generated by his shibboleths. And greater currency hath no shibboleth over the past fifteen years than that of *power.* On a sociopolitical level, we have been bombarded by all manner of groups and populations, each, in turn, extolling the virtues of power, what they believe they have coming or, worse, have been denied. On a more individual level, we all give voice to the desire for more control over our lives and destinies. A book that met with great success a few years ago that played to this sentiment was Michael Korda's *Power: How to Get It, How to Use It.*

The comfort-generating shibboleth of power gives it greater payoff in the running—not the winning—of the race. That is, it is greater balm to seek and anticipate the exercise of power than to get it and discover you don't know what or where "it" is. It is taken for granted that great leaders have power, but what great leader does not realize that first of all he is a follower?

Nowhere is this more apparent than in corporate life. Most people would assume that the chief executive of a large company is the epitome of power. He has decision-making authority on a whole range of matters essential to his corporation's well-being. But closer scrutiny will reveal that most of his decisions require expertise, information, and alternatives that are produced by his subordinates; subordinates whose cooperation and respect he must earn if he is to benefit from their best efforts. Further, no matter what his pet projects or personal convictions, he must follow the demands of the marketplace or be prepared to see his product line go the way of buggy whips. And as you have seen, on all major capital commitments, he must secure the approval of his board of directors.

The point I'm leading up to, as you might expect, is that the executive who finds comfort in the goal of absolute power is riding for a fall. He would be better advised to seek solace in the reality of persuasion rather than the illusion of power. In short, he must win people over to his way, rather than try to bludgeon them into submission.

On several occasions I have been asked by a company concerned with its succession at senior levels to conduct a search for a new president. Typically, I am retained by the current president who will step up to chairman upon the completion of the search when the new president is hired. While such assignments constitute the more glamorous side of my business, they are anything but easy.

The reason for this is that among the most qualified candidates I might unearth for the job, many are adamant against leaving the security of their current positions unless the job in question includes their being named chief executive officer. They want to reduce their sense of uncertainty in making a change by being named to the ultimate power position right off the bat. However, this bestowing of the mantle usually is not in the cards until they prove themselves worthy of it in the new company. Consequently, by backing away, these executives miss out on a prize opportunity to achieve what they want in their careers.

Ironically, their sense of security in their current company isn't based on their occupying the ultimate power position, but on their ability to be persuasive in that setting. If they made the same demand for "power" where they are as they do to my client, they would be fired. But if they exercised the same winning ways with my client as they do where they are, they probably would become chief executive before too long. The lesson is obvious: any executive who is to succeed will find he makes far more headway toward success by developing skills of persuasion rather than grasping for the often illusory exercise of power.

Idealism

It can be said that the perennial optimist is somewhat of an idealist. Also let it be said there is a place for idealism in corporations. It is refreshing to learn that half of all executives believe idealism has a positive impact on their careers. While some idealistic people are not quite earthbound, a measure of idealism as provided by its executives can stretch a corporation beyond banal and cynical concerns and pastimes.

31

Personality, Image, and Luck

Whether we realize it or not, we always react positively or negatively to other people when we first meet them. It's a visceral thing. In the executive search business, some of us call this the *ten-second impression*. Before words ever are exchanged, before ideas ever are expressed, people aid or curse themselves by projecting an image. Their personalities then continue to add or detract from what they've already projected to their audience. In the case of the job or promotion interview, these basic impressions can make the hairsbreadth difference between failure and success.

To determine how much executives believe personality and image matters affect their careers in their corporations, we asked them to rate the impact of the following characteristics:

Good looks.

Charm.

Charisma.

Being a cigarette smoker.

Being a cigar smoker.

Being a pipe smoker.

Being fifteen pounds overweight.

Being fifty pounds overweight.

Being a conservative dresser.

Being unusually well-tailored and -dressed.

For males, being five feet ten or taller.

Table 33
Career Impact of Personality and Image

	TOP EXECUTIVES				
	Very Positive	Somewhat Positive	Neutral	Somewhat Negative	Very Negative
Good looks	3.9	40.6	53.1	1.2	0.0
Charm	8.1	59.4	31.1	0.2	0.0
Charisma	18.5	59.6	19.5	1.0	0.0
Being a cigarette smoker	0.0	0.2	66.1	23.5	4.7
Being a cigar smoker	0.0	0.0	65.0	21.6	7.3
Being a pipe smoker	0.0	0.8	68.4	19.1	5.7
Being 15 pounds overweight	0.0	0.0	67.6	25.3	3.5
Being 50 pounds overweight	0.0	0.6	22.1	44.1	29.0
Being a conservative dresser	9.8	60.9	29.1	0.0	0.0
Being unusually well-tailored & -dressed	12.5	51.9	32.9	2.2	0.0
For males, being 5′ 10″ or taller	1.8	26.5	66.6	0.8	0.2

"Don't Know" responses not included.

Good Looks

There are relatively few cases where having good looks can harm any professional endeavor. Except in the case of the extremely attractive female executive who finds herself up against sexual harassment on the job, or the strikingly handsome man who is automatically and unfairly judged to be vain, good looks are a bonus in dealing with people. However, there are two items to consider when weighing the value of good looks in business activities. First, what is or is not good looking is largely a matter of personal taste. Second, the best-looking members of our species can thoroughly nullify their handsomeness with an ugly attitude.

	MIDDLE MANAGERS				
	Very Positive	**Somewhat Positive**	**Neutral**	**Somewhat Negative**	**Very Negative**
Good looks	5.5	41.2	49.0	0.7	0.5
Charm	8.2	60.8	28.0	0.4	0.4
Charisma	20.0	58.8	18.1	0.5	0.2
Being a cigarette smoker	0.0	0.9	68.7	17.9	6.4
Being a cigar smoker	0.0	0.7	62.9	18.6	9.9
Being a pipe smoker	0.0	0.7	68.8	15.8	6.9
Being 15 pounds overweight	0.0	0.7	67.2	23.6	3.7
Being 50 pounds overweight	0.2	0.0	26.3	41.6	26.3
Being a conservative dresser	10.6	56.9	31.4	0.4	0.0
Being unusually well-tailored & -dressed	16.5	52.7	28.2	1.8	0.0
For males, being 5′ 10″ or taller	1.3	25.9	65.5	1.1	1.4

"Don't Know" responses not included.

No one in his right mind is going to consider good looks a handicap. But without all the other qualifications that more directly produce success, attractiveness is simply a useless prop. Forty-one percent of all executives say being good looking is somewhat positive in affecting advancement. However, 53 percent top executives and 49 percent middle maintain neutrality in rating the value of good looks in influencing promotions. These executives are likely reserving their vote until they have a chance to rate a person's other qualifications. Aggressiveness, brilliance, good performance record, willingness to work long, hard hours, and being talented and well trained are characteristics that certainly would be topped off beautifully with good looks. But a good-looking dunce is useless.

Some women may discover that their good looks simply call attention to their gender rather than their work ability. But most women learn to overcome these handicaps through conservative dress, moderate use of makeup, and most of all through a persistent professional attitude in dealing with peers, bosses, subordinates, customers, and other work associates.

Charm and Charisma

More important than good looks in a professional encounter is the ability to demonstrate charm and charisma. In fact, some people believe these two characteristics are enough in themselves to constitute good looks. It isn't odd to find competent professionals in the business world who can impress their contacts with so much charm that they are thought of as good looking, even though basically they are of average attractiveness. And what is more useful to an executive than being able to make people happy to work for him? An executive with charisma has the magic quality that wins people over to his side. He persuades customers that they are lucky to do business with him, subordinates they are honored to work for him, and bosses they are blessed to have him on their team.

Both charm and charisma are rated fairly high by executives as having impact on advancement in their corporations. Sixty-eight percent top executives and 69 percent middle believe that being charming has a positive impact on their careers. But while charm might dazzle them, charisma is what really helps to get things done. Just under 80 percent of all executives say that having charisma is important to career advancement.

Smoking, Diet, Dress, and Height

You will note that no top executives or middle managers consider smoking to be a positive factor in affecting career advancement. The main position of executives toward smoking as a factor in advancement is neutrality. Executives who smoke themselves are, of course, less likely to judge a smoker harshly. Still, there are some executives who make a case against smoking, viewing it as a negative in affecting promotions. Twenty-eight percent top executives and 24 percent middle say that smoking cigarettes can have negative impact on consideration for advancement. Cigar smokers fare slightly worse in this regard. On the other hand, pipes are slightly more tolerated by executives, who are probably less offended by the aromatic tobaccos.

There are many executives who prefer that smoking not take place in their presence, or particularly in their offices. They consider such smoking bad for their health, a pollutant, and rank for their offices. They are likely to consider the violators of their personal code to be possessed of bad judgment and gross manners.

Obviously, no corporation is going to turn down a superb executive or refuse him a promotion because he is a chronic smoker. But if we consider the well-disciplined behavior patterns that many executives impose on themselves, it is not unreasonable to assume that some of the most successful ones are not smokers. To be able to keep up with their demanding schedules and long work hours, they are more compelled to tend carefully to their physical health. Not smoking is for them a symbol of such tending.

Though smoking is viewed as a compulsive habit (such "lack of control" not being altogether flattering), being overweight is more detrimental to an executive's chances for promotion. The more overweight an executive is, the more negative an impact this has on his advancement. Twenty-nine percent top executives say executives fifteen pounds overweight are negatively affected when being considered for a promotion. But 73 percent top executives and 68 percent middle say being fifty pounds overweight is harmful to an executive's gaining advancement. Concern about poor health of an overweight executive is a factor. A greater one, however, is simply the negative value of the overweight image, and the lack of discipline and judgment of an executive who remains overweight given his knowledge of that image.

As much as being well dressed projects positive images of executives, it also projects positive images of their corporations. Make no mistake about it. Deny it and don't conform at your own peril. Clothes, grooming, and tailoring count in affecting executive advancement. Roughly 70 percent of all executives say being conservatively dressed is of positive influence on career advancement in their companies. And for those who manage to be conservatively dressed in fashionable, well-tailored garb, so much the better. Sixty-four percent top executives and 69 percent middle say being dressed in well-tailored clothes has a positive impact on advancement.

While the importance of dress is confirmed, the adoration of height has proved unfounded. Only a fourth of all executives believe that, among males, being five feet ten or taller is important to career advancement.

The Role of Luck

The profiles of successful executives clearly depict the persistent mobility that is an outcome of their professional growth and achievement. Jan Stockstill's managing to combine personal fulfilment and a successful career is an example of the conquest of obstacles that is characteristic of all executive success stories. For now, her story is rare among women, but as they learn to compete with men in corporations, more women will have similar stories to tell.

Actually, whether executives are men or women, or at top or middle management levels, their chances of achieving distinctive success are relatively slim. And when it is grasped, it is not always kind. Probably one of the greatest ironies about success in an executive's career is that the goal the person has chosen as its most identifiable sign is often reached during a period of personal challenge and consternation. It is no accident that the midlife crisis and mid-career crisis tend to occur simultaneously.

At first glance, many observers are inclined to attribute most executive success to a series of lucky breaks. But the kind of luck executives enjoy depends more on their own persistence in pursuing such favorable fortunes. Legions of executives have had opportunities amply presented to them, but because they are not well equipped and bold enough to make a few risky decisions, they turn away and are destined to enjoy only mediocre professional lives. While the fact is that all successful executives have indeed enjoyed their share of luck, luck needs to be understood as a combination of happenstance and the good fortune to be in the right place at the right time with the right qualifications. The most successful executives are adept at being in such places at such times, ready and able to meet the defined requirements. As Disraeli said, "The secret of success in life is for a man to be ready for his opportunity when it comes."

Executives usually have put abundant energy into finding fortunate circumstances, sometimes having been available and searching for years. Attending a professional seminar, a man might meet a future business associate who provides the final and ultimate turning point in his career. That kind of chance meeting can be categorized as lucky. But an aggressive individual who frequently attends seminars and makes it his business to be known and respected in professional circles related to his business is someone who builds the mold for his luck.

Luck in a career is likely to center on an individual's ability to convert a bad experience or bad break into a pivotal event that leads to long-range success. The essential trait for making this happen is tenacity. As with most people, an executive generally starts his career not quite sure where in the corporate scheme of things it is headed. Despite an uncertain destination, most executives know the kind of business in which they want to toil, and the kind of success for which they are aiming. For the rest, they try to make their strengths productive and strive to be bold when opportunity inevitably presents itself.

More than anything else, career success depends on an executive's making the right choices at the right times. And that choice making is probably the biggest element of what gets called "luck" by envious onlookers.

A November 16, 1981, *Fortune* article, "Luck and Careers," describes several kinds of luck in executive career success that are more reflective of tenacity and unique choice-making ability than out-and-out luck. In the article, several executives describe what they perceive as chance and lucky breaks that directly or indirectly have led them to their current career success. These accounts are mainly for public consumption. After all, who's going to say in a national publication that he made his breaks?

Would you consider the outspoken Felix Rohatyn a modest man? He is chairman of New York City's Municipal Assistance Corporation, director of several large companies, and a partner of Lazard Frères, a top investment bank. In the article, he recalls his first meeting with his subsequent mentor, André Meyer. Meyer, who was his boss for many years, mistook Rohatyn's presence in LF's office one summer night for dedication. Actually Rohatyn was simply killing time while waiting to meet a date—thinking it silly to go all the way home and come back into town. Rohatyn eventually was persuaded by Meyer to join the firm permanently. His rich mentor relationship with Meyer, one which he feels might have been "based on a misunderstanding," is one of the kind many executives report to be significantly responsible for their career success. But in truth, this story tells us more about Rohatyn than it does about luck.

Pluck More than Luck?

Jan Stockstill is convinced that a good portion of her success is attributable to luck—"being in the right place at the right time." But common sense dictates it is not likely she aggressively was seeking to change professions at just the right time. Her thoughts were that the climate in her newly chosen industry would be beneficial to her and facilitate her growth. Aerospace was a new industry then, and Jan believes being in on the ground floor of a new program gave her an unusual opportunity to learn. Yet a lot of other people worked with her on that ground floor. All of those people have not realized the success she can claim today. While there's no question luck is a factor in success for many executives, it seldom comes to those who sit back and wait for it.

In order to gain clearer perspective on the role of luck in most executives' careers, we asked them their beliefs on how the following activities affect their advancement:

Planning your career carefully.

Having a lot of "contacts" in your industry.

Good luck.

Loyalty.

Accepting a job with another company, then returning to your company.

Changing companies prior to joining your corporation.

Being with a small company prior to joining your corporation.

Accepting a job relocation to another city with your company.

Their responses appear in Table 34.

Planning Your Good Luck

If you elect to set out on a long-range career as an executive, it is likely you will be told by at least one advice giver that you have to have a strategy. Even if you don't know exactly where you are headed, as is often the case with new projects that lead to unknown ends, you must devise a well-thought-out plan that will keep you on a general course in accordance with your main goal.

Executives plan their careers carefully. Fifty-six percent top executives and 61 percent middle believe developing a strategy to guide them through their careers is of very or somewhat positive benefit to their advancement. Planning your career carefully entails everything from obtaining the proper specialized education to studying carefully the companies for which you might go to work.

Contacts

After carefully devising a plan that leads to successful employment in a company well suited to his or her values and tastes, an executive begins to make contacts. Most contacts are not planned. Ordinarily, they grow out of impressive job performance inside and outside of one's company. The *Fortune* article on luck tells of Consolidated Foods founder Nate Cummings's "chance meeting 40 years ago in a railroad car" with the fabled Henry Crown. As "luck" would have it, Cummings was en route to Chicago from Baltimore in the hopes of acquiring the large food company Sprague Warner & Company. Crown was so impressed with his ability and lively conversation that he offered to approach his close friend, Colonel Sprague, in Cummings's interest. Would Cummings have been successful in making the acquisition had Crown not interceded on his behalf? No one can answer that. Cummings himself finds the question "damn interesting" today. But it needs to be kept in mind, whatever the answer might be, that Henry

Crown is a hard man to impress. He doesn't make such intercessions for his health.

No matter how young or junior, as soon as a would-be executive joins his first company, contacts begin to unfold from his work efforts. Some of those contacts grow to be influential. Executives who worked effectively with former peers, who convinced former peers and bosses that they were capable and skilled, established valuable contacts—whether these past bosses and peers attained influential stature or not. Through word of mouth, referrals, and valuable recommendations, executives accumulate contacts of varying degrees of influence. Such well-formed contacts are among the most-cited factors in success among executives. Seventy percent top and 73 percent middle say that establishing good contacts is positive and influential in helping them gain career advancement. To be without them leaves an executive feeling bereft of support and sponsors, adrift in treacherous seas.

As for luck, it already has been established that many careers are influenced by an occasional lucky break or well-timed happenstance. But controlling luck is a skill many executives have cultivated. Good executives anticipate that the worst that can happen on a project well may occur. In effect, they are always prepared. So being, they can do the most with seemingly unexpected occurrences and breaks, good or bad. Good luck itself is seen by over half of all executives as having no appreciable effect on their careers.

Changing Jobs

Changing jobs and companies is a fact of life in most executives' career development. This has not always been as true as it is today. A May 4, 1981, *Fortune* article, "Job Hopping to the Top," claims that of the chief executives at the "Fortune 500" companies, only 40 percent, or 192 executives, have spent their entire careers at one company. "At some time in their careers, 145 have worked at another 500 company," the article asserts, "and eight have job-hopped between four or more of the largest U.S. industrials." One executive officer reports that he managed to get considerable diversity by job hopping through six corporations. Edward Hennessey, fifty-four, chief executive of Allied Corporation, learned "acquisitions at Textron and Lear Siegler, financial controls at ITT and Colgate-Palmolive, marketing at Heublein, and operating experience at United Technologies." His broad range of expertise offers rare justification for weaving in and out of companies. And it must be borne in mind this weaving occurred over a period of twenty-seven years. This is far different from the hypothetical executive of Chapter 8 who had five jobs in ten years. Such an executive is given bad

Table 34

Career Impact of Luck and Other Factors

	TOP EXECUTIVES				
	Very Positive	Somewhat Positive	Neutral	Somewhat Negative	Very Negative
Planning your career carefully	9.2	47.2	40.1	1.6	0.0
Having a lot of "contacts" in your industry	14.9	55.2	28.3	0.8	0.0
Good luck	7.8	32.7	54.0	1.6	1.0
Loyalty	49.0	43.5	6.7	0.6	0.0
Accepting a job with another company, then returning to your company	1.6	7.1	37.7	34.7	13.0
Changing companies prior to joining your corporation	1.6	9.3	66.7	14.3	1.4
Being with a small company prior to joining your corporation	1.6	8.3	79.4	3.4	0.6
Accepting a job relocation to another city with your company	19.3	51.4	22.6	1.0	0.8

"Don't Know" responses not included.

marks because it is likely he was fired from some of those jobs, while his career itself displays little, if any, advancement.

Another factor in job hopping is mergers and acquisitions. As they continue to increase among corporations, resulting in increasing executive dislocation, more and more executives are forced to move from one company to another. But as I implied in my comments about Hennessey, the trick in doing so is to assure themselves of professional growth and timely advancement.

	MIDDLE MANAGERS				
	Very Positive	**Somewhat Positive**	**Neutral**	**Somewhat Negative**	**Very Negative**
Planning your career carefully	12.3	48.8	35.1	1.6	0.0
Having a lot of "contacts" in your industry	17.8	55.3	23.1	0.9	0.4
Good luck	5.7	31.3	54.8	2.7	3.6
Loyalty	47.8	44.6	7.3	0.2	0.0
Accepting a job with another company, then returning to your company	1.6	8.4	35.8	30.2	14.3
Changing companies prior to joining your corporation	1.2	9.1	66.2	12.3	2.0
Being with a small company prior to joining your corporation	2.8	10.8	75.2	3.9	0.9
Accepting a job relocation to another city with your company	21.8	40.8	28.3	1.1	0.7

"Don't Know" responses not included.

Sequential Loyalty

Job hopping has not negated the fact that loyalty is a valued characteristic in most corporations, even though it is harder to come by than in times past. This is borne out by executives who leave their companies for more promising positions with others, become disillusioned, and then return to their former employers. Some companies have policies that won't allow such a practice. Nonetheless, those executives who leave and then come back are the ones most likely to damage their chances for subsequent promotion. Forty-eight percent top executives and 45 percent middle say such departure and return has some or very much negative impact on advancement opportunities of executives who do it. The philosophy of corporations regarding these movements goes something like, "If you left us, you can't have loved us." While the increasing incidence of shifting from one job to another has encouraged companies to broaden their hearts and minds toward departing executives, companies still tend to scorn betrayers. For the most part, executives realize this. They develop loyalties and share a sense of identity with their corporations. Whether they have ever left a company or not, they proclaim loyalty to their current one. Ninety-three percent top executives and 92 percent middle believe that being loyal to their organizations helps their chances for advancement somewhat or very much.

In accordance with the frequent job hopping of many executives, little importance is placed on mobility as a negative factor in career growth. Only 16 percent top executives and 14 percent middle think that changing jobs before joining their companies has a negative impact on an executive's advancement potential.

Small Company Experience

Executives who have worked for smaller companies, where they most likely have gained broad experience and valuable management training, receive little extra credence from large corporations. Small companies are the cradle of business. They are places where executives can learn what the "whole" of running a business is all about. Small companies provide executives with broader frames of reference for understanding the entire business spectrum, and are preferable training grounds to overly specialized, large, bureaucratic corporate training methods. Yet most corporations fail to appreciate the benefits of small-business background in an executive's portfolio. Only 10 percent top executives and 14 percent middle say working at a small company before joining their organizations provides positive impact on an executive's advancement potential.

Relocation

You already know that no matter what previous experience an executive has managed to get, no matter how many companies he's been in and out of, he most often can earn advancement through submitting to the demanding sacrifices of relocation. Sixty-three percent top executives and 63 percent middle say being willing to relocate to a job in another city with their company has a positive impact on their career advancement potential.

The evidence is in. The reports from executives make it evident that they consider themselves lucky up to a point in establishing and directing their careers. But by performing well and sacrificing through relocation and hard work, they have managed to control their luck, or in many cases, adapt to bad luck in such a way that they ultimately turn it to their advantage.

32

Management Style, Competition, and Brilliance

The truly ambitious are always as busy on the landings as they
are breathless on the stairs.
—LOUIS KRONENBERGER

Executives who have managed to earn promotion after promotion do not
necessarily share any particular style of management. There are aggressive,
demanding, almost tyrannical executives in the same corporations that house
seemingly passive, easygoing, supportive ones. Management style is a reflection of an executive's own personality and philosophy of effectiveness combined with his interpretation of his corporation's values and objectives. It is
the corporation's challenge to transform its executives' random, varied personalities with their diverse backgrounds and dreams into a body with
sensitivity and awareness of corporate purpose.

Those executives most effective in furthering corporate objectives enjoy
the most success in their companies. Since profit is the main objective of all
corporations, it is the *style* of management in achieving objectives—rather
than the objectives themselves—that varies markedly among corporations
and their executives. But although style can and does vary, any executive
who seeks advancement has to be effective. In his book *The Effective Executive*, Peter Drucker defines effectiveness as the specific function of executives. He sees this function as the line between success and failure for any
executive and, consequently, his corporation. "As executives become effective," he claims, "they raise the performance level of the whole organization." One of Drucker's main points throughout his book is that all executives have to learn to be effective. They can and must acquire the habit of
being effective.

Most crucial to an executive's performing well is knowing how to use his
time well, knowing what is and is not important, addressing what's important and forgetting the rest, and finally, getting results. How executives
accomplish all this is a matter of combining proper style with good timing,
good judgment, and corporate values. In other words, by doing the right
things at the right times in the right ways. This is what constitutes an
324 effective style.

To determine the importance of certain elements of management style, we asked executives to rate the impact of the following functions on career advancement in their corporations:

Managing time well.

Knowing how to set priorities and stick with them.

Being single-minded on a project.

Concentrating on results rather than work.

Shaking things up.

Good judgment.

Being a team player.

Understanding a corporate balance sheet.

Taking financial risks.

Punctuality.

Adhering to deadlines.

Honesty.

Their responses, shown in Table 35, indicate that most of these functions are critical to their success.

Managing Time

You already have seen that executives are pressured with long working hours and strenuous work schedules. No individual can be a good executive if he does not know how to make the best use of his time. Managing time well requires a determined effort to account for every minute spent. Executives who have a habit of wasting a minute here and a minute there will find that within a week's time they have squandered a considerable amount of this resource on someone else's job or a task unimportant to their function. In addressing priorities, executives who manage to dispose of their time in large chunks are the most effective time managers. Working a half hour on one project, then a half on another throughout the day usually doesn't result in much getting done. People who work in this fashion spend more time warming up than accomplishing something substantial.

Drucker says the most effective executives make a periodic recording of where their time goes. They take time out to analyze where their time has gone and how effectively it has been used. Managing time is an essential function of an executive. Ninety-three percent of all executives believe the ability to manage time effectively is instrumental to career success. Of

Table 35
Career Impact of Management Style

	TOP EXECUTIVES				
	Very Positive	**Somewhat Positive**	**Neutral**	**Somewhat Negative**	**Very Negative**
Managing time well	36.1	56.6	6.5	0.6	0.0
Knowing how to set priorities and stick with them	58.1	39.5	2.2	0.2	0.0
Being single-minded on a project	1.4	19.6	29.2	41.0	7.5
Concentrating on results rather than work	39.9	46.6	11.5	1.8	0.0
Shaking things up	4.1	30.8	44.0	17.3	2.4
Good judgment	62.1	36.7	1.3	0.0	0.0
Being a team player	32.8	61.3	5.3	0.4	0.0
Understanding a corporate balance sheet	26.6	57.5	14.6	0.8	0.0
Taking financial risks	2.4	28.0	33.5	28.0	6.1
Punctuality	35.1	55.7	9.0	0.2	0.0
Adhering to deadlines	38.7	57.0	4.1	0.2	0.0
Honesty	75.2	23.0	1.6	0.2	0.0

"Don't Know" responses not included.

course, just because they know how important it is to cultivate the art of time management, that doesn't mean they practice their beliefs. For example, I called ten executives I know and asked them in what ways they misuse their time. All of them are successful. All but one is a vice-president, and that one is president of his company. Here are their replies:

"I convene too many meetings with subordinates on problems where only I can make the decision."

"I spend time on things that are easy to decide and often avoid the tough ones;

	MIDDLE MANAGERS				
	Very Positive	**Somewhat Positive**	**Neutral**	**Somewhat Negative**	**Very Negative**
Managing time well	41.5	51.1	7.3	0.2	0.0
Knowing how to set priorities and stick with them	58.4	37.3	3.7	0.4	0.2
Being single-minded on a project	2.1	12.5	32.0	40.8	9.8
Concentrating on results rather than work	34.0	47.3	14.4	1.8	0.7
Shaking things up	4.3	27.3	41.4	22.3	2.9
Good judgment	57.0	40.0	2.8	0.0	0.0
Being a team player	36.0	54.3	8.0	1.4	0.0
Understanding a corporate balance sheet	19.2	54.4	23.1	0.3	0.0
Taking financial risks	1.4	16.5	37.3	29.0	9.7
Punctuality	40.4	49.7	9.0	0.5	0.0
Adhering to deadlines	45.0	48.0	5.5	0.7	0.0
Honesty	64.7	30.7	3.9	0.4	0.0

"Don't Know" responses not included.

on things that interest me the most, rather than on what's best for the company. I should also cut people off quicker. I worry about their feelings and spend too much time with them."

"I 'big picture' a lot, but I'm not sure that's all it's cracked up to be. I lack hustle."

"It's lonely to sit up on top and be creative. I'm drawn by my deficiencies to relive my earlier successes when being a man of action—a decision maker—got me where I am. But my job is to deal with overall structure and other problems that don't have fast or easy solutions. I avoid these and meddle where I don't belong."

"First thing in the morning, I ask my secretary for my mail, coffee, and *The Wall Street Journal*. It's a bad habit. I don't get off to a running start."

"By treating my in-box as if every piece of paper in it is equal. I rarely ask myself what's the most important thing. When I do, I sure cut out a lot of garbage."

"I set up too many face-to-face meetings that require travel when the face-to-face meeting isn't really required in the first place."

"By not being tough enough with people and telling them, 'That's gonna have to wait.' "

"I agree to too many appointments when I'm interested at the time. Later, I begrudge them and often cancel, wasting everybody's time."

"I spend too much time talking to my people about things not specifically related to what needs to be done now."

Setting Priorities

One of the primary arts in time management is learning how to avoid spreading oneself out too much. This means determining priorities over posteriorities. In setting priorities, executives restrict their decision making to the most important matters before them. While deciding what is important and what isn't may sound ridiculously easy to a lot of people, for executives choosing what to address and what to discard it often is difficult, confusing, and in some cases demands considerable courage.

Because what's important to one person is not always important to another, executives take considerable risk in posteriorizing some projects. They are sure to face criticism eventually from some peers or even superiors for their choices. In setting posteriorities, executives elect not to postpone, but to abandon certain projects. Most executives realize that old projects become stale, and that it is rarely a good idea to go back over a cold trail. Drucker maintains that in setting posteriorities, executives use "not intelligent analysis, but courage." That is because in putting any project on the back burner, executives are damning its completion to oblivion. A merger that might have been a good idea two years ago (but wasn't investigated because of other more important projects) could be harmful to a company in later years under different, less advantageous economic conditions.

Doing something today that affects the future rather than attempting to remedy the past is typical of the priority setting of effective executives. They pride themselves on being positive thinkers, optimists, and innovators in management style. They concentrate on opportunities rather than problems in setting priorities. They don't elect to do merely what their peers and superiors are doing. They take initiative in finding new areas worthy of their energies. They address development not only of new products, but of new techniques and technologies. Such executives are risk takers. They don't hide behind the boundaries of conformity and security. They make choices that affect the future by setting high goals for themselves that they believe in. Obviously, executives who act this way in setting their priorities do not take the safe, easy road to success. They are not "yes" men, even though they act well within the role of cooperative team members.

Whether executives set lofty priorities or not, they all are compelled to narrow the lists of projects which they will address. And once they have decided what to concentrate on and what to put off, they stick to their decisions. Ninety-eight percent top executives and 96 percent middle assert that the ability to set priorities and stick to them has much or somewhat positive impact on their advancement opportunities.

Single-Mindedness

After executives set their priorities, they are once again forced to determine how they should divide their time among them. Some executives do not like to spread themselves too thinly by addressing several projects at once. But few executives have the luxury of being able to concentrate solely on one project. Executives who can direct their efforts to only one project at the same time are of minimal value to their corporations, no matter what excellence their final results reflect. They are not delegating their work effectively enough. They are putting too much energy into routine performance and not enough into decision making; addressing technique rather than making impact.

The most compelling example of single-mindedness in all of literature is Captain Ahab. No more commitment and tenacity to a task could be shown by anyone than is apparent in his words to his crew of the ill-fated *Pequod*: "Stand round me, men. Ye see an old man cut down to the stump; leaning on a shivered lance; propped up on a lonely foot. 'Tis Ahab—his body's part; but Ahab's soul's a centipede, that moves upon a hundred legs." Yet despite his focus and determination, Ahab's mission proved disastrous for him and his crew alike.

Only 21 percent top executives and 15 percent middle believe being single-minded on a project is beneficial to their careers. Roughly 30 percent of both level executives say such limited focus of attention is neutral in affecting advancement. But half of all executives say limiting an executive's attention to one project at a time is ineffective and will have negative impact on achieving success and advancement in the long run.

Results Rather than Work

Ultimately, the name of the game for successful executives is getting results. That is what work is for. By directing his attention to results rather than work, an executive maximizes his opportunities for success. Doing so is a basic premise of any successful competition. If a jogger determines to run three miles tomorrow, rather than the usual two he has been striving for over the last year, he is making progress, but it is slow. His slow progress is mostly attributable to his lack of a goal. But the jogger who wakes up one day and decides that within a year's time he will be a runner—putting in high daily mileage and fast speed—is sure to see more progress because he knows from the beginning what he is working for. His goals are determining his progress, rather than the other way around.

Effective executives take this high-pressured approach to their own goal setting. They know their corporations are counting on them and will judge them on their ability to get specific results from their projects. And rather than just work, they work smart—in areas where they can make a distinctive contribution. To be sure, not all executives share the same appreciation and respect for putting results before all else. But most know that if they don't achieve adequate results, they are left out of the race eventually. Eighty-seven percent top and 81 percent middle aver that by concentrating on results rather than work, they will be able to enhance their success in their companies.

Shaking Things Up

In doing their jobs, executives adopt an array of management styles that affect their relationships with both superiors and subordinates. Style counts at least as much as ability in almost any area that involves people.

Nothing can make the difference in management more than an executive's philosophy about what ignites people's actions and what doesn't. I know a retired chief executive who swore by the theory that a rattled cage works best. He made it his business to shake things up every couple of months. His philosophy was based on a conviction that complacency was almost an out-and-out evil. He saw his most significant role within his office as *the man with the stick* and didn't mind the contempt that most of his subordinates had for him. In fact, he saw it as proof he was doing his job.

In *Wising Up*, Jo Foxworth describes a woman who was forced to take over her husband's business upon his death. The woman shared my friend's conviction that shaking things up is the only way to get things done right. But after she told her late husband's employees, "Things are going to change around here—you're not going to kill me like you killed him," and her executives began leaving the company one by one, she quickly learned that style is paramount.

Certainly, there are some companies that thrive on problems. And there are some executives who create them even if they don't exist. They abide by the philosophy that having problems to solve keeps the adrenaline flowing—and that's the only sure way to high productivity. But there are more companies and executives who think that rattled cages and shaken subordinates are destructive to getting results. By constantly shaking things up, executives force their subordinates to concentrate on intramural battles rather than important ones; sideshows rather than main events. This activity further leads to sidestepping and evasive approaches to work rather than the exercise of initiative.

Creating tension as a management technique is not viewed as a proper approach to management by most executives. Only 35 percent top and 32 percent middle say shaking things up is likely to have positive impact on their careers in their companies. Most executives believe when shaking up is truly necessary, then it must be accepted as such. But they are convinced that, used as a problem solver when need be, it generally has no appreciable effect on their advancement. Just over 40 percent of all executives say the effect of such methods is neutral on advancement. Moreover, 20 percent top executives and 25 percent middle say that shaking things up is more likely to have negative than positive impact on their career growth.

Being a Team Player

Rather than being a shaker and rattler in work relations, most executives find it more worthwhile and productive to join work efforts as a team player. There is almost no company that does not cherish wholeheartedly the attitude and style of an executive who rolls up his sleeves along with his associates and really tackles a project. Such an executive shares his objectives and goals openly with his subordinates, and enthusiastically takes on the challenges of his job. A team player is not secretive and scheming in his approach to overseeing work. He is not obstructionist with subordinates or peers. He cares more about results gained jointly than about hogging credits for himself. Executives find that being a team player is good for their careers. Ninety-four percent top and 90 percent middle claim being a team player has very much or somewhat positive impact on achieving success in their corporations.

Good Judgment

Since executives have to take responsibility for their decisions and the results to which they lead, executives are dependent on making judicious ones. Generally, good judgment has to do with an executive's ability to put problems in proper perspective and to understand the ultimate values and priorities of his corporation. In short, it means doing the right things. Executives who don't do the right things lose out to those who do.

Executives always must consider the outcome and impact of their decisions, both short and long range, on their corporations. Exercising good judgment is generally regarded more as a function of both farsightedness and common sense than of brilliance or talent. Most executives regard weighing matters and trade-offs rationally to come to judicious decisions as invaluable to their success. Ninety-nine percent top and 97 percent middle believe that exercising good judgment has positive impact on their careers.

Understanding a Corporate Balance Sheet

Almost all executives know that understanding the balance sheet of their corporations is important to them. Setting proper priorities and drafting their own departmental or division budgets requires that they be cognizant of their companies' financial position and considerations. Most executives understand the balance sheet. Eighty-four percent top and 74 percent middle say that understanding the corporate balance sheet is important to achieving career success in their corporations. The significantly higher number of top executives than middle managers who make these claims indicates that real understanding of company finances is something that comes with experience, exposure, and higher-level decision making. It is understandable that this kind of understanding comes as executives broaden their scope within the company. In the early stages of an executive's career, he is more likely to be absorbed with his own specialized field. He has limited knowledge about how his job affects and influences the company balance sheet. But executives who rise to the top are required to be more concerned with how their investments and other expenditures affect capital management and company progress.

Taking Financial Risks

Executives know that what they contribute toward profit is a plus on their behalf. They also know that what they spend in making that money is scrutinized. The object of the game is to make as much profit as possible while spending as little as possible. That doesn't mean they cut corners. It means they try to minimize risk and exercise good judgment on how they invest dollars. While that attitude may be healthful in preventing losses, it also may be a deterrent to innovation. The commitment to reduce risks is good in any company, but not so much that playing it safe results in corporate stagnation.

Today, most companies are averse to taking risks. Only 30 percent top executives and 18 percent middle say taking financial risks is helpful to their careers. Thirty-four percent top and 39 percent middle say this kind of risk taking actually is negative to their gaining advancement. You can see from these figures that top executives generally are more secure in taking these kinds of risks. As you would expect, this is because they have more experience, confidence, and greater authority in spending and investment matters.

Time and Timeliness

I have said that exercising good judgment means doing the right things. But doing the right things at the wrong time is sabotaging to the aspiring executive's career. Good timing is essential to getting ahead. I never have met a truly effective executive who lacked a sense of timing. While it has been made clear that managing time well is a mark of executive effectiveness, it also needs to be said that punctuality and adherence to deadlines are signs of the executive who is properly self-directed. This is borne out in the views of all intelligent executives. Over 90 percent of both top and middle state that these traits are important to achieve career success in their companies.

Honesty

Most executives think they are honest. They also think honesty is the best policy where their careers are concerned. Ninety-eight percent top executives and 95 percent middle say that being honest is important to career success in their corporations. However, thinking oneself honest is a subjective determination. A lot of people say they are honest and think they are, but if they examine their purposes, and especially their objectivity in approaching a given situation, they might find that they are less so than they think. Executives are likely to be biased in their actions and attitudes by their vested interest in their corporation's gain or loss resulting from their performance.

What executives typically mean by using the word *honesty* as applied to their daily work, peers, and bosses can be interpreted as their seeing great value in being *sincere* or committed. On the other hand, if their perception of themselves as honest is based on its definition in the moral sense, they could be viewed as fooling themselves. An article entitled "Ethics Without the Sermon" in the November/December 1981 *Harvard Business Review* states that to be completely honest or ethical in business decision making, executives would have to focus their energies into acquiring a less parochial or objective frame of mind.

The article advises executives who want to come to more ethical decisions to attempt to define problems accurately (based on facts rather than loyalties), objectively empathize with opposing points of view, understand the history of a problem, acknowledge loyalties and the biases they entail, understand objects and results of decisions, recognize who might be harmed from a decision, attempt to negotiate with the opposition before making a decision, and be sure as far as possible that this decision will be effective and harmless over time. In addition, Laura L. Nash, writer of the article, suggests that the executive who has made a decision based on these steps should be able to discuss that decision with anyone—CEO, boss, board of directors, family, and even society as a whole. She also cautions executives to realize the symbolic potential of action resulting from a decision. For example, is building a park after being charged as a polluter of water or air within a community likely to be viewed as a peace offering or an attempt to buy off the community?

Is this Pollyanna? You bet. And any executive who takes all of these considerations into account in his decision-making process will probably find himself without a job, not just because of his moral commitments, but because all these activities would be so time consuming he wouldn't be able to carry out his main responsibilities. Nonetheless, I agree strongly that certain business-related issues deserve more ethical approaches from corporations than they get.

Competitive Styles

You have seen that competition abounds in corporations. Middle managers especially—approaching their forties and perhaps struggling with the consternation of a midlife transition—feel the pressures of time as they reach their key hurdles to corporate career success. They are likely to engage in particularly intense competition. However, it is not just among middle managers but among top executives as well that the struggle for professional growth and advancement is constant. Even executives holding top positions within their companies—CEOs—are forced to compete to some extent just to keep their jobs.

To determine some of the ways executives compete for success in their companies, we asked them to rate the impact of the following actions on their careers:

Staying abreast of your field.

Giving talks or speeches at industry conventions and meetings.

Writing professional articles for publication.

Staying late at the office.

Coming to the office on weekends.

Taking work home regularly.

Repeatedly expressing to your superiors that you are ambitious.

Their responses are shown in Table 36.

Staying Abreast

For the most part, executives compete for recognition in their companies by striving to turn in a good performance. No executive can hope to compete with his peers if he does not maintain up-to-date knowledge about his specialized field. Through avid reading of business-related literature, company-sponsored seminars and training programs, and, in some cases, even independent studies through additional formal education, executives strive to keep themselves current on the state of the art within their disciplines. Over 90 percent of all executives say this has a positive impact on their advancement.

Speeches and Articles

Corporations especially like to have their executives receive favorable attention from the business community itself and their social communities as well. A good example of this is provided by David Ogilvy, the charismatic, indomitable founder of Ogilvy & Mather, the top-quality advertising agency, in the June 1978 issue of *Mainliner* magazine. He says, "It is desirable that the heads of all our offices should become personages in their communities. The best way for them to achieve this is by making remarkable speeches. If you make dull speeches, you will not be reported—and you will never be invited to address an important audience. If you make good speeches, you will be widely reported, and you will get your pick of audiences. Take a lot of trouble in preparing your speeches, and don't make more than two a year."

Table 36
Career Impact of Competitive Style

	TOP EXECUTIVES				
	Very Positive	Somewhat Positive	Neutral	Somewhat Negative	Very Negative
Staying abreast of your field	32.4	60.9	6.5	0.2	0.0
Giving talks or speeches at industry conventions and meetings	4.7	48.3	43.4	1.0	0.6
Writing professional articles for publication	2.4	32.5	58.7	2.2	0.6
Staying late at the office	5.1	36.7	54.6	2.0	0.4
Coming to the office on weekends	5.1	27.9	62.9	2.0	0.6
Taking work home regularly	1.8	21.4	69.9	5.1	0.8
Repeatedly expressing to your superiors that you are ambitious	1.0	11.4	34.0	42.2	9.4

"Don't Know" responses not included.

It is well known that Mr. Ogilvy has a keen sense of effective public-image building. But most companies place great value on executives who improve their corporate image among their various publics. By publishing articles and making well-placed and well-received speeches, executives can enhance their reputations within the business community overall, and among superiors who evaluate their worth to the corporation.

If executives don't have the time or ability to write articles or speeches, they increasingly employ the services of public-relations firms to do it for them. One executive at a large citywide bank in the Midwest came to the conclusion that he had gone about as far up in management as he was going to go. The upper echelons of management were in the middle of total change, and he suspected he would be reassigned to less desirable duties. Consequently, he hired a public-relations agent to devise a small campaign

	MIDDLE MANAGERS				
	Very Positive	**Somewhat Positive**	**Neutral**	**Somewhat Negative**	**Very Negative**
Staying abreast of your field	36.2	55.1	8.4	0.4	0.0
Giving talks or speeches at industry conventions and meetings	4.5	42.8	44.6	2.0	1.0
Writing professional articles for publication	3.6	27.7	57.5	2.5	1.6
Staying late at the office	5.0	37.9	50.4	4.3	1.2
Coming to the office on weekends	5.2	30.4	55.7	5.2	1.8
Taking work home regularly	1.2	23.2	64.5	7.0	1.4
Repeatedly expressing to your superiors that you are ambitious	0.7	16.6	33.3	38.3	7.7

"Don't Know" responses not included.

that would both help to promote a new service in his department and at the same time establish an enviable reputation for him among other local banks. His hope was that within the six-month period that top management was reorganizing the bank structure, he would find a suitable, more elevated position elsewhere. His campaign turned out to be so effective that not only did he improve his reputation in the banking community in his city, but he also won approval of his bank's new management regime for his noteworthy performance. After the bank reorganization was completed, he was one of the lucky few promoted.

While some executives certainly can appreciate the benefits of exposure through well-placed articles or well-received speeches, these kinds of activities take extra effort that may not be worth it. Only 53 percent top executives and 47 percent middle say that delivering speeches is helpful to their advancement. Even fewer executives are concerned with writing articles. Thirty-five percent top and 31 percent middle say that such activity has positive impact on their careers.

Hours and Appearances

By now it is well established that companies place high value on executives' putting in long hours. Few corporations care much whether executives put these hours in by coming into the office on weekends, taking work home with them at night, or by staying late at the office. Before any executive can hope to be promoted to top management, he must prove that he can handle a large volume of work efficiently. Long working hours and rigorous work schedules are the trademarks of successful executives. Often being seen working long hours enhances an executive's image as a toiler in the vineyard, possessed of the kind of ambition that leads to his own success and contributes to that of his corporation.

Coming into the office on weekends, or sticking around at night because one knows that the big boss will be there to see his admirable dedication, is considered gimmicky by some and not really characteristic of most good executives. But this certainly is not true in all cases, and an executive had better be aware of which standard applies in his company. In her book *Making Good*, Jane Adams quotes a chief executive wistfully missing the grind and day-to-day action:

> Some nights, when I leave the office at six and see the younger fellows still at it, working away, I almost envy them; they know why they're doing it, or at least they think they do, and there's a kind of camaraderie with the others who are also doing it. As president you don't have that—you're rather isolated at the top. But I will occasionally notice that a very able man doesn't seem to be doing that, and while I know that probably means he has his job under control, is a capable manager, I feel like his commitment to the company is somehow questionable.

Despite the views of this CEO, many executives think they have enough challenge with spreading their time effectively between their jobs, families, and communities without devoting wasted energy to making fraudulent impressions. Yet, I must repeat, those executives should beware of the informal agendas and measures that may be operating. One thing is for sure: long hours never hurt.

Some executives believe it is important to be willing to stay late at the office; so say 42 percent top and 43 percent middle. They also believe it is important to come into the office on weekends; so say 33 percent top and 36 percent middle. And they further believe it is important to take work home; so say 23 percent top and 24 percent middle. But the groups of these executives who say such long hours are important to their advancement are of relatively modest size. While the number of middle managers who rate these activities as important to their promotion possibilities is ever so slightly more than that of top executives, that is because they are doing a little more paperwork (and perhaps footwork) than their top executive counterparts. It also is likely they are extending themselves just a little in the hopes that they will be the lucky ones to be tapped to move up the corporate ladder. The CEO Adams quotes agrees: "When I look at my executives, the younger ones especially, who do what I used to do, I know why they're doing it: because promotion frequently depends on the appearance of effort, at least at the lower levels. As president, I've tried to set limits on that, but it is difficult to make the best men stay within those limits."

Ambition on the Sleeve

There are very few forms of competition that are likely to affect advancement negatively. Corporations where competition is a key characteristic for survival and growth generally do not discourage competitiveness among executives. But most companies and executives considering candidates for promotions respond more favorably to constructive, results-producing, ability-proving competition. Even if executives are capable and bright, constant reminders from them to their bosses about their ambitions are likely to be a turn-off. When we asked executives what effect repeatedly reminding bosses about one's ambitions would have on promotion possibilities, they indicated that such tactics would have a negative influence on advancement. In the area of career hopes, this is the highest rating of negative impact of a competitive gesture or tactic. Fifty-two percent top executives and 46 percent middle say this kind of tactic would prove to have a very or somewhat negative impact on an executive's advancement. Such behavior only makes peers and bosses uncomfortable and even embarrassed for its crudeness. The repeated expression of a longed-for successful future shows that the naive executive hasn't yet grasped the fact that all or most of his peers are at least as ambitious as he is, but far more diplomatic and canny. Resentment among peers and bosses is the only assured result to be had from a campaign of moaning, groaning, and exclaiming ambition. Machiavelli would roll over in his grave . . . these aren't seemly tactics of a solid prince.

Brilliance and Talent

Brilliance per se has a limited role in the success and achievements of an executive. Of course, it is one of those characteristics that can't hurt anyone's career. But without other critical abilities, brilliance is of little assistance in getting a job done, let alone getting a promotion.

Table 37
Career Impact of Brilliance and Talent

	TOP EXECUTIVES				
	Very Positive	Somewhat Positive	Neutral	Somewhat Negative	Very Negative
Brilliance	18.5	54.4	24.8	1.0	0.0
Articulateness	42.5	51.6	5.3	0.6	0.0
Good writing	18.2	55.0	25.4	1.0	0.0
Superior talents	55.8	38.0	5.9	0.4	0.0
	MIDDLE MANAGERS				
	Very Positive	Somewhat Positive	Neutral	Somewhat Negative	Very Negative
Brilliance	17.6	49.2	30.2	1.8	0.2
Articulateness	39.1	51.7	7.6	0.4	0.0
Good writing	20.5	46.1	32.0	1.0	0.0
Superior talents	48.2	41.3	9.6	0.4	0.0

"Don't Know" responses not included.

However, this does not mean that most executives don't appreciate the value of out-and-out superior mental horsepower. They do, but for most their own brilliance is limited to an occasional occurrence rather than a constant state of mind. Generally, executives find they can turn out an astoundingly brilliant performance on some projects (sometimes pleasantly shocking even themselves), but are confined to producing rather mediocre results on others. Seventy-three percent top executives and 67 percent middle say being brilliant helps in career advancement in their companies. While it is not possible statistically for a large number of executives in a corporation to be truly brilliant, most of them obviously recognize the value of that gift in others. When it is combined with tenacity and the heart to overcome difficulties, this makes for a potent force in an individual executive.

Virtually all executives value the ability to be articulate and think of it mainly as skilled oral expression. Being able to speak fluently and clearly is helpful to achieving success. Ninety-four percent top executives and 91 percent middle believe articulateness is given great importance by their corporations. It probably is a strong notion among most executives that by perfecting their oral communication abilities, they also can improve their written communications. While fewer executives place emphasis on writing ability for gaining success than they do on oral articulateness, it remains very important. Since corporations depend heavily on written, formal communications, the ability to write well is desirable. Seventy-three percent top executives and 67 percent middle believe being a good writer can be helpful in advancing their careers. This corroborates the positive value corporations place on writing ability described in Chapter 5.

Most executives have superior talents in areas and specializations that affect their work. Some may have superior technical abilities. Others may have superior "people-handling abilities" that lead them to be effective managers. All executives think they have superior abilities in one area or another. Among the most successful of them, it is fair to presume that these perceived areas of superiority are real.

Ninety-four percent top executives and 90 percent middle say superior talents provide a real leg up for executives in their corporations. Undoubtedly, most executives say this proudly, others enviously. Few executives could achieve success without the self-confidence of believing they excel in some facet of their work and have something distinctive to offer in the way of ability. Such executives know full well, however, that making use of their superior talents—rather than merely having them—has everything to do with what kind of success they can win for themselves.

By possessing superior talents, brilliance, writing ability, or articulateness, executives only are equipped to compete. They still need to call upon all their personal and emotional resources to become successful. While corporations certainly place value on rare gifts and skills, they care more about and reward the utilization of those gifts and skills than their mere possession. A student who earns a straight-A average without even trying is not automatically a better candidate for competitive executive roles. Only if that student has drive, the eye to discern what's important and when, the willingness to admit and learn from his mistakes, and the appetite for excellence will he be successful in the corporate world.

33

Training, Studies, and Advancement

You have seen it is almost mandatory for all young executives aspiring to top executive positions to acquire a quality college or university education that grounds them in the ability to think. This is a bit ironic. While a college education is virtually a prerequisite to success in business, there is a long history of antagonism between the corporate world and members of academia. Executives in the business world resent what they consider the impractical, esoteric, jargon-based focus of most professors. A September 1978 *Consultants News* gives some amusing examples of B-school professorial lingo that constitutes a foreign language to executives. They include: "typology," "heuristic decision making," "B-mod," "paradigm," "contingency management," "organistically oriented intervention," "configural cue utilization," and "asymmetric rivalries." It's no wonder some executives have problems in writing reports and letters once they get into the business world.

Antagonism between ivory towers and executive suites aside, we wanted to know how important executives believe education is to their advancement opportunities. Not only that, but because the most ambitious executives do not relinquish their thirst for knowledge after completing their college or university experience, we wanted to know how important to career advancement they consider continuing study and training.

Specifically, we queried them on the career impact of the following items:

Having the technical training or education necessary to do your job.

A college or university degree.

Taking courses in night school to improve your skills or knowledge.

An M.B.A. degree.

An M.B.A. degree from a prestigious university.

Joining a management trainee program after completing your education.

Learning new disciplines.

Reading heavily in business subjects.

Reading heavily in all subjects.

Being a student of organizations.

The Right Kind of Training

Far and away for executives, having secured the right kind of training or education means having earned a college or university degree. Over 90 percent of all executives say having such a qualifying educational background lends solid support to advancing their careers. A tiny 8 percent say such preparation has no impact on their promotion possibilities. I expect these latter executives are the exceptions that prove the rule. They have made successes of themselves and expect to continue doing so without the aid of a formal degree.

In addition, most executives indicate they have been fairly persistent in updating the kind of study or training that makes them even more valuable to their corporations. Almost 70 percent of all executives claim taking courses in night school to improve their skills or knowledge is looked upon positively by their corporations. Still, the remainder seem to question the value of such continuing education in enhancing their career growth. Roughly 30 percent of executives think continuing education through night school courses has neither positive nor negative impact on their careers.

Roughly two-thirds of both level executives say having an M.B.A. is helpful to their careers. As I have mentioned previously, getting that degree from a prestigious school can be helpful, but is hardly essential to their career prospects. Fifty-six percent of both level executives regard getting an M.B.A. from a prestigious school a boost to their chances for promotion. It is evident that for the most successful executives, learning never stops. Even if they don't seek to educate themselves formally through a university, they are required to stay abreast of developments in their fields and, if they're smart, in the business world as a whole.

Jan Stockstill notes the need to read constantly about technical developments to fulfill her duties on the board of managers at the Baytown refinery.

Table 38
Career Impact of Training and Education

	TOP EXECUTIVES				
	Very Positive	Somewhat Positive	Neutral	Somewhat Negative	Very Negative
Having the technical training or education necessary to your job	49.3	42.2	7.7	0.6	0.0
A college or university degree	40.9	48.6	9.6	0.2	0.0
Taking courses in night school to improve your skills or knowledge	12.8	54.8	30.8	0.6	0.0
An M.B.A. degree	19.0	49.3	28.1	0.8	0.2
An M.B.A. degree from a prestigious university	14.7	41.7	38.9	1.6	0.2
Joining a management trainee program after completing your education	7.3	40.4	47.1	0.4	0.0
Learning new disciplines	12.0	61.0	26.1	0.0	0.0
Reading heavily in business subjects	13.0	61.5	24.4	0.2	0.2
Reading heavily in all subjects	7.5	45.8	45.2	0.8	0.0
Being a student of organizations	2.4	25.8	62.1	2.8	0.2

"Don't Know" responses not included.

"I have to keep up with the technical terminology as well as technical implications of my decisions," she says. To do this, she reads voraciously. "Going to school at night or during the day isn't practical for me anymore."

	MIDDLE MANAGERS				
	Very Positive	**Somewhat Positive**	**Neutral**	**Somewhat Negative**	**Very Negative**
Having the technical training or education necessary to your job	47.0	44.3	7.8	0.5	0.2
A college or university degree	34.6	49.6	13.3	0.4	1.2
Taking courses in night school to improve your skills or knowledge	14.4	52.5	29.9	0.7	0.7
An M.B.A. degree	19.2	48.0	26.7	0.9	2.0
An M.B.A. degree from a prestigious university	16.6	38.9	35.1	2.3	2.1
Joining a management trainee program after completing your education	10.1	42.7	39.5	0.9	0.2
Learning new disciplines	11.0	57.2	29.7	0.7	0.0
Reading heavily in business subjects	11.3	57.6	27.7	1.4	0.4
Reading heavily in all subjects	5.4	43.2	48.0	1.4	0.2
Being a student of organizations	2.7	24.5	60.7	3.0	1.2

"Don't Know" responses not included.

The ultimate objectives of the educational endeavors (formal or informal) of any ambitious executive are (1) keeping abreast of developments in one's field, (2) knowing what applications others in the field are making, (3) generating ideas, and (4) showing oneself as well informed. These objectives cannot be achieved without directing constant attention to learning.

Joining a Management Training Program

Joining a management training program in a corporation that takes it seriously is important to young graduates as they begin their executive careers. Roughly half of all executives say joining a management trainee program is conducive to career success in their corporations. Good programs provide guidance and broad exposure to the budding executives. They round out their college experience.

Some companies have good training programs while others offer mediocre ones. The best ones usually last about two years. They are designed to break in the new recruit to the basic disciplines of business: finance, manufacturing, marketing, and human resources. No executive of any age can approach problem solving in business without having been familiarized with the main concerns of these four areas. Executives who have been exposed to good training programs are better off as they begin their careers than executives who have had only a haphazard introduction to their corporations. They have a broadened view of corporate function, purpose, and problem solving that executives with inferior training may never match.

The 47 percent top executives and 40 percent middle who claim that joining a management training program has neither positive nor negative effect in their companies are likely to be with firms whose training programs are mediocre. Executives who had the good fortune to benefit from a well-rounded and extensive training program are sure to be aware of the added benefits and competitive edges provided them through these training programs.

After an executive has completed an extensive training program and settles into one of the four main disciplines, his training will be extended throughout his career by seminars, continuing education, and various company-sponsored management training courses and programs.

Learning New Disciplines

Learning new disciplines is essential for career growth, particularly if an executive's abilities and interests lie in the direction of general management. Sometimes a company will initiate exposure to new areas or disciplines for newly recruited executives and its middle managers who have been identified as "comers." This guidance of younger, promising executives into new disciplines signifies hope and expectation for their future career growth on the part of the corporation. Executives not tapped for such favorable treatment and pampered guidance are in trouble if they don't find their own way to broaden their knowledge. The object of learning new disciplines is to prepare oneself for general management. How executives elect to do this determines what paths their careers will take. As I pointed out in Chapter 18, there is a difference between broadening skills and preparing for general management.

Young executives who hope to become general managers have to broaden their knowledge *beyond* their own specific areas of specialization. A marketing executive learning financial applications for his or her function in a corporation is one example of such broadening. A financial executive seeking a manufacturing control assignment is another. Executives who attempt to broaden their knowledge base are preparing themselves for profit-and-loss responsibility. In effect, they attempt to learn new disciplines that either relate to or add to their already specialized fields of concentration. Only when executives are exposed to the problems in other fields of concentration do they equip themselves to make broadly based decisions on business trade-offs that affect matters outside their immediate area of competence.

Executives who work in larger corporations usually have to make special efforts to learn new disciplines. Marketing managers at subsidiaries and divisions, for example, may work only with marketing executives at the parent level. They rarely have opportunities to become familiar with the concerns and operations of other departments that affect their work or are affected by their work. The more areas of discipline that an executive has been exposed to and understands, the more prepared he or she becomes for general management. Seventy-three percent top executives and 68 percent middle say that advancement opportunities in their corporations are increased when an executive learns new disciplines.

By making significant horizontal moves within their organizations or by moving to other companies, executives are forced to expose themselves to new areas. Getting this broadening experience can be initiated either by the executive himself or by his company. With most corporations, only executives identified as having unusual potential are maneuvered through one discipline and then another. Therefore, in the main, it is up to the executive to determine what path he wants to follow to the top and make it happen by pushing for expansion in his company. (He should have no fear that by asking for greater responsibility with the idea of making a greater contribution he will be guilty of "ambition on the sleeve.") He also may choose to move to another company where being exposed to other disciplines is likely. Executives who fail to realize the need for such expansion to achieve growth are those who allow themselves to go stale in overly routinized jobs.

In short, the appetite and temperament an executive has for becoming a generalist surely will affect his ability to assume greater responsibility.

Drucker defines a generalist in *The Effective Executive* as "a specialist who can relate his own small area to the universe of knowledge." Executives in marketing, for example, who understand how their marketing decisions will affect the sales, production, and development of the product, and the corporate balance sheet as well, are executives who can cope with the responsibilities of being a general manager.

The Importance of Reading

Executives loaded with heavy schedules have little time for formal education to keep them abreast of their fields and business generally. However, a well-rounded executive is always up to date on business and world matters. In Section III, I have shown that executives often have a narrow sense of self in the world. They limit their attentions to business matters and tend to care little about what occurs outside that narrow focus. Seventy-five percent top executives and 69 percent middle managers say they read heavily in business subjects and this habit has a positive effect on their careers. But only 53 percent top and 49 percent middle say they read heavily in all subjects. Their narrow reading habits assure that their perspective on worldwide issues remains limited. While their busy schedules might justify such limited interests to some extent, many business decisions impinge on social problems and conditions. The failure of an executive to acknowledge the part he plays in the world at large is a failure at fulfilling his requirements as a responsible citizen.

Organizational Unsophisticates

Even in business-related subjects, executives tend to have a narrow view of their immediate universe. Surprisingly few executives pride themselves as being students of organizations. They do not regard knowledge of organization functioning as valuable in achieving success. Understanding why some companies are successful and others are not, why some companies have particular problems and others do not, why some mergers work, but most do not, is priceless in executive decision making.

The fact that only a fourth of all executives place value on this kind of analytical approach to organizations feeds their reputation as narrow thinkers isolated from any world outside of their immediate organizations. Not only are they neglectful of their role in their communities, they are just dimly aware of how their corporations compare to other ones except for, perhaps, a few major competitors. Operating with such limited knowledge of organizational functioning and malfunctioning is a severe handicap for any executive with lofty ambitions.

34

Family and Community

Most successful people adopt life patterns or habits that reflect their preoccupation with professional achievements. Executives are no different from scientists, artists, or other highly specialized professional groups. Their lives are molded around requirements that will lead them to ultimate success within their fields. The one thing that most executives want more than anything else is success—defined as promotion to top executive positions. To accomplish this, they have to set priorities in their personal as well as professional lives.

Probably the most interesting aspect of the life patterns of any person is the degree to which they betray that person's dream for his or her future. In his book, *The Seasons of a Man's Life*, Yale psychologist Daniel Levinson describes the *dream* as "something more formed than fantasy, but less specific in concept and approach than a plan." The dream is usually formed during the preadult (late teens) phase of life. Levinson asserts that in these years most individuals begin to have vague concepts of themselves as adults and how they will fit into the adult world. As they grow older their dreams take on more clearly defined character, but it is a rare occasion when an individual is clearly aware of the exact professional path he will follow. More often than not, individuals are compelled to seek or abandon their dreams with only vague ideas about the direction in which they are headed. Generally, they have little notion of what success will mean by the time they already are making life choices that will influence their attainment or abandonment of those dreams.

Levinson says that of the ten executives he interviewed, only a few "were impelled by a youthful dream." (He also studied ten each of biologists, novelists, and workers over a period of several years.) One executive out of the ten revealed during his extensive and intensive interviews with Levinson's research team that he wanted to get away from his lower-middle-class origins and "become head of a major corporation." But the others confided **349** that they had no particular professional dreams. They indicated that their dreams tended to center more on "community and family" functions within their lives. These executives achieved modest career growth within their corporations while avoiding the strenuous kind of travel and relocation that is characteristic of the most successful executives. They compromised the ultimate growth they might have achieved in their companies in favor of more stable family and community lives. The choices each of these executives made accumulated to form total patterns of living that strongly reflected their early-developed dreams. Levinson's view of the dream as a kind of catalyst for behavior through various life-cycle phases holds a special significance and clarity when applied to the behavior patterns of executives.

The Levinson Study

Dr. Daniel J. Levinson's seminal study of forty men's lives (including ten executives) has led him to classify adult male development into the following age categories. Each stage is not arbitrary, but can vary as much as three years on either end.

Leaving the family (eighteen to twenty-two). This is a transitional period on the border between family and another home base of one's own, where one will exist in a larger world as an adult and not as a child in the parents' home. The task is to make that transition.

Getting into the adult world (twenty-two to twenty-eight). One is now more in the adult world than in the family and is exploring and building the first adult structure—very tentative but a structure. Major tasks are to give form to a dream of self-in-the-world, to find a mentor who will support the young man's dream and assist him in putting it into effect and to find a loved woman who will help to define and carry the dream.

Age thirty transition (twenty-eight to thirty-two). One makes important choices in marriage and occupation, either to deepen commitments or to reject the life one spent much of the twenties putting together.

Settling down (thirty-two to thirty-nine). Life becomes less provisional. He joins a tribe and sets up a timetable for pursuing long-range plans and goals. The second phase, which occurs in the middle to late thirties, is so distinctive as to rate its own name: *Becoming one's own man,* or BOOM. The tasks of BOOM are to find one's own voice as a senior member of one's enterprise and to prune the dependent ties to bosses, mentors, critics, and a wife.

Midlife transition (thirty-nine to forty-three). This is the time one faces the gulf between youthful dreams and actual fulfilment. The feeling is one of suspended animation. It requires reworking the dream and finding ways to connect parts of the self that were not provided for in the old life structure. One of these newly discovered parts is the feminine in himself.

Restabilization and entry into middle age (forty-three to forty-seven). Before this period is out, a new stability is achieved, which may be more or less satisfying. If a man has met the self-confrontation of his early forties and done the work of forging a new life structure, he may well feel renewed. If he stayed put through midlife transition, the crisis will emerge again to pinch around fifty.

For all its pain of self-renewal, the pilgrimage into middle life is a worthy one for those who don't get lost along the way.

As you can see, Levinson's description of life as a journey broken into several cyclical phases of awareness culminates in the midlife transition where the dream is either abandoned as unrealistic, irrelevant, or unattainable, or else is reexamined and/or reapproached in a final attempt at ultimate success. For executives as well as all other professional groups, this particular time is most crucial. This is the period in which most people approach and attain or fail at the kind of success they incorporated into their dreams early in their lives.

Aside from assessing objective and subjective success professionally, this particular life cycle is also encumbered with other crisis-type events that force most individuals to reexamine the state and level of satisfaction contained within their personal lives. This period—busy with the enormous weight of determining professional success or failure—is also the time pocket in which all other aspects of an individual's life come to be jammed and judged as successful or ineffective. This is a time to approach the dream anew or totally abandon it; and all the aspects of life experiences and choices that up to now have remained as the dream's baggage are then kept on board or jettisoned.

The way we order our existence reflects our priorities in both personal and professional lives. Levinson writes about four of the executives who expressed greater interest in their community and family lives than in their professional ones. Their contrast with the more ambitious executives in our study is quite apparent:

All of them spent their novice phase in their original occupation (such as engineering or accounting) and entered middle management in their early thirties. They were of lower middle-class origins and retained strong ties to their pre-adult ethnic worlds. Three of them, in their forties, were living in or near towns where they were born and turned down opportunities to move elsewhere. The fourth had made two major geographical moves, but in his forties was restricting his occupational ambitions in favor of a stable family-community life. All of them worked hard to reconcile the conflicting demands of occupational advancement and family-community stability.

By his own description, Levinson's executives are not typical of the highly mobile executive who traditionally puts his career interests well above community stability and, in some cases, even family stability. Further, their ill-formed plans don't square with our findings. Moreover, a careful reading of his cases produced only one executive whose career, in my opinion, could be called successful. The pinnacles of executive success often are reserved for those whose priorities lie with professional achievement above all else. However, having said that, I believe most successful executives manage to make the trade-offs that render their lives as meaningful and rewarding overall as those of the general population.

Although I do not think Levinson's ten executives are representative of the truly ambitious, none of what I have said is meant to be a repudiation of his total study. I have included his views in this discussion because I think his concept of the midlife transition is important and relevant to executive living.

During the midlife transition, executives alter many aspects of their lives while they rise to moderate or ultimate career success or experience failure. Among these alterations are changed relationships with bosses and subordinates, and rearranged elements of family and community lives. By the time the midlife "crisis" is over, most executives have come to terms with the niches they have carved out for themselves in their organizations, or have completely shifted their goals and aspirations to other companies or even to other careers.

Reordering Priorities

The phenomenon known as "the second career" has been overblown. It really isn't very common. However, neither is it nonexistent. When it occurs in an executive's life, it usually does so during this crisis cycle. How prudently and well planned the decision is made to leave an executive career determines the extent of positive or negative effect on that executive's life. You will remember that in Chapter 8 the hypothetical executive who dropped out of corporate life to run an organic farm in Wisconsin was not enthusiastically received when he sought reentry. Careless wallowing in doubts common to male executives approaching their forties can set them into patterns of behavior that jeopardize their professional lives and otherwise offer them little positive outcome. On the other hand, carefully monitored choices to "take time out" to "reevaluate past accomplishments" and to redirect capable professional efforts can result in highly satisfactory achievements for some executives.

Ken Mason, former president of Quaker Oats, decided to disengage from his career at a time when he was considered by many to be in line to succeed chief executive Bob Stuart upon his retirement. Mason abandoned his corporate activities to ponder his business and life philosophy at North Minnesota's Pine Island. With no regrets or unhappiness about his corporate life, Mason simply wanted to make time to examine his corporate experience, perhaps (but not necessarily) to apply this experience to another business in the future.

Mason's views are discussed in a July 27, 1981, *Fortune* article. He says, "I had a strong desire to have time, before I got too old, to reflect on what my experiences had all been about. . . . I'm a great believer that the examined life is much more worth living."

At fifty-seven, Mason was regarded by those who know him as a valuable idea man in his corporation. But it is his respect for ideas over administrative functions that may have led him ultimately to abandon his career with Quaker. "I am not impressed with the power of a corporate president," the *Fortune* interview reads. "I am impressed with the power of ideas. If you have ideas, they'll find their way whether you're sitting in the president's chair or off in a hut somewhere. Here I have a better chance of developing the theories that are needed than if I were doing the things presidents have to do."

Disengaging from a career is only one form of reaction to midlife transition or crisis. For executives who choose to stay on the well-trod corporate path, this period is one that inevitably affects the factors and functions of successful ascension to the topmost executive positions.

An article in the July/August 1981 *Harvard Business Review* covers the midlife crisis of three executives, and the implications of it for their careers. The article concludes that the symptoms and traumas of executives experiencing this crisis are as varied as the executives themselves. One executive, forced into an unwanted role in his corporation, experienced four years working with a bad boss. His reaction, as he increasingly grew to doubt *his own* competence and abilities, *led to newly established confidence and understanding of his corporation* and his role within it.

Another executive discusses his concern with choices that overaccented his professional priorities at the expense of his family life. After achieving significant success at forty-nine, this executive questioned most of those choices. The corporate success he had valued so much in earlier years had diminished in importance in his eyes. His outside life took on greater importance despite an admitted "mediocre relationship with his wife," and his "only adequate" stature as a father. He slowly concluded that his corporate achievements were merely a harbor to shelter him from confronting failures in his personal life.

The third executive, after going through a divorce while maintaining an even-keel professional life, concluded that he needed to reorder his priorities. He decided to put more energies into rounding out his life, paying more attention to his children.

Family Life and Career Advancement

Wanting to know how family life patterns influence corporate careers, we asked executives to rate the effect of the following items on their promotion possibilities in their companies:

Never marrying.

Getting married.

A strong marriage.

Getting divorced.

Getting remarried.

Professing gayness (homosexuality).

A spouse who is very supportive of your career.

An intelligent and well-educated spouse.

A spouse who will not relocate because of his/her career.

A spouse who will relocate anywhere.

Having your spouse pursue a career as vigorously as you.

Making all major family decisions.

Peace and quiet at home.

Their responses are tallied in Table 39.

The responses to many of these questions corroborate the findings on marriages, spouses, and families of executives that were addressed in slightly different ways in earlier parts of our questionnaire, and which I discussed in Sections I and IV. Rather than report information that is repetitive, I simply want to make a few summary comments and refer you to Table 39 for the figures on any of these questions that are of particular interest to you.

Spouse Support

According to the lion's share of executives, the most career-enhancing connubial state is that of a strong marriage to a spouse very supportive of his or her career. It is even more beneficial to career growth if that spouse is perceived as intelligent and well educated. Of course, spouses abet executive advancement most when they willingly relocate as the need arises. However, nearly half of all executives maintain that while the best spouses will wholeheartedly support their careers, be well educated, bright, and happily relocate across the country if need be, they also should keep peace and quiet in the home. These statistics only tell us what we already know.

Most executives are staunchly traditional when it comes to family life.

Executives depend on marriage as an important framework from which they derive moral support and stability for their mobile and ever-changing careers. For some of them, elements of family life are dictated by the needs presented by their jobs. For others, family needs provide an inspirational motivation—a driving force encouraging, if not demanding, outstanding professional success. You know the old cliché: "Behind every successful man, there's a woman who . . . ." Spouses who support an executive's career are considered to be among the most valuable for advancement by most executives. The report from 82 percent top executives and 76 percent middle that spouse support is very or somewhat helpful to their career advancement explains why roughly 60 percent of all executives say having a strong marriage is important to their careers.

It is no surprise that the more intelligent and better educated a spouse is, the more capable that individual is at sharing the professional and emotional problems of her or his executive mate. Sixty-six percent top executives and 61 percent middle say having an intelligent, well-educated spouse is very much or somewhat beneficial to their advancement. Spouses who are less educated and have less insight into their executive mate's professional problems and dilemmas are least likely to support and participate in the journey to achieving the dream that Levinson describes.

The more a wife shares her husband's dream, the more she is willing to be inconvenienced for the achievement of it. But if, as is common today, a spouse departs from aspiring toward his dream in attempting to achieve a dream of her own, conflict comes into the picture, and attempts to fulfill either dream may be seriously hindered. Generally, support and not competition is what most executives view as valuable in assisting their own career objectives.

Only 14 percent top executives and 17 percent middle say making all decisions at home has a positive impact on their professional careers. But 78 percent top executives and 73 percent middle say decision making at home has no appreciable effect. Rather than magnanimously eschewing the "king of the castle" role at home, these figures simply show that executives want to be free of the concerns, distractions, and problems that inevitably arise in every family. Some evidence for this can be seen by executive preferences when it comes to valuing organization and tranquility in their home lives. Forty-one percent top executives and 43 percent middle say that peace and quiet at home is helpful to them in their careers. While a more tolerant 55 percent top executives and 53 percent middle say such peace and quiet is immaterial to their career concerns, nobody thinks it is harmful to his or her career.

Table 39
Career Impact of Family Life

	TOP EXECUTIVES				
	Very Positive	Somewhat Positive	Neutral	Somewhat Negative	Very Negative
Never marrying	0.2	0.4	78.1	16.0	1.6
Getting married	1.6	24.3	70.2	0.4	0.8
A strong marriage	15.1	49.1	34.8	0.2	0.0
Getting divorced	0.2	0.0	65.9	26.1	3.8
Getting remarried	1.0	11.0	80.5	2.0	1.8
Professing gayness (homosexuality)	0.0	0.0	14.3	25.2	48.5
A spouse who is very supportive of your career	25.3	56.7	16.1	0.4	0.0
An intelligent, well-educated spouse	9.1	56.4	32.9	0.6	0.0
A spouse who will not relocate because of his/her career	0.0	1.6	17.8	48.6	27.7
A spouse who will relocate anywhere	21.4	56.4	19.3	0.2	0.4
Having your spouse pursue a career as vigorously as you	0.0	3.9	80.8	10.4	1.4
Making all major family decisions	1.4	12.6	78.4	4.5	1.0
Peace and quiet at home	8.8	32.0	54.8	0.6	0.2

"Don't Know" responses not included.

	MIDDLE MANAGERS				
	Very Positive	**Somewhat Positive**	**Neutral**	**Somewhat Negative**	**Very Negative**
Never marrying	0.4	0.7	76.1	13.8	2.3
Getting married	1.8	26.1	65.2	0.7	0.9
A strong marriage	15.0	45.3	35.8	0.2	0.5
Getting divorced	0.0	0.2	63.3	26.1	5.0
Getting remarried	0.7	9.9	77.8	2.5	2.0
Professing gayness (homosexuality)	0.0	0.2	14.7	23.6	49.5
A spouse who is very supportive of your career	23.5	52.7	20.7	0.5	0.4
An intelligent, well-educated spouse	9.4	52.0	35.6	0.4	0.5
A spouse who will not relocate because of his/her career	0.2	1.4	21.5	45.6	25.3
A spouse who will relocate anywhere	21.5	52.3	21.1	1.2	0.4
Having your spouse pursue a career as vigorously as you	0.5	4.1	75.9	10.3	2.3
Making all major family decisions	1.4	15.4	72.7	5.7	1.2
Peace and quiet at home	8.0	34.8	52.6	0.7	0.2

"Don't Know" responses not included.

Community Activities and Career Advancement

To determine the importance to their careers of their activities within the community, we asked executives to rate the following functions:

Being active in community affairs.

Being active in a church.

An active social life.

High social status.

Living in the "right" communities.

Driving an expensive automobile.

Getting involved in the public campaign of someone seeking elective office.

Membership in the "right" clubs.

Close friends with no connection to your corporation.

Their responses, outlined in Table 40, indicate that activities contributing to the needs and welfare of the community have more bearing on executive advancement than the ones affecting status. Though executives usually enjoy high status within their communities, boasting about or flaunting it does little to inspire their bosses to promote them.

Community and Social Status

When men discussed their dreams with Levinson, they disclosed that in the main they centered on either (1) occupation or (2) community and family life. The community generally represents different degrees of importance to most executives. However, it could be said that a local community's welfare reflects—favorably or unfavorably—on the executives and their families who work and live in it. The community's welfare likewise reflects to some extent on its corporations. For that reason many corporations view participation in community events and needs by its executives as a virtue. Accordingly, over half of all executives believe being active in community affairs increases their potential very much or somewhat for promotion in their corporations. By meeting needs within their communities, executives increase their social status and the social welfare of their own families (making conditions within the communities more beneficial for their families—especially children) and that of their corporations.

Being active in the community is the major activity that benefits executives in their career growth. Only 21 percent top executives and 27 percent middle claim being active in a church is beneficial to their careers, and only 23 percent top and 29 percent middle say maintaining an active social life is generally supportive to their careers.

Despite the high social status that most executives generally enjoy in their communities, most of them think such status, and especially boasting of it, is of little help to their careers. Only 18 percent top executives and 25 percent middle say that being of high social status is of positive impact to their advancement. A slightly higher 29 percent top and 31 percent middle believe living in the right communities is of very much or somewhat positive influence in their careers. However, ostentatious or conspicuous consumption is of little value to most executives. Only 10 percent top executives and 11 percent middle say driving an expensive auto enhances their careers. Hanging around the right places and hobnobbing with the right people well may provide enjoyment, but they don't help one's executive career in any specific way. Fewer than one executive in four believes having close friends outside his company and belonging to the "right" clubs add impetus to his promotion potential. Even political contacts and activities offer little boosting to an executive's aspirations for promotion. Only 10 percent top executives and 9 percent middle aver that getting involved in a public campaign of someone seeking elective office would be any help to gaining advancement.

Though corporations place little or no value on these social activities, most executives think they are free to engage in any of them to any extent they consider desirable. The main conclusion drawn by executives is that, aside from being active in community affairs, most community-oriented and status and social activities are of little importance to their organizations and, consequently, have been neither positive nor negative in influencing their career advancement.

Table 40
Career Impact of Community Activities

	TOP EXECUTIVES				
	Very Positive	**Somewhat Positive**	**Neutral**	**Somewhat Negative**	**Very Negative**
Being active in community affairs	6.5	45.5	44.7	1.6	0.4
Being active in a church	1.0	20.3	75.4	1.0	0.2
An active social life	1.2	21.8	73.3	2.0	0.2
High social status	2.4	15.7	75.4	3.5	0.4
Living in the "right" communities	2.0	26.5	69.2	0.6	0.2
Driving an expensive automobile	1.0	9.2	84.0	4.3	0.2
Getting involved in the public campaign of someone seeking elected office	0.2	10.2	68.4	14.5	2.6
Membership in the "right" clubs	1.2	15.6	76.8	3.3	0.4
Close friends with no connection to your corporation	3.7	12.6	78.3	1.2	0.0

"Don't Know" responses not included.

	MIDDLE MANAGERS				
	Very Positive	**Somewhat Positive**	**Neutral**	**Somewhat Negative**	**Very Negative**
Being active in community affairs	6.6	44.9	45.3	0.7	0.5
Being active in a church	3.0	23.8	68.4	0.7	0.4
An active social life	2.5	26.6	66.8	1.4	0.5
High social status	2.5	22.6	67.0	4.1	0.9
Living in the "right" communities	2.7	28.0	63.5	1.6	1.4
Driving an expensive automobile	0.4	11.0	77.9	5.1	2.3
Getting involved in the public campaign of someone seeking elected office	0.7	8.3	69.0	11.2	2.1
Membership in the "right" clubs	2.0	20.3	68.1	2.7	2.5
Close friends with no connection to your corporation	4.3	14.4	75.5	1.6	0.7

"Don't Know" responses not included.

35

Mentors and Bosses

Other than one of blood where the power to dispose is present, no relationship affects executive advancement as beneficially as the one between mentor and junior. Few executives fully mature in their skills and management style without the aid of some kind of mentor. Jan Stockstill credits her boss-mentors for most of her professional growth. She believes strongly in the contribution of these figures to her career advances. "Any growing executive needs a person to whom he or she can express frustrations, fears, and concerns without worrying about implications of future growth."

The complexities present in most intimate relationships are also characteristic of mentor interactions. While the act of mentoring seems altruistic, it is as beneficial to the mentor as it is to his or her subordinate. Mentors function as teachers, advisors, and sponsors, as well as grand hosts to newcomers amid the halls of business. But the relationship between a mentor and his or her subordinate is still more complex than that. In the best of relationships, mentors take what appears to be a personal interest in their subordinate's ambitions and goals. By showing faith in a subordinate's ability and potential, a mentor reassures the young person that his goal is realistic.

As a teacher, the mentor functions to enhance the skills and intellectual development of his or her subordinate. As a sponsor, he offers his influence as a senior member of the organization and facilitates the subordinate's advancement. As a host or guide, the mentor welcomes the subordinate into the new corporate world. In short, he takes that special subordinate under his wing. Mentors instruct subordinates in the beginning of their careers on how to relate successfully to their bosses, peers, and their own subordinates. In addition to such basic functions, they facilitate growth for young executives by offering counsel and moral support. Executives share their doubts and stressful problems with their mentor. They learn to resolve controversy and soften conflict with the aid of their mentor's guidance and example.

In order for the mentor relationship to be effective, Daniel Levinson (who

362

has done the pioneer thinking on mentor relationships) suggests it is important that the mentor be several years older than his subordinate. This age difference is essential for fruitful relationships because of the intense interaction between mentors and their subordinates. But he also cautions that he shouldn't be too much older, either. Executives mentoring subordinates twenty to fifty years younger than themselves are likely to react to their subordinates with maternalistic or paternalistic feelings. That kind of relationship is likely to inspire greater conflict and rebellion among the subordinates. Mentors who are too young (less than six to eight years older than the subordinate) are likely to maintain more of a peer relationship with the subordinate, and their function as guide and advisor will be minimal.

In essence, it is important the subordinate respect, admire, and sometimes even love his or her mentor. Most executives are likely to have experienced several mentor relationships by the time they approach their forties, the age of realization of success or failure in corporate careers. The level of intensity in these relationships is sure to vary with each mentor. The role of mentor is always one of transition. Executives maintain these relationships as long as their subordinates are learning from them. Inevitably, however, the give and take between both parties changes to more of a peer basis, and often this is not done in the most amicable fashion.

Mentors eventually might begin to believe their subordinates are not grateful enough, or are trying to outdo or outshine them. They may begin to fear their subordinates might pass them on the corporate ladder. Sometimes a mentor might become disillusioned with his subordinate, suddenly feeling he doesn't try hard enough, or doesn't have the potential previously indicated.

Subordinates are just as likely to become disillusioned with the relationship. They are likely to think their mentors expect too much of them, and are too demanding. If a subordinate has low self-esteem, he might begin to feel like an impostor, being given credit for abilities he doesn't have. More often than not, subordinates are likely to resent the methods and persistence with which mentors try to mold them.

Difficulties aside, executives form a series of beneficial mentor relationships throughout their careers until they approach the midlife transition.

Levinson's *The Seasons of a Man's Life* was published in 1978. At that time, he asserted the role of mentor was almost exclusively filled by men. Since then more women have begun to fill corporate management positions, but the role of female managers as mentors is still minuscule compared to that of male executives. There appear to be several reasons for this. Many women in management feel overburdened by women coming into their corporations seeking career advancement. The small number of female executives cannot possibly be effective mentors to all the women entering corporate communities.

Jan Stockstill suggests this is just as well. Her strong beliefs in the value of mentoring have led her to offer it to some people with whom she works. But she does not like to restrict her mentoring to women and doesn't like to have women depend on her for it based solely on their having gender in common. "Women who require and exclusively seek out mentoring from other women are asking to be viewed as a special case. If you constantly seek to be treated as a special case, you will always be viewed as a special case."

Cross-gender mentoring most commonly occurs between male mentors and female subordinates. But the problems that arise in such cases are likely only to increase as women in larger numbers join corporate competition. Whether mentors are men counseling women or women counseling men, the number of cases of sexual harassment and intimidation because of differing approaches to advising and teaching will have to decline before these relationships can be as universally beneficial for women as they have been for men.

It is because of these kinds of problems that women receive less mentoring than men. Not only are qualified women mentors scarce in most corporations, but they also might have less time for it while they seek their own advancement in a work world dominated by men. Further, Levinson is so sure of the inequality factor that affects mentor relationships between men and women that he cautions of possible hindrances in such relationships. Both the male mentor and female subordinate might have a conviction that she is less gifted than she is, that she is attractive but not gifted, or that she is "a charming little girl, not to be taken seriously."

Actually, anyone involved in a mentor/junior relationship is likely to experience some negative side effects temporarily when that relationship begins to terminate. In the case of a falling out, cooperation between the two becomes strained. Sometimes the relationship can end in so much resentment that the subordinate is better off working under another boss. Rarely does a subordinate realize the benefits received until some time after the relationship has ended.

Despite the sticky ending to many mentor/junior relationships, most executives agree these relationships are a vital part of their training and development. While mentors don't always have to be a boss, they usually are. Ordinarily they initiate the relationship after they have observed an executive they deem of high potential. Sixty-four percent top executives and 60 percent middle believe mentor relationships can have a very beneficial impact on their careers in their corporations.

While young executives might hope to fall into the good graces of an influential mentor, they rarely are in a strong position to initiate such relationships. Such executives might influence the decision of a boss or other top management figure by demonstrating impressive capabilities, but these relationships are based on personality chemistry as well as performance and are difficult to arrive at through sheer politicking.

However, most young executives are hopeful that by demonstrating superior skills and ambition, they can be singled out at least once in their careers by a superior for special tutoring and guidance in their professional activities. There is much evidence to support their seeking to be so identified as "comers." Eighty-one percent top executives and 77 percent middle say being labeled as a "comer" by management offers such a fortunate executive a big boost up the corporate ladder.

Being singled out as a "comer" by top management or for special attention by a mentor is bound to endear bosses to their subordinates. While liking one's boss isn't essential to career advancement, it surely makes corporate life easier! Seventy-five percent of all executives believe "liking your boss" has a positive impact on their promotion potential.

Managing the Boss

Studying the ebb and flow between mentors and juniors makes clear that the kind of relationship an executive establishes with his boss probably has more to do with the speed and likelihood of his advancement than any other factor. The failure to establish quality boss relationships hinders—if it doesn't absolutely prevent—career progress. By establishing one significant or a series of growth-oriented mentor relationships, executives often pave their own way to higher stature and power positions within their organizations. The best possible result from a long, beneficial boss/subordinate relationship is that aspiring executives follow their bosses up the corporate ladder. Following Emerson's advice by hitching one's wagon to a star is among the surest ways an executive can win advancement. For some executives, this kind of tagalong has carried them to the top through part and, in many cases, all of their corporate careers.

Politics: The Art of the Practical

Maintaining good relationships with the various bosses an executive has during his career can mean everything to the kind of success he or she will achieve. In addition to demonstrating impressive technical skills and ability, executives who do best in climbing their corporate ladders are generally those who make the most of the political climate in their corporations.

Politicking has come to be negatively viewed in our society, somehow being associated with dishonest, deceptive practices. There's no question that engaging in politics involves competing for attention and favors in any environment. Politicking in itself is merely a subliminal manner of competing with others for dominant stature within a group. As pejoratively as that activity has come to be viewed by purists, the fact is that wherever two people—and certainly three—are gathered, there is politicking going on. One's failure to engage in this activity, or to acknowledge its value, can mean only subservience for him or her. In the corporate setting, politicking is the essential prerequisite to learning one's nontechnical function within his or her company. It is through politics that people are dealt with, their cooperation won. Engaging in politics is simply getting things done.

Women executives particularly have been hesitant to address themselves to the need to politic. Some naively deny that the diplomatic art of dealing effectively with peers and bosses while managing subordinates involves politics. Jo Foxworth notes in *Wising Up* that the need to be aware of and learn the art of politics in any organization is mandatory for success. Despite the inability of politics alone to carry any executive to the top, she observes, "You'll never get there without it. Neither will you get any other place you have in mind. . . . Call it diplomacy, call it compromise, call it whatever goes down easiest, but political savvy by any name is an absolute essential to success. Without [it]—and the reasonably smooth practice of it—you might as well go home and stay there."

All executives politic as they engage in their daily business with bosses, peers, and subordinates. If they fail to do this, they are eliminated from the hotly contested race, or assigned to peaceful oblivion in a nonjob job. Nowhere in corporate life is politics as important as it is in the relationship an executive develops and maintains with his bosses. These are the people who evaluate him for promotions and determine how deserving he is when it is time for salary reviews. More important, they carry (or suppress) the message of his abilities to their superiors, thereby playing a part in establishing his reputation throughout the corporation. Be he a good boss or a bad one, he will influence important factors in a subordinate's career growth. Good politics says he should be treated accordingly.

To determine how executives set about establishing fruitful relationships with their bosses, we asked them to rate various items that may have an impact on their career advancement in their corporations. Those items are:

Having a mentor.

Being identified as a "comer" by top management.

Liking your boss.

Following your boss up the corporate ladder.

Always agreeing with your boss.

Encouraging your boss.

Making your boss look good to his superiors.

Making your boss look bad to his superiors.

High visibility for your performance with top management.

Executive responses to the first three items already have been discussed. A discussion of the remaining six appears in the next several pages.

Following Your Boss Up the Ladder

Whether your boss is your mentor or not, the best you could hope for is to follow him or her up the corporate ladder. At least for a rung or two. *All* executives hope for this kind of assistance in getting promotions, but of course it's mathematically impossible. If a boss has anywhere between two and ten subordinates, it stands to reason he can take only one of these capable executives with him on his trip to the top. Even so, executives generally compete among peers for this kind of added career benefit. Fifty-five percent top executives and 54 percent middle say following their bosses up the ladder is one of the most favorable ways to get the attention of the brass.

Despite the benefits that executives tend to gain through following their bosses up the ladder, this pattern of advancement is not likely to account for all the promotions an executive hopes to realize in his career. That's just as well. There are various elements of danger in depending too greatly on following one person to the top. No matter how good the relationship between a subordinate and his or her boss might be, there is always the threat of a falling out. Executives who place too much emphasis on their ability to politic with their bosses, to win their favors and to benefit from tagging along at promotion time, will almost surely find themselves isolated at some time in their careers.

While riding his boss's coattails, an executive must nonetheless put much energy into establishing his own power base, his own contacts, and his own style of management. An executive who fails to do this will find his career seriously threatened if disagreement should become serious between himself and his boss. The same kind of threatening situation could arise if the executive's boss leaves the company or falls out of favor with *his* superiors. Unless the subordinate has managed to establish a reputation of his own among his boss's superiors and peers, he will find himself without influence at top management. Moreover, one of the worst things that could happen to an executive would be to follow his boss up through a long series of promotions always reporting to that same person. Exposure to several bosses is a valuable learning process for any executive and necessary to well-rounded development. Working for several bosses throughout a career also forces an executive to learn the art of politics: how it can be important and appropriate; when it can be inappropriate and harmful—to executive and corporation alike.

Table 41
Career Impact of Relations with Bosses

	TOP EXECUTIVES				
	Very Positive	**Somewhat Positive**	**Neutral**	**Somewhat Negative**	**Very Negative**
Having a mentor	18.7	45.0	31.3	1.8	0.2
Being identified as a "comer" by management	20.6	60.2	15.6	0.8	0.2
Liking your boss	20.4	54.8	24.5	0.0	0.4
Following your boss up the corporate ladder	7.0	47.9	40.7	1.8	0.6
Encouraging your boss	16.1	62.7	19.2	1.0	0.2
Always agreeing with your boss	0.4	7.1	29.9	47.7	13.9
Making your boss look good to his superiors	31.6	53.1	14.1	0.4	0.2
Making your boss look bad to his superiors	0.0	1.0	8.4	23.2	66.6
High visibility for your performance with top management	37.6	50.8	10.2	1.0	0.2

"Don't Know" responses not included.

Encouraging Your Boss

You can help establish close relationships with your bosses by offering them support and encouragement. You diplomatically set out to make them look good to *their* superiors. Encouraging your boss proves that you are sensitive to the pitfalls, frustrations, and less obvious problems involved in his job. By demonstrating this kind of insight into the snarls and difficulties your boss faces, it is apparent you surely can fill the requirements of his job someday. That is the kind of impression encouraging your boss can make.

	MIDDLE MANAGERS				
	Very Positive	Somewhat Positive	Neutral	Somewhat Negative	Very Negative
Having a mentor	18.5	41.2	32.1	2.0	0.7
Being identified as a "comer" by management	23.7	53.6	17.4	1.1	0.4
Liking your boss	21.6	53.2	24.5	0.0	0.0
Following your boss up the corporate ladder	8.7	45.0	41.4	1.2	1.1
Encouraging your boss	17.2	60.4	20.2	0.5	0.2
Always agreeing with your boss	1.2	10.8	33.6	42.3	11.0
Making your boss look good to his superiors	32.9	54.9	11.1	0.2	0.2
Making your boss look bad to his superiors	0.0	0.2	7.3	28.4	63.1
High visibility for your performance with top management	36.5	51.7	10.4	0.5	0.0

"Don't Know" responses not included.

Offering encouragement to your boss means giving moral support, expressing faith in his wisdom and ability, relying on his expertise. Encouragement supports his own concept of himself as a leader and guiding factor in steering his department or function to success. To be thoroughly encouraging, you have to be alert to your boss's position in the organization, the implications of his function in relation to his own peers and superiors. For example, when peers are critical of a decision your boss has made, you would be supportive to congratulate him on his courage, his willingness to take the heat. This is not being sycophantic, nor does offering support in one area require that you agree with him in all others. In fact, our findings show (see

Table 40), always agreeing with your boss can be quite harmful to your promotion potential.

Just under 80 percent of both level executives say encouraging their bosses helps their careers very much or somewhat. After establishing bonded relationships with their bosses through offering such encouragement, they also are likely to be privy to the informal kind of information that is valuable to any executive. This puts them in a better position to administer, compete, and negotiate effectively.

Executives encourage their bosses not only by being supportive in times of crisis, but also by making them look good to their superiors. This activity involves subtle behavior in addition to just doing a good job. By getting a job done with favorable results, executives help their bosses present an image of capability to their own superiors. Other ways of contributing to a good image for their bosses involve indirect comments and references that inform their bosses' superiors about their effective leadership. During "chance" meetings, an executive "spontaneously" may marvel at his boss's ability to overcome a difficult situation. The most effective means of enhancing a boss's image to his superiors is to sing his praises behind his back.

Most executives put considerable importance on this kind of activity. Eighty-five percent top and 88 percent middle say giving this kind of stroking has very much or somewhat to do with advancing. On the other hand, making one's boss look bad is the kiss of death to a career. Such is the activity of a fool or conniver.

Of course, making one's boss look bad is totally different from working for a bad boss. Most executives have to work for a bad boss from time to time or at least once in their careers. A bad boss generally is viewed to be one that stifles a subordinate's learning and, worse, hides his ability and performance record from his own superiors. This kind of boss is usually afraid that his subordinate will overshadow him—possibly surpass him in the race to the top. Working for such a boss, and surviving the experience without serious harm to one's own career, is among the most toughening, tempering, maturing exposures an executive can have. To my mind, an executive who can pull this off goes automatically into that small inventory bin of talent labeled "the best."

A case study appearing in the July/August 1981 *Harvard Business Review* discusses the problems that the bad-boss relationship posed for one subordinate. This executive had been forced into a position that nobody else in the company wanted. Up to this point, he had established an excellent record with his company. Being aware, he realized, when he was approached by his superiors, that he was being told to take the job. In addition to his unhappiness because the position was a "nonjob," he experienced considerable despair in his relationship with his new boss. That boss proved to be "the only guy I've ever worked with who made me feel uncomfortable about my conceptual abilities. He was so quick on his feet and so broad in his knowledge. He'd ask questions I couldn't even think of. But we had no rapport at all." Working for such a boss can be a benefit to any executive, offering a rare opportunity to learn and grow. Instead, this executive felt discouraged: "There was no invitation to grow. He treated me as if he was saying, 'I want to show you how dumb you are, kid.' "

Granted, this executive was between a rock and a hard place. But his comments show a grudging admiration for the boss. There is room there, still, for him to make that bad boss into a good one. Likewise, by making every effort to make his bad boss look good, he will win the admiration of those superiors who threw him into that abysmal job in the first place. No executive can grow if he does not secure some kind of visibility for his performance at top management levels. Eighty-eight percent top and middle executives say that visibility for their performance at top management levels contributes very or somewhat positively to their advancement. If executives work for an obstructionist boss who thwarts such visibility, but they can overcome that resistance, they will win double credit at the top for both resourcefulness and moxie.

I have one (and only one) piece of advice for you if you work for a certified scoundrel and feel compelled to make him look bad. In those "chance" encounters you have with his superiors, say *nothing* about him unless asked. If asked, *damn him with faint praise.* Even this isn't safe. I don't recommend it. But if you must do something, do this!

36

Managing Subordinates and Self

The relationships between an executive and his subordinates are not as important to his career growth as his relationship with his own boss, but they come close. An objective for any executive is to inspire cooperation and/or competitive spirit among his subordinates. By stimulating maximum productivity through rivalry and team spirit, while at the same time providing encouragement and positive direction, executives breed the best possible working conditions for their organization's achievements.

We asked executives to rate the following actions as they relate to their subordinates, with an eye to how these actions affect their own career advancement in their companies.

Being demanding with your subordinates.

Encouraging your subordinates.

Protecting and looking out for your subordinates.

Grooming a successor.

Being Demanding

Ogilvy & Mather founder David Ogilvy determined that the future success and longevity of his company were dependent on staffing his office with managers good at, among other things, "grasping nettles." He also concluded that executives who are demanding with subordinates are actually good bosses. He believed (and still does) that "the harder people work, the happier they are. Agencies that frequently work nights and weekends are more stimulating." Executives derive the most productivity from their subordinates by being demanding with tender loving care. With David

Table 42
Career Impact of Relations with Subordinates

	TOP EXECUTIVES				
	Very Positive	Somewhat Positive	Neutral	Somewhat Negative	Very Negative
Being demanding with your subordinates	6.9	56.9	18.4	15.7	2.2
Encouraging your subordinates	44.1	50.6	4.9	0.0	0.0
Protecting and looking out for your subordinates	16.3	60.8	16.9	5.9	0.2
Grooming a successor	34.2	54.8	10.0	0.8	0.0
	MIDDLE MANAGERS				
	Very Positive	Somewhat Positive	Neutral	Somewhat Negative	Very Negative
Being demanding with your subordinates	7.8	48.0	22.0	16.9	4.4
Encouraging your subordinates	40.0	52.9	6.0	0.5	0.0
Protecting and looking out for your subordinates	14.6	62.7	15.1	6.6	0.4
Grooming a successor	27.1	53.6	17.7	0.4	0.0

"Don't Know" responses not included.

Ogilvy, an excellent sense of humor gets thrown in as well. Sixty-four percent top executives and 56 percent middle say they think being demanding with subordinates has very much or somewhat positive impact on their own career growth.

How most executives approach getting the most out of their subordinates, while offering inspiration and encouragement, depends largely on their own personal styles. Nearly all successful executives agree that being encouraging with subordinates is essential to career growth. Over 90 percent of all executives say that being so with their subordinates has a very positive impact on their own potential advancement. In fact, this is the highest such rating of the four subordinate relationship actions we surveyed.

Ogilvy outlines his attitudes regarding the importance of maintaining good relationships with subordinates in the *Mainliner* article. Of first importance, he saw the need to attract and keep extraordinary talent within the company. He saw it as dangerous should the company fail to "promote young men of exceptional promise . . . the loss of an exceptional man can be as dangerous as the loss of a client."

He also deemed it important to equip his organization with the best of top executives—an asset he sees as scarce in many corporations. "Some [top executives] were adept at solving problems, some were said to be good decision makers. . . . But I seldom came across a top man who showed any ability as a leader. All too many of them, far from inspiring their lieutenants, displayed a genius for emasculating them."

The Good Shepherd

To be effective leaders in his organization, Ogilvy advised his top management to make the most of the firm's human resources. "Give them challenging opportunities, recognition for achievement, job enrichment, and the maximum responsibility. Treat them as grown-ups and they'll be grown up. Help them when they're in difficulty. Be affectionate and human."

To be effective leaders, executives engage not only in encouraging their subordinates while being demanding with them, but also in protecting and looking out for these individuals in certain crises. There is probably nothing more admirable or effective than a boss who will stand behind his people in times of crisis. Protecting and looking out for subordinates doesn't mean pampering and sheltering them. But good executives know that to do good creative work, their subordinates occasionally will have to take risks. When executives take risks in decision making, they are in danger of making mistakes. By offering protection and looking out for the welfare of subordinates, executives stimulate imaginative, resourceful approaches to their department's team efforts. Most executives see this supportive action as contributory to their own career growth. Seventy-seven percent of both level executives say they derive positive effects in their careers by maintaining relationships with subordinates that offer protection.

If all goes well in an executive's relationships with his subordinates, he effectively will have groomed a successor from among his or her charges. This ability to groom a successor contributes to the development of both the superior and his subordinates. The superior moves up; a subordinate takes his or her place.

Reports from executives suggest that their being able to groom successors is a general concern within their corporations rather than one on which a specific promotion decision for an executive would be made at a given time. Earlier in the questionnaire, when asked what value their corporations place on executives grooming a successor before they can get promoted, only 50 percent of both level executives responded that this activity was vital before getting a specific promotion. Yet when asked here if grooming a successor is generally helpful to their own career advancement, 89 percent top executives and 81 percent middle say it has a very or somewhat positive impact on such advancement.

Executives who manage to groom a successor prove to their companies that they are effective leaders. They have been able to teach a subordinate well enough to do their own jobs. In doing so, executives assume their share of serving the corporation's need for future leaders.

Taking Ourselves Too Seriously

The self-image we business executives often insist on maintaining—that of single-minded, stoical, hard-bitten drivers—often results in an inability to acknowledge aspects of our whole natures. Our macho façades even serve to fool *ourselves*, keeping us mobilized around the utter seriousness of our jobs and careers. We admit no weakness and abhor exposing ourselves to any vulnerability. But these façades aren't entirely effective. I made mention of this in Chapter 6. I said the corporate and executive outlook that insists on denying any personal weakness causes ambivalence. Energy has its limits. Self-doubts do creep in. Vulnerabilities are felt. Failures do occur. Mistakes are made. Judgment can be faulty. To err is human.

Of course, the most fulfilled executives realize this. They have a sense of the comic in life and don't take themselves so seriously. While committed to their work, they also maintain a distance or detachment from it. Their lives are overlaid with involvements, values, and commitments that allow for them to accept and enjoy their complete humanness, acknowledge their deepest emotions, and have a sense of scale of themselves in relation to creation and history.

Increasingly, I have come to believe that for a person truly to have a sense of humor, he has to be religious. I don't mean he has to be a churchgoer (although there's nothing wrong with that!), but he has a presence in his life that prevents him from being grandiose.

I'm hardly alone or original in this point of view, but am particularly pleased that the two cardiologists who wrote *Type A*—the book on heart disease and prevention that is required reading for executives—also take this position. Drs. Meyer Friedman and Ray Rosenman state that Western society is not merely irreligious but antireligious. They believe that emotions (negative and positive) have a great impact on heart and cardiovascular functioning and that loss of religion also spells loss of positive emotion for people: "Admittedly, millions of Americans are churchgoers, but fewer and fewer of them 'live with their God' in any meaningful way. The myths and rituals of all religions in America have suffered disastrously from the destructive forces of secularization and so-called scientific rationalism."

Peter L. Berger, university professor at Boston University and director of the Seminar on Modern Capitalism, also believes society needs contemporary expressions of religious affirmation. He recently wrote a book about this. Its title alone, *The Heretical Imperative*, shows that such thoughts are considered off the wall by many. In it, however, he hits the bull's eye: *"The most obvious fact about the contemporary world is not so much its secularity, but rather its great hunger for redemption and for transcendence."* No less a light to thinking business executives than Irving Kristol has this to say about religion: "People need religion. It's a vehicle for a moral tradition. A crucial role. *Nothing can take its place."*

In the early seventies, as a young executive recruiter having recently founded my firm, I was quite taken with myself at booking a search for a president of a corporation. I also was scared to death I would flub somehow and show myself to be a fool among the senior executives I would be contacting and interviewing. As I began the assignment, I had occasion to fly out of Chicago to Denver early one morning. There, I was to meet with the president of a company who—as is typical in our business—reluctantly agreed to talk with me and made clear from the start that I was wasting my time and probably his as well.

I arrived at O'Hare Airport with not a lot of time to spare, but enough to board my flight. However, it was during this period that airports around the nation were installing new security measures to prevent the skyjackings that had become epidemic. The result was that I had to queue up in a line about a hundred yards long, was horribly delayed, and finally arrived at the departure gate just in time to see one of Continental's proud birds turn its golden tail to my face as it taxied off to the runway.

Livid, I stalked back to the security officials and lambasted them for their balky procedures. Where my fury came from, of course, was my embarrassment at not being able to meet the routine requirements of boarding a plane on time, and that not only would I look foolish to that big man in Denver, but I had blown the chance to see him since he'd been far from eager to give me his time in the first place.

Perhaps I panicked and became doubly determined. Or maybe it was just the terror in my voice. Whatever, when I got the man's secretary on the phone and told her my troubles but that I was coming on a later flight, she said he would rearrange his schedule and meet with me. As I regained my composure, I began to feel silly at having taken this whole business so seriously. Later, after meeting with that executive, and on a flight headed for Los Angeles, I wrote this bit of doggerel as a lesson to myself.

Airplane bound for Denver,
Outraged I missed the flight,
Deprived of a crucial meeting,
Blaming others for my plight.

What score was I to settle?
What shrewd move was I to make?
How pompous is my raving!
For such a harmless break.

That big exec for my client
A prize candidate would be.
Now lamenting in self-torture,
"I've missed *the* man to see."

What will he think, that big exec
Who busily runs the show?
I'd prevailed on him to squeeze me in,
As three into two won't go.

Worming into the big man's day,
Wit and charm hiding imposition.
Reluctant was he to grant me time,
To hear my proposition.

Now here I stand, inside O'Hare
In peptic consternation.
From panoramic window, watching
Jet-trails spew devastation.

A later flight, Trans World delivers,
Second wind blowing less rancor.
"An hour's delay?" Lunch with *me*?
He cancels the downtown banker.

Over salad and roll, platter and bowl
I render discreet revelation.
In reciprocal form he follows my norm,
And confides without hesitation.

Image of a busy man melts away,
Thawing my ears for hearing.
Imagined pretense, 'twas my own doing,
Obscured how our goals were nearing.

My self-important parody,
Contriving mighty out of meager,
Found me uptight over fate,
Feigning pride as being eager.

A lesson is learned: I've a job to do,
But force and flurry recede.

My professional challenge must never torture,
While I'm meeting my client's need.

This story has a sad, ironic twist. That executive and I got along immediately and well. He was a prince and I determined he was a man of extraordinary administrative ability. After our lengthy discussion and some thought, he concluded my proposition wasn't right for him. I agreed, but was pleased I had made friends with such a quality person.

That executive was Al Feldman, president of Frontier Airlines. I continued to follow his career and cheered at the credits he received for the way he ran that company. After a few years, he was chosen as chief executive of Continental Airlines to continue its fine tradition as the standard of premium customer service for the entire industry. I did a search for him. Early in 1981, the company became embroiled in a bitter struggle to ward off a takeover by Texas International Airlines, a struggle it eventually would lose.

On Tuesday, August 4, 1981, I received a short, warm letter from him thanking me for some words of encouragement I had offered in his takeover battle. The following Monday morning, while beginning a vacation in La Jolla, California—the town where he then lived—I picked up the *San Diego Union* and read on the front page that the night before, he had shot himself.

Let me return now to Peter Berger:

There are times in history when the dark drums of God can barely be heard amid the noises of this world. Then it is only in moments of silence, which are rare and brief, that their beat can be faintly discerned. There are other times. These are the times when God is heard in rolling thunder, when the earth trembles and the treetops bend under the force of his voice. It is not given to men to make God speak. It is only given to them to live and to think in such a way that, if God's thunder should come, they will not have stopped their ears.

It is not appropriate for an author of a business book to use the reader's time espousing his own religious preferences. However, my purpose is not to proselytize for a particular faith, but simply to underscore that the spiritual side of man cannot be satisfied fully by commerce and career. Levinson's concept of midlife transition has made it clear that executives' other dimensions often have gone untended for overcommitment to the almighty job.

My own business has brought me into contact with all kinds of executives who have reached for the brass ring and missed it. Far too many are broken men. (Possibly we'll begin to see more women like this, but I doubt it. Women seem to have more judgment in these matters. I hope we can learn from them as we increasingly work side by side.)

At one end I've seen bullies reduced to tears and utter helplessness when their bluffs were called and they were put out on the street in their fifties.

I've been badgered at the other end by retired, millionaire executives absolutely beside themselves with idleness. Without their jobs and trappings of office, many feel like nobodies. It's sad and also unnecessary. Neither I nor anyone else need offer apology for being serious about our work, for going as far and as fast as we can within the limits of our capacities and meeting our responsibilities to our fellow man. However, it's balance and stability we need, the three-legged stool of work, love, and friendship. These three together give life its full satisfaction and purpose at day's end and as one sidles into retirement. Commitment to the other two life tasks must not be shunned in total deference to our careers.

On my study wall at home hangs a framed plaque I had made up under the title "Essentials for Living." It is a list of six characteristics of the well-balanced, thriving life. They are a distillation of mostly Norman Cousins (derived from his *Anatomy of an Illness*) and some thoughts of my own. I like having this list on display as a reminder of how an enterprising life can be a noble effort with full participation in all the life tasks. I present it here with the hope it will be helpful to you in setting your goals and priorities.

Systematic and full exercise of the affirmative emotions.

A highly developed sense of purpose.

Engagement in creativity.

Ongoing community involvement.

Jogging the innards with laughter.

Taking action.

37

What to Make of It?

Let me turn to finish what I came to do: report on the American corporation in such a way that all interested parties can understand it broadly and, if they so choose, excel within it.

While it seems commonplace to analyze all manner of phenomena in threes, for the time being at least, I'm caught up in threes times two. Having just presented six "essentials for living" to executives who seek a balance between their professional and personal lives, I now would like to offer six conclusions on corporate life I believe are the main ones to draw from this study. These conclusions are not intended as a summary of our findings so much as they are broad, encompassing lessons from them on which we can hang our hats.

The Corporation Is Healthy

Despite the criticisms of the corporation that come incessantly from all camps—including the one within—this entity shows itself to be remarkably robust. Communications within corporations aren't all they could be, but yet they are adequate. Executives and operating units with any resolve have ample autonomy and the opportunity for self-determination. Executives seem basically happy with their work and identify strongly with their companies. While job hopping from one company to another is increasingly common among them, this is more a reflection of the geographical and social mobility and acquisitiveness of American culture than it is of sheer dissatisfaction with one's company. Job hopping is more characteristic of all professions than it was a generation ago.

It is true that corporations' left hands may not know always what their
right hands are doing. However, we only need to think fleetingly of their

enormous size and complexity to realize that the coordination they achieve among their far-flung operating units is worthy of nothing less than high praise. Further, it should be borne in mind that such coordination has been achieved as corporations have mastered rapid growth and adapted to changing attitudes in society and the marketplace and greater government regulation.

What other institution wins the kind of commitment of effort and hours from its managers that the corporation does? And what other institution is so pervasive in its impact on society? President Eisenhower's secretary of defense, Charles E. Wilson, was formerly the president of General Motors. On one occasion he said, "For years I thought what was good for our country was good for General Motors, and vice versa." The press quickly interpreted this to mean, "What's good for GM is good for the country," and he got into hot water. Perhaps Wilson might have been more wary about pridefully associating himself and his former company with the center of the universe, but who can deny that when the economy is sick, when corporations are sick, that the country also is sick?

In spite of its faults and serious lapses in perception and self-understanding, it is the corporation that continues to offer the best hope for the nation and world by offering employment, delivering goods and services in mind-boggling arrays at lightning speed, creating wealth for its founders, income for its investors, technological advances and greater comforts for the people, and still making way for characters straight out of Horatio Alger. Today's executive is no more patrician than he was fifty years ago, and he wasn't patrician then!

Corporate Goals Often Are Fictional

While language is the most essential tool to corporations in their conduct of business, they often use it poorly. One almost could say hyperbole is the language of business except that hyperbole is used intentionally whereas corporate exaggeration is most often engaged in without much or any premeditation.

To be sure, some corporations are out-and-out deceptive to their public and employees, but such malice is rare, and such companies are in a slow walk toward their own graves. However, it also is the case that when one reads most corporations' annual reports, there is never reason to doubt that everything in these firms is humming along in simply the most splendid fashion. Although the corporation practice of putting one's best face to the world is not only harmless but needs to be done *more*, the overstatement typical of annual reports is reflective of a more significant problem.

That problem is that stated corporate goals often are fictional. While they may be drafted sincerely by top management and entered into willingly or even enthusiastically by employees, the gyrations that are necessary on the part of armies of people in and out of the corporation in support of a corporation's goals that aren't its real ones, results in an incalculable amount of wasted motion, misunderstanding, and cost.

I am not castigating corporations. The gap that exists inevitably between what we say we're going to do and what we actually do is a human problem that has been with us since the beginning of man. New Year's resolutions are a standard joke. In my own experience, I know the more I talk about undertaking a project, the less chance there is I will ever do it. It is as if the speaking of my good intentions is reward enough, so I don't need to complete the task itself.

Corporations have a bad case of the "shoulds," "oughts," and "trys," just as most individuals do at New Year's resolution time. The annual plan, made up, as it often is, of objectives chosen by top management because they think these are challenges the corporation *should* meet, or *ought* to meet, or must *try* to meet, is bound to come a cropper.

The reason "Johnny One-Notes" make the best chief executives is they are clear on a single, central, unifying goal for their corporations. While they have to give consistent voice to it, their decibel level can be kept low by virtue of their supporting it with their actions and decisions. Because they are committed to it, and their employees know it, the daily efforts of those employees go into intermediate goals that support rather than conflict with the central one. This makes for a lot less "loose talk" in corporate corridors.

Executives Are Intellectually Self-Limiting

A friend of mine who achieved distinctive success by becoming chief executive of a well-known company in his mid-thirties left that job to serve in a subcabinet level post in the Carter administration. Over lunch one day, I asked him to compare the abilities of cabinet officers with those of corporate chief executives. In reply to my question he said, "Cabinet officers and their senior aides are much, much brighter than corporate senior management and chief executives, but they can't manage worth a damn. When it comes to management, Washington is in perpetual chaos." Despite this capable executive's having far more exposure to Washington and government than I, I doubt that senior cabinet officials are brighter than corporation senior and chief executives. In fact, they may not be as bright. Every compilation of IQ scores I've seen on pure intelligence among professional groups places corporate top executives and medical doctors at the top of the heap. What I suspect, however, is that corporate senior executives are not in the same league with top government officials *intellectually*.

This study has shown at several points that executives display a significant sense of unconnectedness with the world outside of business. Though they have great richness of intelligence itself, that mental horsepower is given to achieving results in pragmatic concerns within a narrow focus. The way corporations function, executives are rewarded for meeting limited objectives based on a meticulously defined division of labor. Corporations are organized in this fashion so no one person or group can wreak havoc to monstrous proportions. This is the corporate form of checks and balances.

This kind of focus in the corporate world makes for an efficient management—which Washington lacks—but generates a bright breed who are formidably incurious and anti-intellectual about a whole host of subjects. This invites a Secretary Baldridge to say that many top executives are "fat, dumb, and happy" and causes me to wonder aloud at many of them "having a need not to know."

This kind of focus also helps explain why so many corporations are not known for their vision, don't find it easy to train general managers, promote the wrong kind of person into their presidencies, and prefer a B average state school business major over a Phi Beta Kappa literature major from Princeton.

Collaborative Management Is Here

Whether a business meeting is small and impromptu, or large and formal, or presided over by a tyrant or someone who acts as if he or she has studied nondirective techniques under a Buddhist master, it is to one degree or another an exercise in collaborative management.

Executives complain about meetings perhaps more than about anything else. Yet no thinking executive can deny his need for them in order to inform, be informed, and arrive at planning and operating decisions. Collaboration—or what could be called committee action—has been criticized by many observers for stifling speed and individual initiative. This can be seen in such one-liners as: "If Moses had been a committee, the Jews would still be in Egypt." Or: "A camel is an animal that looks like it was created by a committee."

Corporations are much too large, complex, broken into too many specialized functions and geographically dispersed for one person or small group of persons at the top of the pyramid to be barking out orders like General Patton. Authoritarianism is a bygone mode. While bureaucracy is a perpetual whipping boy, the need for corporations to organize people and tasks on a large, coordinated scale make it as inevitable as death and taxes. But bureaucracy itself is not immune to change. The old form where I sat in my little box and took care of my responsibility—and nothing more—and you did the same, sitting in your little box, has given way to a newer form that requires your and my talking often to make sure things don't fall between the cracks that separate our boxes. In fact, by meeting and talking, we link up in such a way as to seal the cracks. True, we may slow things down a bit by working to achieve a meeting of the minds, but what we accomplish is more likely to be well conceived and we both feel better about our jobs and our company.

For this kind of collaborative management to function optimally, however, a company has to be clear and determined on a central, unifying goal. This is the glue collaborators must have to seal the cracks.

Women Are Enriching the Executive Suite

It was Carl Gustav Jung's view that women and men were becoming more alike—psychologically and physically. Whether or not Jung ultimately will prove to be right about this is still a matter of lively scholarly debate. Nonetheless, as more women each year are assimilated into the ranks of management, they not only learn from their male colleagues, but have a significant impact on the behavior of those males. In short, male and female executives are becoming more alike.

As I mentioned earlier in the book, perceptive observers such as Marilyn Moats Kennedy and Jo Foxworth point out that many women have a tendency not to work as team players and have an outsized fear of making mistakes. As a result, they try to go it alone and, out of a desire to demonstrate not being hyperdependent, keep themselves out of the circles of influence. Obviously, some women executives have a lot to learn from their more seasoned male counterparts in avoiding this self-defeating behavior.

On the other hand, I fully expect women will have more to teach men than they will learn from them. This will not happen overnight, but the process strikes me as inexorable. While chauvinists (myself included) often have been caught praising certain women executives because they—as we so eloquently put it—think like a man, the art of management in the executive suite is going to be enhanced as more men learn to *think like a woman*!

I part company with women who stridently deny the existence of many "womanly traits." They consider the identification of such traits to be inaccurate and a stereotyping of the worst order. The characteristics I have in mind are those that center on traditional beliefs—right or wrong—that women are more sensitive, intuitive, and less logical than men. Whereas men seem more ready to reduce living creatures to machinelike functions, the women I've known have the capacity to see the world in greater wholeness and give inanimate objects names and "personality." Their "illogic" of two plus two is usually a little more or less than four, depending on circumstances, often works better than a man's cold reason in human enterprise.

This is not the time or place to argue whether such differentiation in male and female traits is predominantly the result of nature or nurture. I simply want to be on record as one who thinks such differences are real and state my opinion that there is not only room in the executive suite for female characteristics, but a distinct *need* for them.

Judgment and Timing Mark the Effective Executive

These two qualities in proper combination are what account for an executive doing the right things at the right time in the right way. And doing the right things at the right time in the right way defines the premier, effective management style.

Judgment and timing in proper combination are more important to career success than talent. They are more important than brilliance. They are more important than education. They are more important than drive. They are more important than sponsorship. They are more important than luck. They are more important than experience.

Below is a checklist of twenty key questions on managing your career. The more of them you can answer "yes," the more your career patterns will match the success-inducing thoughts and actions cited by the executives in this study and the more your management style will display judgment and timing in proper combination.

1. Have you set an ultimate career goal? Yes _____ No _____ If you haven't, your direction is determining your goal rather than your goal determining your direction.

2. Are your next steps in harmony with your ultimate goal? Yes _____ No _____ If they aren't, don't take them.

3. Do you have high expectations for your own achievement? Yes _____ No _____ If you don't, neither will your superiors.

4. Are you willing to risk mistakes and failure, go far out on a limb? Yes _____ No _____ If you aren't, you'll never do anything distinctive.

5. Do you believe you make your own luck? Yes _____ No _____ If you don't, you'll wait in the wings forever for the big break.

6. Are you willing to relocate geographically? Yes _____ No _____ If you aren't, you will severely limit your opportunities in your current company or any other.

7. Do you feel loyal to your current company? Yes ____ No ____ If you don't, you cannot give your best effort.

8. Do you actively cultivate "contacts" throughout your company and the business community? Yes ____ No ____ If you don't, you narrow your vision, resources, and options.

9. Do you direct your efforts to results rather than work? Yes ____ No ____ If you don't, you are more concerned with what you should do instead of what you should accomplish.

10. Do you set and stick with the right priorities? Yes ____ No ____ If you don't, you are engaged in sideshows and are squandering your valuable time.

11. Are you habitually punctual and dependable on deadlines? Yes ____ No ____ If you aren't, you are inconsiderate and an attention getter.

12. Are you tapping currently your superior talents? Yes ____ No ____ If you aren't, you are denying your company your distinctive contribution.

13. Do you have the proper training or education to stay abreast of your field and do your job effectively? Yes ____ No ____ If you don't, you must get it or change jobs.

14. Are you a student of corporate finance? Yes ____ No ____ If you aren't, or won't become one, you never can become an effective top executive.

15. Are you committed to learning new disciplines? Yes ____ No ____ If you aren't, you never can become a general manager.

16. Do you recognize that *politics* is the art of interpersonal competence you must cultivate? Yes ____ No ____ If you don't, you never can become a distinctive leader.

17. Do you actively encourage your boss? Yes ____ No ____ If you don't, you won't find it in yourself to make him look good.

18. Do you actively encourage your subordinates? Yes ____ No ____ If you don't, they will find ways to make you look bad.

19. Can you be happy if you go no farther up the corporate ladder? Yes ____ No ____ If you can't, your life is out of balance.

20. Have you listened to your stomach in setting your ultimate career goal? Yes ____ No ____ If you haven't, that goal really isn't appropriate for you.

Methodology of
The Cox Report

by **Allan Schnaiberg, Ph.D.**
Professor of Sociology
Northwestern University

I. Sample Design

Initial planning for the *Inside Corporate America* study included review of various sampling approaches to the corporate universe. An early decision was made to study sample corporations *in*tensively rather than to spread the sample over a great many corporations. This permitted a variety of cross-checks on the quality of information we would receive from respondents, as well as increasing the possibility of future research using the anticipated data set. Thus, rather than seeking, say, twenty-five respondents from fifty corporations, it was felt preferable to sample fewer corporations but to obtain data from executives in all the divisions and subsidiaries of the same corporation, by obtaining 125 respondents for each of ten corporations.

An ideal sampling frame for creating a probability sample of corporations existed within the lists of the five hundred or a thousand largest American corporations. These lists permitted stratification in a variety of ways, permitting us to generate a *theoretically* ideal sample of a multistage probability type. And so, using this initial approach, we generated a variety of suggested samples.

Two features militated against continuing along these lines. First, it was apparent early in the design of the project that once corporate senior executives had approved participation of their corporations in this study, we would likely move to a quota-type, nonprobability sampling approach within the corporations. This was necessitated by the decision we had earlier made to sample intensively across all organizational units of the corporation. To do a probability sample of top and middle management executives, we would need an extensive list of all such executives, stratified by rank and unit membership. This would have involved extensive negotiation with corporate officials, entailing delays and expenses that were beyond the scope of the project. Therefore, since we were ultimately restricted to a quota sample **387** of executives within the selected corporations, it was not as scientifically valuable to struggle with a probability sample of corporations, since we would be unable to make probability statements about our statistical findings.

Our second pressure to move toward a sophisticated quota sample rather than attempt a multistage probability sample came from initial chief executive officers' responses to early contacts. There was considerable diffidence on the part of a sufficiently large fraction of our initial mailings that we felt that although we could *design* a probability sample of corporations, we would be unlikely to *achieve* it: nonresponse patterns would be sufficiently high to make the achieved sample of corporations problematic as a probability sample.

Hence, these two factors suggested a quota design for both the corporations to be selected, and for the executives sampled within the selected corporations. To maximize responses of the latter—the ultimate respondents in the study—we felt that only corporations whose senior management was enthusiastic about the study should be included in the sample. Since much of the operational details required cooperation of upper managements across *all* offices, subsidiaries, and divisions, we believed that an apathetic top management would lead to erratic response rates, thus diminishing the value of the multistage quota sample we were designing.

Accordingly, we first attempted to estimate the sample size we felt was desirable for the study. A sample of a thousand to twelve hundred was deemed sufficient for our purposes (roughly equivalent to the well-known Gallup poll or Roper national surveys). Since we had committed ourselves to do a quota of five top and five middle management executives in *each* component of the selected corporations, we had considerable uncertainty about the number of such units in the corporations we would ultimately select and operate in. Accordingly, we made some rough estimates of the likely numbers of corporate units, and directly from this set a target for a number of corporations to be chosen: the target was in the range of ten to twenty corporations.

With this range of targets for the corporate quota sampling, we firmed up criteria for quotas. First we set a sales level ($200 million) below which we would not select corporations. Second, we set up strata for corporate products, since it was felt that corporate structures and executives' contexts varied somewhat across types of corporations. Our ultimate strata included consumer products, industrial products, and services (these incorporate a number of finer categories in, for example, the *Fortune* directories).

Using these criteria, the results of earlier mailings, conversations with chief executive officers, and his own extensive corporate contacts, Allan Cox negotiated a final quota of thirteen corporations, distributed as noted in the Preface. The unusually high response rates for both top and middle management respondents indicate the validity of our decisions on sampling. While a probability sample would have been an ideal in order to make statistical probability statements about our survey findings, we have a great deal of confidence about the quality of the samples for *these* corporations selected, and a strong sense that this more than offsets any loss of corporate representativeness entailed in the design. From our review of the existing literature, we have a clear sense that, overall, this is the most representative and comprehensive study of American corporations and their executives yet reported.

II. Questionnaire Design

From an initial set of targets and questions proposed by the study director, the three-member consulting staff (comprised of myself, Dr. Wayne Baker, and Ms. Rosanna Hertz) spent many months refining and extending the questionnaire. Our experience in questionnaire design in other social surveys provided a basis for determining the form and content of questions, the flow of issues, the forms for response (including designs to minimize various response sets such as acquiescence, or "yea-saying" and "nay-saying"). These forms were informally tested on colleagues, students, and friends for general and specific critiques.

An initial draft incorporating these revisions was formally pretested in August 1979 to a group of executives attending an Institute of Management seminar at Northwestern University's Kellogg Graduate School of Management. Participation was voluntary, with approximately 75 percent of the executives responding to our request. In addition to responding to the questionnaire, they were asked to evaluate it as well. They were requested to note both inappropriate questions ("useless, totally inappropriate, or unanswerable"), and problems of question wording ("ambiguous or needs rewording"). Finally, they volunteered often to assess the entire task of completing the questionnaire—as to both length and difficulty. From the twelve completed sets, we derived a set of critiques and revisions for the final version of the questionnaire. We estimated that it would require approximately one to one-and-one-half hours to complete the final questionnaire.

III. Field Organization

The organization of field work was somewhat complex because of the fact that the consulting team and study director did not have direct contact with or control over the actual respondents—the executives in the selected thirteen corporations. For most of the corporations, the study director was provided with lists of corporate units, and responsible executives in each unit. These responsible executives were charged with *distributing* the questionnaires sent them by the study director to top and middle management executives in their units (and presumably, with motivating the selected quotas of executives to respond promptly and accurately).

In order to exact compliance from the selected executives, we recognized the need to ensure absolute confidentiality of responses. This was particularly needed because their corporate superiors were often the agents transmitting the blank questionnaires. Therefore, a fairly complex recording system was established (a) to permit tight control over the distribution and response patterns by the consultants, and (b) to maintain respondents' confidentiality and *their* confidence in this anonymity guarantee.

To facilitate both these goals, the recording system consisted of an identification system for *blocks* of questionnaires. A six-digit identification number identified the corporation, subunit, and the rank (top or middle) to the quota group members. When corporate unit responsible officers were sent a set of questionnaires, these numbers were transmitted by the study director to the consultants. Only when the completed questionnaires were received did the consultants add a seventh number, to provide a unique identification for each respondent. This unique number was for purposes of statistical tabulation only; the *set* of unique numbers gave the consultants a measure of *quota completion.* Thus, where quotas had not been filled after an appropriate period, we informed the study director of this, and he in turn contacted the responsible corporate officers, to ask them to request completion of questionnaires from the unknown set of executive laggards. In some cases, the responsible officer was given extra questionnaires, to fill out the quotas. Thus, we had an ongoing recording system of *quotas,* but no records of identifiable respondents. By this mechanism, we were able to trace quota completion at each stage, from initial mailings by the study director through final submission of completed questionnaires.

All completed questionnaires were mailed by individual respondents to a postal box near Northwestern University. This was true for all thirteen corporations' executive respondents. For the three corporations with internal distribution systems, essentially the same system above was followed, with only minor modifications (e.g., communication with a central officer rather than multiple responsible officials).

IV. Processing of Data

The consultants were in charge of all aspects of processing of completed questionnaires. They arranged for pickup of these from the local postal box on a regular basis, after which each completed questionnaire was assigned a unique last number and the number entered on recording sheets for quota completion. One of the consultants was assigned primary responsibility for supervising coding operations, and coding of each questionnaire was carried out under this supervision. Coders were graduate and undergraduate students at Northwestern University, paid on an hourly basis (essentially three codes were used for the bulk of the coding).

To ensure high intercoder reliability, an extensive coder manual was prepared by the consultants, and updated on a regular basis to maximize homogeneity of coding. The manual indicated codes and mechanisms for dealing with particular kinds of questions. Periodic review of questions was carried out by supervisors, and noted in the manual whenever a change in coding was deemed necessary. Some cross-checking of items was also carried out, to assess the reliability of data being provided. In general, most respondents appeared to have understood all the questions, and to have responded fully and openly (while most questions were close-ended, there were a number of open-ended questions which elicited some especially rich comments).

When all coding and recording had been completed, the coded questionnaires were sent to a professional keypunching service, where they were punched and verified, before being recorded on tapes. The tapes were sent back to the consultants, where they were cross-tabulated to do some consistency checks on both data quality and keypunching accuracy. Where errors were found, they were corrected before the final tapes were prepared.

All data were ultimately processed through Northwestern University's Vogelback Computing Center, under contract with the study director. The consultants carried out all programming and verification as well as data storage and file maintenance. Final reports for each corporation were sent to chief executive officers, along with a final report for the entire sample. Thus, it is possible to state with some certainty that the quality of data processing meets all social scientific standards, and represents an objective assessment of the reports of the cooperating executives. The study thus represents the particular interests of the study director, coupled with professional social science expertise to undergird *Inside Corporate America*.

B

Participating
Corporations

The raw data of this study comes from 1,086 top and middle management executives in 115 operating units in 13 corporations. Three of the corporations are privately held; 10 are publicly held.

Information on the ten publicly held corporations falls into five categories: (1) main products or services, (2) industry standing, (3) actual or estimated sales and net profits for 1981 (some companies' final performance figures for the year were not available until after this book went to press) and estimates for 1982, based on the Value Line Investment Survey, (4) actual or estimated percent return on total capital invested for 1981, also from Value Line, and (5) a thumbnail sketch of each company's chief executive officer. Information on the three privately held corporations (*) does not include sales, profit, or return-on-capital figures.

Allen-Bradley Company*
Milwaukee, Wisconsin

This industrial company is a quiet giant. Founded in 1909 by brothers Lynde and Harry Bradley with support from a family friend, Dr. Stanton Allen, it engages in the manufacture and sale of (1) industrial electrical controls, (2) electronic components, and (3) magnetic materials. It is known as a quality producer that has muscle in its markets. It competes head on with GE and Westinghouse in several product areas. A-B numbers over 13,000 employees who are spread among 10 divisions, including a strong international unit which accounts for about 13 percent of annual sales.

For many years, the company was led by I. A. "Tiny" Rader, who directed it through an enviable growth period. In 1981, he relinquished the chief executive title, but remains chairman of the board. In Milwaukee, where A-B is headquartered, Tiny Rader is an executive who has garnered the highest respect from his fellow chieftains. In addition to being presumed as a very profitable company, A-B has been a large but inconspicuous donor to Milwaukee and Wisconsin social and cultural causes.

A-B's new chief executive is Claude R. "Bud" Whitney. Age fifty-seven, he holds a B.S. degree from the University of Wisconsin. He joined Allen-Bradley in 1969.

Ametek, Inc.
New York, New York

The September 21, 1981, issue of *Forbes* carries a feature article on Ametek that is titled "Boring Can Be Beautiful." The article begins by asking, "What's inside most big Xerox and 3M copiers?" The answer: "A tiny electric motor built by Ametek, Inc., an obscure manufacturing conglomerate." The article goes on to say that Ametek's gauges are part of every Boeing 747, its crushers squeeze tons of grapes for Gallo, and both Du Pont and Monsanto depend on its expertise in custom plastics compounding. The whole point of this, of course, is that while its product line may not seem all that racy to the man on the street, it is a thing of beauty to Ametek's stockholders, who exult in the company's phenomenal success.

Earlier in the year, *Forbes* published its "Annual Report on American Industry." This is a compilation of industry by industry performance statistics—along with the corporations within those industries—for 1980. Ametek is classified as a specialty industrial equipment company and included with such others as Cooper, Rexnord, Ex-Cell-O, and Combustion Engineering. Among this group of 33 companies, Ametek ranked 7th in return on total capital employed, averaged over the past five years. Out of all 1,041 public companies in the *Forbes* compilation, Ametek ranked 175th in return on total capital over the previous 12 months. *Fortune* ranks Ametek as America's 537th largest industrial company in 1980.

Annual sales for 1981 were $448.1 million; net profit, $26.5 million. Those figures for 1982 are $515 million and $30 million respectively. The return in 1981 on total capital invested is estimated at 14.5 percent.

Ametek's chief executive is John H. Lux. Age sixty-three, he holds B.S. and Ph.D. degrees from Purdue University. He has been with the company since 1966.

Anchor Hocking Corporation
Lancaster, Ohio

This company is the largest U.S. producer of glass tableware. Its consumer and technical products group makes glass and plastic drinkware and dinnerware, ceramic dinnerware, and decorative accessories. Its Amerock subsidiary makes decorative hardware. The company also makes glass and plastic containers, plastic and metal closures, and plastic food service components. Radio buffs and sentimentalists will remember that this company sponsored the popular Sunday night program *Meet Corliss Archer* during the forties.

Fortune ranks this company as America's 335th largest industrial corporation in 1980. *Forbes* classifies it with the 17 packaging companies that include Owens-Illinois, Diamond International, and Continental Group. Among this group, AH ranks 5th in return on total capital, averaged over five years.

Annual sales for 1981 are estimated to be $935 million; net profit, $27.7 million. Those figures for 1982 are $975 billion and $30.8 million respectively. Return on total capital invested for 1981 is estimated at 8 percent.

The chief executive of Anchor Hocking is J. Ray Topper. Age fifty-four, he holds a B.S. degree in electrical engineering from Brown University. He has been with the company since 1972.

ARA Services, Inc.
Philadelphia, Pennsylvania

This large, expansive company operates in five major service areas: (1) health care, (2) publications distribution, (3) food and refreshment, (4) textile rental and maintenance, and (5) transportation. ARA does business throughout the United States, Puerto Rico, Canada, Mexico, Western Europe, and the Caribbean.

The company is best known for its food vending and mass feeding operations in corporations, schools, airlines, government institutions, and general public facilities. In the health care area, it provides general management capability where needed along with specialized management services for dietary and other departments of medical institutions. Through its Aratex division the company provides work uniforms and other career apparel to client organizations on a contract rental basis.

Fortune ranks ARA the nation's 21st largest retailer. That is up from 28th in 1979. Annual sales in 1981 were $2.9 billion; net profit, $45.1 million. Those figures for 1982 are estimated at $3 billion and $53.5 million, respectively. Return on total capital invested for 1981 was 7.9 percent.

ARA's chief executive is William S. Fishman. Age 65, he holds a B.S.

degree from the University of Illinois. He has been with the company since 1959.

Consolidated Freightways, Inc.
San Francisco, California

This excellent service company is engaged in two main areas of business: trucking and air freight forwarding. Its motor carrier group provides motor freight service in forty-eight states, including Alaska, as well as eastern and western Canada. CF maintains a fleet of 6,200 power units and 15,862 trailers. Its average haul is 1,416 miles and weighs 1,200 pounds. The CF red, white, and green semitrailers can be seen on all the nation's major roadways. Likewise, the same color-scheme CF Air delivery trucks seem ubiquitous as they serve customers through over 50 company-operated terminals and 200 agents in the U.S. and abroad. The air freight business, begun in 1970, has shown rapid growth and continues to look promising for the company. CF also manufactured Freightliner heavy-duty trucks. But in July 1981, it sold this part of its company to Daimler-Benz.

Fortune ranks CF as the 13th largest transportation company in 1980. Of the top 15, 13 are either airlines or railroads. In its specific group, no trucker is as large. *Forbes* puts the company in its "Truckers and Shippers" category. In this group of 15 that includes companies such as Roadway, Leaseway, and McLean, CF ranks 2nd in return on total capital over the last 5 years.

Annual sales for 1981 were $1.1 billion; net profit, $55.5 million. With the sale of Freightliner being felt for the whole year, those figures for 1982 are estimated at $1.2 billion and $65.5 million, respectively. Its return on total capital invested in 1980 was 10.6 percent. That figure is estimated at 11.5 percent for 1982.

CF's chief executive is Raymond F. O'Brien. Age forty-nine, he holds a B.A. degree from the University of Missouri. He has been with the company since 1958.

Encyclopaedia Britannica, Inc.*
Chicago, Illinois

This company was founded in 1943 by William Benton. Mr. Benton also was cofounder, along with Chester Bowles, of the large advertising agency that still bears their names. He served as assistant secretary of state under President Truman and was instrumental in organizing UNESCO. From 1949 through 1952, he was U.S. senator from Connecticut.

The company is best known for publishing the prestigious encyclopedia for which it is named. In addition, it publishes The Great Books, the brainchild of the learned, prolific, indefatigable Mortimer Adler. The company also publishes the G & C Merriam dictionary. For the most part, its products are marketed through direct-selling efforts of a highly motivated, well-trained sales force. International sales account for a significant portion of the company's annual volume.

EB is owned by the William Benton Foundation of Illinois. Making known his firm commitment to private ownership of the company, the late senator stated in his will: "There are very few companies of any kind of the size and substance of EB which are now wholly in private hands and with no public common stockholders and there is no comparable corporation with EB's significant intellectual interest and responsibilities in the world. In my judgment, no temporary or seeming financial advantage, private or public, which allegedly accrues from public financing will compensate for the long-range disadvantages."

EB's chief executive is Charles E. Swanson. Age fifty-four, he holds a B.S. degree form Northwestern and an M.B.A. from the University of Chicago. He has been with the company since 1962.

Hyatt Hotels Corporation*
Rosemont, Illinois

This company is one of the many ventures of the resourceful Pritzker family of Chicago. The family got into the hotel business in 1957 with a facility near the Los Angeles Airport. However, it was with the opening of its Hyatt Regency in Atlanta in 1967 that the company truly got off the ground.

The Atlanta hotel was designed by John Portman, renowned architect. With its open-atrium lobby and illuminated glass elevators, it was the flagship that set the precedent for the company's bold, striking hotel architecture and fueled its rapid growth.

Known for plush furnishings and attentive service, this chain has 61 hotels with 33,000 rooms in 51 cities. Eleven hotels are under construction. While the Hyatt name is on these hotels, the company manages most of these properties for a fee, and doesn't control them. Forty hotels are majority owned by other companies. Hyatt owns a small interest in some of them. Eight of the 61 are actually controlled by the company. The rest are owned by Pritzker-controlled trusts.

Hyatt's chief executive is J. Patrick Foley. Age forty-nine, he holds a B.A. degree from Washington State University. He has been with the company since 1962.

International Minerals & Chemical Corporation
Northbrook, Illinois

IMC is the world's largest private-enterprise producer of fertilizer materials. It produces phosphate rock, potash, and animal-feed ingredients. Its animal-products group is the nation's largest producer of phosphate feed ingredients. It also produces biochemicals, hydrocarbons, carbon products, petroleum coke, ferroalloys, metals, and various foundry products.

Fortune ranks IMC 201st in size among America's industrial corporations. *Forbes* classifies it with 16 specialty chemicals companies that include Witco, Air Products & Chemicals, and Ethyl. Among this group IMC ranks 10th in return on total capital, averaged over the past five years. Annual sales in 1981 were $2 billion; net profit, $153.8 million. Those figures estimated for 1982 are $2 billion and $128 million, respectively. Return on total capital invested for 1981 was 11.2 percent.

IMC's chief executive is Richard A. Lenon. Age sixty-one, he holds a B.A. degree from Western Michigan. He has been with the company since 1956.

James River Corporation of Virginia
Richmond, Virginia

This company is the largest independent U.S. producer of specialty papers. Only thirteen years old, it has an incredible growth record. During this short time, earnings have risen at a 35 percent annual rate. This has been accomplished while maintaining consistently high profit margins.

Fortune ranks James River as the 558th largest industrial corporation in America in 1980. However, its rapid growth will place it well into the largest 500 industrials in 1981. In its "Annual Report on American Industry," *Forbes* classifies JR as a forest products company and includes it with such companies as Champion International, Kimberly-Clark, Weyerhaeuser, and St. Regis. Among this group of 20 companies, James River ranks 3rd in return on total capital, when averaged over the past five years.

Annual sales for 1981 are estimated at $840 million; net profit, $26.5 million. Those figures for 1982 are $975 million and $32 million, respectively. Return on total capital invested for 1981 is estimated at 10 percent.

JR's chief executive is Brenton S. Halsey. Age fifty-five, he holds a B.S. degree from the University of Virginia. A cofounder, with Robert C. Williams, he has been with the company since its inception in 1969.

The Scott Fetzer Company
Lakewood, Ohio

You may have seen this company's clever ads in the national print media before the ampersand in its name was dropped during 1981. Their main line was: What's a Scott & Fetzer? The ads were well directed because the company is highly diversified and, therefore, hard to classify. It is a maker and marketer of industrial and consumer products grouped in five segments: (1) cleaning systems, (2) educational and household products, (3) fluid transmission, (4) energy and control, and (5) equipment and accessories. Best known among its products are Campbell-Hausfeld air compressors, Wayne burners and water pumps, *World Book* encyclopedias, and Kirby vacuum cleaners.

Fortune ranks it 418th in its list of the largest industrial corporations for 1980. In *Forbes's* 1981 "Annual Report on Corporate Industry," SF is included in the conglomerate grouping of companies along with others such as Litton, Northwest Industries, Tenneco, and Teledyne. Among this group of 45 companies, Scott Fetzer ranks 4th in return on total capital when averaged over the past five years. Within the *Forbes* 1,041 total, it stands 186th in this respect over the previous twelve months.

Annual sales for the company in 1981 were $656.4 million; net profit, $29.1 million. These figures for 1982 are estimated at $700 million and $31 million, respectively. Return on total capital invested in 1981 was 12.6 percent.

SF's chief executive is Ralph E. Schey. Age fifty-seven, he holds a B.S. degree from Ohio University and an M.B.A. from Harvard. He has been with the company since 1974.

The Sherwin-Williams Company
Cleveland, Ohio

This company is the world's largest producer of paints and varnishes. It also manufactures home decorative products and chemicals. S-W has had a dramatic turnaround in profitability since 1979 when John Breen joined the company as chief executive. For that reason, it is particularly appropriate to include the company in this study. Breen had been an executive vice-president at Gould Inc.

The company is not merely snapping back, it's also making exciting acquisitions. In 1980, it purchased the Dutch Boy name and certain assets from the company that held them. In 1981, it acquired Gray Drug Stores. Apart from its new drug chain, S-W has 1,400 company-operated retail stores, 24 domestic plants, and 8 foreign plants. As its old corporate slogan boasted, S-W "covers the earth."

Fortune ranks S-W as the 264th largest American industrial corporation. *Forbes* classifies it with building materials companies that include Evans Products, Johns-Manville, and Masonite. In this group of 14, S-W ranks dead last in return on total capital, averaged over five years. However, the turnaround is on. By the end of 1981, *Forbes* ranked it 7th in this respect in the same group. Annual sales for 1981 were at $1.5 billion; net profit, $31.4 million. Those figures for 1982 are $2 billion and $35.5 million respectively. Return on total capital invested in 1981 was 7.5 percent. That figure, estimated for 1982, is 8 percent.

John G. Breen, age forty-seven, holds a B.S.B.A. degree from John Carroll University and an M.B.A. from Case-Western Reserve.

Taft Broadcasting Company
Cincinnati, Ohio

This company owns radio and TV stations, owns and operates amusement parks, makes motion pictures, produces broadcast software, and distributes various entertainment properties. It is best known for its highly profitable entertainment group, which includes Hanna-Barbera Productions. H-B is the producer of all the company's animated programs and well-known characters such as Fred Flintstone, Scooby-Doo, and Yogi Bear. Programs produced by H-B occupy approximately 50 percent of all children's programing aired by the three national networks on Saturday morning. QM (Quinn Martin) Productions, acquired by Taft in 1979, is the creator of *Barnaby Jones, Streets of San Francisco, The FBI, Cannon,* and many other action-adventure favorites. In the past two years, QM has concentrated on producing such TV specials as *Senior Trip* and *Help Wanted, Males,* as well as programing for pay television.

Taft owns and operates the following amusement parks: Canada's Wonderland (Toronto), Carowinds (Charlotte), Hanna-Barbera's Marineland (Los Angeles), Kings Dominion (Richmond), Kings Island and Old Coney (Cincinnati). The company also operates the College Football Hall of Fame in Cincinnati and is half-owner of the Philadelphia Phillies professional baseball team.

Annual sales for the company during 1981 are estimated at $360 million; net profit $38 million. Those figures for 1982 are $390 million and $38 million, respectively. Its estimated return on total capital invested in 1981 is 10.5 percent. That figure for 1982 is 10 percent.

Taft's chief executive is Charles S. Mechem, Jr. Mechem is fifty-one years old, and has a B.A. degree from Miami University (Ohio) and a law degree from Yale. He has been with the company since 1962.

Woodward & Lothrop, Inc.
Washington, D.C.

This quality, contemporary retailer is the major and largest general department store chain servicing the Washington, D.C., area. It operates one large (744,000 sq. ft.) downtown store in the city and 15 suburban outlets in the greater metropolitan area.

Whereas many well-known names in retailing such as Bloomingdale's, Neiman-Marcus, The Emporium, and Bullock's are part of larger chains, W&L is free standing. Despite increased competition from some of these chains, such as Bloomingdale's, the company has been increasing its market share.

Sales for 1981 were $334.8 million; net profit, $10.2 million. Those figures estimated for 1982 are $375 million and $11.5 million respectively. Estimated return on total capital invested in 1981 is 7 percent.

Woodies' chief executive is Edwin K. Hoffman. Age fifty-nine, he holds a B.S. degree from Northwestern. He has been with the company since 1968.

THE COX CORPORATION PROFILE QUESTIONNAIRE

This questionnaire is designed to elicit a broad array of information from top and middle management executives in complex corporations. The information it seeks about *you and your corporation* is divided into six categories:

- Corporate Relations
- Corporate Values
- Corporate Organization & Functioning
- Corporate Goals & Activities
- Personal Background & Employment Criteria
- Career Advancement

Because this questionnaire is comprehensive, it should provide a learning exercise relative to your career and your corporation.

Your personal identity is not asked for in this questionnaire, and every measure has been taken to ensure the confidentiality of your response.

ALLAN COX & ASSOCIATES
400 North Michigan Avenue
Chicago, Illinois 60611

Copyright © 1980 by Allan Cox & Associates. All rights reserved. Reproduction in any form, including photocopying and via data retrieval systems, is prohibited.

• PLEASE USE BLACK OR BLUE INK ONLY

*• NOTE THAT NUMBERS IN PARENTHESES
ARE FOR DATA PROCESSING ONLY*

CARD-01

If you are an executive of [*check one*]:

[ ] A PARENT COMPANY   *Begin on*   (10)
                                          Page I-1

[ ] A DIVISION OF A   *Begin on*
     PARENT COMPANY   *Page I-2*

[ ] A SUBSIDIARY   *Begin on*
                                          Page I-4

[ ] A DIVISION OF A   *Begin on*
     SUBSIDIARY COMPANY   *Page I-2*

CORPORATE PARENT RELATIONS

Please circle the one response number that most clearly matches your opinion.

A. *Parent-Subsidiary Relations* (11-15)

1. In general, how much autonomy do your subsidiaries have in relation to your parent company?
   [1] a little   [2] some   [3] a fair amount   [4] a great deal

2. In general, how has the level of subsidiaries' autonomy changed over the past ten years or so?
   [1] much less   [4] somewhat less   [3] stayed same   [4] somewhat more   [5] much more

3. Overall, how much input do your subsidiaries have in policy-making that affects them?
   [1] little input   [2] some input   [3] a fair amount of input   [4] a great deal of input

4. How much do your subsidiaries vary in their autonomy?
   [1] a little   [2] some   [3] a fair amount   [4] a great deal

5. How are the divisions of your subsidiaries administered?
   [1] inappropriate: no subsidiaries or divisions
   [2] wholly through subsidiary headquarters
   [3] primarily through subsidiary headquarters
   [4] primarily through parent office
   [5] wholly through parent office

B. *Parent-Subsidiary Communications* (16-21)

6. Do you feel your organization has adequate communication with your subsidiaries for getting your job done?
   [1] less than adequate   [2] adequate   [3] more than adequate

7. How would you evaluate the overall quality of communication between the parent company and its subsidiaries?
   [1] very poor   [2] low   [3] adequate   [4] good   [5] excellent

8. What is the mix of formal communication (i.e., memos, periodic reports, scheduled meetings) and informal communication (i.e., phone calls, unscheduled conversations, grapevine) between the parent company and its subsidiaries?
   [1] mostly informal   [4] more formal than informal
   [2] more informal than formal   [5] mostly formal
   [3] about equal

9. How much has your organization adopted new communication technology (word processing, direct lines, etc.)?
   [1] a little   [2] some   [3] a fair amount   [4] a great deal

10. Has the *quality* of communication between the parent company and its subsidiaries improved in recent years?
    [1] greatly reduced quality   [4] somewhat improved quality
    [2] somewhat reduced quality   [5] greatly improved quality
    [3] no change

11. Has the *quantity* of communications between the parent company and its subsidiaries changed in recent years?
    [1] greatly reduced quantity   [4] somewhat increased quantity
    [2] somewhat reduced quantity   [5] greatly increased quantity
    [3] no change

C. *Intra-Parent Communications* (22-26)

12. How would you evaluate the overall quality of communications within the parent company?
    [1] very poor   [2] low   [3] adequate   [4] good   [5] excellent

13. Do you feel you have adequate communication with relevant others within the parent company to get your job done?
    [1] less than adequate   [2] adequate   [3] more than adequate

14. What is the mix of formal and informal communication within your parent company?
    [1] mostly informal   [4] more formal than informal
    [2] more informal than formal   [5] mostly formal
    [3] about equal

15. How has the *quality* of communication within the parent company changed in recent years?
    [1] greatly reduced quality   [4] somewhat improved quality
    [2] somewhat reduced quality   [5] greatly improved quality
    [3] no change

16. How has the *quantity* of communication within the parent company changed in recent years?
    [1] greatly reduced quantity   [4] somewhat increased quantity
    [2] somewhat reduced quantity   [5] greatly increased quantity
    [3] no change

(SKIP TO PAGE II-1)

CORPORATE DIVISION RELATIONS

If you are in a division of a parent company, think of the following questions *only* in terms of parent-division relations. If you are in a division of a subsidiary (of a parent company), think of the following questions *only* in terms of subsidiary-division relations. (This applies to sections A, B, and C below). Please circle the one response number that most clearly matches your opinion.

A. *Divisional Autonomy*   (27-29)

1. In general, how much autonomy does your division have?
   [1] a little   [2] some   [3] a fair amount   [4] a great deal

2. In general, how has the level of your division's autonomy changed over the past ten years or so?
   [1] much less   [2] somewhat less   [3] stayed same   [4] somewhat more   [5] much more

3. How much input does your division have in policy-making that affects your division?
   [1] little input   [2] some input   [3] a fair amount of input   [4] a great deal of input

B. *Divisional Communications*   (30-35)

4. Do you feel you have adequate communication with your parent company (or subsidiary) for getting your job done?
   [1] less than adequate   [2] adequate   [3] more than adequate

5. How would you evaluate the overall quality of communications between your division and its parent (or subsidiary)?
   [1] very poor   [2] low   [3] adequate   [4] good   [5] excellent

6. What is the mix of formal communication (i.e., memos, periodic reports, scheduled meetings) and informal communication (i.e., phone calls, unscheduled conversations, grapevine) between your division and its parent (or subsidiary)?
   [1] mostly informal   [4] more formal than informal
   [2] more informal than formal   [5] mostly formal
   [3] about equal

7. How much has your organization adopted new communication technology (word processing, direct lines, etc.)?
   [1] a little   [2] some   [3] a fair amount   [4] a great deal

8. Has the *quality* of communication between your division and its parent (or subsidiary) improved in recent years?
   [1] greatly reduced quality   [4] somewhat improved quality
   [2] somewhat reduced quality   [5] greatly improved quality
   [3] no change

9. Has the *quantity* of communication between your division and its parent (or subsidiary) changed in recent years?
   [1] greatly reduced quantity   [4] somewhat increased quantity
   [2] somewhat reduced quantity   [5] greatly increased quantity
   [3] no change

C. *Intra-Divisional Communications*   (36-40)

10. How would you evaluate the overall quality of communication within your division?
    [1] very poor   [2] low   [3] adequate   [4] good   [5] excellent

11. Do you feel you have adequate communication with relevant others within your division to get your job done?
    [1] less than adequate   [2] adequate   [3] more than adequate

12. What is the mix of formal and informal communication within your division?
    [1] mostly informal   [4] more formal than informal
    [2] more informal than formal   [5] mostly formal
    [3] about equal

13. How has the *quality* of communication within your division changed in recent years?
    [1] greatly reduced quality   [4] somewhat improved quality
    [2] somewhat reduced quality   [5] greatly improved quality
    [3] no change

14. How has the *quantity* of communication within your division changed in recent years?
    [1] greatly reduced quantity   [4] somewhat increased quantity
    [2] somewhat reduced quantity   [5] greatly increased quantity
    [3] no change

D. *Divisional Statistics*
   15. What percentage of total company
       sales was your division sales
       (last fiscal year)?

   _____*For parent-*
   division executives % of
   parent company sales

   (41-43)

   _____*For subsidiary-*
   division executives % of
   subsidiary sales

   16. What percentage of total company
       before-tax profit came from
       your division profit in the last
       fiscal year?

   _____*For parent-*
   division executives % of
   parent company before-tax
   profit

   (44-46)

   _____*For subsidiary-*
   division executives % of
   subsidiary before-tax
   profit

   17. What is the total number of
       persons employed in your
       division?

   _____

   (47-52)

(SKIP TO PAGE II-1)

CORPORATE SUBSIDIARY RELATIONS

Please circle the one response number that most clearly matches your opinion.

A. *Subsidiary-Parent Autonomy* (53-55)

1. In general, how much autonomy does your subsidiary have in relation to the parent company?
   [1] a little   [2] some   [3] a fair amount   [4] a great deal

2. In general, how has your subsidiary's level of autonomy changed over the past ten years or so?
   [1] much less   [4] somewhat more
   [2] somewhat less   [5] much more
   [3] stayed same

3. How much input does your subsidiary have in policy-making that affects your subsidiary?
   [1] little input   [3] a fair amount of input
   [2] some input   [4] a great deal of input

B. *Subsidiary-Parent Communications* (56-61)

4. Do you feel you have adequate communication with your parent company for getting your job done?
   [1] less than adequate   [2] adequate   [3] more than adequate

5. How would you evaluate the overall quality of communication between your subsidiary and the parent company?
   [1] very poor   [2] low   [3] adequate   [4] good   [5] excellent

6. What is the mix of formal communication (i.e., memos, periodic reports, scheduled meetings) and informal communication (i.e., phone calls, unscheduled conversations, grapevine) between your subsidiary and parent company?
   [1] mostly informal   [4] more formal than informal
   [2] more informal than formal   [5] mostly formal
   [3] about equal

7. How much has your organization adopted new communication technology (word processing, direct lines, etc.)?
   [1] a little   [2] some   [3] a fair amount   [4] a great deal

8. Has the *quality* of communication between the parent company and its subsidiaries improved in recent years?
   [1] greatly reduced quality   [4] somewhat improved quality
   [2] somewhat reduced quality   [5] greatly improved quality
   [3] no change

9. Has the *quantity* of communication between the parent company and its subsidiaries changed in recent years?
   [1] greatly reduced quantity   [4] somewhat increased quantity
   [2] somewhat reduced quantity   [5] greatly increased quantity
   [3] no change

C. *Intra-Subsidiary Communications* (62-66)

10. How would you evaluate the overall quality of communication within your subsidiary?
    [1] very poor   [2] low   [3] adequate   [4] good   [5] excellent

11. Do you feel you have adequate communication with relevant others within your subsidiary to get your job done?
    [1] lesss than adequate   [2] adequate   [3] more than adequate

12. What is the mix of formal and informal communication within your subsidiary?
    [1] mostly formal   [4] more formal than informal
    [2] more informal than formal   [5] mostly formal
    [3] about equal

13. How was the *quality* of communication within your subsidiary changed in recent years?
    [1] greatly reduced quality   [4] somewhat improved quality
    [2] somewhat reduced quality   [5] greatly improved quality
    [3] no change

14. How has the *quantity* of communication within your subsidiary changed in recent years?
    [1] greatly reduced quantity   [4] somewhat increased quantity
    [2] somewhat reduced quantity   [5] greatly increased quantity
    [3] no change

. *Subsidiary Statistics*

15. What percentage of total
    company sales was your
    subsidiary sales
    (last fiscal year)? _____ % (67-69)

16. What percentage of total
    company before-tax profit
    came from your subsidiary
    profit in the last fiscal
    year? _____ % (70-72)

17. What is the total number
    of persons employed in
    your subsidiary? _____ % (73-78)

SKIP TO PAGE II-1)

CORPORATE VALUES

The items in this section are designed to help us understand what publicly-held corporations value. In considering each item, please respond by keeping in mind to what degree you believe *your* corporation collectively values these matters.

For each numbered item below, please circle the one response number that most clearly matches your opinion on the corporation that presently employs you.

A. *Recruitment Policies and Practices:*

In your opinion, how much does your corporation support the recruitment of:

CARD
(10-2

	Strong support	Some support	No position	Some opposition	Strong opposition	Don't know / Inapplicable
1. Executives with degrees from prestigious colleges and universities.	1	2	3	4	5	6
2. Executives with Master of Business Administration degrees.	1	2	3	4	5	6
3. Executives having another type of advanced degree (master's level or above).	1	2	3	4	5	6
4. Executives having an undergraduate engineering or technical degree.	1	2	3	4	5	6
5. Executives having an undergraduate liberal arts or humanities degree.	1	2	3	4	5	6
6. Senior executives from outside the company.	1	2	3	4	5	6
7. Executives having high social status family backgrounds.	1	2	3	4	5	6
8. Executives having low social status family backgrounds.	1	2	3	4	5	6
9. Executives from one region in the U.S.	1	2	3	4	5	6
10. Executives who are women.	1	2	3	4	5	6
11. Executives who are not overweight.	1	2	3	4	5	6
12. A male executive only after evaluating his wife.	1	2	3	4	5	6
13. A female executive only after evaluating her husband.	1	2	3	4	5	6

Promotion Policies and Practices (23-43)

In general, how much does your corporation support promoting:

	Strong support	Some support	No position	Some opposition	Strong opposition	Don't know Inapplicable
To senior position (v.p. or above) from within its executive ranks.	1	2	3	4	5	6
a senior position (v.p. above) a top executive om the following partments:						
a. Personnel/human resources	1	2	3	4	5	6
b. Manufacturing (operations or production)	1	2	3	4	5	6
c. Field operations in general	1	2	3	4	5	6
d. Sales	1	2	3	4	5	6
e. Marketing	1	2	3	4	5	6
f. Finance	1	2	3	4	5	6
g. Research & Development	1	2	3	4	5	6
h. Legal	1	2	3	4	5	6
i. General Management	1	2	3	4	5	6
j. Line Positions	1	2	3	4	5	6
k. Staff Positions	1	2	3	4	5	6
senior positions execu- es who are:						
a. over 35 years of age	1	2	3	4	5	6
b. between 51 and 55 years of age	1	2	3	4	5	6
c. between 46 and 50 years of age	1	2	3	4	5	6
d. between 41 and 45 years of age	1	2	3	4	5	6
e. between 35 and 40 years of age	1	2	3	4	5	6
f. under 35 years of age	1	2	3	4	5	6
Women to senior management.	1	2	3	4	5	6
Women to middle manage-ment (managers, directors, and supervisors of depart-ments and functions).	1	2	3	4	5	6
An executive only after he/she groomed a successor.	1	2	3	4	5	6

Assume you were considering the following people for positions in the departmental function or division for which you are responsible. Indicate how highly you would rate them.

(44-

	Disquality	Very poor candidate					Excellent candidate
	1	2	3	4	5	6	7
20. A woman executive with appropriate experience.	1	2	3	4	5	6	7
21. A woman with a liberal arts degree, no business experience, but says she wants to be your gopher and will earnestly study the business.	1	2	3	4	5	6	7
22. The woman above, who has been an elementary school district supervisor for 10 years.	1	2	3	4	5	6	7
23. A hospital chaplain who wants to get into business and who strikes you as a natural leader.	1	2	3	4	5	6	7
24. A woman whose children have grown up and who has just completed a Master of Business Administration degree.	1	2	3	4	5	6	7
25. An executive who "dropped out" from corporate life for two years to run an organic farm in northern Wisconsin.	1	2	3	4	5	6	7
26. A 24 year old male student who just finished his Master of Business Administration degree at a B-School you know little about.	1	2	3	4	5	6	7
27. The student above, from Harvard.	1	2	3	4	5	6	7
28. A 24 year old female student who just completed her Master of Business Administration degree at Wharton.	1	2	3	4	5	6	7

	Disqualify	Very poor candidate					Excellent candidate
	1	2	3	4	5	6	7

An executive who:

29. was fired from his last job.	1	2	3	4	5	6	7
30. was fired from his last two jobs.	1	2	3	4	5	6	7
31. has had jobs with five different companies in the last 10 years.	1	2	3	4	5	6	7
32. comes to your job interview with scuffed or unpolished shoes.	1	2	3	4	5	6	7

A male executive who:

33. comes to your job interview with a mustache.	1	2	3	4	5	6	7
34. comes to your job interview with a beard.	1	2	3	4	5	6	7
35. comes to your job interview wearing a bracelet or neck chain.	1	2	3	4	5	6	7
36. orders an alcoholic drink when you take him to lunch.	1	2	3	4	5	6	7

A female executive who:

37. comes to your job interview in a semi-transparent blouse.	1	2	3	4	5	6	7

	Disqualify	Very poor candidate					Excellent candidate
	1	2	3	4	5	6	7

An executive who:

38. comes to your job interview five minutes late.

1	2	3	4	5	6	7

39. comes to your job interview 15 minutes early.

1	2	3	4	5	6	7

40. asks reflective questions about your company during your job interview.

1	2	3	4	5	6	7

41. was recommended to you by your employment agency.

1	2	3	4	5	6	7

42. was recommended to you by your executive search firm.

1	2	3	4	5	6	7

43. was recommended to you by your personnel department.

1	2	3	4	5	6	7

44. called you at home one evening, told you he admired you and wanted to work for you.

1	2	3	4	5	6	7

45. A senior graduating from Princeton, Phi Beta Kappa in literature, who wants a career in business.

1	2	3	4	5	6	7

46. A senior graduating from Dartmouth with a C average, who majored in political science, and wants a career in business.

1	2	3	4	5	6	7

47. A senior graduating from a large state university with a B average, who majored in business administration.

1	2	3	4	5	6	7

48. A graduating Master of Business Administration student from Stanford whose undergraduate major was in liberal arts at a small church-related college.

1	2	3	4	5	6	7

49. The son of your college roommate who just graduated from your alma mater with a C+ average and majored in sociology.

1	2	3	4	5	6	7

C. *Executive Work Styles*
Does your corporation encourage or discourage the following:

	Strongly encourage	Somewhat encourage	No position	Somewhat discourage	Strongly discourage	Don't know / Inapplicable
50. Working in suit coats.	1	2	3	4	5	6
51. Being a good writer.	1	2	3	4	5	6
52. Taking only short vacations (one week or less).	1	2	3	4	5	6
53. Heavy business traveling (130 nights per year away from home and family).	1	2	3	4	5	6
54. Sixty-hour or more work-weeks.	1	2	3	4	5	6
55. Following an active physical fitness exercise program.	1	2	3	4	5	6
56. Speed in decision-making.	1	2	3	4	5	6
57. Consistently displaying energy and a fast pace on the job.	1	2	3	4	5	6
58. Executives being "well liked" by their peers.	1	2	3	4	5	6
59. Executives being feared by their subordinates.	1	2	3	4	5	6
60. Understaffing of executives for the workload.	1	2	3	4	5	6

D. *Policies for Executives*
How typically does your corporation engage in the following policies:

	Always done	Usually done	Often done	Seldom done	Never done	Don't know / Inapplicable
61. Firing marginally performing executives.	1	2	3	4	5	6
62. Providing career planning and counseling for its executives.	1	2	3	4	5	6
63. Transferring its executives only after careful consideration.	1	2	3	4	5	6
64. Encouraging its executives to add to their formal education.	1	2	3	4	5	6
65. Providing adequate coverage in its health care policy for psychological counseling.	1	2	3	4	5	6

	Always done	Usually done	Often done	Seldom done	Never done	Don't know / inapplicable
66. Providing counseling for its executives experiencing drinking problems.	1	2	3	4	5	6
67. Company-sponsored management education, development and training.	1	2	3	4	5	6
68. Articulating its intended corporate destiny and business strategy for all its employees.	1	2	3	4	5	6

E. *Executive Life Styles*
How much importance does your corporation attach to the following behavior of its executives: (29-42)

	Very important	Somewhat important	Somewhat unimportant	Not important at all	Don't know
69. Marriage for males.	1	2	3	4	5
70. Marriage for females.	1	2	3	4	5
71. Avoiding divorce.	1	2	3	4	5
72. Executive involvement in community activity.	1	2	3	4	5
73. Executives' spouses' involvement in community activity.	1	2	3	4	5
74. Socializing with other executives.	1	2	3	4	5
75. Membership in a church.	1	2	3	4	5
76. Avoiding extramarital affairs.	1	2	3	4	5
77. Avoiding discovery of extramarital affairs.	1	2	3	4	5
78. Having large families (four or more children).	1	2	3	4	5
79. Having small families (two or fewer children).	1	2	3	4	5
80. Maintaining active hobbies off the job.	1	2	3	4	5
81. Living in a prestigious residential area for senior executives.	1	2	3	4	5
82. Living in a prestigious residential area for middle-level executives.	1	2	3	4	5

Corporate Images (43-46)

How much concern exists in your corporation for the following public image issues:

	A great deal of concern	Moderate amount of concern	Relatively small concern	No concern	Don't know/ inapplicable
3. Being perceived as a socially responsible company.	1	2	3	4	5
4. Being perceived as an innovative company.	1	2	3	4	5
5. Being perceived as a high-technology company.	1	2	3	4	5
6. Having media attention regarding corporate stances on industry issues.	1	2	3	4	5

What extent does your corporation pay attention to the following items: (47-52)

	Much attention	Some attention	Little attention	No attention	Don't know/ inapplicable
7. Having quality art work (paintings, prints, sculpture) displayed in executive offices.	1	2	3	4	5
8. Architecture of the corporate building(s).	1	2	3	4	5
. Landscaping around corporate facilities.	1	2	3	4	5
. Decor and furnishings of the facilities.	1	2	3	4	5
. Supporting the arts financially.	1	2	3	4	5
. Contributing funds to community social service agencies.	1	2	3	4	5

. If you could describe your company as an animal, what would that animal be? _____ (53-54)

. What characteristics of that animal make it a good analogy for your company? _____

_____

_____

_____

_____ (55-64)

CORPORATE ORGANIZATION & FUNCTIONING

A. *Corporate Activity and Structure*

Please provide to the best of your knowledge the following information on your present corporation. *(circle one)*

1. Generally, how strong do you consider the board of directors in exercising its responsibilities?   (65)
   [1] very strong   [2] moderately strong   [2] moderately weak   [4] very weak

2. What number of executives report directly to your parent company president?   _____   (66-

3. What number of executives report to the CEO if different person from President?   _____   (70-

4. In your present position, to whom do you report?
   [1] report directly to CEO/chairman
   [2] report directly to CEO/president
   [3] report to someone who reports directly to CEO   (73)
   [4] report to someone who does not report directly to CEO

B. *Executive Position and Perquisites*

Please provide us with the following information about your present position in your corporate organization.   CARI

5. Are you a vice president?   (10)
   [1] yes   [2] no

6. Do you have a title in the parent company?   (11)
   [1] yes   [2] no *(Skip to 7)*
   6a.   What is it?   _____   (12-

7. Do you have a title in a subsidiary?   (14
   [1] yes   [2] no   *(Skip to 8)*
   7a.   What is it?   _____   (15-

8. Do you have a title in a division of the parent?   (17
   [1] yes   [2] no   *(Skip to 9)*
   8a.   What is it?   _____   (18

9. Do you have a title in a division of a subsididary?   (20
   [1] yes   [2] no *(Skip to 10)*
   9a.   What is it?   _____   (21

10. In what functional area do you work? *(select only one)*
    [1] general field operations   [7] manufacturing (operations or production)   (23
    [2] finance   [8] research and development
    [3] general management   [9] sales
    [4] legal   [10] other *(please specify)*
    [5] personnel/human resources   _____   (24
    [6] marketing

11. Are you primarily a staff executive?   (2(
    [1] yes   [2] no

12. Are you primarily a line executive?   (27
    [1] yes   [2] no

13. What was the total amount of cash compensation paid to you by your company (or by all your companies if you worked for more than one) in last calendar year? $_____   (2(

14. Was all of this amount salary?   (3(
    [1] yes *(Skip to 15)* [2] no
    14a.   What amount was bonus? $_____   (32

Please indicate all items below that you are eligible to receive from your present employer: *(circle as many as apply)* (37-72)

    [1] Company-paid country club membership
    [2] Company-paid city club membership
    [3] Company-paid automobile
    [4] Frequent use of company-owned or rented limousine
    [5] Stock purchase plan
    [6] Interest-free or low-interest loans to buy company stock
    [7] Loans to purchase a new home
    [8] Company-paid brokerage fees for the sale of your home when relocating
    [9] Company makes up difference in any loss incurred in selling your home when relocating
    [10] All moving expenses paid when relocating
    [11] One or more business trips per year when spouse's expenses are paid by company
    [12] Company finds suitable employment for spouse when relocating
    [13] Use of company-owned or leased aircraft for business trips
    [14] Use of company-owned or leased aircraft for personal trips
    [15] Company-paid estate and financial planning
    [16] Company-paid income tax preparation
    [17] Lodge and vacation facilities
    [18] Other *(please specify perquisites)* _____

    _____   **CARD-05**

    _____   (10-19)

    _____   (20-21)

What is your immediate boss' title? _____

16a. Does the title above refer to a position in the parent company? (22)

    [1] yes *(Skip to 17)*   [2] no

16b. Does your immediate boss have any title in the parent company? (23)

    [1] yes   [2] no *(Skip to 17)*

16c. What is your boss' title in the parent company? _____ (24-25)

In what functional area of the corporation does your boss serve? *(select one)* (26)

    [1] general field operations   [7] manufacturing (operations or production)
    [2] finance   [8] research and development
    [3] general management   [9] sales
    [4] legal   [10] other *(please specify)* (27-28)
    [5] personnel/human resources   _____
    [6] marketing

What number of executives, including you, report directly to your boss?_____ (29-32)

Do you report to more than one person? (33)

    [1] yes   [2] no *(Skip to 20)*

19a. How many in total? _____ (34-35)

How many executives report directly to you? _____ (36-39)

Approximately what number of people work for you overall in your area of responsibility? _____ (40-44)

Generally, how many hours per week do you work? (45)

    [1] 40-45 hours   [2] 46-50 hours   [3] 51-60 hours   [4] over 60 hours

What percentage of the total hours you work per week do you work at home? _____ (46-48)

Do you have budget responsibilities? (49)

    [1] yes   [2] no *(Skip to 26)*

What is the amount of your current annual budget that you are responsible for? $_____ (50-53)

Is there a specified limit for expenditures you can make without getting your boss' approval? (54)

    [1] yes   [2] no *(Skip to 27)*

26a. What is this limit? $_____ (55-57)

Rank the frequency with which you use the following means to reach decisions in your areas of responsibility. *($\underline{1}$ = most frequent; $\underline{3}$ = least frequent)* (58-60)

    [ ] Alone   [ ] In meetings with your subordinates   [ ] One-to-one with your boss

C. *Relationships with Higher Executives*

Indicate the general pattern of communication and decision making you and your boss are involved in. (61
(circle one)

	Always	Usually	Sometimes	Seldom	Never	Don't know
28. Does your boss make major decisions on a one-to-one basis with his subordinates?	1	2	3	4	5	6
29. Will your boss call meetings of all direct reporting subordinates for discussion on major decisions?	1	2	3	4	5	6
30. Do you and your boss share information essential to the business that is not shared with your department peers (who also report to your boss)?	1	2	3	4	5	6
31. Does your boss and at least one of your department peers share information essential to the business that is not shared with the rest of you?	1	2	3	4	5	6
32. Is your boss too slow in responding to your recommendations?	1	2	3	4	5	6
33. Are you free to exchange operating information with your peers in other functions without the approval of your boss?	1	2	3	4	5	6

34. Does anyone besides your immediate boss evaluate your work?
    [1] yes   [2] no *(Skip to 36)*
35. If so, what are their titles? _____
    _____
36. Does your authority generally match your responsibility on projects you are assigned?
    [1] yes *(Skip to 37)*   [2] no
    36a. Do you think it should?
    [1] yes   [2] no
37. Are your opinions sought by your boss as often as you would like?
    [1] generally yes   [2] it varies   [3] generally no
38. Do you have a voice in initiating new products or services?
    [1] yes *(Skip to 39)*   [2] no
    38a. Do you think you should?
    [1] yes   [2] no
39. Do you have contact with your company's customers?
    [1] yes *(Skip to 40)*   [2] no
    39a. Do you think you should?
    [1] yes   [2] no
40. Do you have a voice in setting the objectives for your area of responsibility?
    [1] generally yes   [2] it varies   [3] generally no
41. Do you feel you are in a job with limited potential for advancement?
    [1] yes   [2] uncertain   [3] no

(25-30)

42. Do you consider yourself in competition with your department peers?
    - [1] always   [4] never
    - [2] usually   [5] not applicable (no peers)
    - [3] sometimes

43. Do you consider yourself in cooperation with your department peers?
    - [1] always   [4] never
    - [2] usually   [5] not applicable (no peers)
    - [3] sometimes

44. Do you and your department peers collectively consider your function in competition with other functions in your division or company?
    - [1] always   [4] never
    - [2] usually   [5] not applicable (no peers)
    - [3] sometimes

45. Do you believe yourself to be a candidate for your boss' job when he is promoted or vacates it for some reason?
    - [1] yes   [2] uncertain   [3] no

46. Do you believe some or all of your peers who also report to your boss are likewise candidates for his job?
    - [1] yes   [2] uncertain   [3] no

D. *Relationships with Subordinates*

47. Do you have subordinates working for you?
    - [1] yes   [2] no *(Skip to 57)*

(31-39)

Indicate the general frequency with which you act in making decisions. *(circle one)*

	Always	Usually	Sometimes	Never	Don't know
48. Do you call meetings of all your direct reporting subordinates for discussion on major decisions?	1	2	3	4	5
49. Do you make major decisions without consulting all your direct subordinates present in meetings?	1	2	3	4	5
50. Do you make major decisions on a one-to-one basis with your subordinates?	1	2	3	4	5
51. Do you make major decisions without consulting your subordinates at all?	1	2	3	4	5
52. Do you think your subordinates are too impatient for your responses to their recommendations?	1	2	3	4	5
53. Do you share information essential to the business with certain of your subordinates that is not shared with the rest of your subordinates?	1	2	3	4	5
54. Do you accept on faith the competence of a subordinate in your company with whom you have never worked?	1	2	3	4	5
55. Do you believe your subordinates should circumvent the chain of command?	1	2	3	4	5

56. What type of authority do you have concerning hiring and firing your subordinates?
    - [1] sole authority   [3] collective decision of department
    - [2] joint authority   [4] don't have any authority

E. *General Management Strategies*
Evaluate your corporation on the following dimensions, based on your knowledge of its structure. *(circle one)*

	Strongly agree	Agree	Uncertain	Disagree	Strongly disagree
57. The department for which you have responsibility operates efficiently.	1	2	3	4	5
58. The group or function for which your boss has responsibility operates efficiently.	1	2	3	4	5
59. Your parent company operates efficiently.	1	2	3	4	5
60. Formal controls within the corporation are necessary to curb corruption.	1	2	3	4	5
61. Meetings are too much a "way of life" in your company.	1	2	3	4	5
62. Throughout your company, too many people have too little discretionary authority.	1	2	3	4	5
63. Influence in having things go your way in your company is largely due to time-in-grade.	1	2	3	4	5
64. Getting promoted in your company is largely due to time-in-grade.	1	2	3	4	5

F. *Evaluation of Female Executives*
As contrasted to male executives with equivalent qualifications, female executives in your corporation are
likely to: *(circle one)*

	Strongly agree	Agree	Neutral	Disagree	Strongly disagree	Don't know/ Inapplicable
65. Advance faster.	1	2	3	4	5.	6
66. Advance at the same rate.	1	2	3	4	5	6
67. Enter at a higher level.	1	2	3	4	5	6
68. Need greater sponsorship for promotion.	1	2	3	4	5	6
69. Have a lower risk of being fired.	1	2	3	4	5	6
70. Be more successful if they remain single.	1	2	3	4	5	6
71. Be at a disadvantage if they have children.	1	2	3	4	5	6

In general, how much does your corporation support promoting female executives who are:

	Considerable support	Some support	No position	Some opposition	Considerable opposition	Don't know / Inapplicable
2. over 55 years of age.	1	2	3	4	5	6
3. between 51 and 55 years of age.	1	2	3	4	5	6
4. between 46 and 50 years of age.	1	2	3	4	5	6
5. between 41 and 45 years of age.	1	2	3	4	5	6
6. between 35 and 40 years of age.	1	2	3	4	5	6
7. under 35 years of age.	1	2	3	4	5	6
at any age.	1	2	3	4	5	6

CORPORATE GOALS & ACTIVITIES

In the left-hand block (I) below, indicate how *important* this item is as a *goal* of your corporation.

Regardless of how you ranked these goals, indicate in the right-hand block (II) what are your corporation's typical *activities* in the market and society.

A. *Economic*

I. How important is this for your corporation? *(circle one)*

II. How often does your corporation do this? *(circle one)*

(62-7

	No importance at all	Very little	Fair amount	Very important	Among highest goals	Not applicable		Rarely or never	Sometimes	Frequently	Generally	Virtually always	Not applicable
1. Making acquisitions.	1	2	3	4	5	6		1	2	3	4	5	6
2. Avoiding being acquired by another company.	1	2	3	4	5	6		1	2	3	4	5	6
3. Increasing total annual sales volume.	1	2	3	4	5	6		1	2	3	4	5	6
4. Increasing before-tax profit.	1	2	3	4	5	6		1	2	3	4	5	6
5. Increasing return on assets.	1	2	3	4	5	6		1	2	3	4	5	6
6. Expanding international business activities.	1	2	3	4	5	6		1	2	3	4	5	6
7. Survival as a distinctive corporate entity.	1	2	3	4	5	6		1	2	3	4	5	6
8. Retaining members of the board of directors who are not members of management.	1	2	3	4	5	6		1	2	3	4	5	6
9. Planning for the long-range.	1	2	3	4	5	6		1	2	3	4	5	6
10. Fulfilling capital commitment objectives.	1	2	3	4	5	6		1	2	3	4	5	6
11. Providing incentive compensation for its executives.	1	2	3	4	5	6		1	2	3	4	5	6
12. Driving its competitors out of business.	1	2	3	4	5	6		1	2	3	4	5	6
13. Expanding into and creating new markets.	1	2	3	4	5	6		1	2	3	4	5	6
14. Producing products/services of high quality.	1	2	3	4	5	6		1	2	3	4	5	6
15. Developing new products/services.	1	2	3	4	5	6		1	2	3	4	5	6

CARD
(10-2

	I. How important is this for your corporation? (circle one)						II. How often does your corporation do this? (circle one)					
	No importance at all	Very little	Fair amount	Very important	Among highest goals	Not applicable	Rarely or never	Sometimes	Frequently	Generally	Virtually always	Not applicable
6. Marketing new products/services.	1	2	3	4	5	6	1	2	3	4	5	6
7. Adapting to changing market demands.	1	2	3	4	5	6	1	2	3	4	5	6
8. Staying abreast of the state of the art in technology relevant to your corporation's business.	1	2	3	4	5	6	1	2	3	4	5	6
9. Providing income for its stockholders.	1	2	3	4	5,	6	1	2	3	4	5	6
10. Managing its financial controls.	1	2	3	4	5	6	1	2	3	4	5	6
11. Having good union relations.	1	2	3	4	5	6	1	2	3	4	5	6
12. Having good information flow necessary to decision-making.	1	2	3	4	5	6	1	2	3	4	5	6

(26-39)

Social Welfare

(40-53)

	No importance at all	Very little	Fair amount	Very important	Among highest goals	Not applicable	Rarely or never	Sometimes	Frequently	Generally	Virtually always	Not applicable
Providing goods and services for society's needs and wants.	1	2	3	4	5	6	1	2	3	4	5	6
Creating jobs.	1	2	3	4	5	6	1	2	3	4	5	6
Advancing the technological sophistication of society.	1	2	3	4	5	6	1	2	3	4	5	6
Contributing funds to community facilities such as schools, hospitals, parks, etc.	1	2	3	4	5	6	1	2	3	4	5	6
Articulating its needs to the public.	1	2	3	4	5	6	1	2	3	4	5	6
Being aware of the public's image of the corporation.	1	2	3	4	5	6	1	2	3	4	5	6
Educating the public on the free enterprise system.	1	2	3	4	5	6	1	2	3	4	5	6

	I. How important is this for your corporation? (circle one)						II. How often does your corporation do this? (circle one)					
	No importance at all	Very little	Fair amount	Very important	Among highest Goals	Not applicable	Rarely or never	Sometimes	Frequently	Commonly	Virtually always	Not applicable
30. Making life less burdensome for the poor in the society.	1	2	3	4	5	6	1	2	3	4	5	6
31. Improving the quality of life for members of society.	1	2	3	4	5	6	1	2	3	4	5	6

C. *Governmental Relations*

32. Paying its share of taxes to governments.	1	2	3	4	5	6	1	2	3	4	5	6
33. Legally reducing its share of taxes to governments.	1	2	3	4	5	6	1	2	3	4	5	6
34. Working to limit State and Federal government regulation of its business.	1	2	3	4	5	6	1	2	3	4	5	6
35. Working cooperatively with governments and governmental regulatory agencies.	1	2	3	4	5	6	1	2	3	4	5	6
36. Reorganizing production to reduce energy needs.	1	2	3	4	5	6	1	2	3	4	5	6
37. Complying with environmental regulations.	1	2	3	4	5	6	1	2	3	4	5	6

(54-69)

CARD-08
(10-23)

D. *Hiring and Training of Minorities for Executive Positions*

38. Hiring Blacks.	1	2	3	4	5	6	1	2	3	4	5	6
39. Hiring Hispanics.	1	2	3	4	5	6	1	2	3	4	5	6
40. Hiring American Indians.	1	2	3	4	5	6	1	2	3	4	5	6
41. Hiring Orientals.	1	2	3	4	5	6	1	2	3	4	5	6
42. Hiring women.	1	2	3	4	5	6	1	2	3	4	5	6
43. Training Blacks for senior management.	1	2	3	4	5	6	1	2	3	4	5	6
44. Training Hispanics for senior management.	1	2	3	4	5	6	1	2	3	4	5	6

	I. How important is this for your corporation? (circle one)						II. How often does your corporation do this? (circle one)					
	No importance at all	Very little	Fair amount	Very important	Among highest goals	Not applicable	Rarely or never	Sometimes	Frequently	Generally	Virtually always	Not applicable

(24-45)

	No importance at all	Very little	Fair amount	Very important	Among highest goals	Not applicable	Rarely or never	Sometimes	Frequently	Generally	Virtually always	Not applicable
5. Training American Indians for senior management.	1	2	3	4	5	6	1	2	3	4	5	6
6. Training Orientals for senior management.	1	2	3	4	5	6	1	2	3	4	5	6
7. Training women for senior management.	1	2	3	4	5	6	1	2	3	4	5	6

Personnel Relations

	No importance at all	Very little	Fair amount	Very important	Among highest goals	Not applicable	Rarely or never	Sometimes	Frequently	Generally	Virtually always	Not applicable
8. Helping its executives attain "self-actualization."	1	2	3	4	5	6	1	2	3	4	5	6
9. Helping its executives broaden their skills.	1	2	3	4	5	6	1	2	3	4	5	6
10. Matching up executives' positions with executives' personality traits.	1	2	3	4	5	6	1	2	3	4	5	6
11. Preparing its executives for general management responsibilities.	1	2	3	4	5	6	1	2	3	4	5	6
12. Providing proper safety measures for its workers.	1	2	3	4	5	6	1	2	3	4	5	6
Articulating its corporate strategy to all its employees.	1	2	3	4	5	6	1	2	3	4	5	6
Rewarding its superior achievers.	1	2	3	4	5	6	1	2	3	4	5	6
Building morale of its executives.	1	2	3	4	5	6	1	2	3	4	5	6

	I. How important is this for your corporation? *(circle one)*						II. How often does your corporation do this? *(circle one)*					
	No importance at all	Very little	Fair amount	Very important	Always helpful	Not applicable	Rarely or never	Sometimes	Frequently	Generally	Virtually always	Not applicable

(46-

Providing a "feeling of belonging" for its:

56. top management.	1	2	3	4	5	6	1	2	3	4	5	6
57. middle management.	1	2	3	4	5	6	1	2	3	4	5	6
58. clerical staff.	1	2	3	4	5	6	1	2	3	4	5	6
59. first-line supervisors.	1	2	3	4	5	6	1	2	3	4	5	6
60. hourly workers.	1	2	3	4	5	6	1	2	3	4	5	6
61. Encouraging a collaborative style of management as opposed to an authoritarian one.	1	2	3	4	5	6	1	2	3	4	5	6
62. Gaining the maximum performance from newly recruited executives.	1	2	3	4	5	6	1	2	3	4	5	6
63. Creating an atmosphere of openness to new ideas by top management.	1	2	3	4	5	6	1	2	3	4	5	6

EXECUTIVE BACKGROUND & EMPLOYMENT CRITERIA

he human dimension of corporations is best represented by executives. Therefore, we would like to know
mething about the background you bring to your position and some of the strategies you have developed
r merging private and corporate concerns. *(circle one)*

1. What is your age as of your last birthday?
   [1] 25-30 yrs.   [4] 51-60 yrs.
   [2] 31-40 yrs.   [5] 61-67 yrs.
   [3] 41-50 yrs.   [6] 68 + yrs.

2. What is your marital status?
   [1] single   [2] married   [3] remarried   [4] divorced   [5] widowed

3. What is your sex?
   [1] male   [2] female

4. What is your height?
   [1] 5'5" and under   [2] 5'6" to 5'8"   [3] 5'9" to 5'11"   [4] 6' to 6'3"   [5] 6'4" and over

5. What is your weight (in lbs.)?
   [1] 109 and under   [6] 166 to 185
   [2] 110 to 120   [7] 186 to 200
   [3] 121 to 130   [8] 201 to 225
   [4] 131 to 149   [9] 226 and over
   [5] 150 to 165

(15-19)

6. What is your current resident zip code? _____

(20-21)

7. At what age did you first consider a career in business? _____

8. How old were you when you accepted a full-time corporate position? _____

(22-23)

9. Do you have a high school degree?
   [1] yes   [2] no *(Skip to 13)*

(24-27)

   9a. Was this school:
   [1] public   [2] private or prep

10. Did you attend college?
   [1] yes, degree granted   [2] some college *(Skip to 13)*   [3] no *(Skip to 13)*

   10a. Type of degree
   [1] B.A.   [2] B.S.   [3] two year degree

   10b. Major field
   [1] liberal arts   [5] science
   [2] fine arts   [6] business
   [3] engineering   [7] other *(please specify)*
   [4] social science   _____

(28)

(29-30)

   10c. How would you rate this school?
   [1] Ivy League   [4] other state
   [2] other prestigious   [5] other private
        private   [6] other *(please specify)*
   [3] prestigious state   _____

(31)

(32-33)

11. Did you attend a Master's or Professional program?
   [1] yes, degree granted
   [2] non-matriculating or some courses *(Skip to 13)*
   [3] no *(Skip to 13)*

(34)

   11a. Type of degree
   [1] business   [4] social sciences
   [2] engineering   [5] other *(please specify)*
   [3] law   _____

(35)

(36-37)

   11b. Major field
   [1] finance   [5] management
   [2] accounting   [6] other *(please specify)*
   [3] marketing   _____
   [4] organizational behavior

(38)

(39-40)

   11c. How would you rate this school?
   [1] Ivy League   [4] other state
   [2] other prestigious   [5] other private
        private   [6] other *(please specify)*
   [3] prestigious state   _____

(41)

(42-43)

12. Did you attend a post-Master's program?
   [1] yes, degree granted   [2] yes, degree not completed *(Skip to 13)*   [3] no *(Skip to 13)*

(44)

   12a. Type of degree
   [1] Ph.D.   [2] M.D.   [3] LL.B. or J.D.   [4] other *(please specify)* _____

(45)

(46-47)

12b. How would you rate this school? (48)

[1] Ivy League   [4] other state

[2] other prestigious   [5] other private
    private   [6] other *(please specify)*

[3] prestigious state   _____ (49-50)

13. Did you interrupt your career to return to school?

[1] yes   [2] no *(Skip to 14)* (51)

    13a. When did you interrupt your career? *(give start and finish month and year)*

      From: _____/_____To: _____/_____ (52-59)
          mo.   yr.   mo.   yr.

14. What was your level of formal education when you first began your business career full time? (60-63)

[1] high school   [4] Master's or equvalent

[2] some college   [5] Doctorate

[3] Bachelor's

15. What was your mother's highest level of schooling?

[1] elementary   [5] Master's

[2] high school   [6] LL.B. or J.D.

[3] some college   [7] Doctorate or M.D.

[4] Bachelor's

16. What was your father's highest level of schooling?

[1] elementary   [5] Master's

[2] high school   [6] LL.B. or J.D.

[3] some college   [7] Doctorate or M.D.

[4] Bachelor's

17. Did you receive any degrees while working full-time?

[1] yes   [2] no *(Skip to 18)*

    17a. What degrees: *(circle as many as apply)* (64-69)

    [1] Bachelor's   [4] Engineering

    [2] Master's   [5] M.B.A.

    [3] LL.B. or J.D.   [6] other *(please specify)* (70-73)

          _____

CARD-10

    17b. Year of degrees: 1st_____/ 2nd_____/ 3rd_____ (10-15)

18. How many siblings did you have at age 12?

#_____brothers   #_____sisters *(If none, skip to 19)* (16-17)

    18a. Are you:

[1] the oldest   [2] in the middle   [3] the youngest (18)

19. Was your mother ever a corporation executive?

[1] yes   [2] no (19)

20. Was your father ever a corporation executive?

[1] yes   [2] no (20)

21. Do you have one or more siblings in a corporate executive position?

[1] yes   [2] no *(Skip to 22)* (21)

    21a. How many?_____ (22-23)

22. Thinking back to when you took your first full-time job with a corporation, indicate the means by which you were introduced to that company.

[1] employment agency

[2] executive search consultant (24)

[3] campus recruiter

[4] you responded to a magazine or newspaper advertisement

[5] you responded to a radio or television advertisement

[6] a friend or relative arranged it

[7] you contacted the company directly

[8] other *(please specify means)* _____ (25-28)

_____

23. Is this first corporation your present employer?

[1] yes *(Skip to 25)*   [2] no (29)

24. How were you first introduced to your *present* employer?

[1] employment agency

[2] executive search firm

[3] you responded to a magazine or newspaper advertisement

[4] you responded to a radio or television advertisement (30)

[5] a friend or relative arranged it

[6] you contacted the company directly

[7] other *(please specify means)* _____ (31-34)

5. If you directly contacted the corporation where you are now employed, did you make use of a direct mail campaign in doing so? (35-41)
  [1] yes   [2] no *(Skip to 26)*   [3] did not contact corporation directly
  25a. Did a career counseling firm have any involvement in the planning or execution of the campaign?
    [1] yes   [2] no

6. Do you have a resume prepared currently that includes a description of your present job title and responsibilities?
    [1] yes *(Skip to 27)*   [2] no
  26a. Are you likely to prepare one soon?
    [1] yes   [2] no   [3] don't know

7. What is your present spouse's highest level of schooling?
    [1] elementary   [4] Bachelor's
    [2] high school   [5] Master's
    [3] some college   [6] Doctorate
    [7] not currently married *(Skip to 30d)*

. Did she/he obtain a degree after you were employed in an executive position?
    [1] yes   [2] no

. Has she/he ever been employed after your marriage?
    [1] never employed *(skip to 30c)*
    [2] not employed now
    [3] part-time employment
    [4] full-time employment
  29a. What was her/his most recent employment? _____ (42-43)
  29b. What was her/his most recent title?_____ (44-45)
  29c. In what ways has your present spouse's work affected your career?_____
  _____
  _____
  _____
  _____
  _____
  _____ (53-62)
  _____

  29d. In what ways has your career affected her/his work?
  _____
  _____
  _____
  _____
  _____
  _____ (56-65)
  _____

What is her/his current employment status? CARD-11
    [1] currently working full-time
    [2] currently working part-time
    [3] not currently working, but is planning to (10)
    [4] neither working nor planning to *(Skip to 30c)*
  30a. Will her/his employment situation influence your relocation decisions in the future? (11)
    [1] very strongly   [2] strongly   [3] somewhat   [4] very little   [5] not at all
  30b. How much importance do you attach to your current spouse's employment, relative to your own?
    [1] mine is much more important
    [2] mine is somewhat more important
    [3] about equal
    [4] spouse's is more important (12)
    [5] spouse's is much more important
  30c. How old is your present spouse? _____years (13-14)
  30d. How many children do you have currently living with you? (15-16)
    Number_____ None_____ *(Skip to 31)*
  30e. What are the ages of the youngest and oldest? _____ _____ (17-20)
    (youngest)   (oldest)

31. Over your total period of marriage, did/has your spouse actively supported your career? (21)

[1] never married   [4] sometimes supported
   (Skip to Part VI)   [5] never supported
[2] always supported   *(Skip to Part VI)*
[3] usually supported

31a. How important has this support been for your career advancement? (22)

[1] very important   [3] marginal at most
[2] somewhat important   [4] don't know

31b. What type of support did/has your spouse provided? *(circle as many as apply)*

(23-32)

[1] dinners, parties, or other similar entertaining of business-related people
[2] participation in volunteer work related to your corporation
[3] moral support and encouragement
[4] willingness to relocate
[5] maintaining a well-run household
[6] socializing with other executives' spouses
[7] financial support
[8] relieving you of household duties
[9] keeping children quiet when you work at home
[10] other *(please specify)*

_____

_____

_____

_____

_____

_____ (33-4

CAREER ADVANCEMENT IN THE CORPORATE WORLD

CARD-12

. *Recent Career History*

(10-11)

1. In how many corporations have you worked in an executive capacity?_____

tarting with your current position and working back through *three* prior positions, please write the
ppropriate response number in the space provided.

	Current position	Last position	Second-to-last	Third-to-last	
2. Was this career change a geographic relocation? [1] Yes [2] No					(12-15)
3. Was this position: [1] Promotion only [2] Promotion & Transfer [3] Transfer only [4] Move to another firm [5] Other *(specify)*					(16-19) (20-23)
4. Location of Firm: [1] Corporate Town [2] Central City [3] Suburb [4] Other *(specify)*					(24-27) (28-31)
5. No. of Years in Position:					(32-35)
6. Type of Firm: [1] Parent [2] Division or Subsidiary [3] Other *(specify)*					(36-39) (40-43)

7. Firm's Principal Activity:
   (i.e., aerospace, banking, extractive, etc.)

    7a. in current position _____ (44-45)

    7b. in last position _____ (46-47)

    7c. in second-to-last position _____ (48-49)

    7d. in third-to-last position _____ (50-51)

8. Your title:

    8a. in current position _____ (52-53)

    8b. in last position _____ (54-55)

    8c. in second-to-last position _____ (56-57)

    8d. in third-to-last position _____ (58-59)

B. *Attributes of Career Success*

Consider the career success you have experienced up to now. For each item below, please circle the one response category that most closely matches your view of these qualities and characteristics for executive career success in your present corporation. *(circle one)*

CARD

(10-

(1) Personal Qualities and Characteristics	Very positive	Somewhat positive	Neither positive nor negative	Somewhat negative	Very negative	Don't know
9. Good-looks	1	2	3	4	5	6
10. Charm	1	2	3	4	5	6
11. Charisma	1	2	3	4	5	6
12. Articulateness	1	2	3	4	5	6
13. Optimism	1	2	3	4	5	6
14. Persuasiveness	1	2	3	4	5	6
15. Idealism	1	2	3	4	5	6
16. Superior talents	1	2	3	4	5	6
17. Good writing	1	2	3	4	5	6
18. Brilliance	1	2	3	4	5	6
19. Positive thinking	1	2	3	4	5	6
20. Being a cigarette smoker	1	2	3	4	5	6
21. Being a cigar smoker	1	2	3	4	5	6
22. Being a pipe smoker	1	2	3	4	5	6
23. Being 15 pounds overweight	1	2	3	4	5	6
24. Being 50 pounds overweight	1	2	3	4	5	6
25. [If a male executive] Being 5'10" tall or taller	1	2	3	4	5	6
26. Honesty	1	2	3	4	5	6
27. Punctuality	1	2	3	4	5	6
28. Conservative dresser	1	2	3	4	5	6
29. Unusually well-tailored and dressed	1	2	3	4	5	6
30. High expectations for your own achievement	1	2	3	4	5	6
31. Overcoming a serious personal problem	1	2	3	4	5	6
32. Drive	1	2	3	4	5	6
33. Aggressiveness	1	2	3	4	5	6
34. Rebounding from adversity	1	2	3	4	5	6

(2-

	Very positive	Somewhat positive	Neither positive nor negative	Somewhat negative	Very negative	Don't know
35. Perceptiveness about people	1	2	3	4	5	6
36. Knowing how to set priorities and stick with them	1	2	3	4	5	6
37. Good luck	1	2	3	4	5	6
38. Staying abreast of your field	1	2	3	4	5	6
39. Shaking things up	1	2	3	4	5	6
40. Coming to the office on weekends	1	2	3	4	5	6
41. Staying late at the office	1	2	3	4	5	6
42. Planning your career carefully	1	2	3	4	5	6
43. Taking work home regularly	1	2	3	4	5	6
44. Concentrating on results rather than work	1	2	3	4	5	6
45. Loyalty	1	2	3	4	5	6
46. Accepting a job relocation to another city with your company	1	2	3	4	5	6
47. Accepting a job with another company, then returning to your company	1	2	3	4	5	6
48. Being single-minded on a project	1	2	3	4	5	6
49. Repeatedly expressing to your superiors that you are ambitious	1	2	3	4	5	6
50. Understanding a corporate balance sheet	1	2	3	4	5	6
51. Giving talks or speeches at industry conventions and meetings	1	2	3	4	5	6
52. Writing professional articles for publication	1	2	3	4	5	6
53. Identification early in your career by management as a "comer"	1	2	3	4	5	6
54. Good judgment	1	2	3	4	5	6
55. Being with a small company prior to joining your company	1	2	3	4	5	6
56. Managing time well	1	2	3	4	5	6

	Very positive	Somewhat positive	Neither positive nor negative	Somewhat negative	Very negative	Don't know
57. A lot of "contacts" in your industry	1	2	3	4	5	6
58. Changing companies of employment prior to joining your company	1	2	3	4	5	6
59. Taking financial risks	1	2	3	4	5	6
60. Being a team-player	1	2	3	4	5	6
61. Adhering to deadlines	1	2	3	4	5	6

(2) Education and Training

	Very positive	Somewhat positive	Neither positive nor negative	Somewhat negative	Very negative	Don't know
62. Having the technical training or education necessary to your job	1	2	3	4	5	6
63. Taking courses in night school to improve your skills or knowledge	1	2	3	4	5	6
64. Reading heavily in business subjects	1	2	3	4	5	6
65. Reading heavily in all subjects	1	2	3	4	5	6
66. Learning new disciplines	1	2	3	4	5	6
67. Joining a management trainee program after completing your education	1	2	3	4	5	6

	Very positive	Somewhat positive	Neither positive nor negative	Somewhat negative	Very negative	Don't know
68. A college or university degree	1	2	3	4	5	6
69. A Master of Business Administration degree	1	2	3	4	5	6
70. A Master of Business Administration degree from a prestigious university	1	2	3	4	5	6
71. Being a student of organizations	1	2	3	4	5	6

(3) Life-Style Characteristics

	Very positive	Somewhat positive	Neither positive nor negative	Somewhat negative	Very negative	Don't know
72. Being active in community affairs	1	2	3	4	5	6
73. Being active in a church	1	2	3	4	5	6
74. An active social life	1	2	3	4	5	6
75. High social status	1	2	3	4	5	6
76. Membership in the "right" clubs	1	2	3	4	5	6

	Very positive	Somewhat positive	Neither positive nor negative	Somewhat negative	Very negative	Don't know
77. Living in the "right" communities	1	2	3	4	5	6
78. Driving an expensive automobile	1	2	3	4	5	6
79. Having your spouse pursue a career as vigorously as you	1	2	3	4	5	6
80. Getting involved in the public campaign of someone seeking elective office	1	2	3	4	5	6
81. A strong marriage	1	2	3	4	5	6
82. Getting divorced	1	2	3	4	5	6
83. Getting remarried	1	2	3	4	5	6
84. Never marrying	1	2	3	4	5	6
85. Getting married	1	2	3	4	5	6
86. Professing gayness (homosexuality)	1	2	3	4	5	6
87. Close friends with no connection to your corporation	1	2	3	4	5	6
88. A spouse who is very supportive of your career	1	2	3	4	5	6
89. Making all major family decisions	1	2	3	4	5	6
90. An intelligent, well-educated spouse	1	2	3	4	5	6
91. A spouse who will not relocate because of his/her career	1	2	3	4	5	6
92. Peace and quiet at home	1	2	3	4	5	6
93. A spouse who will relocate anywhere	1	2	3	4	5	6

Relations with Work Associates

	Very positive	Somewhat positive	Neither positive nor negative	Somewhat negative	Very negative	Don't know
94. Following your boss up the corporate ladder	1	2	3	4	5	6
95. Encouraging your boss	1	2	3	4	5	6
96. Making your boss look good to his superiors	1	2	3	4	5	6
97. Making your boss look bad to his superiors	1	2	3	4	5	6

	Very positive	Somewhat positive	Neither positive nor negative	Somewhat negative	Very negative	Don't know
98. Liking your boss	1	2	3	4	5	6
99. Always agreeing with your boss	1	2	3	4	5	6
100. Being demanding with your subordinates	1	2	3	4	5	6
101. Protecting and looking out for your subordinates	1	2	3	4	5	6
102. Grooming a successor	1	2	3	4	5	6
103. High visibility for your performance with top management	1	2	3	4	5	6
104. Encouraging your subordinates	1	2	3	4	5	6
105. Having a mentor	1	2	3	4	5	6

106. Up to now, you have been asked for your responses in a structured way. If this exercise has prompted thoughts or ideas you would like to express on corporations, careers, business, etc., please feel free to do so below in whatever form you like.

(39-4

Bibliography

Adams, Jane. *Making Good.* New York: Morrow, 1981.

Adler, Alfred. *The Science of Living,* ed. Heinz L. Ansbacher. New York: Doubleday Anchor, 1969.

Berger, Peter L. *The Heretical Imperative.* New York: Anchor Press/Doubleday, 1979.

Cahn, William. *Out of the Cracker Barrel.* New York: Simon and Schuster, 1969.

Cousins, Norman. *Anatomy of an Illness.* New York: W. W. Norton, 1979.

Dalton, Melville. *Men Who Manage.* New York: Wiley, 1959.

Drucker, Peter F. *Concept of the Corporation.* New York: John Day, 1946.

_____ *Landmarks of Tomorrow.* New York: Harper & Brothers, 1957.

_____ *The Effective Executive.* New York: Harper & Row, 1967.

Epictetus. *The Discourses of Epictetus,* trans. George Long. Great Books of the Western World, Vol. 12. Chicago: Encyclopaedia Britannica, 1952.

Florman, Samuel C. *The Existential Pleasures of Engineering.* New York: St. Martin's, 1976.

Foxworth, Jo. *Wising Up.* New York: Delacorte, 1980.

Friedman, Meyer, and Rosenman, Ray. *Type A Behavior and Your Heart.* New York: Alfred A. Knopf, 1974.

Harris, Sara, and Allen, Robert F. *The Quiet Revolution.* New York: Rawson, 1977. (A fascinating account of the working conditions reforms among the Coca-Cola Company's migrant workers.)

Hoffer, Eric. *Reflections on the Human Condition.* New York: Harper & Row, 1973.

Kipling, Rudyard. *The Lesson.* New York: Doubleday, Page, 1901.

Korda, Michael. *Power: How to Get It, How to Use It.* New York: Random House, 1975.

Levinson, Daniel J., et al. *The Seasons of a Man's Life.* New York: Alfred A. Knopf, 1978.

Livesay, Harold C. *American Made.* New York: Little, Brown, 1979.

McDonald, Forrest. *The Phaeton Ride.* New York: Doubleday, 1974.

McLuhan, Marshall. *Understanding Media.* New York: McGraw-Hill, 1964.

_____ *Culture Is Our Business.* New York: McGraw-Hill, 1970.

437

Malamud, Bernard. *Dubin's Lives.* New York: Farrar Straus & Giroux, 1979.

Melville, Herman. *Moby Dick.* Great Books of the Western World, Vol. 48. Chicago: Encyclopaedia Britannica, 1952.

Moskowitz, Milton, Katz, Michael and Levering, Robert. *Everybody's Business, An Almanac.* New York: Harper & Row, 1980.

Synge, John Millington. *The Aran Islands.* Dublin: Maunsel & Co., 1906.

Tarshis, Barry. *The "Average American" Book.* Atheneum/SMI, 1979.

Warner, W. Lloyd, and Abegglen, James C. *Big Business Leaders in America.* New York: Harper & Brothers, 1955.

Wilson, Sloan, *The Man in the Gray Flannel Suit.* New York: Simon and Schuster, 1955.

Index

439